OXFORD ENGLISH MONOGRAPHS

'Strandentwining Cable'

Joyce, Flaubert, and Intertextuality

SCARLETT BARON

OXFORD
UNIVERSITY PRESS

OXFORD

UNIVERSITY PRESS

Great Clarendon Street, Oxford OX2 6DP

Oxford University Press is a department of the University of Oxford.
It furthers the University's objective of excellence in research, scholarship,
and education by publishing worldwide in

Oxford New York

Auckland Cape Town Dar es Salaam Hong Kong Karachi
Kuala Lumpur Madrid Melbourne Mexico City Nairobi
New Delhi Shanghai Taipei Toronto

With offices in

Argentina Austria Brazil Chile Czech Republic France Greece
Guatemala Hungary Italy Japan Poland Portugal Singapore
South Korea Switzerland Thailand Turkey Ukraine Vietnam

Oxford is a registered trade mark of Oxford University Press
in the UK and in certain other countries

Published in the United States
by Oxford University Press Inc., New York

British Library Cataloguing in Publication Data
Data available

Library of Congress Cataloging in Publication Data
Data available

Typeset by SPI Publisher Services, Pondicherry, India
Printed in Great Britain
on acid-free paper by
MPG Books Group, Bodmin and King's Lynn

ISBN 978–0–19–969378–8

1 3 5 7 9 10 8 6 4 2

In loving memory of my mother
Stephanie Baron
(1943–2007)
and
for my father
Christopher Baron

Acknowledgements

This book is a revised version of a doctoral thesis written under the auspices of a number of remarkable institutions and organizations. I am particularly grateful to Christ Church, the Oxford college of all my student years, and to Magdalen College, Oxford, which provided an ideal research environment for my work on the project's final stages. I profited immeasurably from time spent with the Équipe Joyce of the Parisian Institut des Textes et Manuscrits Modernes in 2006: I am especially indebted to Daniel Ferrer for making very fruitful suggestions about my various lines of inquiry, and for helping me to decipher VI.B.8, that most thrillingly Flaubertian of *Finnegans Wake* notebooks. I am full of gratitude for the time I spent at the Zurich James Joyce Foundation in the summer of 2007: there I was able to draw daily on the knowledge and wise counsel of Fritz Senn and his team—Ruth Frehner, Ursula Zeller, and Frances Ilmberger—as well as on an exceptional treasure trove of resources. I am also thankful for grants from the Arts and Humanities Research Council, the Oxford English Faculty, the International James Joyce Foundation, the Trieste James Joyce Summer School, and the Dublin James Joyce Summer School.

More people than I can justly acknowledge have helped me think through, compose, and revise this book. Above all, I am enormously grateful to my D.Phil. supervisor, Ron Bush, for meticulous readings of my work at many different stages, for invaluable guidance and advice proffered at every turn, and for kind and stalwart support throughout the project.

I am deeply grateful to others who have perused various fledgling versions of this book and enriched it by their suggestions: to my D.Phil. examiners, Jeri Johnson and Geert Lernout, for their thoughtful and productive questions and comments; to my anonymous readers at Oxford University Press for their searching and subtle responses to my manuscript; and to Michael Silk, for his illuminating scrutiny of the text.

During my first trip to the National Library of Ireland in 2005, Luca Crispi and Gerard Long provided information which enabled me to get in touch with Alexander Neubauer, who has been extremely generous in sending me pictures of Joyce's signed copies of *Madame Bovary* and *L'Éducation sentimentale* and allowing me to reproduce them in this book. My thanks to all three for turning an accident of circumstance into so great a boon to my detective endeavours.

Many members of the warm and vibrant community of Joyce scholarship—many more than I could list—have become friends and regular academic interlocutors. This book bears the traces of many a delightful and challenging conversation. I am grateful for all such discussions, including those that may have slipped my memory. In addition to the individuals already mentioned, I would like to express especial thanks to Marco Camerani, Ronan Crowley, Vincent Deane, Finn Fordham, Hans Walter Gabler, Michael Groden, Brandy Kershner, Amanda Sigler, Robert Spoo, Dirk Van Hulle, and Wim Van Mierlo.

The genealogy of this book stretches back in time beyond the D.Phil. years: it is connected by strandentwining cables to myriad crucial figures from earlier periods of my life. I wish to thank those who nurtured my academic interests long before they led to doctoral research: Jennifer Merlino, who taught me English in a French-speaking school with passion and dedication; the staff of the English National Programme at the Lycée International de Ferney-Voltaire, for providing a stimulating springboard to university study in England; Christopher Butler, who made the discovery of *Ulysses* an excitement and a pleasure; Belinda Jack and Christopher Robinson, who introduced me to the genius of Flaubert; and Bart van Es, who applied a much-needed scalpel to the florid style of my undergraduate essays.

I am grateful to my commissioning editors, Jacqueline Baker and Ariane Petit; to Kathleen Kerr and Brendan Mac Evilly, who oversaw the final stages of production; to my copy-editor, Richard Mason; and to my proofreader, Javier Kalhat.

Every effort has been made to ensure that all quotations from copyright material fall within the definition of fair dealing for the purposes of literary criticism. I am grateful to the editors of the following journals for allowing me to draw on articles published in their pages: *Dix-Neuf, Genetic Joyce Studies*, the *James Joyce Quarterly*, *Modern Fiction Studies*, and *Papers on Joyce*. Thanks also to Finn Fordham and Rita Sakr for granting me permission to include material from an essay that first appeared in *James Joyce and the Nineteenth-Century Novel* (Amsterdam and New York: Rodopi, 2011).

I have been fortunate in having a buoying and buoyant circle of wonderful and steadfast friends. For literary talk and frivolous diversion, for precious support and meaningful levity, for all the joys of close exchange and warm companionship, my heartfelt thanks go to Michael Allingham, Joshua Billings, Andrew Blades, Melanie Caruso, Ronan Crowley, Catherine David, Conor Dwan, Alexandra Harris, Andrew Hay, Hong Xia Li, Fiachra Mac Góráin, William May, Alisa Miller, John Morgenstern, Jacqueline Papo, Amanda Sigler, Benjamin Skipp, Christopher Stephens, Eleanor Thompson, and Susan Williams.

My deepest gratitude goes to my family. To my sister, Justine. To my father, who read every word of this book countless times to advise and reassure. And to my mother, who read every word for as long as she could, whose enthusiasm and encouragement meant the world to me, and who would have loved to see the project complete.

Contents

List of Illustrations

List of Abbreviations

For ease of reading, all references (including references to Joyce's and Flaubert's works) are given in footnotes to the main body of the text.

WORKS AND LETTERS BY JAMES JOYCE

APA   'A Portrait of the Artist', in *Poems and Shorter Writings*, ed. Richard Ellmann and others (London: Faber and Faber, 2001), 211–218.

D   *Dubliners* (Harmondsworth: Penguin Classics, 2000).

E   *Exiles* (London: Jonathan Cape, 1952).

FW   *Finnegans Wake* (London: Faber and Faber, 1975). References are given in the following form: *FW* page number: line number.

JJA   *The James Joyce Archive*, ed. Michael Groden and others, 63 vols (New York and London: Garland, 1977–9). References are given in the following form: *JJA* volume number.

L1   *Letters of James Joyce*, vol. 1, ed. Stuart Gilbert (London: Faber and Faber, 1957).

L2   *Letters of James Joyce*, vol. 2, ed. Richard Ellmann (London: Faber and Faber, 1966).

L3   *Letters of James Joyce*, vol. 3, ed. Richard Ellmann (London: Faber and Faber, 1966).

OCPW   *Occasional, Critical, and Political Writing*, ed. Kevin Barry (Oxford: Oxford University Press, 2000).

P   *A Portrait of the Artist as a Young Man*, ed. Jeri Johnson (Oxford: Oxford University Press, 2000).

SH   *Stephen Hero*, ed. Theodore Spencer (1944), revd edn incorporating additional manuscript pages from Yale and Cornell University libraries, ed. John J. Slocum and Herbert Cahoon (New York: New Directions Publishing Corporation, 1969).

SL   *Selected Letters of James Joyce*, ed. Richard Ellmann (London: Faber and Faber, 1975).

U   *Ulysses*, ed. Hans Walter Gabler with Wolfhard Steppe and Claus Melchior (New York: Random House, 1986). References are given in the following form: *U* episode number: line number.

WORKS AND LETTERS BY GUSTAVE FLAUBERT

BP/DIR   *Bouvard et Pécuchet*, with the *Dictionnaire des Idées Reçues* (Paris: Flammarion, 1999).

C1   *Correspondance*, ed. Jean Bruneau (Paris: Gallimard, 1973–2007), vol. 1 (1973).

C2   *Correspondance*, ed. Jean Bruneau (Paris: Gallimard, 1973–2007), vol. 2 (1980).

C3   *Correspondance*, ed. Jean Bruneau (Paris: Gallimard, 1973–2007), vol. 3 (1991).

C4   *Correspondance*, ed. Jean Bruneau (Paris: Gallimard, 1973–2007), vol. 4 (1998).

C5   *Correspondance*, ed. Jean Bruneau and Yvan Leclerc (Paris: Gallimard, 1973–2007), vol. 5 (2007).

ES   *L'Éducation sentimentale* (Paris: Gallimard, 1965).

MB   *Madame Bovary* (Paris: Gallimard, 1972).

MB 1910   *Madame Bovary* (Paris: Louis Conard, 1910).

SAL   *Salammbô* (Paris: Garnier-Flammarion, 1964).

TA   *La Tentation de saint Antoine* (Paris: Pocket, 1999).

TC   *Trois Contes* (Paris: Gallimard, 1973).

TRANSLATIONS OF WORKS AND LETTERS BY GUSTAVE FLAUBERT

BPE/DIRE   *Bouvard and Pécuchet*, with the *Dictionary of Received Ideas*, trans. A. J. Krailsheimer (Harmondsworth: Penguin, 1977).

ESE   *A Sentimental Education*, trans. Douglas Parmée (Oxford: Oxford University Press, 2008).

FS1   *The Letters of Gustave Flaubert 1830–1857*, trans. Francis Steegmuller (London: Faber and Faber, 1981).

FS2   *The Letters of Gustave Flaubert 1857–1880*, trans. Francis Steegmuller (London: Faber and Faber, 1984).

GW   *Selected Letters*, trans. Geoffrey Wall (Harmondsworth: Penguin, 1997).

MBE   *Madame Bovary*, trans. Margaret Mauldon (Oxford: Oxford University Press, 2004).

SALE   *Salammbo*, trans. A. J. Krailsheimer (London: Penguin, 1977).

TAE   *The Temptation of St Antony*, trans. Kitty Mrosovsky (Harmondsworth: Penguin, 1980).

TCE   *Three Tales*, trans. A. J. Krailsheimer (Oxford: Oxford University Press, 1991).

SECONDARY AND CRITICAL LITERATURE

CJ   Ellmann, Richard, *The Consciousness of Joyce* (London: Faber and Faber, 1977).

F&J   Cross, Richard K., *Flaubert and Joyce: The Rite of Fiction* (Princeton: Princeton University Press, 1971).

HJWFW	*How Joyce Wrote 'Finnegans Wake': A Chapter-by-Chapter Genetic Guide*, ed. Luca Crispi and Sam Slote (Madison: University of Wisconsin Press, 2007).
JJ	Ellmann, Richard, *James Joyce*, revd. edn (Oxford: Oxford University Press, 1982).
JJQ	*James Joyce Quarterly* (Tulsa: University of Tulsa, 1963–).
P/J	Pound, Ezra, *Pound/Joyce: The Letters of Ezra Pound to James Joyce: with Pound's Essays on James Joyce*, ed. Forrest Read (London: Faber and Faber, 1968).
'Scribble' 2	Jacquet, Claude, and André Topia (eds), *'Scribble' 2: Joyce et Flaubert* (Paris: Minard, 1990).
Stoics	Kenner, Hugh, *Flaubert, Joyce, and Beckett: The Stoic Comedians* (London: W. H. Allen, 1964).
Workshop	Scholes, Robert E., and Richard M. Kain (eds), *The Workshop of Daedalus: James Joyce and the Raw Materials for 'A Portrait of the Artist as a Young Man'* (Evanston: Northwestern University Press, 1965).

Note on Translations

Quotations from French-language texts are given in translation. The original is given in square brackets in the footnotes, with a page reference to the relevant French edition. Where part of a published translation is inadequate, my own translation is given in italics in square brackets within the relevant quotation. Where no translation is available, my own has been provided. All translations for which no reference is given are my own.

From Flaubert's Works
Translations from Flaubert's works are drawn from the following widely accessible standard editions:

BPE/DIRE   *Bouvard and Pécuchet* (including the *Dictionary of Received Ideas*), trans. A. J. Krailsheimer (Harmondsworth: Penguin, 1977).

ESE   *Sentimental Education,* trans. Douglas Parmée (Oxford: Oxford University Press, 2008).

MBE   *Madame Bovary,* trans. Margaret Mauldon (Oxford: Oxford University Press, 2004).

SALE   *Salammbo,* trans. A. J. Krailsheimer (London: Penguin, 1977).

TAE   *The Temptation of St Antony,* trans. Kitty Mrosovsky (Harmondsworth: Penguin, 1980).

TCE   *Three Tales,* trans. A. J. Krailsheimer (Oxford: Oxford University Press, 1991).

From Flaubert's Letters
Not all of Flaubert's letters have been previously translated, and those that have been appear in different editions. Translations have been provided from the following sources. Geoffrey Wall's translations have been privileged when more than one version is available.

FS1   *The Letters of Gustave Flaubert 1830–1857,* trans. Francis Steegmuller (London: Faber and Faber, 1981).

FS2   *The Letters of Gustave Flaubert 1857–1880,* trans. Francis Steegmuller (London: Faber and Faber, 1984).

GW   *Selected Letters,* trans. Geoffrey Wall (Harmondsworth: Penguin, 1997).

Proper Names
Proper names are spelt in the same way as they appear in the listed translations: Antony, Félicité, Frédéric, Julian, Herod, Herodias, Mâtho, Pécuchet, Regimbart, Salammbo, Salome. In the case of *La Tentation de saint Antoine*, this leads to some

inconsistencies in spelling, for though Kitty Mrosovsky opts for 'Antony', many literary critics refer to 'Anthony'. Joyce himself uses the latter spelling in two jottings referring to Flaubert's saint among notes compiled in preparation for the composition of 'Circe' (see Chapter 5). The name is also spelt in this way in *Stephen Hero* (page 57) and in *Finnegans Wake* (page 86). As there is no evidence that Joyce owned an English-language copy of the text—such as, for instance, G. F. Monkshood's *The Temptation of Saint Anthony* (London: Greening, 1910)—it seems likely that the translated spelling was his own, effected from the French version of the text purchased in Trieste in 1913–14.

Introduction: Strandentwining Cables

In the fifth and final chapter of James Joyce's first novel, *A Portrait of the Artist as a Young Man*, Stephen Dedalus grandiloquently rephrases the most famous dictum of Gustave Flaubert's theory of authorial impersonality. Ambling through the streets of Dublin with his friend Lynch at his side, Stephen declares that:

> The artist, like the God of creation, remains within or behind or beyond or above his handiwork, invisible, refined out of existence, indifferent, paring his fingernails.[1]

The statement flamboyantly echoes a view expressed in one of Flaubert's most quoted letters. In 1857, the French author adamantly asserted that:

> The author in his work must be like God in creation, invisible and all-powerful; you can sense him everywhere but you cannot see him.[2]

In the 'Proteus' episode of *Ulysses*, a disheartened Stephen, still very much the impecunious littérateur, walks alone and dejected along Sandymount Strand. His abstruse philosophical thoughts, conveyed through the medium of interior monologue, feature a return to the train of his earlier musings about creation. Prompted by the blurry sight of two figures on the beach whom he mistakenly imagines to be midwives, Stephen contrasts the godly simplicity and abstraction of 'Creation from nothing' with the sprawling complexity and messy materiality of human birthing and its 'trailing navelcords'.[3] Although Stephen, rehearsing the dangerously tempting words of the biblical serpent, briefly entertains the fantasy of being 'as gods'—much as he had at the end of *A Portrait*—he acknowledges to himself that in human reality 'The cords of all link

---

[1] *P*, 181.
[2] Flaubert to Mlle Leroyer de Chantepie, 18 March 1857, *GW*, 258 ['L'artiste doit être dans son oeuvre comme Dieu dans la création, invisible et tout-puissant; qu'on le sente partout, mais qu'on ne le voie pas.' (C2, 691)].
[3] *U* 3: 35–6.

back', forming a 'strandentwining cable of all flesh'.[4] Stephen's mind envisages the originating matrix from which the cable proceeds and to which all cords return as both human and textual: it is Eve's 'belly without blemish', a blank surface of 'taut vellum'.[5]

This striking nexus of imagery reads as an apt extended metaphor for the exceptionally dense and wide-ranging intertextuality of Joyce's writing, which constantly 'link[s] back' to precursor texts, absorbing and entwining the strands of foreign linguistic materials. Stephen's insight regarding the connections and continuity that characterize both human and literary creation is unwittingly reprised by Leopold Bloom, who in the 'Ithaca' episode of *Ulysses*, thinking about the relations between men and women, reaches the realization that:

> each one who enters imagines himself to be the first to enter whereas he is always the last term of a preceding series even if the first term of a succeeding one, each imagining himself to be first, last, only and alone whereas he is neither first nor last nor only nor alone in a series originating in and repeated to infinity.[6]

Like Stephen Dedalus and Leopold Bloom, Joyce's work acknowledges, accepts, and affirms the contexts in and out of which life and literature emerge and take shape, assuming its position within tightly woven nets of intertextual reference with arch and serene self-consciousness.

This book is about Joyce's relations to Flaubert. The Flaubertian oeuvre constitutes but one among the theoretically infinite number of framing, forming, and informing contexts to Joyce's work. Yet this particular link in the chain has a significance that extends beyond itself—not only inflecting Joyce's writing in each consecutive work, but also playing a key role in the crystallization of his thinking about textual relations. By focusing closely on those moments in Joyce's writing which act as 'cords' that 'link back' to Flaubert's works, this study sheds light on the dynamics of a complex and evolving literary relationship, outlining the ways in which it enabled Joyce to become an extreme and serene practitioner of intertextuality, as well as one of the theory's crucial midwives.

Joyce and Flaubert: the names conjure two of the most admired and mythologized masters of nineteenth- and twentieth-century prose. In one sense, to probe the relations between such towering geniuses is to do the obvious. Their great renown naturalizes the assumption of a connection between them: if both authors have been deemed worthy of so unques-

---

tioned an elevation into the canon of Western fiction, then surely a consideration of both can tell us something about what excellent prose, an excellent novel, or outstanding literature might be. On the other hand, the very suggestion that Joyce and Flaubert may have much in common has the power to mystify, for the differences between the contexts, textures, plots, structures, and tonalities of their various works—as well as between their lives in terms of place, time, and event—are substantial, and can make the existence of any significant intertextual connection between them seem unlikely. But an awareness of such discrepancies in no way invalidates the hypothesis that a strong Flaubertian strand runs through Joyce's web. Indeed, the combination of sameness and difference inherent to all intertextual relations will be one of the leitmotifs of this study. The aim will not be to force Joyce and Flaubert into systematic alignment, but to be sensitive to the ways in which Joyce's response to his precursor involves both convergence and divergence, continuation and deviation.

Although Joyce and Flaubert met in art, they did not meet in life. Flaubert died in 1880. Joyce was born in 1882. Their encounters, mediated by the texts and cultures of the late nineteenth and early twentieth century, took place through the written word alone.

Flaubert witnessed at first hand a number of the political upheavals in France's tumultuous nineteenth-century history. Born in the Norman town of Rouen in 1821, he looked on as the popular revolution of 1848 brought an end to the reign of Louis-Philippe, as Louis-Napoleon Bonaparte was elected President of the Second Republic and subsequently seized power as Emperor Napoleon III in 1852. Flaubert despaired as France was invaded by the Prussians in 1870, watched as the Empire collapsed in 1871, and fumed when chaotic Communard fighting ensued. Against this agitated backdrop, he led a life of contrasts, dividing his time between periods of intense, fiercely protected isolation stolidly devoted to writing in his quiet pavilion in Croisset (a little hamlet on the outskirts of Rouen), and trips to Paris where he increasingly found himself at the heart of a coterie of fellow literary luminaries. Flaubert reacted to contemporary events with escalating disgust, resolving to make *L'Éducation sentimentale* 'the moral history of the men of my generation'[7] and to use his *Dictionnaire des Idées Reçues* to shame his readers into silence.

Flaubert was at his writing desk when he died—an almost uncannily fitting end to a life given over to art. For Flaubert had lived by and for his craft. As he explained to Louise Colet in a letter written at the beginning of

[7] Flaubert to Mlle Leroyer de Chantepie, 6 October 1864, *GW*, 304 ['l'histoire morale des hommes de ma génération' (*C3*, 409)].

his work on *Madame Bovary*: 'I am a creature of the quill. I feel through it, because of it, in relation to it, and much more with it.'[8] Throughout his life, Flaubert remained single-mindedly committed to the creation of artistic beauty ('Above all, I seek *beauty*'[9]) in spite of the torture that the quest for the *mot juste* entailed for him ('Style is achieved only by dint of atrocious labour'[10]). His first novel, *Madame Bovary*, published when he was thirty-six years old, remains his most widely regarded. After being serialized in *La Revue de Paris* in 1856, the book was brought to trial in 1857 for constituting an offence against morality and religion. Flaubert and his publishers were acquitted, but the sulphurous aura of the court-room turned *Madame Bovary* into an instant best-seller. Flaubert did not welcome the personal notoriety that followed: it was not the acclaim per se that he resented, but his sharp sense that he had become a household name for the wrong reasons—that sales of his book were being driven solely by the reading public's eagerness to own a modish *succès de scandale*.

After *Madame Bovary* came *Salammbô* (1862), a luxuriant, epic retelling of the Carthaginian wars, partly inspired by Flaubert's long continuous travels through the Middle East in 1849 and 1850, and further fuelled by a research trip to Carthage itself in 1858; *L'Éducation sentimentale* (1869), a fictionalized account of recent political events; *La Tentation de saint Antoine* (1874), a wildly phantasmagorical closet drama written on the formal template of a medieval morality play; *Trois Contes* (1877), a triptych of stories dealing with contemporary French life, medieval legend, and antiquity respectively; and (posthumously in 1881) *Bouvard et Pécuchet*, the story of two copying clerks' quest for knowledge, within which was to feature the *Dictionnaire des Idées Reçues*, a lampooning list of some of the most howling clichés of the age.

Almost as much as for his novelistic works, Flaubert is known to posterity for his letters. Mario Vargas Llosa calls the Flaubertian *Correspondance* 'the most lucid and profound treatise on narrative art ever to be written'.[11] Often composed late into the night, after hours spent on the rack of fictional creation, the letters expound a fervent and intransigent aesthetic theory. In 1893 Henry James published a review of the first edition of the letters in *Macmillan's Magazine*, emphasizing the centrality

---

[8] Flaubert to Louise Colet, 31 January 1852, *GW*, 172 ['Je suis un homme-plume. Je sens par elle, par rapport à elle et beaucoup plus par elle.' (*C2*, 42)].

[9] Flaubert to George Sand, 31 December 1875, *GW*, 401 ['Je recherche par-dessus tout, *la Beauté*' (*C4*, 1,000)].

[10] Flaubert to Louise Colet, 14–15 August 1846, *FS1*, 65 ['On n'arrive au style qu'avec un labeur atroce' (*C2*, 303)].

[11] Mario Vargas Llosa, 'Flaubert, Our Contemporary', in *The Cambridge Companion to Flaubert* (Cambridge: Cambridge University Press, 2006), 222.

of artistic concerns in Flaubert's epistolary writing and marvelling at 'so much vivid and violent testimony to an intensely exclusive passion'. Along with Flaubert's 'almost insanely excessive' dedication to the idea of an absolute style, James noted his love of prose over poetry, his reverence for style, his 'aggressive pessimism', his horror of cliché. Analyzing the elements of Flaubert's practice as a craftsman, he mused with both admiration and unconcealed bafflement at his immovable adherence to the principle of impersonality in art, his commitment to documentary research as a necessary preparation for fictional writing, and his perfectionist attention to the subtlest details of sound and rhythm.[12]

There is much in this analysis that is evocative of James Joyce, despite the tracts of space and time that separate the two authors' writing lives. Born in 1882 into an Ireland riven with divisions, Joyce led a life that, like Flaubert's, was overridingly devoted to art. Like Flaubert, and despite spending much of his adult life in exile, Joyce followed the political upheavals of his day: the fall of Charles Stewart Parnell and the failure of the system of Home Rule he had championed in 1891, the Easter Rising of 1916, the proclamation of the Irish Free State in 1922. But unlike Flaubert—who expressed strong reactions to contemporary events in his letters, if not in his art—Joyce's observation of 'real world' events was carried out with an inscrutable aloofness. For Joyce as for Flaubert, the composition of a book meant long hours and long years of intensive work. For him as for Flaubert, the masterful organization of words into styles was a central preoccupation. And for him as for Flaubert, reading was a prerequisite for writing. Joyce's writing, like Flaubert's, is unstintingly impersonal. Although Joyce was far less prolix than was Flaubert about his aesthetic beliefs and motivations, some of his statements do bear distinctly Flaubertian inflections. When Frank Budgen, a close friend of the author's during the years he spent in Zurich (1915–1919), asked whether his day had been spent in search of the *mot juste*, Joyce replied: 'I have the words already. What I am seeking is the perfect order of words in the sentence. There is an order in every way appropriate.'[13] Similarly, his statement, also to Budgen, that he wanted 'the reader to understand always through suggestion rather than direct statement',[14] could have been drawn straight out of one of Flaubert's letters, which consistently advocate the abrogation

---

[12] Henry James, 'Gustave Flaubert', *Macmillan's Magazine*, vol. 67, no. 401 (March 1893), 333, 336. I am grateful to Finn Fordham for drawing my attention to this review.

[13] Frank Budgen, *James Joyce and the Making of 'Ulysses'* (London: Grayson and Grayson, 1934), 19–20.

[14] Budgen, *James Joyce and the Making of 'Ulysses'*, 21.

of explicit authorial guidance: 'a novelist ~~hasn't the right to express his opinion~~ on anything whatsoever'.[15]

As well as painting a picture of the artist, Henry James's review of Flaubert's letters reflected on the nature of Flaubert's legacy. It identified him as 'a writer's writer', 'one of the artists to whom an artist will always go back', and enjoined aspiring writers to '*use* him, to feel him, to be privately glad of his message', to 'swallow him whole', and to 'cherish him as a perfect example'. Flaubert, he maintained, invites 'imitation of the practical kind', offering an opportunity for 'a sort of mystical absorption', and the nurturing of a 'fruitful secret'.[16]

This study's emphasis on Joyce's response to Flaubert's work is not intended to occlude or minimize his strandentwining relations to other texts and authors. Indeed its arguments are advanced in full agreement with Brandon Kershner's view that:

> more than the work of any other major author, Joyce's writings are permeated by quotations, citations, literary allusions, and other traces of texts or voices.[17]

Accordingly, the following pages proceed in recognition of the throng of echoes that resonate through Joyce's writings. This dimension of the author's works was apparent even to his earliest critics, and the drive to understand this aspect of Joyce's texts has remained unabated over the decades, with many continuing with the annotative inquiries inaugurated by, for example, Adaline Glasheen, James Atherton, Weldon Thornton, Roland McHugh, Don Gifford, and Robert Seidman.[18] Numerous studies have concerned themselves with Joyce's relations with other

---

[15] Flaubert to George Sand, 5 December 1866, *FS2*, 94 ['un romancier *n'a pas le droit d'exprimer son opinion* sur quoi que ce soit.' (*C3*, 575)].

[16] Henry James, 'Gustave Flaubert', 333, 339, 340, 342.

[17] R. Brandon Kershner, 'Dialogical and Intertextual Joyce', in *Palgrave Advances in James Joyce Studies*, ed. Jean-Michel Rabaté (Basingstoke and New York: Palgrave Macmillan, 2004), 183.

[18] Adaline Glasheen, *A Census of 'Finnegans Wake': An Index of the Characters and their Roles* (Evanston: Northwestern University Press, 1956, with 2nd and 3rd edns in 1963 and 1977); James Atherton, *The Books at the Wake: A Study of Literary Allusions in James Joyce's 'Finnegans Wake'*, 3rd edn (London: Faber and Faber, 1959); Weldon Thornton, *Allusions in 'Ulysses': An Annotated List* (Chapel Hill: University of North Carolina Press, 1961); Roland McHugh, *Annotations to 'Finnegans Wake'* (London: Routledge and Kegan Paul, 1980, with 2nd and 3rd edns in 1991 and 2006); Don Gifford with Robert J. Seidman, *'Ulysses' Annotated: Notes for James Joyce's 'Ulysses'*, 2nd ed (New York: E. P. Dutton, 1974; revd. edn, Berkeley/Los Angeles, and London: University of California Press, 1988).

authors—Dante, Ibsen, Mallarmé, Milton, Rabelais, Shakespeare, Shaw, Wyndham Lewis, to name but a few.

The increasing accessibility of manuscript material has considerably expanded the field of material relevant to such inquiries, enabling critics to gain insights into the genesis of Joyce's works. The publication of the 63-volume *James Joyce Archive* between 1977 and 1979 marked the beginning of a process that has since substantially altered the Joycean critical landscape.[19] The type of research that subtended the compilation and publication of the *Archive* paved the way for significant editorial overhauls—such as the still much debated 'synoptic edition' of *Ulysses* published by Hans Walter Gabler in 1984—and facilitated the application of nascent critical approaches, such as genetic criticism, to the field of Joyce studies.

Genetic criticism emerged in the late 1960s. While some were proclaiming the death of the author, the earliest genetic critics were, not unrelatedly, advocating a mode of inquiry that disregards a writer's choice to privilege one (usually final) version of a text over others. Discarded drafts are submitted to scrutiny, the ultimate aim of the endeavour being to reach an understanding of the composition process itself. In the field of Joyce studies, genetic criticism and source studies have always been closely linked, an association evidenced by the pages of *A 'Finnegans Wake' Circular*, which ran from 1985 to 1992. The journal's first editorial called for the 'complete and accurate transcription of the Buffalo notebooks and identification of their sources'.[20] The edition of *The 'Finnegans Wake' Notebooks at Buffalo*, which began in 2001, is motivated by the same aspirations and continues to exemplify the detective curiosity that characterized earlier source-hunting enterprises:[21] the editors' mission is not just to transcribe the notebooks, but also, crucially, to furnish indications of source.[22] As David Hayman points out, genetic critics are, in some respects, 'like archeologists': the 'necessary spadework'[23] and empirical stockpiling they perform in their implicit drive to sketch a complete map of Joyce's reading ultimately aims to lay the foundation for the study of the processes by which words extracted from a source travel 'upstream'

---

[19] For David Hayman, 'the pressure of such data has effectively changed the face of Joyce criticism'—'Genetic Criticism and Joyce: An Introduction', in *Probes: Genetic Studies in Joyce*, ed. David Hayman and Sam Slote, in *European Joyce Studies* 5 (Amsterdam: Rodopi, 1995), 6.

[20] Vincent Deane, 'Editorial', *A 'Finnegans Wake' Circular*, vol. 1, no. 1 (1985), 1.

[21] *The 'Finnegans Wake' Notebooks at Buffalo*, ed. Vincent Deane, Daniel Ferrer, and Geert Lernout (Turnhout: Brepols, 2001–).

[22] Vincent Deane, Introduction, *The 'Finnegans Wake' Notebooks at Buffalo*.

[23] Hayman, 'Genetic Criticism and Joyce', 8, 14.

through successive notebooks before reappearing under new guises in the published text.[24]

Twenty-first-century critical discussions of literary relations are faced with a choice between two contending paradigms: influence on the one hand, intertextuality on the other. This introduction will differentiate between these terms in such a way as to render explicit the rationale behind the titular focus on intertextuality.

In 1966 Julia Kristeva, drawing on the earlier writings of the Russian theorist Mikhail Bakhtin, coined the term 'intertextuality' to designate the notion that 'any text is constructed as a mosaic of quotations': 'any text', she stated, 'is the absorption and transformation of another'.[25] Two years later Roland Barthes echoed her definition in his provocative proclamation of 'The Death of the Author', asserting that 'the text is a tissue of quotations'.[26] In 1969 Michel Foucault probed similar conceptual terrain in an essay entitled 'What is an Author', stressing the 'voluntary effacement' of the subject involved in the act of writing.[27] Spearheaded by this trio of theorists writing from the fringes of the French academy, intertextuality took the literary critical world by storm, rapidly acquiring a currency that has endured despite the debates and contortions which have marked its fifty-year history. Initial interest in the concept continued unabated in subsequent decades, with numerous critics (among them Jacques Derrida, Jonathan Culler, Harold Bloom, Antoine Compagnon, Gérard Genette, Michael Riffaterre)[28]

---

[24] Geert Lernout provides a history of the evolution of Joycean genetic criticism and its various schools of thought in 'The *Finnegans Wake* Notebooks and Radical Philology', in *Probes: Genetic Studies in Joyce*, ed. David Hayman and Sam Slote, *European Joyce Studies* 5 (Amsterdam: Rodopi, 1995).

[25] Julia Kristeva, 'Word, Dialogue, and Novel', in *Desire in Language: A Semiotic Approach to Literature and Art*, ed. Leon S. Roudiez, trans. Thomas Gora, Alice Jardine, and Leon S. Roudiez (New York: Columbia University Press, 1980), 66 ['tout texte se construit comme mosaïque de citations, tout texte est absorption et transformation d'un autre texte' ('Le Mot, le dialogue, et le roman', *Séméiótiké: Recherches pour une sémanalyse* [Paris: Editions du Seuil, 1969, 85].

[26] Roland Barthes, 'The Death of the Author', in *Image Music Text*, ed. and trans. Stephen Heath (London: Fontana, 1977), 146 ['le texte est un tissu de citations' ('La Mort de l'auteur', in *Le Bruissement de la langue* [Paris: Editions du Seuil, 1984], 67)].

[27] Michel Foucault, 'What is an Author?', in *Textual Strategies: Perspectives in Post-Structuralist Criticism*, ed. Josué V. Harari (London: Cornell University Press, 1979), 142 ['effacement volontaire' ('Qu'est-ce qu'un auteur?', in *Dits et Écrits 1954–1988*, 4 vols [Paris: Gallimard, 1994], vol. 1, 793)].

[28] Jacques Derrida, *De la grammatologie* (Paris: Editions de Minuit, 1967), *L'écriture et la différence* (Paris: Editions du Seuil, 1967); Jonathan Culler, 'Presupposition and Intertextuality', in *The Pursuit of Signs: Semiotics, Literature, Deconstruction*, augmented edn (New York and Ithaca: Cornell University Press, 2002); Harold Bloom, *The Anxiety of Influence: A Theory of Poetry* (New York: Oxford University Press, 1973); Antoine Compagnon, *La Seconde Main: ou Le Travail de la citation* (Paris: Editions du Seuil, 1979); Gérard Genette, *Palimpsestes: La Littérature du second degré* (Paris: Editions du Seuil, 1982); Michael

proposing new formulations of the term's implications and applications. Yet the value of the notion, which is still considered a merely faddish synonym for influence in some quarters,[29] remains contested.

This continuing confusion is in large part attributable to the fact that it is practically impossible to draw a neat and sustainable dividing line between the concepts of influence and intertextuality. Kristeva and Barthes tried in vain to impress upon their readers the need for intertextuality to be kept distinct from the well-established notion it had been coined to transcend.[30]

Despite this generalized haziness, some fundamental differences do obtain between these two treacherously related concepts. Influence is defined by agency and causality: 'It presumes a source, an origin, an agency that flows into or acts upon another',[31] emphasizing the importance of the precursor at the expense of that of the successor. Intertextuality, on the other hand, takes a bird's-eye view of the texts involved, exploding the binary structure that sits at influence's conceptual heart. Whereas influence functions within what Jay Clayton and Eric Rothstein call 'dyads of transmission',[32] intertextual theory envisages literary history as a matter of 'meshing systems',[33] and texts as infinitely plural sites: in the transition from one notion to the other, the spectrum of literary connectivity broadens out from a binary into infinity. Yet acting on this theory in critical terms proved more difficult than the theorists had expected.

Riffaterre, 'Compulsory Reader Response: The Intertextual Drive', in *Intertextuality: Theories and Practices*, ed. Michael Worton and Judith Still (Manchester and New York: Manchester University Press, 1990), 'Interpretation and Undecidability', *New Literary History*, 12 (2) (1980), 'Intertextual Representation: On Mimesis as Interpretive Discourse', *Critical Inquiry*, 11 (1) (1984).

[29] See William Irwin, 'Against Intertextuality', *Philosophy and Literature*, 28 (2004).

[30] Kristeva's frustration at the amalgamation of the two notions even led to her proposal of a new word which she hoped might escape the semantic blurring that already plagued intertextuality: 'since this term has often been understood in the banal sense of "study of sources", we prefer the term *transposition*', *Revolution in Poetic Language*, trans. Margaret Walker (New York: Columbia University Press, 1984), 60 ['puisque ce terme a été souvent entendu dans le sens banal de "critique des sources" d'un texte, nous lui préférons celui de transposition' (*La Révolution du langage poétique: l'avant-garde à la fin du XIXe siècle: Lautréamont et Mallarmé* [Paris: Éditions du Seuil, 1974], 59–60)].

[31] Susan Stanford Friedman, 'Weavings: Intertextuality and the (Re)Birth of the Author', in *Influence and Intertextuality in Literary History*, ed. Jay Clayton and Eric Rothstein (Madison: The University of Wisconsin Press, 1991), 152.

[32] Clayton and Rothstein (eds), *Influence and Intertextuality*, 3.

[33] Clayton and Rothstein (eds), *Influence and Intertextuality*, 17.

Kristeva herself, for instance, tellingly followed the template of the traditional influence study in her very efforts to illustrate the new concept.[34]

Harold Bloom's *The Anxiety of Influence: A Theory of Poetry*, published in 1973, provided further evidence of the endurance of such established modes of reading. Asserting that 'Criticism is the act of knowing the hidden roads that go from poem to poem',[35] Bloom advocates the continuing pertinence of the influence binary. Accordingly, his own theory of poetic influence—or poetic 'misprision' as he prefers to call it – focuses narrowly on (Freudian, and specifically Oedipal) relations of 'misreading', 'creative correction', and 'misinterpretation' between 'strong poets' and their precursors.[36] Bloom's conception of literary relations as a family affair rests on shaky premises, but there are elements within it, such as the dominant trope of the precursor author as a father figure, which speak to Joyce's (and Stephen Dedalus's) fascination with the question of paternity.

Joyce's thinking about literary relations (as it laconically transpires from his essays and private jottings), as well as his writing practices, resist reduction to any overly schematic literary theory. It is for this reason that the far-reaching ambit, or infinite compass, of intertextuality offers a more satisfactory way of understanding his complex compositional procedures. As Culler explains:

> The study of intertextuality is thus not the investigation of sources and influences as traditionally conceived; it casts its net wider to *include* anonymous discursive practices, codes whose origins are lost, that make possible the signifying practices of later texts.[37]

For all its emphasis on 'perspectives of unmasterable series, lost origins, endless horizons',[38] Culler's description of intertextuality refuses to dismiss traditional modes of inquiry from the new theoretical domain: the source or influence study fall within its infinite realm. Intertextuality emerges as an extension ad infinitum of the various domains that had previously been covered by other paradigms of literary connectivity.

The present study is informed by this view of the relations between the two paradigms: traditional manifestations of influence, such as quotation, imitation, echo, and allusion, whether accidental or intentional or merely perceived, are seen as belonging to the wider set of textual practices and events envisaged by the intertextual theorists of the 1960s. That an echo of

---

[34] Julia Kristeva, 'Poésie et Négativité' (1968), in *Séméiótiké*, 195.
[35] Bloom, *Anxiety of Influence*, 96.
[36] Bloom, *Anxiety of Influence*, 130.
[37] Culler, 'Presupposition and Intertextuality', 103 (my emphasis).
[38] Culler, 'Presupposition and Intertextuality', 111.

Flaubert in Joyce's works may be pinpointed and demonstrated to have been deliberately inscribed—the fact, in other words, of it being an allusion—will not preclude its description as an instance of intertextuality.

The inflections brought to bear on the definition of 'intertextuality' by later theorists, such as Gérard Genette and Michael Riffaterre,[39] are also relevant to this study's use of the word. Both critics reinstate authorial intention as a phenomenon worthy of critical consideration. Under their sway, intertextuality re-emerged in the 1980s and 1990s as a word that could be used to describe both a set of intentional authorial procedures and the status of all linguistic systems. In their analyses, as in Culler's account of the theory's original tenets, literary phenomena such as influence, quotation, and allusion are viewed as subsets within the overarching field of intertextuality.

This study's adherence to such a formulation of the intertextual paradigm also responds to the fact that Joyce's own understanding of literary relations shifts from an early concern with his own place within the literary tradition—within currents of influence and lines of artistic descent—towards an increasingly complex, proto-intertextual conceptualization of textual relations, in which the inevitability of repetition and relationality is acknowledged and embraced. Thus although this study's critical eye will be trained exclusively on Joyce's relations to Flaubert, it is not an influence study. While it relates certain Joycean styles and devices to relevant sections of the Flaubertian oeuvre rather than to any other literary corpus, this is not intended to imply that connections to other authors are invalid, or that certain Joycean structural and technical features arose from acquaintance with Flaubert's works alone. Intertextual events need nor—indeed should not—be thought of in exclusive terms: the aim of this book is merely to highlight what is particularly Flaubertian about certain aspects of Joyce's writing, irrespective of what other sources may have come into play at the same time.

Moreover, this study's concentrated focus on Flaubert should not be taken to suggest that Joyce's thoughtful and experimental response to his works is a matter of straightforward replication. As the following pages will show, literary repetition always comes with a difference. The textual interchange between two of the greatest masters of prose fiction is neither a question of plagiarism nor of banal reiteration: Joyce's adoption of Flaubert is always also an adaptation. Such, in a sense, is always the case in literary creation—as Jorge Luis Borges's *Pierre Menard* memorably

---

[39] See especially Genette, *Palimpsestes*, and Riffaterre, 'Interpretation and Undecidability', 'Intertextual Representation: On Mimesis as Interpretive Discourse', and 'Compulsory Reader Response: The Intertextual Drive'.

shows. André Topia notes in the context of a discussion of 'the intertextual problem' that the act of borrowing does not leave a reused fragment unchanged: 'echo is not repetition, re-utilization is not restitution', and the transplanted snippet 'becomes a graft [. . .] which takes root in its new environment and weaves organic connections within it'.[40]

What is known of Flaubert's place in the vast crucible of Joyce's writing? Flaubert was identified as a significant precursor to Joyce from the earliest days of his works' critical reception. Ezra Pound excitedly placed Joyce in the line of Flaubert's descent as soon as he became acquainted with *Dubliners* and the opening chapters of *A Portrait of the Artist as a Young Man*. In a review of *Dubliners* written for *The Egoist* in 1914, Pound marvelled at Joyce's realism and at his 'clear hard prose', ranking him among those 'followers of Flaubert [who] deal in exact presentation'.[41] Two years later, his review of *A Portrait* expressed the opinion that 'James Joyce produces the nearest thing to Flaubertian prose that we have now in English'.[42] Pound's conviction of the importance of the connection never relented. Indeed, his statements on the matter became ever more adamant as each of Joyce's works reached publication. In 1933 he even went so far as to invoke the image of paternity to describe the relationship: 'Joyce,' he declared, 'went back to Papa Flaubert.'[43]

Anecdotal biographical evidence tends to corroborate Pound's intuition. Constantine Curran states that when both men were students 'Flaubert frequently cropped up in our talk'.[44] In *James Joyce and the Making of 'Ulysses'* Frank Budgen reports his claim to have read every word Flaubert ever published, adding that 'Of all the great nineteenth-century masters of fiction Joyce held Flaubert in highest esteem.'[45] Another friend of Joyce's, the Polish writer Jan Parandowski, remembers him declaiming page upon page from one of Flaubert's stories entirely from memory.[46] In his monumental, if latterly much debated, biography, *James Joyce*, Richard Ellmann gives an account of an evening in a Parisian restaurant during which Joyce gleefully but mistakenly pointed out what he took to be

---

[40] André Topia, 'The Matrix and the Echo: Intertextuality in *Ulysses*', in *Post-structuralist Joyce*, ed. Derek Attridge and Daniel Ferrer (Cambridge: Cambridge University Press, 1984), 105.

[41] Ezra Pound, '*Dubliners* and Mr James Joyce', in *P/J*, 27–8.

[42] Ezra Pound, 'James Joyce, At Last the Novel Appears', in *P/J*, 89.

[43] Ezra Pound, 'Past History', in *P/J*, 248.

[44] Constantine Curran, *James Joyce Remembered* (London: Oxford University Press, 1968), 29.

[45] Budgen, *James Joyce and the Making of 'Ulysses'*, 186, 184.

[46] Jan Parandowski, 'Meeting with Joyce', in *James Joyce: Portraits of the Artist in Exile*, ed. Willard Potts (Dublin: Wolfhound Press, 1979), 159–60.

grammatical errors in Flaubert's short stories (such close attention to Flaubert's syntax may have been prompted by an article entitled 'A Propos du Style de Flaubert', which Marcel Proust had published in the *Nouvelle Revue Française* in January 1920).[47]

The first academic study to take up the baton from Ezra Pound's enthusiastic analogies was a doctoral thesis by Haskell M. Block entitled 'Théorie et technique du roman chez Flaubert et James Joyce',[48] submitted to the Sorbonne in 1948. Block sees Joyce as a 'direct inheritor of the end of the nineteenth century',[49] and particularly emphasizes the influence of the 'art for art's sake' movement in England and France. Block considers Flaubert's own direct impact on Joyce, but also considers how his influence was refracted through the works of a number of English, Irish, and American writers, most notably Walter Pater, George Moore, Henry James, Oscar Wilde, and Arthur Symons. The thesis provides a useful survey of some of the channels by which Joyce may have come to hear and read about Flaubert's works. Block identifies the publication of his correspondence in the 1880s and 1890s as:

> the most important factor in the development of Flaubert's reputation at the end of the nineteenth century.[50]

As well as eliciting an eloquent if perplexed response from Henry James, the letters were very positively reviewed by Walter Pater. It is to the influence of the latter that Block attributes the high esteem in which Flaubert was held by the English public in the 1890s. Block's study is historical and bibliographical in emphasis: what it gains in breadth it loses in detail—close readings of the text, for instance, are conspicuous by their absence. But this is not a loss in Block's own terms, for his ultimate aim is not so much to demonstrate that Flaubert exerted an influence on Joyce as to show, far more nebulously, that both belong to a literary tradition devoted to 'the enrichment of life'.[51]

This humanist attitude—which emphasizes both authors' (putatively) affirmative message, rather than the nuts and bolts of the connections between them—is also evident in Richard Cross's *Flaubert and Joyce: The*

---

[47] *JJ*, 492; Marcel Proust, 'A Propos du Style de Flaubert', in *Chroniques* (Paris: Gallimard, 1927), 202.

[48] Haskell M. Block, 'Théorie et technique du roman chez Flaubert et James Joyce' (unpublished doctoral thesis, University of Paris, Sorbonne, 1948).

[49] ['héritier direct de la fin du dix-neuvième siècle' (Block, 'Théorie et technique', 2)].

[50] ['le facteur le plus important dans le développement de la réputation de Flaubert à la fin du dix-neuvième siècle' (Block, 'Théorie et technique', 55)].

[51] ['l'enrichissement de la vie' (Block, 'Théorie et technique', 247)].

Rite of Fiction (1971), to date the only full-length study of the two authors to have appeared in print. Cross's study, like Block's, does not attempt to explore Flaubert's role as a possible source or influence for Joyce. Such a task, in fact, is dismissed as futile:

> I am not suggesting a need for *Quellenforschungen* [source studies]; efforts to unravel the many strands of influence in an *oeuvre* as complex as Joyce's are likely to prove unproductive.[52]

Cross hits the nail on the head as regards the impossibility of trying to unravel *all* the intertextual strands of Joyce's writing, yet an awareness of this insuperable difficulty need not invalidate more focused analyses of the intertextual cords that connect authors to each other. Cross's interest, however, is not in points of linguistic or formal intersection but in areas of likeness. His inquiries replicate Block's concern with similarities of plot, theme, and characterization, and the author is content to stress 'the pervasive affinity of mind and art which places both writers in a common literary tradition'.[53] Cross's study, in other words, is a resolutely comparative reading, which stops short of suggesting that the experiments carried out by Joyce may have been prompted or shaped by Flaubert's prior innovations, or—to put the matter in intertextual terms—that aspects of Joyce's writing may read as an elaboration of the phrases and structures of his French precursor.

Hugh Kenner's *Flaubert, Joyce, and Beckett: The Stoic Comedians* (1964) proposes a fundamentally different account of the two authors' relations. On Kenner's reading, Flaubert, Joyce, and Beckett represent three major points along a specific spectrum of literary development, 'each scorching in turn the earth where his successor would sow his crop'.[54] Flaubert is cast as the 'comedian of the Enlightenment', Joyce as the 'comedian of the Inventory', Beckett as the 'comedian of the Impasse'.[55] For Kenner, Flaubert—'the patron saint of the rigid fictional machine' and 'the most meticulous craftsman of prose fiction the world has ever seen'[56]—is the first great author to respond to revolutionary changes in book printing, the first to create works that revolve around words as individual units. This explains the enduring association of his name with the mystique of the *mot juste*: 'Our interest in the *mot juste*', holds Kenner:

---

[52] *F&J*, v.
[53] Haskell M. Block, 'Theory of Language in Gustave Flaubert and James Joyce', *Revue de littérature comparée*, xxxv (1961), 202, quoted in *F&J*, vi.
[54] *Stoics*, xviii.
[55] *Stoics*, 1, 30, 67.
[56] *Stoics*, 104–5, 12.

is a function of our concern with the single word, its look, feel, weight, history, range, and denotation.[57]

Joyce, he continues, 'pick[s] up Flaubert's fascination with the encyclo-paedic and the meticulous', but does so without 'the Frenchman's famous ecstasy of disgust [. . .] but with admiration and joy'.[58] In effect, Kenner's perception of this line of artistic descent replicates Pound's genealogical understanding of Joyce's relationship to Flaubert, articulating a concep-tion of literary relations in which authors influence each other, need each other, and are knowingly and willingly enmeshed in evolutionary currents involving their own responses to the discoveries of their predecessors. Like Pound, Kenner sees Joyce as 'the heir of Flaubert', asserting that with Joyce 'we move beyond Flaubert', and that 'Joyce chose to raise Flaubert to a higher power'.[59]

Although the intertextual reading of the works of Joyce and Flaubert offered in the following pages has no book-length precedent, it is indebted to a number of shorter studies, either as exponents of the inductive approach adopted here or for their prior identification of Flaubertian echoes in Joyce's writing. These are mentioned wherever apposite—in the main body of the text or in the footnotes, and in the bibliography. However, the most important antecedent to my analyses, a collection of essays edited by Claude Jacquet and André Topia in 1990, should be singled out for special mention. '*Scribble' 2: Joyce et Flaubert* is disparate in the way such compilations necessarily are, and does not, as such, give either a comprehensive or a consistent account of Joyce's relationship to Flaubert. Yet despite its fragmentariness the collection provides the begin-nings of a detailed intertextual approach.[60] Crucially, '*Scribble' 2* draws attention to David Hayman's momentous discovery of three 'Flaubert' jottings in one of the *Finnegans Wake* notebooks.[61] One of these states: 'G. F can rest having made me.'[62] Coming from an author obsessed with the themes of origins and paternity, the significance of this private

---

[57] *Stoics*, 42.

[58] *Stoics*, 62, 72.

[59] *Stoics*, 70, 52, 106.

[60] Particularly valuable contributions include Claude Jacquet, 'Joyce et Flaubert'; David Hayman, 'Toward a Postflaubertian Joyce'; André Topia, 'Flaubert et Joyce: les affinités sélectives'; Richard Brown, 'Shifting Sexual Centres: Joyce and Flaubert'; Jean-Michel Rabaté and Pierre-Marc de Biasi, 'Joyce, Flaubert et *Exiles*'.

[61] These had already been disclosed, without comment, in Hayman's Introduction to notebook VI.B.8 in *JJA 30* (1978), xviii.

[62] James Joyce, *Finnegans Wake* notebook VI.B.8, 42; *JJA 30*, 315.

acknowledgement of Flaubert as a literary father, cryptic though it is, should not be underestimated.

Another essay, by one of the editors of 'Scribble' 2, merits acknowledgement here. André Topia's 'The Matrix and the Echo: Intertextuality in *Ulysses*' situates Joyce's intertextuality in the wake of changes to the status of quotation effected by nineteenth-century writing in general, and by Flaubert's works in particular.[63] Topia holds that:

> In the evolution towards a literature of the intertextual, Flaubert occupies a strategic position: he is among the first to have deliberately blurred the hierarchy between the original text and the secondary text.[64]

In Flaubert's and Joyce's texts, techniques such as free indirect discourse and interior monologue bring about 'an increasing instability in the notion of origin: discourses weave through the text in such a way that one cannot really distinguish the original from its more or less distorted version'.[65] Although he sketches an important connection between Joyce and Flaubert, Topia's overriding interest is in 'discourse', rather than in specifically literary prior writing, in *Ulysses*'s integration of:

> fragments of popular songs, folk ballads, operatic arias or religious hymns; scraps of quotations from poems, novels, plays, nursery rhymes; bits of magazine and newspaper articles; proverbial phrases, maxims of popular wisdom.[66]

In examining the social dimension of Joyce's intertextuality in the spirit of the notion's first theorists (both Kristeva and Barthes reiterate the social emphases of Bakhtin's earlier work on the concepts of dialogism and heteroglossia), Topia shines a spotlight on an aspect of his writing that blossoms in the wake of Flaubert's ground-breakingly intertextual compositional methods.

---

[63] Topia, 'The Matrix and the Echo'. Topia's opening statement that 'since the end of the nineteenth-century, the status of quotation has been one of the most crucial and problematic aspects of writing' (103) is amply supported by recent analyses. In *The Copywrights: Intellectual Property and the Literary Imagination* (London and Ithaca: Cornell University Press, 2003), for instance, Paul Saint-Amour argues that the mode of highly self-regarding intertextual writing which blossomed in modernist texts followed from regular extensions to copyright law over the two preceding centuries. In *Original Copy: Plagiarism and Originality in Nineteenth-Century Literature* (Oxford: Oxford University Press, 2007), Robert MacFarlane shows that the second half of the nineteenth century saw a swing in favour of recombinative poetics, which only later became entrenched in the canonical works of high modernism.

[64] Topia, 'The Matrix and the Echo', 104.

[65] Topia, 'The Matrix and the Echo', 104.

[66] Topia, 'The Matrix and the Echo', 112.

Adding its analyses and interpretations to those that precede it, this study offers more than an account of Joyce's working methods or of one strand of his artistic formation. Its findings have the potential to inflect the reader's actual experience of Joyce's works: not, or not solely, by drawing attention to specific Flaubertian intertextual moments in Joyce's fiction (which the reader may or may not be equipped to recognize and respond to), but by ushering in a new awareness of the dense intertextual weave of his writing: heightening one's sense of the finesse of his linguistic ear, the precision of his recall, and his transformative genius in the use of other authors' discoveries. With any one of Joyce's works, one is not merely in the presence of a single text, nor even of a dazzling Flauberto-Joycean duet of texts, but within an infinite, veritably symphonic echo chamber of literary reverberations.

The book is organized into six chapters, which follow the sequence of Joyce's works. This chronological approach highlights the ways in which Joyce's relationship to Flaubert evolved over the course of his writing career.

The first chapter identifies and analyses traces of Flaubert in Joyce's early writing—the critical essays (written as a student of University College, Dublin, between 1899 and 1902); entries in the 'Paris and Pola Commonplace Book' that Joyce kept in 1902–3 and then 1903–4; the short snippets of dramatic or narrative writing, collected between 1900 and 1903, to which he referred as 'epiphanies'; and *Stephen Hero*, the bulky, 64-chapter draft of what would eventually become *A Portrait of the Artist as a Young Man*. Contrary to W. B. Yeats's assertion that Flaubert's works were difficult to obtain in early twentieth-century Dublin,[67] this chapter establishes that a number of Flaubert's books were available to Joyce at the National Library of Ireland at that time, and, even more significantly, that Joyce purchased his own copies of both *Madame Bovary* and *L'Éducation sentimentale*, in original French editions, as early as 1901. Even at this early stage, Flaubertian echoes adumbrate the importance of Joyce's intertextual relationship to his French precursor in later works.

Chapter 2 is devoted to a close intertextual reading of both authors' collections of stories, *Trois Contes* (1877) and *Dubliners* (1914). The argument focuses on the word 'gnomon', which famously appears in italics in the opening paragraph of the first story in Joyce's collection ('The Sisters'), and which affiliates it to Flaubert's short story, 'Hérodias', in which it also features. The use of this rare word is read as a gesture of

---

[67] W. B. Yeats, 'The Reform of the Theatre', in *Samhain: An Occasional Review* (September 1903), 11. See also Haskell M. Block, 'Flaubert, Yeats, and the National Library', *Modern Language Notes*, vol. 67, no. 1 (January 1952).

acknowledgement on Joyce's part, indicating a subtle but extensive semantic, thematic, symbolic, and structural intertextuality between his and
Flaubert's short stories. The chapter also considers Joyce's response on a
technical level, exploring the modes of his elaborations on Flaubert in such
areas as the splicing of the realistic and the symbolic, the blurring of the
boundaries between the static and the dynamic, and the deployment of
cinematographic writing.

Chapter 3 examines Flaubertian intertextuality in *A Portrait of the Artist
as a Young Man*. It considers references to Flaubert in the novel and argues
that although Stephen Dedalus may be wrestling with something resem-
bling Harold Bloom's 'anxiety of influence', Joyce himself had already,
even at this relatively early stage in his writing career, come to see his
relationship to Flaubert as a matter of playful engagement rather than of
rivalrous angst.

Chapter 4 explores the significance of a jotting made by Joyce in the
notebook he kept in preparation for the composition of his only play,
Exiles (1918). It considers the implications of Joyce's view of *Madame
Bovary* as a watershed literary event—a tale of adultery in which 'the centre
of sympathy appears to have been shifted from the lover or fancyman to
the husband or cuckold'. Joyce's note goes on to state that 'This change is
utilized in *Exiles*'.[68] Chapter 4's analysis of the play investigates the
relationship Joyce sought to establish between Richard Rowan and the
theatre-going public, contrasting Joyce's unsteady control of audience
sympathy in the play with his masterful orchestration of such responses
in *Ulysses*. Noting the absence in *Exiles*, and presence in *Ulysses*, of legally
contracted marriage as a frame for the study of adultery, the chapter
analyses Joyce's negotiation and interrogation of what was arguably
the most pivotal of nineteenth- and early twentieth-century bourgeois
institutions.

Chapter 5 is divided into three sections and focuses on some of the
numerous Flaubertian intertextual moments in Joyce's *Ulysses*. The first
section registers the literary marks of Joyce's reading of Flaubert's *La
Tentation de saint Antoine*, of which a record survives in the *Ulysses*
notesheets at the British Library in London. It begins by looking in detail
at Joyce's references in the book to a cluster of third- and fourth-century
church heresiarchs in the light of Flaubert's grouping of the same three
figures in *La Tentation*, before examining Joyce's extensive engagement
with *La Tentation* in the 'Circe' episode. The chapter's second section
aligns the 'citizen' of the 'Cyclops' episode of *Ulysses* with the character

---

[68] *E*, 165.

referred to as '*le Citoyen*' in *L'Éducation sentimentale*, and suggests that both characters embody their authors' sceptical evaluation of some of the political and philosophical offshoots of the Enlightenment. In a similar vein, the third section of Chapter 5 explores the intertextual relations between *Bouvard et Pécuchet*, the *Dictionnaire des Idées Reçues*, and the 'Eumaeus' and 'Ithaca' episodes of *Ulysses*, showing that these texts portray blind belief in facts and the catalogability of all knowledge as a nineteenth-century bourgeois perversion of Enlightenment intellectual ideals, as most notably exemplified by the era's newly systematic encyclopaedias.

Chapter 6 is divided into two sections. The first examines *Finnegans Wake* notebook VI.B.8, in which Joyce made the 'Flaubert' jottings discovered by David Hayman. It relates these to Joyce's travels through Normandy (home to Flaubert as well as Emma Bovary and Bouvard and Pécuchet) in the summer of 1925, and suggests that both the journey and the jottings reflect Joyce's preoccupation with Flaubert and with issues of intertextuality in the early stages of his work on *Finnegans Wake*. The second section considers allusions to Flaubert in the *Wake*: these are read as knowing indications of a connection between the radical intertextuality deployed by Joyce in his final work and the precedent of Flaubert's *Bouvard et Pécuchet*.

The conclusion draws together the implications of the intertextual strands examined in the preceding chapters to suggest that throughout his writing Joyce uses Flaubert to think through the dynamics of any text's inevitable relations to other texts, and that these reflections inform the self-consciousness of his increasingly intertextual practices. Ultimately, it is argued that the ever more radical nature of Joyce's intertextuality paved the way for the emergence of intertextual theory in the 1960s.

1

Early Writing

A primary concern in setting out to identify traces of Flaubert's impact on Joyce's early writing is to establish a plausible bibliographical foundation to support such a line of inquiry. Many of the most likely sources of information regarding the nature and extent of Joyce's familiarity with Flaubert's work before his departure from Ireland in 1904 fail to yield relevant facts. The National Library of Ireland, where Joyce, like most of the students of University College, was 'a frequent reader',[1] holds no record of the books he consulted. Similarly, although Richard Ellmann states that Joyce 'spent his days' at the Bibliothèque Nationale during the months he spent in Paris in 1902 and 1903,[2] Joyce's name does not appear on the library's readers' register. Ellmann's claim concerning this reading routine is corroborated by Joyce's reader's card, dated 24 January 1903.[3] The absence of Joyce's name from the register may indicate that he confined his reading to books that were available on open shelves rather than ordering volumes from the library stacks. The Bibliothèque Sainte-Geneviève, where Ellmann claims Joyce 'spent his nights'[4] during the same period, kept no readers' records for the first decades of the twentieth century. Public-library documents, therefore, offer no clues as to what Joyce may have read as a young man. Surviving private records do testify to some of Joyce's literary interests. He compiled lists of authors, for instance, in his 'Paris and Pola Commonplace Book'[5]—but Flaubert does not feature.

The apparent dearth of evidence concerning Joyce's reading of Flaubert is compounded by suggestions that Flaubert was an author whose works may have been difficult to obtain in turn-of-the-century Dublin. In

---

[1] *JJ*, 117. The library of University College, in which Joyce was enrolled, was practically non-existent at the end of the nineteenth century.

[2] *JJ*, 120.

[3] *JJ*, 120. The card is reproduced in *JJ*, Plate VI.

[4] *JJ*, 120.

[5] James Joyce, 'Paris and Pola Commonplace Book', Dublin, National Library of Ireland, NLI MS 36,639/2/A, 16–18.

Stephen Hero the protagonist encounters 'through the medium of hardly procured translations the spirit of Henrik Ibsen'.[6] There are reasons to think that Flaubert's work may also have been hard to procure. Translations, for one thing, were scarce and slow to appear in print. *Madame Bovary*, which went through numerous French editions and reprints in the second half of the nineteenth century, was not translated into English until 1886, when the task was undertaken by Eleanor Marx (a connection that, if he knew of it, may have appealed to the socialist leanings of Joyce's youth).[7] As a student of French from 1899, Joyce would probably have been less impeded by the small number of available translations than by the predominantly Catholic context of Ireland: *Madame Bovary* had caused Flaubert to be tried (and acquitted) in court in 1857 for 'offences against public morality and religion', and in 1864 both *Madame Bovary* and *Salammbô* had been added to the Vatican Index of Prohibited Books.[8] Suspicions concerning the difficulty of obtaining copies of Flaubert's books in Joyce's Ireland are exacerbated by a statement published by W. B. Yeats in 1903. In September of that year Yeats wrote an article for *Samhain* in which he vehemently condemned the censorship of Balzac and Flaubert in Ireland, drawing particular attention to the conspicuous absence of any of Flaubert's works at the National Library:

> Every educated man knows how great a portion of mankind is in Flaubert and Balzac, and their books have been proscribed in the courts of law, and I found some time ago that our own National Library, though it has two books on the genius of Flaubert, had refused on moral grounds to have any books written by him.[9]

Such testimony, coming from an engaged public intellectual, had the potential to exert considerable influence: to raise awareness of censorship, to impart a sense of the value of Flaubert's and Balzac's works, and to ensure that the missing books were purchased. But Yeats, it seems, was wrong about the National Library's attitude to Flaubert, as is attested by

---

[6] *SH*, 40.

[7] Gustave Flaubert, *Madame Bovary*, trans. Eleanor Marx-Aveling (London: Vizetelly, 1886). See Ronald Bush, 'James Joyce, Eleanor Marx, and the Future of Modernism', in *The Future of Modernism*, ed. Hugh Witemeyer (Ann Arbor: University of Michigan Press, 1997). Other translations followed in 1896 and 1902. For discussions of Joyce's politics and early socialist inclinations, see *CJ*, especially Chapter III, 'Joyce', 73–96, and Dominic Manganiello, *Joyce's Politics* (London: Routledge and Kegan Paul, 1980), especially Chapter 3, 'Perspectives: Socialism and Anarchism', 67–114.

[8] *Index Librorum Prohibitorum, 1600–1966*, ed. J. M. De Bujanda with Marcella Richter (Montréal: Médiaspaul, 2002), 349.

[9] W. B. Yeats, 'The Reform of the Theatre', 11. See also Block, 'Flaubert, Yeats, and the National Library'.

the institution's acquisition record. Indeed the shelf-marks and accession stamps of certain volumes still held at the National Library today prove that at least some of Flaubert's works were available to readers of the library at the turn of the century, and that these included the two (*Madame Bovary* and *Salammbô*) that had been denounced by the Vatican. The Library holds French copies of *Salammbô* in an edition of 1897 (acquired in 1899), *Trois Contes* in an edition of 1899 (acquired in 1900), and *Madame Bovary* in an edition of 1903 (acquired in 1903). It also holds copies of two of the four volumes of Flaubert's *Correspondance* (series I and III, published in 1891 and 1892 respectively) that were then available (figs. 1–5).[10] In the light of these records, Yeats's outrage regarding the Library's putative ban on Flaubert appears to have been misinformed.

In 2005 the National Library of Ireland was offered a right of first refusal on two books by Flaubert bearing Joyce's signature—these had recently emerged for sale in the United States after being held for decades in private ownership. The books are original French editions of *Madame Bovary* (1900) and *L'Éducation sentimentale* (1901), published in Paris by Bibliothèque-Charpentier.[11] The copy of *Madame Bovary* bears two signatures. The first appears on the inside front endpaper and is dated 'June 1901'. The second appears at the top right-hand corner of the artwork that decorates the front wrapper. The copy of *L'Éducation sentimentale* is signed once on the half-title page and the signature is dated 1901. It seems likely, given the proximity in the editions' respective publication dates and in the dates inscribed in the books in Joyce's hand, that both copies were purchased at the same time (figs. 6–11). The books, acquired by Joyce at the age of nineteen, constitute the earliest evidence of his interest in Flaubert. They have featured neither in catalogues of Joyce's various libraries nor in accounts of his reading.[12] They have now been resold into private ownership.

---

[10]   All of these books were published in Paris by Bibliothèque-Charpentier, from 1891 to 1903.

[11]   Gustave Flaubert, *Madame Bovary* (Paris: Bibliothèque-Charpentier, 1900); Gustave Flaubert, *L'Éducation sentimentale* (Paris: Bibliothèque-Charpentier, 1901). These books previously belonged to the personal library of Thomas Quinn Curtiss, best known for his work as theatre critic for the *International Herald Tribune* and *The New York Times*. Curtiss acquired the books from the Irish critic Ernest Boyd, whose signature appears on the copy of *Madame Bovary*.

[12]   The main catalogues of Joyce's libraries are: Thomas E. Connolly, *The Personal Library of James Joyce: A Descriptive Bibliography* (Buffalo: University of Buffalo, 1957); *CJ*; Michael Patrick Gillespie, *Inverted Volumes Improperly Arranged: James Joyce and his Trieste Library* (Ann Arbor: UMI Research Press, 1983); Michael Patrick Gillespie, with the assistance of Erik Bradford Stocker, *James Joyce's Trieste Library: A Catalogue of Materials at the Harry Ransom Humanities Research Centre*, ed. Dave Oliphant (Austin: Harry Ransom Humanities Research Centre, 1986).

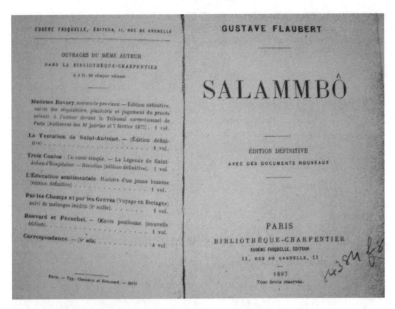

Fig. 1. Title page, 1897 edition of *Salammbô*, acquired by the National Library of Ireland in 1899.

Constantine Curran's published recollections of James Joyce provide additional information concerning his knowledge of Flaubert, and his preferences for certain corners of the oeuvre over others. Thus:

> it was Joyce who made me read *La Légende de saint Julien l'Hospitalier*, that ingenious piece of literary *vitrail* [. . . .] But he himself, as an apprentice craftsman, was more interested in the fatuous doings of Bouvard and Pécuchet, in Flaubert's collection of 'cases'. And in what Elizabeth Bowen calls 'the exquisite compilation of a *cliché* dictionary for additions to which one strained one's ears at gatherings'. He was already collecting 'epiphanies'.[13]

From the evidence thus pieced together from different sources, Joyce's reading of Flaubert appears to have been remarkably comprehensive. He seems to have been well versed in those of Flaubert's works conventionally considered to be his masterpieces (*Madame Bovary*, *L'Éducation sentimentale*, *Bouvard et Pécuchet*, and *Trois Contes*). As we have seen, he had other

---

[13] Curran, *James Joyce Remembered*, 28–30. Ellmann's account of Curran's memories on this matter (identical in both editions of Joyce's biography) is rather different, privileging *La Tentation de saint Antoine* over *Bouvard et Pécuchet*: 'He was interested in Flaubert, less in *Madame Bovary*, according to Curran, than in "La Légende de saint Julien l'Hospitalier" and *La Tentation de saint Antoine*.'—*JJ*, 75. No source is given for this statement.

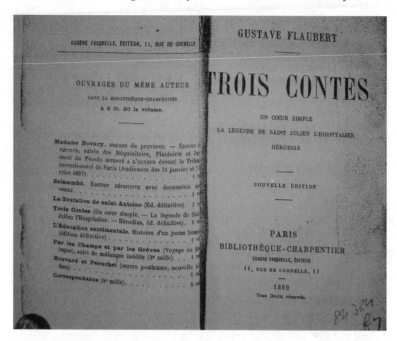

Fig. 2. Title page, 1899 edition of *Trois Contes*, acquired by the National Library of Ireland in 1900.

Flaubertian texts, most notably *Salammbô* and the *Correspondance*, within reach at the National Library. The only key text of which there is no trace either at the National Library or in Joyce's own Dublin library, or in accounts of his reading at this time, is *La Tentation de saint Antoine* (which is not to say, of course, that he did not read it).[14]

In 'The Reform of the Theatre' Yeats mentioned 'two books on the genius of Flaubert' which he had found at the National Library. There are three studies in the National Library's possession today that might be those to which Yeats alludes. The first is John Charles Tarver's study, *Gustave Flaubert as Seen in his Works and Correspondence*, which was acquired by the Library in April 1896.[15] Haskell M. Block describes Tarver's work as 'the first English study of Flaubert', accurately noting

---

[14] Ellmann reports Joyce's purchase of a copy of *La Tentation de saint Antoine* in Trieste in 1913 or 1914—*JJ*, 779. This acquisition, and the impact it had on Joyce's writing, is explored in detail in Chapter 5.

[15] John Charles Tarver, *Gustave Flaubert as Seen in his Works and Correspondence* (London: Archibald Constable & Company, 1895).

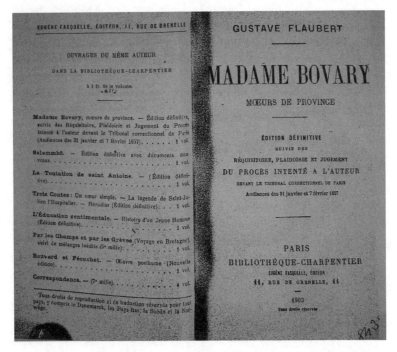

Fig. 3. Title page, 1903 edition of *Madame Bovary*, acquired by the National Library of Ireland in 1903.

that the study's biographical narrative 'is more or less entirely based on the *Correspondance*, from which abundant translations enrich the text'. Flaubert's works are also 'paraphrased at length and illustrated by quotations'. Tarver's book, in other words, 'lets Flaubert do the talking',[16] thereby providing a general and largely reliable Flaubertian primer for an English-speaking audience (although the published letters on which Tarver's account is founded had already been censored by Flaubert's niece, and Tarver warns that he himself has excised passages from Flaubert's letters which 'might incline the English reader to avert his gaze').[17] The second of the books Yeats may have had in mind is Maxime Du Camp's two-volume *Souvenirs littéraires*,[18] which was acquired by the Library at

---

[16] ['la première étude anglaise sur Flaubert'; 'se base à peu près complètement sur la *Correspondance* dont des traductions abondantes enrichissent le texte'; 'paraphrasés longuement et illustrés de citations'; 'laisse Flaubert parler' (Block, 'Théorie et technique', 178)].

[17] Tarver, *Gustave Flaubert*, Introductory Note, xvi.

[18] Maxime Du Camp, *Souvenirs littéraires*, 2 vols (Paris: Hachette et Cie, 1882–3).

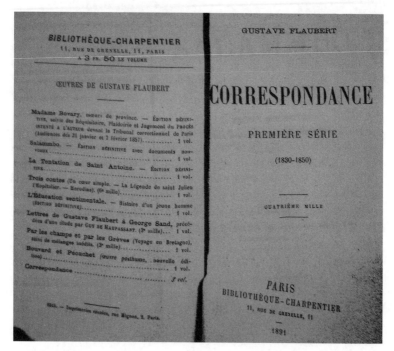

Fig. 4. Title page, 1891 edition of Flaubert's *Correspondance* ('Première Série'), acquired by the National Library of Ireland in 1900.

the time of its publication in 1882 and 1883, and which contains extensive recollections of Du Camp's friendship with Flaubert. These 'souvenirs' are now widely deemed to form an untrustworthy account of the two men's relationship, and the solid friendship portrayed to have in fact been fluctuating and ambivalent. The third book to which Yeats may have been referring is a volume entitled *Studies in European Literature, being the Taylorian Lectures 1889–1899*, which was acquired by the Library between January and June 1901. One of these lectures, given by Paul Bourget, was devoted to Flaubert. (However, because only one of the book's sections is specifically concerned with Flaubert, it seems rather less likely that Yeats should have had this book in mind when he wrote his article.)[19] Bourget's account of the man and artist is broad in scope, analytical, and fervently laudatory. His address begins by singling Flaubert out as:

[19]   Paul Bourget, 'Gustave Flaubert', in *Studies in European Literature, being the Taylorian Lectures, 1889–1899* (Oxford: Clarendon Press, 1900).

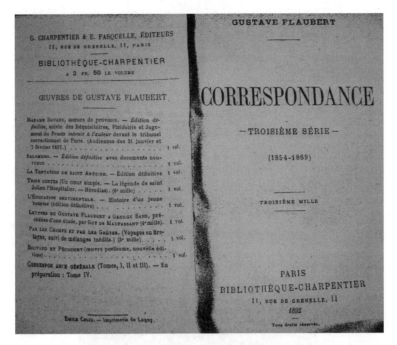

Fig. 5. Title page, 1892 edition of Flaubert's *Correspondance* ('Troisième Série'), acquired by the National Library of Ireland in 1900.

the most scrupulous and accomplished prose writer to have appeared in print in our country in this second half of the century[20]

and it closes on a note of even more absolute endorsement, with Bourget identifying the novelist both as 'the most magnificent example of a passionate, exclusive love of literature' and as 'the greatest, the purest, most complete of our literary artists'.[21] Bourget succinctly and eloquently surveys the landscape of Flaubert's poetics and accomplishments, evoking his 'aesthetic of total truth', his 'religion of literature', his affiliation to 'Art for Art's Sake', his writing's combination of romantic and scientific tendencies, his hatred of bourgeois mediocrity, and the carefully crafted, resplendent beauty of his prose:

---

[20] ['le prosateur le plus scrupuleux aussi et le plus accompli qui ait paru chez nous dans cette seconde moitié du siècle' (Bourget, 'Gustave Flaubert', 254)].

[21] ['le plus magnifique exemple d'amour passionné, exclusif pour la littérature'; 'le plus grand, le plus pur, le plus complet de nos artistes littéraires' (Bourget, 'Gustave Flaubert', 274)].

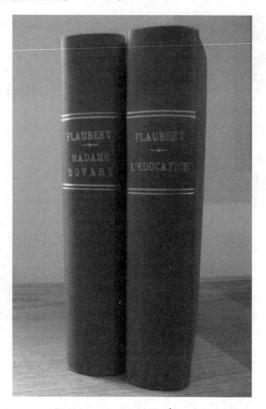

Fig. 6. Joyce's copies of *Madame Bovary* and *L'Éducation sentimentale* (rebound).

This impeccable prose, alternately coloured like a Flemish painting, sculpted like a Greek marble statue, rhythmic and supple as a phrase of music.[22]

Particular emphasis is placed on Flaubert's commitment to impersonality and on the rigorously expounded theory of art set forth in his *Correspondance*. Bourget quotes from several of Flaubert's letters to highlight his famous dedication to the ideal of godlike, artistic impassibility, for instance adducing his assertions that 'the Artist must no more appear in his work than God does in the world'[23] and that:

---

[22] ['esthétique du vrai total'; 'religion des lettres'; 'l'Art pour l'Art'; 'Cette prose impeccable, tour à tour colorée comme une peinture flamande, taillée en plein marbre comme une statue grecque, rythmée et souple comme une phrase de musique' (Bourget, 'Gustave Flaubert', 254, 255, 263, 272, 273, 267)].

[23] Flaubert to George Sand, late December 1875, *GW*, 401 ['l'Artiste ne doit pas plus apparaître dans son oeuvre que Dieu dans la nature' (*C4*, 1,000), quoted in Bourget, 'Gustave Flaubert', 263].

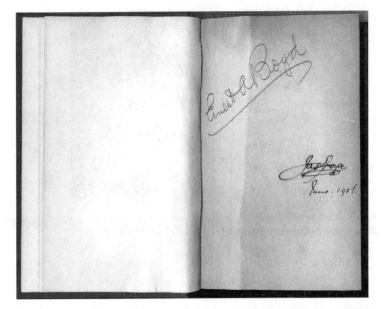

Fig. 7. Joyce's signature, dated June 1901, in his copy of *Madame Bovary* (inside front endpaper).

An author in his book must be like God in the universe, present everywhere and visible nowhere. Art being a second Nature, the creator of that Nature must behave similarly. In all its atoms, in all its aspects, let there be a sense of hidden, infinite impassivity [impassibility].[24]

There is much in this short essay that may have shaped Joyce's understanding of Flaubert. If he read it, he may, along with the salient facts of Flaubert's biography and literary philosophy, have made note of a quotation from the letters in which his precursor expressed the premonition that his endeavours might be completed by an artistic successor:

the task which I am undertaking will be carried through by someone else. I will have shown somebody the way, someone more gifted and more *born for it* than I am.[25]

---

[24] Flaubert to Louise Colet, 9 December 1852, *FSI*, 173 ['L'auteur dans son oeuvre doit être comme Dieu dans l'univers, présent partout et visible nulle part. L'art étant une seconde nature, le créateur de cette nature-là doit agir par des procédés analogues. Que l'on sente dans tous les atomes, à tous les aspects, une impassibilité cachée, infinie.' (*C2*, 204), quoted in Bourget, 'Gustave Flaubert', 264].

[25] Flaubert to Louise Colet, 27 March 1835, *GW*, 203 ['la tâche que j'entreprends sera exécutée par un autre. J'aurai mis sur la voie quelqu'un de mieux doué et de plus *né*.' (*C2*, 287), quoted in Bourget, 'Gustave Flaubert', 266].

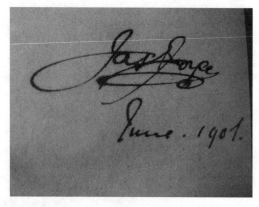

Fig. 8. Close-up of Joyce's signature, dated June 1901, in his copy of *Madame Bovary* (inside front endpaper).

THE EARLY ESSAYS

Although Joyce's knowledge of some of Flaubert's letters (whether acquired through such secondary sources as were available at the National Library[26] or from the *Correspondance* itself) is manifest in his early writing, it was by reference to the novels themselves that his interest first became apparent. Indeed, even had Joyce's own copy of *Madame Bovary* not come to light, 'The Day of the Rabblement' (dated 15 October 1901), one of Joyce's first published essays, makes his familiarity with that most scandalous of Flaubertian novels a matter of ascertainable fact. Joyce refers to *Madame Bovary* in the context of a discussion of George Moore (1852–1933), whose novels he dismisses as outdated. Moore's work is criticized for its lack of novelty—for coming at the tail-end of a tradition inaugurated by Flaubert:

> Mr Moore is really struggling in the backwash of that tide which has advanced from Flaubert through Jakobsen [*sic*] to D'Aununzio [*sic*]: for two entire eras lie between *Madame Bovary* and *Il Fuoco*.[27]

For David Hayman, Joyce's gesture of rejection inadvertently discloses the real allegiances discernible in his (much later) first novel, *A Portrait of the Artist as a Young Man* (1916):

---

[26] There are many more such sources than can be listed here. To name but one example, the National Library was a subscriber to *Macmillan's Magazine*, in which Henry James's review of Flaubert's letters had appeared in 1893.

[27] James Joyce, 'The Day of the Rabblement', in *OCPW*, 51.

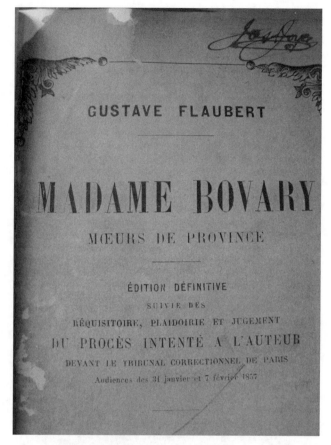

GUSTAVE FLAUBERT

MADAME BOVARY

MŒURS DE PROVINCE

ÉDITION DÉFINITIVE
SUIVIE DES
RÉQUISITOIRE, PLAIDOIRIE ET JUGEMENT
DU PROCÈS INTENTÉ A L'AUTEUR
DEVANT LE TRIBUNAL CORRECTIONNEL DE PARIS
Audiences des 31 janvier et 7 février 1857

Fig. 9. Joyce's signature in his copy of *Madame Bovary*, at the top right-hand corner of the artwork on the front endpaper.

    There is more to this rather pontifical statement than the value judgement of a nineteen-year-old initiate. Here, for the convenience of later critics, Joyce has listed some of the major literary forebears of his own novel.[28]

Joyce's confidence in castigating George Moore as a follower of Flaubert certainly suggests a more than casual acquaintance with the text that anchors his statement: *Madame Bovary*. It should be noted that Joyce does not bring into question the value of Flaubert, nor of the Danish novelist, poet, and scientist Jens-Peter Jacobsen (1847–1885), nor of the

---

[28] David Hayman, '*A Portrait of the Artist as a Young Man* and *L'Éducation sentimentale*: The Structural Affinities', *Orbis Litterarum* XIX, no. 4 (1964), 161.

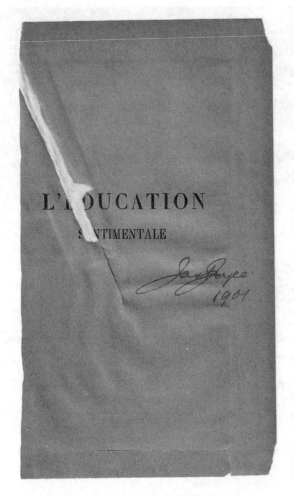

Fig. 10. Joyce's signature, dated 1901, on the half-title page of his copy of *L'Éducation sentimentale*.

Italian poet, novelist, journalist, and political figure Gabriele D'Annunzio (1863–1938): he points out, rather, that if literature advances in tides, then the particular tide of which they are the principal exponents has receded. Joyce's genealogy of nineteenth-century prose writing seems to have more to do with the urge to deprecate Moore, an Irish contemporary rival, as a mere imitator of other authors' artistic experiments and achievements, than with the wholesale rejection of his

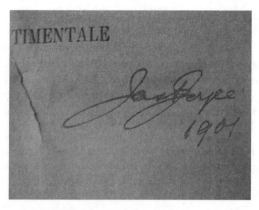

Fig. 11. Close-up of Joyce's signature, dated 1901, on the half-title page of his copy of *L'Éducation sentimentale*.

predecessors.[29] There is no indication that Joyce considers Moore's European masters to be flawed—only that Moore himself is misguided in being a backward-looking replicator rather than an innovator:

> Mr Moore [. . .] has wonderful mimetic ability [. . .] his new impulse has no kind of relation to the future of art.[30]

Joyce's disdain for Moore arises from three related observations. Firstly, Moore, like Edward Martyn, is not a writer 'of much originality'. Secondly (and relatedly), Moore is praised with cutting irony for 'ha[ving] wonderful mimetic ability'. Thirdly, Joyce condemns him on grounds of artistic fickleness: 'the quest for a new impulse', Joyce wryly speculates, 'may explain his recent startling conversion'.[31] The 'startling conversion' described here was to the cause of the Irish Literary Revival, with whose doctrinaire agenda Joyce resolutely refused to align himself. For Moore to join the ranks of the Revivalists was, to Joyce's mind, to make himself a follower once more. Beneath all this lies an unspoken agenda: the essay constitutes Joyce's effort to carve out a niche for himself in contemporary literature by implying his own commitment to originality, and differentiating himself from his most obvious Irish contender (a rival with whom—for all his tacit denial—he shared a strong interest in the continental

---

[29] The opinion Joyce articulates regarding Moore's imitative relation to Flaubert is one with which subsequent criticism has concurred. As C. Heywood has shown, Flaubert's influence on Moore is particularly obvious in *A Mummer's Wife* (1885)—'Flaubert, Miss Braddon, and George Moore', *Comparative Literature*, vol. 12, no. 2 (Spring 1960).

[30] 'Rabblement', *OCPW*, 51.

[31] 'Rabblement', *OCPW*, 51.

literature that the essay seeks to present as irrelevant[32]). Moore's regard for the same figures was a source of annoyance to Joyce, and 'The Day of the Rabblement' betrays his attempt to position himself within a separate tradition. Indeed Joyce's map of Moore's literary heritage stands in contrast to the idealized chart of genealogical descent outlined at the end of the essay, in which Joyce features as the self-proclaimed successor to the great dramatic names of Henrik Ibsen (1828–1906) and Gerhart Hauptmann (1862–1946):

> Elsewhere there are men who are worthy to carry on the tradition of the old master dying in Christiania. He has already found his successor in the writer of *Michael Kramer*, and the third minister will not be wanting when his hour comes. Even now that hour may be standing by the door.[33]

The prophetic tone of this desired scenario functions as an implicit reiteration of Joyce's dismissal of the artistic path adopted by George Moore.

Although rivalry may partly explain Joyce's relegation of prose realism to an inferior literary realm, other motives also prompted Joyce's flamboyant tribute to the leading figures of avant-garde European theatre. The impassioned homage to Ibsen and Hauptmann at the end of 'The Day of the Rabblement' accords with Joyce's high valuation of the concept of 'drama'—to the detriment of 'literature'—at this time in his life. 'Drama' is first defined by Joyce in 'Royal Hibernian Academy "Ecce Homo"':

> if a play, or work of music, or picture concerns itself with the everlasting hopes, desires and hates of our widely related nature, then it is drama.[34]

Prose does not feature in the subsequent enumeration of the arts to which the concept of 'drama' applies:

> It is a mistake to limit drama to the stage; a drama can be painted as well as sung or acted, and 'Ecce Homo' is a drama.[35]

In Joyce's next essay, 'Drama and Life' (which is dated 10 January 1900 and which Joyce read before University College's Literary and Historical Society on 20 January), 'drama' and 'literature' are more starkly opposed:

---

[32] Stanislaus Joyce, for instance, recalls his brother's passionate admiration for D'Annunzio, whose *Il Fuoco* he reportedly 'considered the highest achievement of the novel to date'—*My Brother's Keeper* (London: Faber and Faber, 1958), 154. Joyce's own copies of a number of D'Annunzio's books, purchased in Dublin in 1900, are held by the library at University College.

[33] 'Rabblement', *OCPW*, 52.

[34] James Joyce, 'Royal Hibernian Academy "Ecce Homo"', in *OCPW*, 17.

[35] 'Ecce Homo', *OCPW*, 18.

Human society is the embodiment of changeless laws which the whimsical-ities and circumstances of men and women involve and overwrap. The realm of literature is the realm of these accidental manners and humours—a spacious realm; and the true literary artist concerns himself mainly with them. Drama has to do with the underlying laws first, in all their nakedness and divine severity.[36]

Literature, in other words, deals in transient superficialities, the passing fashions of the day; drama, by contrast, is deemed to deal in absolute essences. The phrase 'true literary artist' has insensibly become an insulting tag. Later on in the essay Joyce becomes more frank, ridiculing 'litterateurs [*sic*]' as 'matchless serio-comics'.[37] Truth is at the heart of Joyce's conception of drama. Drama is 'the interplay of passions to portray truth';[38] truth will lead the drama of the future to be 'at war with convention';[39] art is deemed to be 'true to itself when it deals with truth'.[40] Because of this emphasis on truth, the timeless uniformity of life and its perpetual routinely common-places, however seemingly banal, are central to Joyce's notion of art:

> out of the dreary sameness of existence, a measure of dramatic life may be drawn. Even the most commonplace, the deadest among the living, may play a part in a great drama.[41]

Such statements foreshadow Joyce's elaboration of the new (if largely private) literary form of the 'epiphany', as embodied in those short passages of prose or drama that the protagonist of *Stephen Hero* defines as 'spiritual manifest-ation[s]' arising from 'the vulgarity of speech or gesture'.[42]

'Drama' does not long retain the privileged importance accorded to it in these early essays. In 'James Clarence Mangan' (published in May 1902 in *St Stephen's*, University College's student magazine), 'literature' is distin-guished from 'ephemeral writing', and what had been called 'drama' in Joyce's earlier pieces is referred to as 'poetry' and 'philosophy':

> Literature is the wide domain which lies between ephemeral writing and poetry (with which is philosophy), and just as the greater part of verse is not literature, so even original writers and thinkers must often be jealously denied the honourable title.[43]

---

[36] James Joyce, 'Drama and Life', in *OCPW*, 23–4.
[37] 'Drama and Life', *OCPW*, 25. The '[*sic*]' is Joyce's.
[38] 'Drama and Life', *OCPW*, 24.
[39] 'Drama and Life', *OCPW*, 25.
[40] 'Drama and Life', *OCPW*, 27.
[41] 'Ecce Homo', *OCPW*, 28.
[42] *SH*, 211.
[43] James Joyce, 'James Clarence Mangan (1902)', in *OCPW*, 54. As David Weir suggests, Joyce's denigration of 'literature' is expressed by way of a phrase most likely

In the following pages Joyce proceeds to define 'poetry' in almost exactly the same terms as he had previously used to define 'drama':

> Poetry, even when apparently most fantastic, is always a revolt against artifice, a revolt, in a sense, against actuality [...] it is often found at war with its age.[44]

Finally, in his scathing review of the poems of William Rooney (published as 'An Irish Poet' in the Dublin *Daily Express* of 11 December 1902), Joyce refers to neither 'poetry' nor 'verse' nor 'philosophy', but to 'literature', and the term is used not, as one might have expected, to belittle Rooney's poetry, but on the contrary to describe that artistic domain to which his work, as bad art, constitutes an affront. 'The written word' is at stake, and Joyce deplores that 'the region of literature is assailed so fiercely by the enthusiast and the doctrinaire'.[45] Thus Joyce's critique of 'literature' comes full circle. His use of the word rejoins common usage: no longer a condescending designation for inferior art, it becomes a 'region' to be defended against the damaging incursions of unworthy writers (a group here represented by William Rooney, who, like the Revivalists and like George Moore, mixes art with causes and dogmas rather than devoting himself to it for its own sake).

These modulations in the emphases of Joyce's essays are mirrored by a shift from drama to prose within the sequence of surviving epiphanies. These variations arguably indicate a realization on Joyce's part that the medium most suited to his own writing was prose and that such a mode need not be disparaged as the realm of the mere 'man of letters'.[46]

THE EPIPHANIES

Of Joyce's forty extant epiphanies, nineteen are dramatic, consisting of dialogue preceded by names or character descriptions, and accompanied by

---

adopted from Paul Verlaine, who in 'L'Art Poétique' dismisses lower forms of artistic expression as mere 'literature': 'Et tout le reste est littérature' ['And all the rest is literature']—*James Joyce and the Art of Mediation* (Ann Arbor: University of Michigan Press, 1996), 16. The connection is supported by the fact that Joyce goes on to praise Verlaine later in the same paragraph: Verlaine's songs, like Shakespeare's, are 'the rhythmic speech of an emotion otherwise incommunicable'. Joyce's understanding of 'literature' in 'James Clarence Mangan' is closely echoed in *Stephen Hero*: 'he imagined the domain of art to be cone-shaped. The term "literature" now seemed to him a term of contempt and he used it to designate the vast middle region which lies between apex and base, between poetry and the chaos of unremembered writing.'—*SH*, 78.

[44] 'Mangan', *OCPW*, 59.
[45] James Joyce, 'An Irish Poet', in *OCPW*, 61.
[46] *SH*, 211.

short descriptive phrases akin to stage directions; the remainder are written in continuous prose. This near-perfect balance between the number of dramatic and prose epiphanies does not reflect the actual unevenness of the collection, wherein the emphasis, as Hans Walter Gabler has noted, shifts from drama to lyric and from scene to narrative.[47] This progression is noticeable even if one considers only the twenty-two epiphanies that survive in Joyce's hand at Buffalo, half of which privilege the dramatic mode and half the narrative mode. The first half of the collection, which opens with the 'Apologise/Pull out your eyes' epiphany and follows a trajectory from childhood to adolescence to adulthood, consists mainly of dramatic snippets. Midway through the collection, the 'Two mourners' epiphany marks the onset of a predominantly narrative mode. The epiphanies inscribed in one of Stanislaus Joyce's 'Commonplace Books', entitled 'Selections in Prose from Various Authors',[48] appear to confirm this evolutionary model. All the epiphanies in Stanislaus's book are written in the narrative mode. Although this has been attributed to Stanislaus's personal preference (on no particular grounds), there is good reason to think that the collection may reflect a chronological ordering.[49] It opens with a series of epiphanies inspired by Joyce's short trips to Paris in 1902 and 1903. A piece about departure, the 'spell of arms and voices' epiphany,[50] is the first to feature. It is followed by 'They pass in twos and threes',[51] a Baudelairean description of a French boulevard. Then come 'I lie along the deck',[52] which was written after Joyce's hurried return home following receipt of the telegram informing him of his mother's illness on 10 April 1903, and the 'Two mourners' epiphany, which was (according to Stanislaus) inspired by May Joyce's funeral in August 1903.[53] For Gabler, the fact that these appear in chronological order suggests:

---

[47] Hans Walter Gabler, Preface, *JJA 7*, xxvii. Gabler is positive in dating the inscription of the twenty-two Buffalo epiphanies to 1903 and 1904, although some may have been originally composed in 1902—Gabler, Preface, *JJA 7*, xxiii–xxiv. These epiphanies are printed in *Workshop* and reproduced in *JJA 7*.

[48] Stanislaus Joyce's 'Commonplace Book' is held at Cornell University Library. For a detailed description, see *The Cornell Joyce Collection: A Catalogue*, ed. Robert E. Scholes (Ithaca: Cornell University Press, 1961), 8–9. In addition to quotations from various other writers, the commonplace book contains twenty-four Joycean epiphanies, seventeen of which are different from those in Joyce's hand at Buffalo. Cornell also holds a fortieth (draft) epiphany belonging neither to the Buffalo set nor to Stanislaus's collection—Gabler, Preface, *JJA 7*, xxv. These epiphanies, like those held at Buffalo, are printed in *Workshop* and reproduced in *JJA 7*.

[49] Gabler, Preface, *JJA 7*, xxiv.

[50] *Workshop*, 40.

[51] *Workshop*, 43.

[52] *Workshop*, 47.

[53] *Workshop*, 31; Stanislaus Joyce, *My Brother's Keeper*, 235.

a genuine progression within Joyce's self-created genre from the scene of dramatic immediacy to the prose miniature mediated in the narrative mode.[54]

Considered in conjunction with the shift from 'drama' to 'literature' in the early essays, the evolution from dramatic to narrative form in the epiphanies would seem to enact Joyce's gradual renunciation of one medium in favour of the other. Joyce's adoption of the prose medium is confirmed by *Stephen Hero*, which, with the exception of a few scattered duologues, unfolds in continuous realistic prose, and *A Portrait of the Artist as a Young Man*, in which the dramatic element recedes even further (surviving mainly in the Christmas scene of Chapter 1 and in the aesthetic disquisitions of Chapter 5). Some of the epiphanies chronicle these evolving preferences more clearly than has yet been shown, and lend additional credence to the hypothesis that Joyce's reading of Flaubert played a significant part in this development.

The epiphany numbered 65 in Joyce's handwritten collection presents intertextual connections to Flaubert. Written in prose, the epiphany divides into two parts. The first locates the narrator on the deck of a ship cruising off the coast of France. The second describes thoughts that spring from the contemplation of these surroundings:

> I lie along the deck, against the engine-house, from which the smell of lukewarm grease exhales. Gigantic mists are marching under the French cliffs, enveloping the coast from headland to headland. The sea moves with the sound of many scales. . . . Beyond the misty walls, in the dark cathedral church of Our Lady, I hear the bright, even voices of boys singing before the altar there.[55]

This interweaving of outer world and inner mind is central to Stephen's conception of the role of the artist as expressed at the beginning of *Stephen Hero*. 'The artist', Stephen therein declares, stands 'in the position of mediator between the world of his experience and the world of his dreams'.[56] It is also a mode of writing typical of Flaubert, who uses *style indirect libre* (that is, free indirect discourse, 'a manner of presenting the thoughts or utterances of a fictional character as if from that character's point of view'[57]) to move seamlessly between the description of 'externals' and the thoughts and feelings aroused by such 'externals'[58] in his characters.

---

[54] Gabler, Preface, *JJA* 7, xxvii.

[55] *Workshop*, 47.

[56] *SH*, 77.

[57] 'free indirect style', in Chris Baldick, *The Oxford Dictionary of Literary Terms*, 3rd edn (Oxford: Oxford University Press, 2008), 135–6.

[58] The term is Stephen's in *Stephen Hero*. Thinking about 'literature' in the same deprecating vein adopted by Joyce in his early essays, Stephen decides that 'its merit lay in its portrayal of externals'—*SH*, 78.

According to Stanislaus, the 'ship' epiphany was composed on Joyce's hasty return from Paris in April 1903.[59] Richard Ellmann notes that Joyce 'attended mass that day at Notre-Dame'.[60] But there may be another reason for the mention of the cathedral in the epiphany. Indeed, the passage is highly reminiscent of the beginning of Flaubert's *L'Éducation sentimentale*. The opening of Flaubert's novel, like Joyce's epiphany, describes the beginning of a journey taken by boat—and a journey also taken to get away from, rather than to, Paris. In Flaubert's novel, the engine of the departing boat is steaming hard ('belching clouds of smoke'), and people cluster around it for heat ('a few were clustered round the engine-room'[61]). Moreover, the landscape is shrouded in the same concealing mists as mar the vision of Joyce's narrator, so that Frédéric Moreau only just catches a glimpse of Notre-Dame before Paris disappears out of sight:

> Through the haze he was observing church towers and other notable build-ings whose names he didn't know. Then, as Paris slipped swiftly away behind him, he cast one final backward glance over the Île-Saint-Louis, the Cité, and Notre-Dame, and breathed a heavy sigh.[62]

In Joyce's epiphany, the sentence that effects the transition between the two parts of the narrative relies on a pun (fish scales, musical scales) to transport the reader from the scene of the event to the inner precincts of the mind. The present tense instils a sense of simultaneity between the two scenes but at the same time blurs the boundary between memory and imagination (the reader, that is, cannot tell whether the scene is imagined or remembered). An incongruous biographical fact buttresses suspicions that Joyce may have had Flaubert ringing in his ears as he wrote these lines. Ellmann reports that during his time in Paris, Joyce:

> was able to take two trips away from the city. One was to Nogent, where he watched the confluence of the Seine and the Marne.[63]

That Joyce should have taken such a journey is puzzling: then as now, Nogent is unspectacular and holds no special tourist appeal. The very banality of the place, however, is precisely why Flaubert chose the town as

---

[59] Stanislaus Joyce, *My Brother's Keeper*, 227.

[60] *JJ*, 128.

[61] *ESE*, 3 ['fumait à gros tourbillons'; 'quelques-uns, debout, se chauffaient autour de la machine' (*ES*, 19–20)].

[62] *ESE*, 3 ['A travers le brouillard, il contemplait des clochers, des édifices dont il ne savait pas les noms; puis il embrassa, dans un dernier clin d'oeil, l'île Saint-Louis, la Cité, Notre-Dame; et bientôt, Paris disparaissant, il poussa un grand soupir.' (*ES*, 19)].

[63] *JJ*, 126. In the first edition of Ellmann's biography, Clamart is stated to have been Joyce's destination on this trip. No reason is given for the change from one edition to the next—Richard Ellmann, *James Joyce* (New York: Oxford University Press, 1959), 131.

a backdrop to the provincial scenes of L'Éducation sentimentale:[64] Nogent
is Frédéric Moreau's home town in the novel and the place to which he
is returning in its opening pages. That Joyce's journey also involved a boat
trip adds to the likelihood that the epiphany intertwines two lived experiences, as well as Flaubertian reminiscence.

Two further epiphanies seem to bear traces of Joyce's reading of
Flaubert. The first of these is extant only in Stanislaus's commonplace
book, and describes the dancing of a young boy before a multitude of
onlookers. This 'dream-epiphany'—to use Robert Scholes's description of
the piece in The Workshop of Daedalus[65]—refers explicitly to Herodias,[66]
the mother of the child-temptress Salome, whose name provides Flaubert
with the title and female protagonist of the third of his Trois Contes.
'Hérodias' tells of Salome's role in the seduction of Herod and of her
request, on her mother's behalf, for the beheading of Iaokanann (John the
Baptist).[67] That the dance scene at the heart of 'Hérodias' made a strong
impression on Joyce is clear from the testimony of Jan Parandowski, who
recalls his declamation of precisely the relevant passage:

> he himself began to recite. It was a page from Flaubert's 'Hérodias'—the
> dance of Salomé. His delivery of the passage sounded splendid; he recited it
> vigorously with his full voice and broke it off shortly and sharply, the way
> Flaubert always concludes his long, swollen sentences.[68]

Although the narrator of Joyce's epiphany emphasizes the difference
between the boy's silent dance and the dance of Salome, echoes between
the two texts are noticeable:

---

[64] Flaubert himself was familiar with Nogent—as the home of some of his family
relatives—from childhood.

[65] Workshop, 33.

[66] David Hayman has noted Joyce's interest in 'Hérodiade', the poem by Stéphane
Mallarmé on the same biblical theme, and traced its repercussions in Finnegans Wake—
Joyce et Mallarmé, 2 vols (Paris: Lettres Modernes, 1956), vol. 2, 'souvenirs d'Hérodiade',
25–30. Yeats also referred to 'Herodias's daughters' in his poem 'Nineteen Hundred and
Nineteen'. But that poem, originally published in The Dial and The London Mercury in
1921, was written almost two decades after Joyce's epiphany.

[67] The reasons for Flaubert's adoption of a variant of the Hebrew spelling of the saint's
name (Yohanan) are discussed in Ron E. Scrogham, 'The Echo of the Name "Iaokanann"',
The French Review, vol. 71, no. 5 (April 1998).

[68] Jan Parandowski, 'Meeting with Joyce', 159–60. Parandowski met Joyce only once, in
Paris, in 1937, after the PEN meeting at which Joyce had presented a paper on authorial
rights. Before their publication in English in Willard Potts's Portraits of the Artist in Exile in
1979, Parandowski's recollections of the encounter appeared in German in 1957, in Polish
in 1959, and in Italian in 1971. When Joyce pointed out the grammatical errors he had
identified in Trois Contes, the last word of 'Hérodias' (and thus of the whole collection),
'alternativement' ['alternately'], was one of the usages he queried—JJ, 492.

That is no dancing. Go down before the people, young boy, and dance for them . . . He runs out darkly-clad, lithe and serious to dance before the multitude. There is no music for him. He begins to dance far below in the amphitheatre with a slow and supple movement of the limbs, passing from movement to movement, in all the grace of youth and distance, until he seems to be a whirling body, a spider wheeling amid space, a star. I desire to shout to him words of praise, to shout arrogantly over the heads of the multitude 'See! See!'. . . . His dancing is not the dancing of harlots, the dancing of the daughters of Herodias. It goes up from the midst of the people, sudden and young and male, and falls again to earth in tremulous sobbing to die upon its triumph.[69]

The dances depicted in each are remarkably similar in their form: while Salome's performance resembles 'the sorceresses' spinning top',[70] Joyce's dancer is a 'whirling body'. The performances are also alike in their anonymity. In Flaubert's story, Salome, like the young boy of Joyce's epiphany, remains unnamed at the time of her dance, making her first appearance simply as 'A young girl'. Only later is she referred to by name, and then only by way of her mother's, from whose youthful self she is deemed indistinguishable: 'It was Herodias, as she used to look in her youth.'[71] By referring to the 'daughters of Herodias' only as nameless harlots, Joyce effectively replicates Flaubert's onomastic choice, subsuming the identity of the archetypal female temptress (which is further diluted by the epiphany's evocation of various undifferentiated siblings) to that of her mother.

Other parallels relate to the role of the audience in these two dances. The word 'multitude', which is twice repeated in Joyce's epiphany, features in Flaubert's story at the point at which the crowd of feasting onlookers responds to the frenzied final stages of Salome's dance: 'the throng responded with applause'. This is shortly followed by a synonym, 'the crowd'. Similarly, Joyce's mention of 'the people' is identical to the word used by Flaubert to denote the assembled crowd in 'Hérodias': 'The people grew more excited.'[72] In both texts sexuality, prophecy, and death are interwoven. Even the wording of the narrator's reaction to the boy's dance ('I *desire* to shout to him words of praise') echoes the 'lust' and 'pleasure' that are at the heart of Flaubert's sexually charged story. Furthermore, in each text desire leads to peculiarly parallel utterances.[73]

[69] *Workshop*, 33.
[70] *TCE*, 102 ['le rhombe des sorcières' (*TC*, 181–2)].
[71] *TCE*, 101 ['Une jeune fille'; 'C'était Hérodias, comme autrefois dans sa jeunesse.' (*TC*, 179–80)].
[72] *TCE*, 102, 100 ['la multitude y répondit par des acclamations'; 'la foule'; 'L'exaltation du peuple grandit.' (*TC*, 181, 178)].
[73] *TCE*, 102 ['convoitise'; 'volupté' (*TC*, 181–2)].

While Herod calls to Salome, 'Come! Come!',[74] Joyce's narrator craves to call out: 'See! See!' The enjoinder to 'see' bears mystical, prophetic overtones, and this also may be related to Flaubert's text, as 'Hérodias' is a story about a prophecy, and about a prophet who, like Joyce's dancer, dies for his prophecy. In 'Hérodias', Herod's call to Salome precipitates a tightening of plot that leads to death. The exclamation uttered in Joyce's epiphany also leads to a (sexualized) kind of death, as the boy's dance 'die[s] upon its triumph'.[75]

The narrator's insistence on the difference between the 'distant', 'male' dancing of the boy and 'the dancing of harlots' begs the question: 'what'— to quote Gabriel Conroy in 'The Dead'—are the dancer and his dance 'symbol[s] of?'[76] Might the dancer be a symbol of the kind of rhythmic, serious art, produced for art's sake only, which Joyce hoped he might produce? On such a reading, the dancer and the dance represent an ideal in which art is formal, impersonal, and entirely its own *raison d'être*. Flaubert's tale seems to have stirred in Joyce a complex reflection about aesthetics, poetics, and his own artistic ambitions.

GEORG BRANDES: A MEDIATOR OF INFLUENCES?

The formative roles played by Flaubert in Joyce's early creative life may be related to his reading of the works of Georg Brandes (1842–1927), a widely respected Danish critic and prolific popularizer of nineteenth-century continental literature. Constantine Curran places Brandes at the 'critical vanguard' of the 'Danish literary movement of the 1880s'. Joyce, as he remembers, was thoroughly versed in Brandes's writings: he read 'the Scandinavians in 1899 and the years immediately after' and 'covered Brandes extensively'.[77] Brandes's name appears twice in letters written by Joyce during the early years of his stay in Trieste (1905–15). In February 1905 he stated to Stanislaus that:

> by the time my novel [*Stephen Hero*] is finished I shall be a good German and Danish scholar, and if Brandes is alive, I shall send it to him.[78]

---

[74] *TCE*, 102 ['Viens! Viens!' (*TC*, 182)].

[75] The pattern of rise and fall enacted in the last sentence of the epiphany is reminiscent of William Blake's *Songs of Innocence and Experience*, anticipates some of the more sexualized passages in *A Portrait of the Artist as a Young Man*, and to some extent adumbrates the structure of tumescence and detumescence that is a feature of all of Joyce's works.

[76] *D*, 211.

[77] Curran, *James Joyce Remembered*, 116.

[78] *SL*, 56. The second mention of Brandes occurs in November 1906—*SL*, 128.

Brandes was by then the author of numerous works, including a mono-
graph on Ibsen; an influential six-volume study entitled *Main Currents in
Nineteenth-Century Literature* (published in English between 1901 and
1905,[79] and which, despite the breadth suggested by the title, makes
mention of neither Flaubert nor Ibsen); and *Creative Spirits of the Nineteenth Century*, which devotes a chapter to Flaubert (VI) and a chapter to
Ibsen (IX). *Creative Spirits of the Nineteenth Century* was first published in
German in 1882 as *Moderne Geister, literarische Bildnisse aus dem 19ᵗⁿ
Jahrhundert*; the fact that the book was not available in English until 1924
may explain why Joyce expressed the hope of being a 'good German and
Danish scholar' by the time *Stephen Hero* (which occupied his novelistic
energies between 1904 and 1907) would be ready to send to Brandes.[80]
Reading Joyce's early works with his high regard for Brandes in mind
brings into focus the extent of his debt to the Danish critic.

Curran writes at some length about the likelihood of Brandes having
served as the main channel for Joyce's acquaintance with Ibsen.[81] But
although some of Brandes's statements about Ibsen in *Creative Spirits* do
make their way into Joyce's early works,[82] close analysis suggests a more
substantial debt to the critic's account of Flaubert.[83] Indeed there are
conspicuous instances of overlap between the chapter Brandes devotes to

---

[79] Georg Brandes, *Main Currents in Nineteenth-Century Literature* (Danish original,
1872–1890; German version, 1872–1876), English translation, 4 vols (London: William
Heinemann, 1901–1905).
[80] Georg Brandes, *Creative Spirits of the Nineteenth Century* (German original, 1882),
trans. Rasmus B. Anderson (London: T. Fisher Unwin, 1924).
[81] Curran, *James Joyce Remembered*, 117, 119.
[82] Brandes's allusion to the 'placing of torpedoes under the ark' in *Brand*, for instance,
finds an echo in Stephen's comment about his paper in *Stephen Hero*: 'This is the first of my
explosives.'—*Creative Spirits*, 375; *SH*, 81. In the same way, when Brandes describes Ibsen
as being 'on a war footing with his surroundings' and evokes the author's 'contempt for his
fellow-creatures', one is reminded of Joyce's claim, in 'Drama and Life', that the drama of
the future will be 'at war with convention', and of the disdainful tones of 'The Day of the
Rabblement'—*Creative Spirits*, 358; *OCPW*, 35 and 50–2. Brandes's quotation from
Ibsen's *The Enemy of the People* ('The fact is, you see, the strongest man in the world is
he who stands absolutely alone') and his comments regarding Ibsen's cult of the egotistic
personality and 'exaltation of the ego as an intellectual force' prefigure a statement that
features in both 'A Portrait of the Artist' (1904) and *Stephen Hero*: 'Isolation is the first
principle of artistic economy.'—*Creative Spirits*, 362 and 357; *APA*, 215; *SH*, 33. Similarly,
just as Ibsen is reported to have been a great believer in Europe, Stephen thinks excitedly
about 'some movement already proceeding out in Europe'—*SH*, 35.
[83] It is notable that although Brandes's essay on Flaubert makes no mention of Ibsen, his
essay on Ibsen evokes Flaubert twice. In the Ibsen piece, the two authors are judged similar
for their disgust for humankind and shared exasperation with stupidity: 'To Flaubert,
mankind is wicked because it is stupid, to Ibsen, on the other hand, it is stupid because
it is wicked.'—*Creative Spirits*, 359. The second mention of Flaubert concerns his coldly
scientific treatment of religion, which is presented 'from the dark side' as 'a hallucination, in
which one believes'—*Creative Spirits*, 379.

Flaubert and Joyce's early writing, especially *Stephen Hero*. The most striking example of this consists in the use of the word 'plesiosaur' in both Brandes's book and in Joyce's draft novel. Describing Flaubert's close friendship with the French poet and dramatist Louis Bouilhet (1822–1869), and both men's interest in antiquity, Brandes evokes Bouilhet's capacity for conjuring 'the pterodactyls, the ichthyosaurs and plesiosaurs, the mammoths and mastodons, without calling them by name'.[84] But Brandes names them for us, and in *Stephen Hero* the incongruous image of the plesiosaurus rears its head again, as Stephen's mind traverses time in an imaginative excursion into art's prehistory:

> He doubled backwards into the past of humanity and caught glimpses of emergent art as one might have a vision of the pleisiosauros [*sic*] emerging from his ocean of slime.[85]

There are other points of overlap between Brandes's survey of Flaubert's writing and Joyce's early thoughts and practice. Brandes quotes and comments on the famous passage in *Madame Bovary* in which the narrator appears to let fall for a moment the mask of impersonality to lament language's inadequacy as a means of expressing emotion. The tone of these comments is uncharacteristically personal:

> as though the abundance of the soul did not at times overflow in the most vapid similitudes, as though any one could reproduce the exact measure of his needs, conceptions, or sufferings, since human language is but a cracked kettledrum, upon which we hammer out melodies that sound as though they were played for a bear-dance, when it is our wish to move the stars.[86]

In *Stephen Hero* the protagonist manifests the same tolerant insight concerning the connection that may obtain between cliché and genuine feeling. It is precisely such an awareness of the sincerity that is frequently bound up in the most commonplace utterances which prevents Stephen from berating his mother for her platitudinous response to Ibsen ('I think that Ibsen . . . has an extraordinary knowledge of human nature . . .'): 'Stephen had to be contented with this well-worn generality as he recognised in it a genuine sentiment.'[87] Similarly, Brandes's description of Flaubert's handling of the commonplace ('which involved elevat[ing] his materials through the artistic manner of his treatment'[88]) arrestingly prefigures Joyce's own view of the role of the artist as one who 'convert[s]

---

[84] *Creative Spirits*, 246.
[85] *SH*, 33.
[86] *Creative Spirits*, 243–4; *MBE*, 170; *MB*, 253.
[87] *SH*, 87.
[88] *Creative Spirits*, 229.

the bread of everyday life into something that has a permanent artistic life of its own',[89] or who, in Stephen Dedalus's equally transcendentalizing analogy, acts as 'a priest of the eternal imagination, transmuting the daily bread of experience into the radiant body of everliving life'.[90]

Brandes's repeated defence of Flaubert against allegations that his art was 'photographic'—photography being a medium which Flaubert himself refused to admit as artistic (though he relented somewhat in later years)—may have shaped Joyce's analogous view of the matter, as expressed in the short 'Ithaca'-like dialogue that features in the 'Paris and Pola Commonplace Book':

Question: *Can a photograph be a work of art?*
Answer: A photograph is the disposition of sensible matter and may be so disposed for an aesthetic end but it is not a human disposition of sensible matter. Therefore it is not a work of art.[91]

It was precisely the mechanical aspect of photography that was at the root of Brandes's dismissal of any possible connection between Flaubert's art and the emerging medium:

He had the bias and the capacity for the study of nature and for historic study, the scrutinizing eye which no relation between details escaped. To speak now of photography in connection with him was impossible. For study implies activity, ardour, and an eye for the essential; while photography on the other hand, is something passive, mechanical, and totally indifferent to the distinctions between essential and non-essential matters.[92]

Words from this passage, including the crucial image of the 'scrutinizing eye', are deployed in *Stephen Hero* when the protagonist evokes the 'mechanism of esthetic apprehension' that is mobilized in the process of epiphanic vision, the stages of which are likened to 'the gropings of a spiritual eye which seeks to adjust its vision to an exact focus'. The value of concentrated attention is emphasized when Stephen declares that 'The apprehensive faculty must be scrutinised in action.'[93] Brandes's concerns about the inability of a machine to make distinctions between the essential and the inessential are also echoed in Joyce's draft novel when Stephen asserts that the artist must be 'gifted with twin faculties, a selective faculty and a reproductive faculty'.[94]

---

[89] Stanislaus Joyce, *My Brother's Keeper*, 116.
[90] *P*, 186.
[91] *Workshop*, 55.
[92] *Creative Spirits*, 241–2.
[93] *SH*, 211–2.
[94] *SH*, 77–8.

Brandes's eagerness to clear Flaubert from imputations of a connection between his writing and photographic art seems to be underpinned by his admiration for the novelist's impersonal method—a method that, as he insists, should not be confused with photographic technique. Whereas the Ibsen essay in *Creative Spirits* makes only one reference to 'objectivity',[95] and none at all to 'impersonality', the latter features no less than four times in the Flaubert chapter.[96] This is significant in the light of the fact that 'impersonal' is the adjective chosen by Joyce to explain Stephen's fervent admiration for Ibsen in *Stephen Hero*: 'It was the very spirit of Ibsen himself that was discerned moving behind the *impersonal* manner of the artist.'[97]

These references to photography and to impersonality tie in closely with the most prominent leitmotif of Brandes's article on Flaubert: the theme of literary art as scientific practice. In a letter of 18 March 1857 Flaubert writes with passion of the need to impart to art the rigour of science:

> It is time to give Art—by a pitiless method—all the precision of the physical sciences![98]

This attitude to writing is widely thought to have inflected Flaubert's description of 'le docteur Larivière' in *Madame Bovary* as a man whose understanding of humanity is sharper than the most incisive of surgical tools:

> His gaze, more piercing than his scalpel, penetrated straight into your soul, and prised out, from beneath the allegations and evasions, every lie.[99]

---

[95] *Creative Spirits*, 381.
[96] *Creative Spirits*, 236, 239.
[97] *SH*, 41 (my emphasis).
[98] Flaubert to Mlle Leroyer de Chantepie, 18 March 1857, *GW*, 248 ['Il est temps de lui donner, par une méthode impitoyable, la précision des sciences physiques!' (*C2*, 691)]. Flaubert's statement very clearly anticipates Zola's later manifesto for the naturalist novel, *Le Roman expérimental* (1880), which called for just such an application of the scientific method to the production of literature: 'we must operate on characters, on passions, on human and social facts, as the chemist and the physician operate on their inorganic bodies, as the physiologist operates on living bodies'; 'why should literature itself not become a science, thanks to the experimental method?'; 'The experimental method alone can get the novel out of the lies and errors in which it languishes.' ['nous devons opérer sur les caractères, sur les passions, sur les faits humains et sociaux, comme le chimiste et le physicien opèrent sur les corps bruts, comme le physiologiste opère sur les corps vivants'; 'pourquoi la littérature elle-même ne deviendrait-elle pas une science, grâce à la méthode expérimentale?'; 'La méthode expérimentale peut seule faire sortir le roman des mensonges et des erreurs où il se traîne.' (Émile Zola, *Le Roman expérimental* [Paris: Flammarion, 2006], 60, 71, 79)].
[99] *MBE*, 285 ['Son regard, plus tranchant que ses bistouris, vous descendait droit dans l'âme et désarticulait tout mensonge à travers les allégations et les pudeurs.' (*MB*, 406)].

Lavishing praise on Flaubert, whom he hails as a 'master of modern fiction' whose work 'marks a step in the history of the novel',[100] Brandes compares his art to the medical sciences of surgery, anatomy, physiology. Brandes's similes make their first entry into the text in the form of a kind of free indirect style that ventriloquizes the outraged attitude of the French people to *Madame Bovary* when it was first published:

> It was rather a reminder of surgery, of anatomy [...] people found in his novels only the merciless, inexorable physiology of everyday life in its sorrowful ugliness.[101]

Brandes aptly captures the shocked, hostile, or parodic tenor of some of the responses aroused by Flaubert's work. One of the better-known nineteenth-century representations of Flaubert was a caricature, published in 1869 (fig. 12), which represents him as the coldly impersonal, scalpel-wielding dissector of Madame Bovary's diseased heart: twelve years after the novel's publication, this view of Flaubert still dominated public perceptions of his art.[102] Having used the image of surgery to convey a sense of Flaubert's reception in France, Brandes goes on to deploy the analogy in his own account. Flaubert's pen is a 'dissecting-knife'; 'the surgeon, in the text, without the slightest manifestation of sympathy, is lacerating and tearing to pieces'.[103] It seems significant, in the light of such sketches, that Stephen should invoke vivisection as the cornerstone of the artistic modernity to which he aspires:

> The modern spirit is vivisective. Vivisection itself is the most modern process one can conceive. The ancient spirit accepted phenomena with a bad grace. The ancient method investigated law with the lantern of justice, morality with the lantern of revelation, art with the lantern of tradition. But all these lanterns have magical properties: they transform and disfigure. The modern method examines its territory by the light of day.[104]

The statement looks ahead to Joyce's development of Flaubertian free indirect style—to his 'vivisective' rendering (often in the simulated real-time of interior monologue) of consciousnesses such as that of, for example, Leopold Bloom. Not for nothing does Mrs Bellingham turn upon him in the 'Circe' episode of *Ulysses* (which carries out its own vivisection of the characters' subconscious in the starkly defamiliarizing

---

[100] *Creative Spirits*, 223.
[101] *Creative Spirits*, 225.
[102] A. Lemot, 'Flaubert disséquant Madame Bovary', *La Parodie*, 5–12 December 1869.
[103] *Creative Spirits*, 239, 226, 228.
[104] *SH*, 186.

GUSTAVE FLAÜBERT

Fig. 12. 'Flaubert disséquant *Madame Bovary*', by A. Lemot, first published in *La Parodie*, 5–12 December 1869.

mode of internalized drama) and enjoin The Honourable Mrs Mervyn Talboys to 'Vivisect him'.[105]

The intertextual relevance of Brandes's essay on Flaubert is not confined to Joyce's early writing: his account adumbrates Joyce's later artistic practices at numerous points. Brandes mentions the increasing importance of encyclopaedism in Flaubert's works ('With Flaubert the encyclopaedia gradually supplants the emotions'); the increasing difficulty of his texts (certain parts of *La Tentation de saint Antoine* 'are only thoroughly intelligible to savants, and seem almost unreadable to the general public');

---

[105] *U* 5: 1,115.

the reliance of his imagination on documented fact ('his accuracy of description and information was rooted in a peculiar precision of the imagination'); the musicality of his sentences ('a style which was at once as clear as a mirror and as pleasant to the ear as harmonious music'); and the creation of images that hover uncertainly between the static and the dynamic (representing 'simultaneously the visible and the audible, the tableau and the mobile life'[106])—all of which characteristics could easily be said to apply to Joyce's writing.

CINEMATOGRAPHIC CUTS AND STRUCTURAL PATTERNS

Over and above the localized echoes traceable to Joyce's reading of Flaubert or of books and essays about Flaubert, the earlier writer's impact is discernible on a broader, technical level in the later's use of simultaneous narrative. The first systematic development of the technique is often ascribed to Flaubert, usually with reference to the famous 'comices agricoles' (or 'agricultural fair') episode of *Madame Bovary* (although it is used at various other points in the novel as well). In that episode, the seduction of Emma Bovary by Rodolphe is synchronized with the speeches of the officials presiding at the fair in such a way that the clichés of romantic love and public life are intertwined, with each discourse mirroring the manipulative banality of the other. This splicing of the narrative presents analogies with cinematographic montage, as Sergei Eisenstein observes. Placing Flaubert at the origin of a trend that influenced early cinema as well as subsequent literary writing, Eisenstein noted that:

> it was Flaubert who gave us one of the finest examples of cross-montage of dialogues [...] This is the scene in *Madame Bovary* where Emma and Rodolphe grow more intimate. Two lines of speech are interlaced: the speech of the orator in the square below, and the conversation of the future lovers.[107]

Variants of this technique are put to use throughout *Madame Bovary* and *L'Éducation sentimentale*. There are two principal kinds of narrative situation in which simultaneity may be mobilized. It may be established either between two concurrent strands of 'action' (as in the example of the agricultural fair), or between what is happening in the 'real world' on the one hand and a character's private response to such events on the

---

[106] *Creative Spirits*, 250, 263, 241, 226, 230.
[107] Sergei Eisenstein, 'Through Theatre to Cinema', in *Film Form: Essays in Film Theory*, ed. and trans. Jay Leyda (London: Dennis Dobson, 1949), 12.

other. *L'Éducation*, for instance, telescopes a character's mental world with the 'real world' in this fashion when Frédéric, travelling back to Paris, imagines what his inheritance will make possible: 'he drew up his plans for his future [. . .] sunk in contemplation of such a rich array he lost all sense of the outside world'. It is with surprise that he notes, after the vision recedes, that so little time has passed and so little distance been covered while it elapsed: 'they'd only done five kilometres, at best!'.[108]

Flaubert's predilection for breaking up narrative into simultaneous strands is replicated in two of Joyce's lyrical epiphanies. In these short pieces simultaneity is implied by the discrepancy between events witnessed in the visible world and the thoughts to which they give rise in the narrator's mind. Thus, an epiphany that begins by describing 'an April company' of young girls in highly imaged language ('the prattle of trim boots', 'the pretty rescue of petticoats', 'a light armoury', 'a white rosary of hours') suddenly breaks off with trailing suspension marks ('the fair promises of Spring, that well-graced ambassador . . .'). The following paragraph transports us to an entirely different place, leaving the reader to wonder what element of the outside world could have prompted the private vision that arises next, and to weigh up the possible meaning of the contrast between the two vignettes:

> Amid a flat rain-swept country stands a high plain building, with windows that filter the obscure daylight. Three hundred boys, noisy and hungry, sit at long tables eating beef fringed with green fat and vegetables that are still rank of the earth.[109]

The same pattern of contrastive juxtaposition is discernible in the epiphany that describes Joyce's return from Paris: the scene in which the narrator 'lie [s] along the deck'[110] is replaced by the static vision of a standing choir of singers from which he himself is absent. In this case, the description of the physical objects ('misty walls') that stand between the narrator and the interior of Notre-Dame Cathedral makes the transition highly cinematographic:[111] the reader is rushed through space and time to hear 'the bright,

---

[108] *ESE*, 111 ['il arrangea, d'avance, sa vie. [. . .] cette contemplation était si profonde, que les objets extérieurs avaient disparu [. . .] On n'avait fait que cinq kilomètres, tout au plus.' (*ES*, 121)].

[109] *Workshop*, 35.

[110] *Workshop*, 47.

[111] For an extended study of 'cinematographic writing', see Alan Spiegel, *Fiction and the Camera Eye: Visual Consciousness in the Film and the Modern Novel* (Charlottesville: University Press of Virginia, 1976). The term 'cinematographic' may seem anachronistic when applied to nineteenth-century writers, but Spiegel traces the roots of cinematographic writing to the 1850s, identifying Flaubert as the tradition's key precursor. Spiegel has written more specifically about connections between Joyce's and Flaubert's 'cinematograph-

even voices of boys singing before the altar there'.[112] Something similar happens in *Stephen Hero* when Stephen is suddenly reminded of a trip taken to Mullingar earlier on in the novel:

> Stephen halted at the end of a narrow path beside a few laurel bushes, watching at the end of a leaf a tiny point of rain form and twinkle and hesitate and finally take the plunge into the sodden clay beneath. He wondered was it raining in Westmeath. He remembered seeing the cattle standing together patiently in the hedges and reeking in the rain.[113]

These sudden transitions between descriptions of the physical world and the inner mind constitute Curran's most vivid impression of *Stephen Hero* (though he identifies Jacobsen rather than Flaubert as the likely source for Joyce's practice):

> Such abrupt transitions from reverie and subjective intricacy to external reality are, as I have said earlier, perhaps my clearest recollection of my reading of the MS. of *Stephen Hero*.[114]

This manner of inserting fragments of memory within a chronologically ordered narrative may be connected to a related technique of which a hint is discernible in *Stephen Hero* but which is more extensively developed in *A Portrait of the Artist as a Young Man*. The technique is discussed by David Hayman in his comparison of *A Portrait* and *L'Éducation sentimentale*.[115] Hayman argues that in both books the 'epiphany' (Hayman uses the term loosely to describe moments of exaltation) acts as a structuring device. Hugh Kenner's description of the contrapuntal structure of *A Portrait* has become a commonplace in critical interpretations of the novel. Stephen reaches the end of each chapter in a state of rapture, only to reappear despondent at the opening of the next: 'Each chapter closes with a synthesis of triumph which the next destroys.'[116] A similar pattern governs the structure of *L'Éducation sentimentale*, with the exhilaration that marks the opening of a section gradually giving way to disillusionment.

The technique juxtaposes a character at different points in time, in different states of mind. It is widely thought to have been an innovation of which Joyce conceived during the writing of *A Portrait*, yet some of the early epiphanies already perform juxtapositions of a related kind. An even

ic writing' in 'Flaubert to Joyce: Evolution of a Cinematographic Form', *NOVEL*, vol. 6, no. 3 (Spring 1973).

112 *Workshop*, 47.
113 *SH*, 74.
114 Curran, *James Joyce Remembered*, 117.
115 David Hayman, '*A Portrait of the Artist as a Young Man* and *L'Éducation sentimentale*'.
116 Hugh Kenner, *Dublin's Joyce* (London: Chatto and Windus, 1955), 129.

more obvious prefiguration of the later technique may be found in the Mullingar episode of *Stephen Hero* (a section of the draft novel whose realistic characteristics beg analogy to the provincial, agrarian sections of *Madame Bovary*). The opening words of the first extant page of the manuscript (fig. 13)[117] are identical to those of the second half of the epiphany of 'The spell of arms and voices',[118] apparently inserted unchanged (except for variations in punctuation and capitalization) from Joyce's notes. The text starts with the word 'nations' and ends, as in the epiphany, with the phrase 'exultant and terrible youth'. This marks the end of the paragraph. The next, which sees Stephen set forth on his journey, opens with the laconic observation that: 'From the Broadstone to Mullingar is a journey of some fifty miles.' The contrast between the exalted tone of the epiphany ('shaking the wings of their exultant and terrible youth') and the bleak denotative prose that immediately follows anticipates the pattern of rise and fall that characterizes the structure of *A Portrait*. Indeed the same epiphany was cribbed again during the writing of *A Portrait*, where it features in one of the concluding diary entries.[119] The *Stephen Hero* manuscript bears the traces of this later use: the words 'Departure for Paris' are scrawled in Joyce's hand across the paragraph break.[120] This transfer of text into *A Portrait*, where the rise-and-fall pattern plays such an important structural role, adds weight to the hypothesis that Joyce's jotting on the manuscript records his first realization of the use to which the technique of contrastive juxtaposition might be put. Whereas *Stephen Hero* sets up an indubitable and immediate disparity between Stephen's successive moods of excitement and disappointment, *A Portrait*'s use of the epiphany denies the reader any such certainty. In accordance with the published novel's poetics of impersonality, the end of the novel withholds final actualization of the sequence, leaving the reader to infer that a fall will, if the precedents of previous structural counterpoints are to be trusted, ultimately thwart the realization of those grand dreams with which Stephen's departure for Paris is infused. It is only in the 'Scylla and Charybdis' episode of *Ulysses* that the fall is confirmed by Stephen's interior monologue:

---

[117] *JJA* 8, 1 and *SH*, 237.

[118] *Workshop*, 40. The full text reads as follows: 'The spell of arms and voices—the white arms of roads, their promise of close embraces and the black arms of tall ships that stand against the moon, their tale of distant nations. They are held out to say: We are alone,—come. And the voices say with them: We are your people. And the air is thick with their company as they call to me their kinsman, making ready to go, shaking the wings of their exultant and terrible youth.'

[119] *P*, 213.

[120] *JJA* 8, 1 and *SH*, 237.

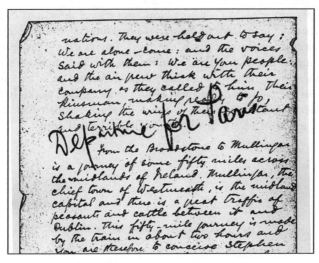

Fig. 13. The first extant page of the *Stephen Hero* manuscript fragment, with the second half of the 'spell of arms and voices' epiphany at the top of the page, and 'Departure for Paris' scrawled across the paragraph break in blue crayon; reproduced from *JJA 8*, 1.

> Fabulous artificer. The hawklike man. You flew. Whereto? Newhaven-Dieppe, steerage passenger. Paris and back. Lapwing. Icarus. *Pater, ait.* Seabedabbled, fallen, weltering. Lapwing you are. Lapwing be.[121]

The sensation of fall registered here is one that Stephen has been experiencing throughout his fictional life.

Joyce's early writing years were a time of aesthetic flux and experimentation. In theory (the early essays) and in practice (the epiphanies and *Stephen Hero*), Joyce moves away from an initial predilection for 'drama' towards a more general espousal of 'literature', the 'written word', and the medium of prose. His first attempt at a novel, in the form of the bulky, autobiographical draft of *Stephen Hero*, bears the strong imprint of that nineteenth-century continental realism that Joyce appears to dismiss in 'The Day of the Rabblement'. The novel seems to seek a place in that tradition, or at least to find itself emulating some of its hallmark characteristics both in its espousal of the genre of the *Bildungsroman* and in its unembellished account of the life of a young Dubliner at the turn of the twentieth century. The grim descriptive tenor of certain passages in *Stephen Hero*—especially the trip to the provincial outpost of Mullingar—

---

[121] *U* 9: 952–4.

are highly evocative of Flaubert's bleak, impersonal depictions of bourgeois country life in *Madame Bovary*. As a budding craftsman of language,
Joyce swiftly begins to incorporate technical lessons learnt from Flaubert,
emulating his precursor's use of simultaneous and cinematographic narrative in ways that, however embryonically, look forward to his increasingly
sustained and masterly deployment of such modes in later works. It was to
the short stories of *Dubliners*—a genre to which Flaubert had applied
himself in *Trois Contes*—that he was to devote himself next.

2

Dubliners

In December 1913 Ezra Pound wrote to Joyce for the first time, to inquire as to whether he had any ready writing which he would like placed in one of the small magazines for which he was then acting as an agent. Within a fortnight Pound wrote again, this time with high praise for Joyce's poem, 'I Hear an Army', which Yeats had just drawn to his attention.[1] On the wings of these encouraging missives a correspondence was initiated between Pound and Joyce that would last decades. In January 1914 Joyce sent Pound the manuscript of his unpublished *Dubliners*. Within a month of the volume reaching print in June 1914, Pound published an excited review of the collection in *The Egoist*, commenting ecstatically on the precision and economy of Joyce's style (his 'rigorous selection' and 'exclusion of all unnecessary detail') and lauding his lucid, unsentimentalizing rendition of the world ('He gives the thing as it is').[2] Pound's critical instinct was immediately to situate Joyce within a literary context. He placed him, without hesitation, within the European prose tradition. Joyce, he stated, 'writes as a contemporary of continental writers', and, more specifically, as a 'follower of Flaubert'.[3] Years later, in 'James Joyce et Pécuchet', an article published in the highly regarded *Mercure de France* on the occasion of the Flaubertian centenary in 1922, Pound reasserted his view of Joyce as a descendant of Flaubert, specifically aligning *Dubliners* with *Trois Contes* (as well as *A Portrait* with *L'Éducation sentimentale*):

> Joyce himself, in *Dubliners* and *A Portrait of the Artist as a Young Man*, is writing like Flaubert, but does not surpass *Trois Contes* or *L'Éducation*.[4]

---

[1] *P/J*, 17–19; *JJ* 349–50.
[2] Pound, '*Dubliners* and Mr James Joyce', *P/J*, 28–9.
[3] Pound, '*Dubliners* and Mr James Joyce', *P/J*, 27.
[4] ['Joyce, lui-même, dans *Dubliners* et dans *A Portrait of the Artist as a Young Man*, fait du Flaubert, mais ne dépasse pas les *Trois Contes* ni *L'Éducation*.' (Ezra Pound, 'James Joyce et Pécuchet', in *P/J*, 202)].

The phrasing is telling: Pound does not say that Joyce is merely like Flaubert, or an excellent imitator of Flaubert: Joyce, in his eyes, 'does' Flaubert in English.

In spite of Pound's instantaneous and adamant identification of a Flaubertian quality in Joyce's first published work, the relations between *Dubliners* and *Trois Contes* have remained largely uncharted.[5] This lacuna is surprising given the close generic fit between the two volumes. The most obvious reason for the link having been left unexplored is simply that there are few easily recognizable allusions to *Trois Contes* in *Dubliners*. But the critical lapse may also have something to do with the notion that these works are not 'the heart of the matter'—that the best of Flaubert and Joyce is to be found in the novelistic masterpieces, in *Madame Bovary* and *L'Éducation sentimentale*, in *A Portrait*, *Ulysses*, and *Finnegans Wake*. Finally, the relative silence on the matter may have to do with the fact that the two collections were produced in such different personal contexts as may make a connection between them seem implausible.

Trois Contes (1877) was Flaubert's last finished work. *Dubliners* (1914) was the first of Joyce's works of prose fiction to reach publication (after almost a decade of acrimonious wrangling with potential printers and publishers). As he wrote *Trois Contes*, Flaubert was ageing (or at least felt himself to be so—and was indeed but a few years from death), impoverished, lonely, depressed, and utterly disillusioned by the failure of his previous works to raise the French people out of their bourgeois apathy (for in his own way he had hoped, as Joyce would later hope in relation to *Dubliners*, to shake his countrymen out of some of their most idiotic ideas). In *Trois Contes* Flaubert laid down the burden of the disgusted scourge. The composition of his three short stories was undertaken as a bulwark against personal despair and to soothe nerves raw from the torment of work on *Bouvard et Pécuchet*. The exercise provided the desired relief, and the excitement Flaubert experienced during the writing of *Trois Contes* was unprecedented: 'It seems to me that French Prose can achieve an inconceivable *Beauty*.'[6] As well as seeking respite from the exhaustion brought on by *Bouvard et Pécuchet*, Flaubert was motivated by the wish to please his friend George Sand, who had long pleaded against what she considered to be the chill impersonality of his works, against those immovable principles that so strongly forbade him from expressing a view on his characters or their actions. In one of their many warm

[5] Cross devotes a chapter to the two collections: 'Dead Selves: Epiphanies in *Trois Contes* and *Dubliners*'—*F&J*, 17–32.

[6] Flaubert to Ivan Turgenev, 25 June 1876 ['Il me semble que la Prose française peut arriver à une *beauté* dont on n'a pas l'idée?' (*C5*, 60)].

epistolary exchanges (one of the few solaces of Flaubert's later years), she had, in her typically open, straightforward fashion, found fault with Flaubert's precious doctrine: 'supreme impartiality is anti-human, and a novel must above all be human'.[7] Flaubert was prompt to reiterate his position:

> As for divulging my personal opinion of the people I put on stage, no, no, never in a thousand years! I do not think I have *any right* to do that.[8]

But he later assured Sand:

> You will see from my *Story of a Simple Heart* (in which you will recognize your own direct influence) that I am not as stubborn as you believe. I think you will like the moral tendency, or rather the underlying humanity, of this little work.[9]

There was indeed more sympathy and less corrosive irony than usual in Flaubert's story of the self-sacrificing life of a country servant. George Sand died before the story was finished, but the softer tones of *Trois Contes* were welcomed by critics and ordinary readers alike. Théodore de Banville's laudatory comments—'These tales are three absolute and perfect master-pieces'[10]—were typical, and the book ran to five editions within a year of its first publication in April 1877.

Joyce's intentions and ambitions during the composition of *Dubliners* were substantially different. The censorious ending of 'A Portrait of the Artist', with its haughty condemnation of 'the general paralysis of an insane society',[11] gives a flavour of the vituperative intent of the stories that shortly followed. Joyce's letters about *Dubliners* testify to his belief in the power of his 'chapter of the moral history' of Ireland, with its 'special odour of corruption',[12] to 'forge [...] the uncreated conscience of [his] race'[13] (an attitude and aspiration that arrestingly recall Flaubert's aim to

---

[7] George Sand to Flaubert, 12 January 1876, *FS2*, 229 ['la suprême impassibilité est une chose anti-humaine, et un roman doit être humain avant tout' (*C4*, 8)].

[8] Flaubert to George Sand, 6 February 1876, *GW*, 404 ['Quant à laisser voir mon opinion personnelle sur les gens que je mets en scène, non, non, mille fois non! Je ne m'en reconnais *pas le droit.*' (*C5*, 12)].

[9] Flaubert to George Sand, 29 May 1876, *FS2*, 234 ['Vous verrez par mon *Histoire d'un coeur simple* où vous reconnaîtrez votre influence immédiate que je ne suis pas si entêté que vous croyez. Je crois que la tendance morale, ou plutôt le dessous humain de cette petite oeuvre vous sera agréable!' (*C5*, 42)].

[10] ['Ces contes sont trois chefs d'oeuvre absolus et parfaits' (Théodore de Banville, *Le National*, 14 May 1877, quoted in *TC*, 209)].

[11] *APA*, 218.

[12] Joyce to Grant Richards, 5 May 1906 and 15 October 1905, *L2*, 134, 123.

[13] *P*, 213.

write 'the moral history of the men of my generation' in *L'Éducation sentimentale*[14]). Although the intensity of Joyce's quarrel with Ireland can be seen to mellow even within the collection itself (in keeping with changes in his attitude to the country he had left behind),[15] his treatment of Dublin and its inhabitants was offensive enough to cause many bitter disputes and delays over the decade the volume took to reach publication.[16] In these political respects Joyce's first published work lends itself more naturally to analogy with Flaubert's earlier works and to *Bouvard et Pécuchet* than it does to *Trois Contes*, which stands out as something of an anomaly in its more gentle treatment of its characters. Irony does not disappear in the stories, but is more neutrally, more sympathetically deployed.

Stark discrepancies of theme and plot obtain between the two collections. Flaubert's *Trois Contes* span vast tracts of time and space. The first of his stories, 'Un Coeur simple' ('A Simple Heart'), tells the story of Félicité, a female servant in a French provincial town who over time loses so many of her faculties—both physical and mental—that the Holy Spirit and her stuffed parrot gradually merge in her mind until they join in one hovering vision above her head as she dies. The second story, 'La Légende de saint Julien l'Hospitalier' ('The Legend of Saint Julian Hospitaller'), is a telling (or the writing of a telling) of the legend of Saint Julian. As a child and as a young man, Julian harbours a darkly mysterious passion for hunting wild animals. After one particularly brutal scene of carnage, Julian hears a prophecy predicting that he will kill his parents. He travels far from home in an effort to escape fulfilment of the fearsome forecast, but fate catches up with him and the double murder is duly committed despite his best precautions. Flaubert's last story, 'Hérodias', recounts the biblical story of John the Baptist's foretelling of the coming of the Messiah in highly historical and politicized terms. The dance of Salome leads to John the Baptist's decapitation at a luxurious banquet.

Superficially, Joyce's stories in *Dubliners* would seem to form a more tightly unified whole. All twelve, as indicated by the title, are about

---

[14] Flaubert to Mlle Leroyer de Chantepie, 6 October 1864, *GW*, 304 ['l'histoire morale des hommes de ma génération' (*C3*, 409)].

[15] Richard Ellmann notes that by the time he set to work on 'The Dead', 'Joyce had come to a more indulgent view of Ireland.'—*JJ*, 230. In a letter of 25 September 1906 Joyce wrote to Stanislaus: 'Sometimes thinking of Ireland it seems to me that I have been unnecessarily harsh. I have reproduced (in *Dubliners* at least) none of the attraction of the city [...] I have not reproduced its ingenuous insularity and its hospitality. The latter "virtue" so far as I can see does not exist elsewhere in Europe. I have not been just to its beauty: for it is more beautiful naturally in my opinion than what I have seen of England, Switzerland, France, Austria or Italy.'—*L2*, 166.

[16] See James Joyce, 'A Curious History' (September 1911), in *OCPW*, 160–2.

Dublin and its people. All are set at the turn of the century. They are further bound together by the impression they initially convey of a narrative constructed around a single nebulous figure: the Dubliner. The effect is deliberate, for Joyce's aim was:

> to present Dublin to the indifferent public under four of its aspects: childhood, adolescence, maturity and public life.[17]

Whereas Flaubert's stories move back in time—from present-day Normandy to medieval France to the pre-Christian Middle East—Joyce's stories bear an infinitesimal sense of progression forwards, if only in the sense that the initial narrator seems to grow up over the first three stories. Flaubert's stories manifest the author's willingness (already on display in *Salammbô* and *La Tentation de saint Antoine*) to produce lavishly detailed portrayals of distant times and places, and, through painstaking research, to conjure situations apparently far removed from the contexts of everyday life. *Dubliners*, by contrast, is—for all Joyce's careful cultivation of an impersonal stance—more obviously underpinned by the will to make something happen. As Joyce explained to Grant Richards:

> I seriously believe that you will retard the course of civilization in Ireland by preventing the Irish people from having one good look at themselves in my nicely polished looking-glass.[18]

His intention—much like Flaubert's in his novels of contemporary life—was to be absolutely, uncompromisingly true to his vision of Dublin and its problems:

> I have written it for the most part in a style of scrupulous meanness and with the conviction that he is a very bold man who dares to alter in the presentment, still more to deform, whatever he has seen and heard. I cannot do any more than this. I cannot alter what I have written.[19]

In a sense Flaubert's and Joyce's stories could be described as occupying opposing places and embodying starkly differing attitudes in their authors' lives, with *Dubliners* relating more closely to the scathing (if concealed) intent of *Madame Bovary* and *L'Éducation sentimentale*, and with the more impeccable neutrality of Joyce's later works bearing a stronger tonal affinity to *Trois Contes*. The diagnostic determination that motivates Joyce's stories involves precisely the uncompromising sense of mission from which Flaubert, in *Trois Contes*, was taking a break.

---

[17] Joyce to Grant Richards, 5 May 1906, *L2*, 134.
[18] Joyce to Grant Richards, 23 June 1906, *L1*, 64.
[19] Joyce to Grant Richards, 5 May 1906, *L2*, 134.

These differences in the conception and reception of *Trois Contes* and *Dubliners* may make a significant intertextual relationship between the two collections seem unlikely. But Pound's intuition of an influence is correct: examined closely, the stories reveal a complex web of linguistic, thematic, structural, and technical echoes.

'GNOMON'

A number of these revolve around the word 'gnomon', which occurs in the very first paragraph of 'The Sisters', Joyce's opening story:

> Every night as I gazed up at the window I said softly to myself the word *paralysis*. It had always sounded strangely in my ears, like the word *gnomon* in the Euclid and the word *simony* in the Catechism.[20]

The rare word appears in exactly the same form in 'Hérodias', in the context of a heated discussion, at Herod's banquet, of a miracle performed by Jesus. Time, in the shape of a gnomon, is at the heart of the story:

> And he had found her standing at the threshold; she had got up from her sickbed when the palace sundial [gnomon] marked the third hour, the very moment when he approached Jesus.[21]

The word 'gnomon' refers to the sundial that frames and defines the Messianic miracle. Not only has Jesus healed a sick girl, but he has done so at a great distance, her father having made the journey to Capernaum to implore his help. The part played by Messianic agency in the ailing daughter's recovery is indicated by the gnomon, which confirms that she rose from her bed at the very same moment ('the third hour') as her father was making his appeal to Jesus. The gnomon, in other words, seals the miracle as miracle. As in 'The Sisters', the gnomon is associated with the danger of imminent death. It is invoked in Flaubert's story to emphasize liminal times and liminal states: not for nothing is the daughter found standing 'at the threshold'. Unlike Father Flynn in 'The Sisters', the saved girl does not succumb to a third stroke, but instead rises from her deathbed on the stroke of three (although the progression of time, in Flaubert's story as in Joyce's, is measured by the silent play of light and shadow rather than by audible strokes).

---

[20]   *D*, 1.
[21]   *TCE*, 95 ['Et il l'avait trouvée sur le seuil, étant sortie de sa couche quand le gnomon du palais marquait la troisième heure, l'instant même où il abordait Jésus.' (*TC*, 171)].

The extreme rarity of the word 'gnomon' in all contexts suggests that the echo in *Dubliners* may not be innocent, in spite of the fact that the narrator of 'The Sisters' specifically relates his knowledge of the word to 'the Euclid'—a reference to source that ensures the plausibility of the child's knowledge of the word but in no way occludes other meanings. One of these, as illustrated by Flaubert's story, relates to time. According to the *OED*, the first meaning of 'gnomon' is 'a pillar, rod, or other object which serves to indicate the time of day by casting its shadow upon a marked surface; especially the pin or triangular plate used for this purpose in an ordinary sundial'. This definition ties in nicely with the imagery of the opening paragraph of 'The Sisters', in which the boy looks up at the blank surface of a window in search of a mark (a matter of light and shadow, as on a sundial) of death, of time passing:

> Night after night I had passed the house (it was vacation time) and studied the lighted square of window: and night after night I had found it lighted in the same way, faintly and evenly. If he was dead, I thought, I would see the reflection of candles on the darkened blind, for I knew that two candles must be set at the head of the corpse.[22]

The *OED*'s second definition of the word states that 'gnomon' is 'occasionally applied to other instruments serving as "indicators"', and according to a French dictionary[23] 'gnomon' designates the complete sundial rather than its reflecting rod alone—this explains the use made of the word in 'Hérodias', in which 'gnomon' refers to the time-keeping device as a whole. It is clear, in view of these definitions, that Joyce puts the image of the gnomon to use even before the word itself occurs in the text. In symbolic terms the window of Father Flynn's house itself is a gnomon, as the frame on which the candles—multiple gnomons, measures of the passage of time, signs of death—will appear 'at the head of the corpse' to mark the end of life. The meaning foregrounded by the text, of the Euclidian gnomon as 'the part of a parallelogram which remains after a similar parallelogram is taken away from one of its corners' (*OED*) adds to the word's connotative density. An image of both partial presence and partial absence, like the window that so captivates the boy's morbid wonder, the geometrical gnomon stands for incompleteness and lack—prominent themes in a story in which secrecy and its grammatical counterpart, aposiopesis, prevail.

Yet another meaning of the word 'gnomon' seems pertinent to readings of 'The Sisters'. In ancient Greek, 'gnomon' is a noun meaning 'interpreter'.

---

[22] *D*, 1.
[23] *Le Trésor de la langue française informatisé*, http://atilf.atilf.fr/ (July 2011).

It is related to the verb 'gignôskein', which means 'to perceive, judge, know'. As Fritz Senn points out, the opening of 'The Sisters' is full of words that invite interpretative labour:[24] 'I'll tell you my opinion', 'I have my own theory', 'My idea is', 'That's my principle'.[25] The narrator records his bafflement regarding the gnomonic statements that act as tantalizing screens to his understanding of the situation ('I puzzled my head to extract meaning from his unfinished sentences'). His bond with Father Flynn is based largely on the pursuit of meaning: 'he had explained to me the meaning of the different ceremonies'. The boy's inquisitiveness, his desire to know more—to 'gnomon'—fade as the story unfolds. In the end he listens in silence to the conversation of dissimulating adults, defeated—'crossed' and 'resigned',[26] like the priest, to the bewildering lack or inscrutability of signs.

The epistemological meaning of 'gnomon' adumbrated by its Greek roots has bearing on the window which captivates the narrator of 'The Sisters' at the story's opening. Indeed, the window so intently scrutinized in fact performs its function in the story by acting as the opposite of a window: a screen. The site of a haunting lack of signs, 'uncanny' (like Father Flynn[27]) because of the faintness and evenness of its lighted square, the window is anything but transparent. It is relevant, therefore, to the question of impossible knowledge, irretrievable meaning: a question of gnomon. As a screen to knowledge and as a symbol of the lack of knowledge resulting from its screening, the window seems intertextually related to the second of Flaubert's short stories, 'La Légende de saint Julien l'Hospitalier'—a literary recasting of the story of the saint as represented on the stained-glass window of Rouen Cathedral. Like Joyce's story, the tale emphasizes the opacity of windows (this opacity is naturalized by realistic detail: the medieval stained-glass windows of Flaubert's legend are, by definition, not transparent). Even the closing sentence, in which the narrator names the cathedral window as his source, implicitly admitting to a certain amount of inevitable distortion in the transposition of the tale from one medium to another ('And that is the story of Saint Julian the Hospitaller, *more or less* as it can be found in the stained-glass window of a church in my part of the world.'[28]), seems to act as a veil, shutting away from memory the text's

---

[24] Fritz Senn, 'Dynamic Adjustments in *Dubliners* "(as Joyce clearly states)"', in *New Perspectives on 'Dubliners'*, ed. Mary Power and Ulrich Schneider, *European Joyce Studies* 7 (Amsterdam: Rodopi, 1997), 17.

[25] *D*, 1–2.

[26] *D*, 1, 3, 5, 9, 7.

[27] Old Cotter refers to Father Flynn as 'uncanny'—*D*, 1.

[28] *TCE*, 70 (my emphasis) ['Et voilà l'histoire de saint Julien l'Hospitalier, telle *à peu près* qu'on la trouve, sur un vitrail d'église, dans mon pays.' (*TC*, 129)].

earlier, more problematic stained-glass windows. References to these cluster around the scene of Julian's parricide. While Julian is away on his second great hunt, his parents arrive at the castle gate and are invited by his wife to spend the night in the younger couple's bed. The narrator comments on their sleep as if he were positioned within the chamber: 'Day was about to break, and behind the glass, the little birds were beginning to sing.'[29] The emphasis, as Shoshana Felman has shown, is on border lines, border times—inside and outside, night and day, life and death.[30] As in 'The Sisters' (and as, to some extent, in 'The Dead'), the window symbolizes the divide between the living and the dead. Both windows intimate impending change, and both reverse the usual mode of gnomonic time-telling: it is not shadow that will reveal, but light. The ludicrous motto incorrectly attributed to Pope Leo XIII in 'Grace', another of the *Dubliners* stories, takes on a strange ironic relevance to these windows: '*Lux upon Lux*',[31] light upon light. It is the light of the candles superimposed upon the already illuminated window that is to signify death in 'The Sisters', just as the light of day striking the stained-glass window of 'La Légende' will signify death by marking the time of Julian's return. By an ironic twist of plot, Julian returns before the light of dawn is bright enough. The window, in this instance, is literally a screen, shutting out the shafts of incipient daylight that might have prevented the double murder: 'The leaded lights dimmed the pale gleam of dawn.'[32] And so, with Julian 'lost in darkness', the killings take place, their violence multiplied by the window's refraction of the light, which, too late, shines in at full strength:

> The crimson reflection from the stained-glass window, just then catching the sun, lit up these red patches and scattered others still more plentifully about the room.[33]

Anticipating the rapprochement effected by Flaubert's closing sentence between the art of stained glass and the art of prose, the window here provides both an image and a reverse parallel for his own art: it is by its refracting agency that the violence of the scene is magnified, just as, analogously, Flaubert's own writing turns the muted representation of murder on the window of Rouen Cathedral into a bloodbath.

---

[29] *TCE*, 59 ['Le jour allait paraître, et, derrière le vitrail, les petits oiseaux commençaient à chanter.' (*TC*, 112)].

[30] Shoshana Felman, 'Flaubert's Signature: *The Legend of Saint Julian the Hospitable*', trans. Brian Massumi et al., in *Flaubert and Postmodernism*, ed. Naomi Schor and Henry F. Majewski (Lincoln and London: University of Nebraska Press, 1984), 66.

[31] *D*, 166.

[32] *TCE*, 62 ['Les vitraux garnis de plomb obscurcissaient la pâleur de l'aube.' (*TC*, 116)].

[33] *TCE*, 62–3 ['perdu dans les ténèbres'; 'Le reflet écarlate du vitrail, alors frappé par le soleil, éclairait ces tâches rouges, et en jetait de plus nombreuses dans tout l'appartement.' (*TC*, 116–17)].

Joyce's story echoes this image of intense patterned light, in a moment that also features after death has occurred. The boy in 'The Sisters' enters the death chamber and stands on the other side of the illegible window, only to discover that it is still a screen, no more amenable to being seen through from the inside than it had been from the outside:

> The room through the lace end of the blind was suffused with dusky golden light amid which the candles looked like pale thin flames.[34]

The synecdochic use of the word 'blind' in lieu of 'window' acts as a closing reminder of the extent to which windows, in this story as in Flaubert's, have impeded rather than enabled vision.

In neither of these two collections is the importance of the gnomon merely semantic, thematic, or symbolic. Indeed, as David Weir[35] has shown by highlighting another of its meanings, the gnomon is an apt figure for the structures of these stories as well. Taking a textbook of Euclid's *Elements*—of which Joyce owned a copy[36]—as his starting point, Weir infers from its diagrams and definitions that Joyce is likely to have had a rather different geometrical conception of the gnomon (relating to the missing corner of a parallelogram) from that which his critics have for the most part assumed.[37] As is the case with many geometrical figures, the definition of a gnomon varies. One of these definitions calls the gnomon a figure formed by the prolongation of the diagonal running from one point of a parallelogram through the opposite point and beyond to a third point, and the use of this third point to construct a new parallelogram containing the first. Inversely, the third point may be taken on the diagonal within the original parallelogram, so that a new, smaller parallelogram is formed, contained within the larger (fig. 14). The gnomon is thus related to notions of expansion and contraction, of progression towards ever greater units or towards ever smaller units contained within each other. Weir adduces the metaphysical thoughts of Giordano Bruno (a philosopher Joyce greatly admired, as testified by an early review essay of 1903[38]) on the subject of the gnomon: 'The gnomon is that which, added or substracted enlarges or diminishes a figure without changing its

---

[34] *D*, 6.

[35] David Weir, 'Gnomon is an Island: Euclid and Bruno in Joyce's Narrative Practice', *JJQ*, vol. 28, no. 2 (Winter 1991).

[36] H. S. Hall and F. H. Stevens, *A Textbook of Euclid's Elements for the Use of Schools*, 2nd edn (London: Macmillan, 1892). Joyce owned the 1900 edition—*CJ*, 111.

[37] In this widely held view, 'gnomon' is taken to designate 'the part of a parallelogram which remains after a similar parallelogram is taken away from one of its corners' (*OED*)—a figure of lack easily applicable to the lives portrayed in *Dubliners*.

[38] James Joyce, 'The Bruno Philosophy', in *OCPW*.

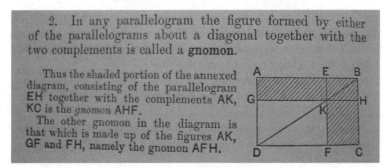

2. In any parallelogram the figure formed by either of the parallelograms about a diagonal together with the two complements is called a **gnomon**.

Thus the shaded portion of the annexed diagram, consisting of the parallelogram EH together with the complements AK, KC is the *gnomon* AHF.

The other gnomon in the diagram is that which is made up of the figures AK, GF and FH, namely the gnomon AFH.

Fig. 14. Diagram and definition of a geometrical gnomon as figured in H. S. Hall and F. H. Stevens, *A Textbook of Euclid Elements for the Use of Schools* (1887) (London: Macmillan, 1903), 128.

form.'[39] Weir convincingly argues that the gnomon is made to function structurally at various points in *Dubliners*. He identifies Farrington, the protagonist of 'Counterparts', as an exponent of two meanings of the word 'gnomon'. Firstly, Farrington, in his capacity as an office clerk, is the practitioner of a kind of failed, gnomonic mimicry. Farrington's job is to copy, but his copying is lacunary: he fails to reproduce documents completely. His account to his friends of his witty repartee to his boss Mr Alleyne, which omits his humiliating forced apology, is also lacunary. The other application of the gnomon to 'Counterparts', derived from Bruno's definition, focuses on Farrington's behaviour at home when he rolls up his sleeves (as he had done in the pub)[40] to beat his son, a younger and safer counterpart than his rival Weathers had been. Weir suggests that Farrington's oppressive relationship to his son is but a smaller-scale version of the oppression to which he is himself submitted by Weathers (with his conspicuously English-sounding name) and by his colleagues at the office, and that these relationships figure Ireland's gnomonic status in relation to Britain (both as a geographical corner of the empire, and as an oppressed political minority). In this schematic reading, Farrington's son Tom is the first in a series that would also include Farrington, Weathers, The Office, Dublin, Catholic Ireland, Protestant Ireland, England, in that order—the largest gnomonic unit being constituted by the English oppressors. In other stories—such as 'A Little Cloud', with its condescending continental visitor,

---

[39] Giordano Bruno, *De Triplici Minimo*, quoted in Weir, 'Gnomon is an Island', 348.
[40] *D*, 92, 94.

and 'After the Race', in which 'clumps of people raised the cheer of the gratefully oppressed' as 'the Continent sped its wealth and industry' through Ireland's 'channel of poverty and inaction'[41]—'the Continent' features as the largest of these oppressing gnomonic structures.

A similar structure underpins 'The Dead', in which the collection's east-west antagonism reaches its climax before being reversed in the closing paragraphs. After brief skirmishes with Miss Ivors and his wife about the west of Ireland and its desirability as a holiday destination, Gabriel's view freezes in a moment of realization brought on by his wife's confession, before beginning to move slowly westward (the rhythm of his thought and imagination seemingly governed by the cadence of the snowfall):

> The time had come for him to set out on his journey westward. Yes, the newspapers were right: snow was general all over Ireland.[42]

The sequence of the two sentences suggests that the gnomon of the west of Ireland, that part of the country which Gabriel had blotted out of his mind as unsuited to his ambitions and self-image, must be restored: Ireland appears whole again, and the 'corner', to use the uncle's phrase in 'The Sisters', is 'box[ed]'.[43]

This, however, is only one application of the word 'gnomon'. As in 'Counterparts', the interpretation derived from Bruno yields an interesting perspective. In such a reading, the dreams of the east represented throughout *Dubliners* (as figured by phantasms of Persia in 'The Sisters', the bazaar in 'Araby', admiration for 'successful Gallicism' in 'After the Race', a penchant for Turkish Delight in 'A Mother', the imagined glamour of continental life in 'A Little Cloud') decrease to a minimum in Joyce's final story. Gabriel in 'The Dead' not only puts in a good word for his country, but also inverts this geographical dynamic by apparently resolving to head westward after all. The emphasis in the closing paragraphs of the story is on reduction, fading, disappearance, as though a gnomonic series were reaching its infinitesimal limit: 'His own identity was fading out [...] the solid world [...] was dissolving and dwindling'.[44] The diminution ends when the snow taps against the window: it is prompted by the sight of the flakes—those tiny units of matter—that Gabriel's thoughts pan out over Ireland's 'central plain' and 'treeless hills', and then 'farther westward': the gnomonic progression, that is, begins to move in an opposite direction. In this movement through a

---

[41] *D*, 35.
[42] *D*, 225.
[43] *D*, 2.
[44] *D*, 224–5.

flake-sized point zero, the reconciliation of the living and the dead occurs, fulfilling Bruno's doctrine of the identity of opposites: 'the maximum and the minimum come together into one existence'.[45] The moment of Gabriel's maximum awareness paradoxically occurs at the moment of minimum consciousness: '[he] watched sleepily', '[h]is soul swooned slowly'.[46]

An analogous, gnomonic, subterranean structure subtends the narratives of Flaubert's *Trois Contes*. All three of Flaubert's tales display tensions between minima and maxima. In 'Un Coeur simple' the pattern is obvious: Félicité's world gradually closes down around her, by dint of successive hardships and bereavements, until she remains entirely alone with her dead, stuffed parrot. The worsening of her circumstances continues as her health (her hearing and eyesight in particular) and her mental faculties deteriorate ('The narrow range of her ideas shrank even further'[47]). In time, even the stuffed parrot is affected by decay ('he was all worm-eaten'[48]). Yet when the situation reaches its lowest possible point, the minimum—Félicité's final agony—turns into the maximum—the moment of greatest exaltation:

> as she breathed her last, she thought she saw, as the heavens opened, a gigantic parrot hovering over her head.[49]

A comparable pattern governs the structure of 'La Légende de saint Julien l'Hospitalier'. The prophecies of sainthood and military greatness for Julian that mark the story's opening give way to the realities of exile—isolation, self-disgust, and extreme self-abnegation. In the final section of the legend, the Leper[50] presents the protagonist with an opportunity for maximum self-chastisement. When Julian joins the Leper in a strange embrace that subsumes all selfhood, the skies open up, and from the minimum of utter selflessness comes the maximum exaltation of godly favour:

> delights in abundance, a superhuman joy came flooding into the soul of Julian, who lay in a swoon; [...] Julian rose up into the blue of space, face to face with our Lord Jesus, who bore him off to heaven.[51]

---

[45] J. Lewis McIntyre, *Giordano Bruno* (London: Macmillan, 1903), quoted in Weir, 'Gnomon is an Island', 348. Joyce's essay, 'The Bruno Philosophy' was a review of McIntyre's book.

[46] *D*, 225.

[47] *TCE*, 31 ['Le petit cercle de ses idées se rétrécit encore' (*TC*, 65)].

[48] *TCE*, 38 ['les vers le dévoraient' (*TC*, 75)].

[49] *TCE*, 40 ['quand elle exhala son dernier souffle, elle crut voir, dans les cieux entrouverts, un perroquet gigantesque, planant au-dessus de sa tête' (*TC*, 79)].

[50] ['le Lépreux']. The capital is Flaubert's.

The conjunction of maximum elation, minimum selfhood, and minimum consciousness (Gabriel swoons, Julian is 'pâmé', Félicité's eyes are closed) at the end of these stories is perfectly summed up by the strikingly gnomonic phrase that is at the heart of 'Hérodias', the story in which the word 'gnomon' features: 'For him to increase, I must decrease.'[52]

The self-consciousness of the gnomon-related intertextuality between *Dubliners* and *Trois Contes* is reinforced by both collections' insistent use of geometrical vocabulary. The openings of each of the *Trois Contes* abound in such terms. In 'Un Coeur simple' boxes and cartons are stacked up to form 'a pyramid of piled-up boxes and cartons'. Julian's castle is set 'in the middle of a forest, on the slope of a hill': Flaubert emphasizes its squareness ('The towers at each of the four corners'), the neatness of the tiles in the castle's churchyard, the grounds' endless enclosures. Similarly, 'Hérodias' opens with a flurry of geometrical terms: 'a conical peak', 'its base within the circle of a wall', 'a zigzag path', 'numerous angles', 'the outlines', 'slopes', 'cube', 'arid plain'.[53] These semantic clusters have counterparts in *Dubliners*, such as the 'gnomon' and the 'square' of the lighted window in 'The Sisters', the thrice repeated 'crossing of the lines' in 'A Painful Case', the quincuncial arrangement in which the five men sit in 'Grace'. The parallel is more obvious in 'The Dead', in which quadrilles are danced, Freddy Malins is described as having a 'convex' face, and the food on the table is arranged in ostentatiously geometrical patterns: 'parallel lines of side-dishes', 'a solid rectangle of Smyrna figs', 'in the centre [. . .] a pyramid of oranges', and on the 'square piano', 'squads of bottles [. . .] with green transverse sashes'. Echoing Herod's view of the 'arid plain', Gabriel thinks of Ireland's 'dark central plain', and of the graveyard's 'crooked crosses'.[54] It is as though the author were reminding us, in extremis, of the geometrical theme that has run through the entire collection, not least in the form of the gnomonic structures derived from *Trois Contes*.

---

[51] *TCE*, 70 ['une abondance de délices, une joie surhumaine descendait comme une inondation dans l'âme de Julien pâmé; [. . .] Julien monta vers les espaces bleus, face à face avec Notre-Seigneur Jésus, qui l'emportait dans le ciel.' (*TC*, 128–9)].

[52] *TCE*, 74, 105 ['Pour qu'il grandisse, il faut que je diminue.' (*TC*, 138, 185)].

[53] *TCE*, 3, 41, 71–2 ['un tas pyramidal' (*TC*, 20); 'au milieu des bois, sur la pente d'une colline. Les quatres tours aux angles' (*TC*, 83–4); 'pic', 'cône', 'base', 'cercle', 'zigzag', 'angles', 'contours', 'surfaces', 'cube', 'plaine aride' (*TC*, 133–4)].

[54] *D*, 1, 109, 172, 183–4, 197, 225.

EPIPHANIC ENDINGS

Endings, as exemplified by the foregoing analysis, manifest a heightened degree of intertextual connection between *Trois Contes* and *Dubliners*. The endings of Joyce's stories are often referred to as epiphanies. Although there has been considerable debate as to whether this constitutes an accurate way of describing the moments of arrest that conclude his stories,[55] the definitions of epiphany at the end of *Stephen Hero* help clarify some of the similarities between Flaubert's and Joyce's endings. The definition Stephen gives is twofold. He first describes the epiphany as 'a sudden spiritual manifestation, whether in the vulgarity of speech or gesture or in a memorable phase of the mind itself'.[56] The section of Stephen's definition most relevant to Flaubert's endings comes next and relies on an implicit photographic analogy: 'Imagine my glimpses at that clock as the gropings of a spiritual eye which seeks to adjust its vision to an exact focus.'[57]

Flaubert's conclusions betray just such an effort to achieve the right focus. The adjustment is effected by an unusual use of verbal tenses, which blurs the distinction between narration and description. Thus, the presumed momentariness of Félicité's vision of her parrot hovering above her head is undermined by the admixture, amid the *passé simple* (past historic) that one would expect (as the French narrative tense par excellence), of other verbal forms, which slow the rhythm of the scene, imparting to the vignettes the static quality of a tableau. Thus in 'Un Coeur simple' the imperfect tense in 'ses lèvres souriaient' ['her lips smiled'] and the present participle in 'planant au-dessus de sa tête' ['hovering over her head'] have a congealing effect also cultivated by similes cast in an immortalizing *présent de vérité générale* (universalizing present), such as 'comme une fontaine s'épuise, comme un écho disparaît' ['like a fountain running dry, like an echo fading'].[58] The reader's lasting impression, as a result, is of a parrot hovering eternally— as it might on a hologrammatic photograph—above the bed-bound, spellbound Félicité. The same ambivalence obtains in the penultimate sentence of 'La Légende', which alternates between imperfect and past historic:

[55] Robert Scholes advocates a more rigorous use of the word 'epiphany' which would confine use of the term to the description of those pieces to which Joyce himself referred as epiphanies—*Workshop*, 4.

[56] *SH*, 211.

[57] *SH*, 211.

[58] *TC*, 78–9 [*TCE*, 40].

Le toit *s'envola*, le firmament *se déployait*;—et Julien *monta* vers les espaces bleus, face à face avec Notre-Seigneur Jésus, qui *l'emportait* dans le ciel.[59]

The process of aesthetic apprehension itself ('The apprehensive faculty', according to the Stephen of *Stephen Hero*, 'must be scrutinised in action'[60]) is discernible in this use of static verbal tenses in scenes that would seem to call for active forms.

'Two Gallants' mobilizes analogous means to epiphanic ends. The story's conclusion certainly depicts a 'vulgarity of gesture':

> Then with a grave gesture he extended a hand towards the light and, smiling, opened it slowly to the gaze of his disciple. A small gold coin shone in the palm.[61]

While the mention of gold and of a disciple seems to invite ironic comparison with the original, Christian Epiphany, the emphasis on the 'gaze' accords with Stephen's definition of epiphany. An obvious adjustment of focus takes place in the final sentences. Corley's hand offers itself 'slowly' to Lenehan's gaze, which is in play despite his eyes and face being outside the field of vision delineated by the narration; the closing sentence in effect offers a close-up of the hand with the coin shining in it. The same effect of frozen permanence is achieved as in the Flaubertian endings—a combination of the slowed rhythm and zoom-like gaze that govern the narration, and of the sudden suspension of the narrative. The palm never closes. The coin shines forever. Just as the reader of *Trois Contes* is unlikely to forget the endings of the stories even after the events leading up to them fade from memory, so the reader of 'Two Gallants' will, if nothing else, remember the gold coin shining in the hand.

Epiphanic moments such as these—the eternally hovering parrot, Julian's endless soaring assumption, the burden of John the Baptist's heavy severed head being shared alternately between its porters as it is carried away from Herod's palace, the pilfered coin gleaming in the hand, Little Chandler forever crying with remorse—epitomize a pervasive kind of intertextuality between Joyce's and Flaubert's work in the short story mode that involves the splicing of the realistic and the symbolic. The epiphanic moments at the end of the stories maximize the resonance of such intertwining. The readerly bafflement cultivated by both authors is accentuated by the short-story genre. With its demands of extreme artistic

---

[59] *TC*, 128–9 (my emphases) ['The roof flew off, the firmament unfolded—and Julian rose up into the blue of space, face to face with our Lord Jesus, who bore him off to heaven.' (*TCE*, 70)].
[60] *SH*, 212.
[61] *D*, 54.

economy, the short story places maximum stress on every object, character, feeling, and encounter described; every word is submitted to the pressure to mean something, and with such pressure comes the concomitant danger, for the reader, of over-interpretation. As neither Flaubert nor Joyce pass comment on the actions they depict, the ambivalence of the stories is akin to the effect of Joyce's stand-alone epiphanies as described by Peter Garrett:

> In themselves these fragments are not properly epiphanic. They manifest almost nothing, remaining merely small slices of life cut in an apparently arbitrary manner.[62]

Unlike the Christian Epiphany, Joyce's epiphanies (and those moments in Flaubert's stories that fit Stephen's definition of epiphany) 'manifest almost nothing', and the nature of what they do manifest remains ultimately unknowable, utterly contingent on interpretation. The sense of bewilderment evoked by Garrett recalls W. H. Auden's definition of the symbolic:

> A symbol is felt to be such before any possible meaning is consciously recognized, i.e. an object or event which is felt to be more important than the reason can immediately explain, is symbolic.[63]

Such is the impression conveyed by many of the objects featured in Flaubert's and Joyce's stories (the stuffed parrot, the stained-glass window, the severed head, the coin, the clay in 'Clay', the bicycle pump in 'Araby'). Both authors deny the symbolizing urge its satisfaction—the stories' open endings, in particular, postpone meaning indefinitely. This is the typical effect of the irony pervading these stories. The selection and arrangement of their elements suggests significance, but the stories provide no sure ground from which to deduce what that significance may be. Like the boy in 'The Sisters', the reader struggles to 'extract meaning' while resisting assumptions that would lead to over-interpretation. As Jeri Johnson points out in her discussion of 'Eveline', the narrator's suggestive traps (calling the male character 'Frank', for instance) must be resisted if misinterpretation is to be avoided: 'we see what she [Eveline] sees, and cannot see what she does not see or avoids seeing or does not understand *unless* we extrapolate from what we are given, unless, that is, we risk interpretation'.[64]

[62] Peter Garrett, *Scene and Symbol from George Eliot to James Joyce* (Yale: Yale University Press, 1969), 222.

[63] W. H. Auden, *The Enchafèd Flood* (London: Faber and Faber, 1951), 61.

[64] Jeri Johnson, Introduction, *Dubliners*, ed. Jeri Johnson (Oxford: Oxford University Press, 2000), xxv.

INTERPRETATIVE GAMBLING AND
REVERSIBLE ENDINGS

Christopher Prendergast calls this aspect of Joyce's and Flaubert's writing 'reversibility'[65]—the quality of writing that lends itself equally to multiple and opposing interpretations. To illustrate the notion, Prendergast adduces an example from Flaubert's *L'Éducation sentimentale*[66] in which the narrator describes Mme Dambreuse's inscrutable social graces:

> if she did happen to utter a platitude, it was so conventionally phrased that you could take it ironically or as sheer politeness.[67]

As Flaubert's deliberately tautological phrasing suggests, Mme Dambreuse has a gift for making clichés sound even more clichéd than they normally would: in her mouth, commonplaces sound even more commonplace than they normally would. Her impeccable handling of social situations replicates the 'reversibility' of the novel as a whole, reflexively highlighting the way in which its various discourses leave the reader struggling to know whether to take a phrase at face value or read it ironically. It is significant that *Dubliners* should closely rephrase this key Flaubertian statement. In 'Two Gallants' Lenehan is described in strikingly similar terms as Mme Dambreuse:

> A shade of mockery relieved the servility of his manner. To save himself he had the habit of leaving his flattery open to the interpretation of raillery.[68]

In this telling intertextual moment, Joyce manifests a Flaubertian self-consciousness regarding the hermeneutical efforts demanded by the text, drawing attention to the interpretative gamble that any act of reading entails.

The end of 'La Légende de saint Julien l'Hospitalier' constitutes one example of such a gamble, demanding that the reader adjudicate between naive and ironic readings of Julian's assumption. As A. E. Pilkington has shown, Flaubert leaves both possibilities open, allowing rationalistic, psychological readings, as well as Christian, providentialist interpretations.[69]

---

[65] The 'citational method' involves extensive quotation from 'the discourse of received ideas', which 'can be said to invade the whole texture of the writing'—Christopher Prendergast, *The Order of Mimesis* (Cambridge: Cambridge University Press, 1986), 202.

[66] Prendergast, *Order of Mimesis*, 207.

[67] *ESE*, 393 ['s'il lui échappait des lieux communs, c'était dans une formule tellement convenue que sa phrase pouvait passer pour une déférence ou une ironie' (*ES*, 392)].

[68] *D*, 46.

[69] A. E. Pilkington, 'Point of View in Flaubert's "La Légende de saint Julien"', *French Studies* 29 (1975).

By making the predictions addressed to Julian's parents accord seamlessly with what we know of their personalities, Flaubert enables both prophecies to be viewed as hallucinations rather than real events. Psychological explanations are also facilitated by the dream-like atmosphere that dominates the great hunting expeditions: Julian's own encounter with the soothsaying great stag occurs amid surreal events that question its reality. Even Julian's private thoughts leave the story open to a realistic, psychological interpretation. Indeed Julian seems less afraid of the predicted parricide than of the possibility that he might actually *want* to kill his parents:

> 'No! no! no! I could never kill them!' Then he thought: 'But supposing I wanted to? . . .' and was afraid that the Devil might prompt such a wish.[70]

These tensions between divine providence and personal responsibility, the medieval and the modern, belief and scepticism, are emphasized by Julian's schizophrenic state of mind after the carnage:

> He did not rebel against God who had inflicted such a deed upon him, and yet he was in despair at the fact that he had been able to do it.[71]

In a tale that invites such conflicting responses the reader can neither embrace nor dismiss the Christian explanation for the Leper's appearance and the ecstatic, liberating death the Messianic figure seems to bring.

Janus-like irony (as a mode of narrative uncertainty rather than of ridicule) makes the adoption of a secure interpretative standpoint similarly impossible in 'Un Coeur simple'. Is Félicité a victim for whom we are encouraged to feel sympathy, or is Flaubert's portrait predominantly ironic? Her name is a good example of irony coming full circle. At first, the appellation appears to be deeply ironic, given the pain and struggles that characterize Félicité's life; but this initial view gradually gives way to the realization that the name is fitting because Félicité, despite her poverty, her personal losses, and her physical ailments, is not unhappy—is, astonishingly, contented, and does not stand in the same analytical and critical relationship to her life as does the reader. In fact, Flaubert seems to undercut the validity of a straightforwardly ironic reading of Félicité by his viciously satirical treatment of Bourais, a retired lawyer and respected acquaintance of Félicité's employer, Mme Aubain. Bourais responds to Félicité's childish questions with pedantic smiles ('He put on a pedantically superior smile at Félicité's bewilderment'[72]), and when Félicité

---

[70] *TCE*, 52 ['"Non! Non! Non! Je ne peux pas les tuer!" puis, il songeait: "Si je le voulais pourtant? . . ." et il avait peur que le Diable ne lui en inspirât l'envie.' (*TC*, 101)].

[71] *TCE*, 65 ['Il ne se révoltait pas contre Dieu qui lui avait infligé cette action, et pourtant se désespérait de l'avoir pu commettre.' (*TC*, 122)].

[72] *TCE*, 20 ['il avait un beau sourire de cuistre devant l'ahurissement de Félicité' (*TC*, 48)].

asks to be shown her nephew's house on a world map, Bourais (to whom the narrator, by yet another ironic twist, seems to join himself) bursts into loud mocking laughter:

> Bourais flung up his arms, sneezed, laughed uproariously; [...] Félicité could not understand why—her intelligence was so limited that she might even be expecting to see her nephew's portrait![73]

The reader reacts against this laughter: sympathy proceeds precisely as a reaction against an irony that seems gratuitously cruel. This anticipates another potential act of reading-against-the-grain at the very moment of epiphanic closure, when the narrator distances himself from Félicité's final vision by introducing it with the doubtful verbal locution 'elle crut voir'. The paradoxical effect of this caution, as Jonathan Culler points out, is to cause the reader to invest more in the vision, already compelling in its suspended stasis, in a sympathetic gesture that injects meaning—a retrospective telos—into Félicité's life:

> by implying 'she only thought she saw a parrot, of course, being stupid and deluded', the text prevents the reader from having to entertain such disagreeable sentiments [...] Saying something that needed saying, it prevents us from having to say it ourselves and allows us to accept the other view, now that it has been appropriately tested.[74]

But however committed the reader may be, or may empathetically want to be, to the truth of Félicité's vision of a hybrid form of parakeet and Paraclete, the parrot motif cannot be purged of its ambivalence. Ironic readings, as Victor Brombert points out, are inevitable where the assimilation of the parrot to the Holy Ghost is concerned. That psittacism—meaningless mimicking, repetition, cliché—should be so closely associated with the Holy Spirit, even if the reader tries to confine the association within the bounds of Félicité's mind, opens the gates to innumerable satirical overtones.[75]

This Flaubertian trait—the ability to make irony cut both ways—is everywhere apparent in *Dubliners*. Should Gabriel Conroy be read sympathetically, ironically, or both? Is his moment of realization genuine, or is it a role he plays to himself in order to enact that generosity for which Gretta so cleverly praises him before making her disclosure about Michael

---

[73] *TCE*, 21 ['Bourais leva les bras, il éternua, rit énormément; [...] Félicité n'en comprenait pas le motif,—elle qui s'attendait peut-être à voir jusqu'au portrait de son neveu, tant son intelligence était bornée!' (*TC*, 49)].

[74] Jonathan Culler, *Flaubert: The Uses of Uncertainty* (London: Paul Elek, 1974), 210.

[75] Victor Brombert, *The Novels of Flaubert: A Study of Themes and Techniques* (Princeton: Princeton University Press, 1966), 240–1.

Furey?[76] How are we to read Gretta's gnomonic story? What are we to make of Father Flynn in 'The Sisters', Frank and Eveline in 'Eveline', Little Chandler in 'A Little Cloud', Maria in 'Clay', Duffy in 'A Painful Case'? The stories reveal nothing so clearly as their own indecipherability, their resistance to any final judgement.

BLURRING THE BOUNDARIES: CINEMATOGRAPHIC WRITING

Trois Contes and *Dubliners* are also intertextually related by their use of a range of techniques elaborated by Flaubert, developed by Joyce, which establish a tension between the static and the dynamic, or the photographic and the cinematographic. Both authors have predilections for images of motion that verge on the static. In Joyce's case, this is reflected in the musings about art as stasis inscribed in the 'Paris and Pola Commonplace Book', as well as in Stephen's disquisitions about epiphany and aesthetic stasis in *Stephen Hero* and *A Portrait*.[77] According to Isabelle Daunais, 'the image [. . .] constitutes the basic unit of narrative' in Flaubert's works .[78] In the *Correspondance* this predilection is obvious, for instance, in cases where the description of some—usually comic—scene is followed by the ironic, immobilizing exclamation: 'Tâbleau!'[79] (the onomatopoeic use of the circumflex drawing attention to the bourgeois pretentiousness Flaubert mimics at such moments).

While static moments have pride of place in both the Flaubertian and the Joycean stories, such scenes are often also in some way animated. Flaubert provides us with a perfect word for this hybrid quality in 'Un Coeur simple'. Describing the intimacy between Félicité and her parrot, Flaubert turns them into a kind of vibrating unit, relying, as in previously quoted examples, on a mixture of imperfect and present participle to create a paradoxical congealing effect:

---

[76] 'You are a very generous person, Gabriel, she said. [. . .] Generous tears filled Gabriel's eyes.'—*D*, 219, 224.

[77] *Workshop*, 53 ('All art, again, is static for the feelings of terror and pity on the one hand and of joy on the other hand are feelings which arrest us.'); *SH*, 211–13; *P*, 172 ('Beauty [. . .] awakens, or ought to awaken, or induces, or ought to induce, an ideal pity or an ideal terror, a stasis called forth, prolonged and at last dissolved by what I call the rhythm of beauty.').

[78] ['l'image constitue [. . .] l'unité de base du récit' (Isabelle Daunais, *Flaubert et la scénographie romanesque* [Paris: Nizet, 1993], 14)].

[79] See, for example, Flaubert's letter to Louise Colet, 25 November 1853, *C2*, 468.

as she bent forward, wagging her head as nurses do, the wide wings of her bonnet and those of the bird quivered in unison.[80]

The shaking movement of the head depicted by the verb but arrested by its present participle 'wagging' ('branlant') is refined in the final clause by the verb 'quivered' ('frémissaient'). The effect of this static yet quivering image is, strictly speaking, neither photographic nor cinematographic— being too static for the cinema (the term is used metaphorically as Flaubert's writing antedates the inception of the medium by several decades), too dynamic for photography. Flaubert plays with the boundary between these states, telescoping the human and the animal. This merging is related to a whole set of techniques he employs to make the animate and the inanimate coalesce to surreal effect. For André Topia, 'The blurring between what is living and what is inanimate is a constant feature of Flaubert's writing' and 'this blurring between the organic and the inorganic is also a constant in Joyce's writing'.[81] Writing about the near-merger of Félicité and her parrot, Topia notes that 'The bonnet and the bird, the inanimate and the living, become a kind of dual creature'.[82] Another striking instance of this occurs towards the beginning of 'Un Coeur simple' when Félicité is described as a kind of automaton: she 'looked like a wooden dummy, driven by clockwork'.[83]

In 'Hérodias' similarly grotesque effects derive from the fragmentation of bodies into individual parts, with each taking on a life of its own, most notably as the subjects of active verbs. In the passage devoted to Salome's dance, for instance:

> Her feet slipped back and forth [. . .] Her arms curved round in invitation to someone [. . .] The jewels in her ears leapt about, the silk on her back shimmered [. . .] her chin brushed the floor.[84]

---

[80] *TCE*, 31 ['comme elle penchait son front en branlant la tête à la manière des nourrices, les grandes ailes du bonnet et les ailes de l'oiseau frémissaient ensemble' (*TC*, 66)].

[81] ['Le brouillage entre le vivant et l'inanimé est une constante de l'écriture flaubertienne'; 'ce brouillage entre organique et inorganique est aussi une constante de l'écriture joycienne' (Topia, 'Flaubert et Joyce', 54, 56)].

[82] ['Le bonnet et l'oiseau, l'inanimé et le vivant deviennent une espèce de créature double' (Topia, 'Flaubert et Joyce', 54)].

[83] *TCE*, 4 ['semblait une femme en bois, fonctionnant d'une manière automatique' (*TC*, 22)].

[84] *TCE*, 101–2 ['Ses pieds passaient l'un devant l'autre [. . .] Ses bras arrondis appelaient quelqu'un [. . .] Les brillants de ses oreilles sautaient, l'étoffe de son dos chatoyait; [. . .] son menton frôlait le plancher' (*TC*, 180–1)].

According to Topia :

> a dislocation springs the locks which kept the body unified as a homogeneous whole, and transforms it into a new quasi-monstrous, half-organic, half-inorganic whole.[85]

Conversely, the scene suddenly resolves itself into near-stasis when Salome's body is compared to an inert, inorganic statue at the very height of its frenzied movement:

> Her lips were painted, her eyebrows very black, her eyes almost frightening, and the drops on her forehead looked like a vapour on white marble.[86]

This 'monstrous' effect, all-pervasive in Flaubert's *Tentation de saint Antoine* and in the 'Circe' episode of *Ulysses*, is discernible in *Dubliners* as well. 'Two Gallants' and 'Counterparts' offer particularly salient examples. In 'Two Gallants' Lenehan and Corley are described in mechanistic terms. Laughter is reduced to a passive phenomenon, and Lenehan becomes a surface taken over by convulsion: 'Little jets of wheezing laughter followed one another out of his convulsed body.' Corley's awkward movements are described in even more acutely dehumanizing terms: not only is it 'necessary for him to move his body from the hips', but his face, when turning towards the woman he is courting, moves 'like a big ball revolving on a pivot'.[87] In 'Counterparts', which is set in a work environment never free from 'the clicking of the machine' and reliant on the 'tube' as a means of communication between the upper and lower levels of the office, the most caricatural treatment is reserved for the boss, Mr Alleyne, whose 'polished skull' is first described as 'a large egg reposing on the papers' and later as 'the head of the manikin'. The motif reaches its most extreme expression during the altercation with Farrington, which sees Mr Alleyne's anger manifest itself in surreal robotic jerks: 'He shook his fist in the man's face till it seemed to vibrate like the knob of some electric machine.'[88] As in Flaubert, the use of such similes, as well as the use of gerunds ('the clicking of the machine') and present participles, whether adjectival ('wheezing laughter') or not ('reposing'), confers an air of the static to the narration. As Roger Huss and André Topia remark, Joyce's present participles yield

---

[85] ['une dislocation fait sauter les verrous qui maintenaient le corps unifié en un ensemble homogène, et le transforme en un nouvel ensemble, mi-organique, mi-inorganique' (Topia, 'Flaubert et Joyce', 56)].

[86] *TCE*, 102 ['Ses lèvres étaient peintes, ses sourcils très noirs, ses yeux presque terribles, et des goutelettes à son front semblaient une vapeur sur du marbre blanc.' (*TC*, 182)].

[87] *D*, 43, 45, 50.

[88] *D*, 86, 82, 83, 82, 87.

analogous effects to Flaubert's anomalous use of the imperfect as a narrative tense.[89] For Topia:

> The action, it seems, need never end. [...] The present participle functions like an echo which vibrates and circulates through the whole scene.[90]

Topia's description of the sense of vibration created by the use of certain verbal tenses accurately reflects what happens at the end of 'The Dead'. In the closing paragraphs of the story, the rhythm of the narrative slows dramatically. Past continuous and present participle are closely related verbal forms in English and the two alternate here to generate a sense of unending infinitesimal movement:

> the flakes [...] falling obliquely against the lamplight [...] It was falling on every part of the central plain [...] falling softly upon the Bog of Allen and, farther westward, softly falling.[91]

The numerous, often chiastic repetitions and the length of the sentences in this passage contribute to the impression of unified, almost imperceptible movement. The scene, which invites one—like Gabriel—to gaze at the snowfall from behind the hotel window, places the reader behind a metaphorical lens (the window, as a symbol of insight, so different from the opacity of the windows in 'The Sisters' and 'La Légende', suggests a move away from the pessimism of the earlier stories). The closing paragraphs, as John Huston's film adaptation demonstrates,[92] lend themselves to filmic interpretation. Moreover, Gabriel's imaginative movement outwards and westwards, which sweeps over Irish landscapes before homing in on Michael Furey's grave, is suggestive of a camera's panning-out and zooming-in, the last few words, with their lullingly alliterative, repetitive cadences ('the descent to their last end', 'the living and the dead'[93]) even suggestive of cinematographic fade-out. The figurative camera-eye in this instance is situated in Gabriel's eye and, indeed, in his mind's eye—as much of the description is imagined rather than seen. Here, in other words, is a technique that renders the description of the outside world subjective—a technique that Pierre Danger, noting its prevalence in Flaubert's works, has termed 'caméra subjective'.[94] This is

---

[89] Roger Huss, 'Some Anomalous Uses of the Imperfect and the Status of Action in Flaubert', *French Studies* 31 (1977).

[90] ['L'action semble ne jamais devoir prendre fin. [...] Le participe présent a l'effet d'un écho qui vibre et circule dans toute la scène.' (Topia, 'Flaubert et Joyce', 59, 61)].

[91] *D*, 225.

[92] John Huston, dir., *The Dead* (Liffey Films: Vestron UK, 1987).

[93] *D*, 225.

[94] Pierre Danger, *Sensations et objets dans le roman de Flaubert* (Paris: A. Colin, 1973), 218.

precisely the procedure that governs the beginning of 'Hérodias'. The description of the territories surrounding the citadel of Machaerous is focalized through Herod, with the verb 'regarda' introducing both the focalization and the cinematographic quality of the sentences that follow. The narrator draws attention to every camera-like movement of the character's gaze: 'The Tetrarch looked away to the right to gaze at the palm trees of Jericho.'[95] The technique makes for a description that is at once subjective and panoramic.

Cinematographic techniques can impact more strikingly on the narration. In an early passage from 'Un Coeur simple', Théodore, Félicité's one-time 'gallant', kisses her for the first time. The event is not recounted directly but by evasion. Instead of showing the kiss, Flaubert employs a suggestive image substitution: the horses Théodore is steering behave unpredictably ('Then, unbidden, they turned off to the right.'),[96] leaving the reader to infer that he has been distracted from his driving by his attentions to Félicité. Théodore kisses Félicité again, and another typically cinematographic trick, the black-out, is drawn out of the hat: 'He kissed her again. She vanished into the darkness.'[97] These effects (image substitution, black-out) are related to focalization. The lack of visual content at this point in the story, the lack of any information at all, in fact, apart from the aberrant trajectory of Théodore's cart, reflects Félicité's own (presumably entirely pre-verbal) embarrassment and confusion. It is this type of effect which inspires Danger to hail Flaubert's 'remarkable prefiguration of a new writing technique'.[98]

Something very similar happens in 'An Encounter'. The deliberate (mis)direction of the narrator's gaze (to which numerous references are made in the build-up to the story's central incident) leads to a complete omission of what, by the sound of it, constitutes a confirmation of the narrator's (and the reader's) unrest:

> I continued to gaze towards the foot of the slope, listening to him. [...]
> without changing the direction of my gaze, I saw him walking slowly away
> from us [...]
> 'I say! Look what he's doing!'
> As I neither answered nor raised my eyes, Mahony exclaimed again:
> 'I say ... He's a queer old josser!'[99]

[95] *TCE*, 71 ['Le Tétrarque en detourna la vue pour contempler, à droite, les palmiers de Jéricho' (*TC*, 134)].

[96] *TCE*, 6 ['Puis, sans commandement, ils tournèrent à droite.' (*TC*, 25)].

[97] *TCE*, 6 [Il l'embrassa encore une fois. Elle disparut dans l'ombre.' (*TC*, 25)].

[98] ['préfiguration remarquable d'une nouvelle technique d'écriture' (Danger, *Sensations et objects*, 186)].

[99] *D*, 18.

The technique of letting the sound run on while keeping the camera-eye immobile is quintessentially cinematographic; the character's gaze determines the visual substance of the narration, which, in this case, remains bafflingly blank.

The camera-eye style of narration can (as illustrated in the example from 'Un Coeur simple') entertain ambiguous relations to a character's point of view. Indeed, the onset of cinematographic techniques does not necessarily coincide with the use of free indirect style. It can, on the contrary, signal a rupture in focalization. Raymonde Debray-Genette refers to this phenomenon as 'focalisation externe'.[100] Where 'caméra subjective' cultivates an intimacy between the character and the reader, 'focalisation externe' has an alienating effect. Two instances are representative. In Flaubert's 'Légende' this effect occurs after the parricide, when Julian attends his parents' funeral. Over the preceding paragraphs, Julian's first name (the narrator's usual mode of reference to the protagonist) gives way to the personal pronoun 'il'. We see Julian take leave of his wife coldly, 'in a voice unlike his own'.[101] Yet none of this prepares the reader for the disorienting effect produced by the switch to what one might call a 'caméra objective' mode of narration, whereby the narrator withdraws from his character, considering him from an entirely external point of view, even, it seems, affecting not to recognize him:

A monk, with his cowl pulled down over his face, followed the cortege, at a distance from everyone else, and no one dared to speak to him.[102]

The narrator's gaze (represented by the impersonal pronoun 'on', which implicitly includes other witnesses) still focuses on the estranged protagonist, describing his dramatic mourning posture: 'prostrated in the middle of the doorway, arms extended and face in the dust.'[103] The narrator's cinematographic gaze follows him—in a move that has become common in film-making—until he disappears out of sight:

After the burial, he was seen taking the road which led to the mountains. He turned round several times, and finally disappeared.[104]

The concluding verb adds to the suggestion of a final fade-out. The fade-out is narrative, as the story has reached an important turning point,

---

[100]   Raymonde Debray-Genette, 'Du mode narratif dans les *Trois Contes*', in *Travail de Flaubert*, ed. Gérard Genette and Tzvetan Todorov (Paris: Seuil, 1983), 163–4.

[101]   *TCE*, 63 ['d'une voix différente de la sienne' (*TC*, 118)].

[102]   *TCE*, 63 ['Un moine en cagoule rabattue suivit le cortège, loin de tous les autres, sans que personne osât lui parler.' (*TC*, 118–19)].

[103]   *TCE*, 64 ['à plat ventre au milieu du portail, les bras en croix, et le front dans la poussière.' (*TC*, 119)].

[104]   *TCE*, 64 ['Après l'ensevelissement, on le vit prendre le chemin qui menait aux montagnes. Il se retourna plusieurs fois, et finit par disparaître.' (*TC*, 119)].

but also psychological. Indeed, as in the case of Félicité in 'Un Coeur simple', these sentences should not be taken to signify a complete divorce between the narrator and his protagonist. As much as the narrator's distance from his character, the linguistic indicators of estrangement reflect Julian's own extreme self-alienation, the chaos of his shattered selfhood.

An exactly analogous estrangement between character and narrator occurs in Joyce's 'Counterparts'. For much of the first part of the narrative, set in the office, Farrington is referred to by the narrator simply as 'the man', and this in spite of the fact that other characters address him and refer to him by his surname. The move to the pubs of Dublin seems to instigate a new closeness between narrator and character, and Farrington is referred to by his name, and more frequently by the pronoun 'he', which blurs the boundaries between the narrator's discourse, free indirect discourse, and third-person narration inflected by the Uncle Charles Principle (the Joycean technique wherein items of idiom and syntax appear to belong to a character, rather than to the narrator).[105] With a new change of setting, which takes Farrington off the streets and home to his family, the narrator reverts to the estranged mode of narration that prevailed at the opening. It is as though the camera-eye reporting the beating of the child were adjusting its focus to the actions perpetrated by the protagonist. The return to the use of 'the man' effects a coldness suggestive of the narrator's efforts to maintain distance and detachment, with possibly even a hint of condemnation: 'The man jumped up furiously and pointed to the fire [. . .] the man followed him and caught him by the coat'.[106] Here again, the 'caméra objective' mode of narration signals the character's confusion and self-disgust as well as the distancing of narrator from protagonist.

The 'focalisation externe' that governs these two instances also accounts for the cinematographic summaries and cuts that fast-forward the plots of both the Flaubertian and the Joycean stories. On several occasions in 'Un Coeur simple' years are summed up in a single sentence: 'Many years went by.'[107] The same thing happens in 'A Painful Case': the paragraph that follows the end of Duffy's relationship with Emily Sinico begins by stating that 'Four years passed'.[108] In 'Eveline' a blank space, analogous to a momentary cinematographic black-out, cuts out the interval between Eveline's reflections and the moment of final decision, maximizing the

---

[105] As defined by Hugh Kenner, 'The Uncle Charles Principle entails writing about someone much as that someone would choose to be written about.'—*Joyce's Voices* (London: Faber and Faber, 1978), 21.
[106] *D*, 94.
[107] *TCE*, 36 ['Bien des années se passèrent.' (*TC*, 73)].
[108] *D*, 108.

dramatic impact of the final scene. Marcel Proust referred to such cuts in Flaubert's works in terms of white space: 'In my view, the most beautiful thing in *A Sentimental Education* is not a sentence but a blank.'[109] In 'A Little Cloud', 'Counterparts', and 'Grace', the procedure becomes more overt, as white spaces are figured in the text by lines of dots separating one scene (Little Chandler's encounter with Gallaher, for instance) from the next (the scene at home with his wife and child). The increasing frequency of these highly visible cuts suggests a heightened self-consciousness on Joyce's part concerning the use of such cinematographic techniques.

Joyce's intertextual response to Flaubert in his first published prose work is both concentrated and wide-ranging. It also appears to have been both deliberate and self-conscious because of Joyce's willingness to sign-post his engagement with Flaubert by inclusion of the word 'gnomon' in his first paragraph. The connection between the 'gnomon' of 'Hérodias' and the 'gnomon' of Joyce's 'The Sisters' is confirmed by many other 'strandentwining cables' between the two collections. Joyce weaves thematic preoccupations upon resonant structural trellises, splicing the realistic and the symbolic, fusing the static and the dynamic, and mobilizing cinematographic modes of writing—all within the constraining requirements of a genre in which economy is essential. For all these reasons, *Dubliners* is thoroughly emblematic of Joyce's continued and continuing interest in both the minute detail and the overarching themes, techniques, and structures of Flaubert's works.

---

[109] Marcel Proust, 'A Propos du Style de Flaubert', 205 ['A mon avis la chose la plus belle dans *L'Éducation sentimentale*, ce n'est pas une phrase mais un blanc.']. Proust refers to the episode in *L'Éducation* in which Frédéric witnesses the murder of Dussardier by Sénécal. Frédéric's astounded recognition of Sénécal as the perpetrator of the killing gives way to both a literal 'blanc'—as the scene is the last of Part III, section V—and to a large narrative ellipsis that intimates the extent of Frédéric's shock. The reader is informed only that 'He travelled.'—*ESE*, 455 ['Il voyagea.' (*ES*, 450)].

3

A Portrait of the Artist as a Young Man

The review of *Dubliners* through which Pound introduced Joyce to the world in July 1914, recommending him to *The Egoist*'s readership by way of enthusiastic Flaubertian analogies, was written with at least some of *A Portrait of the Artist as a Young Man* in mind. Writing from Trieste, Joyce had sent the first chapter of the novel along with *Dubliners* to Pound's London address in January 1914. The second chapter followed in March. It would not have escaped Joyce's attention (needy for congratulation and encouragement as he always was) that Pound's immediate reaction to the materials he received was to praise the novel above the stories. Pound's excitement about the opening of *A Portrait* is patent in a letter written just days after his receipt of Joyce's dispatch:

> I think your novel is damn fine stuff [. . .]
> I am sending it off at once to THE EGOIST [. . .]

Pound's praise for *Dubliners* was more moderate, and his assessment of the stories' chances of publication less optimistic:

> I think the stories good—possibly too thorough, too psychological or subjective in treatment to suit that brute in New York.[1]

But every chapter of *A Portrait* that Joyce sent to Pound elicited renewed assurances of the poet's admiration:

> Dear Joyce: Your second chapter has arrived O.K., you know how good I think your work is so I needn't go into that.[2]

Pound's review of *Dubliners* addresses an audience that he also assumed to be familiar with Joyce's novelistic writing, as the early instalments of *A Portrait* had been appearing in *The Egoist* since February:

---

[1] Pound to Joyce, 17 and 19 January 1914, *P/J*, 24; 'that brute in New York' referred to by Pound was the editor of *The Smart Set*, to whom he shortly afterwards sent 'An Encounter', 'The Boarding House', and 'A Little Cloud'—*P/J*, 25.

[2] Pound to Joyce, 1 April 1914, *P/J*, 25.

The readers of THE EGOIST, having had Mr Joyce under their eyes for some months, will scarcely need to have his qualities pointed out to them.

Pound's article makes few references to *Dubliners*, focusing instead on the general qualities of Joyce's prose.[3] Joyce could not but have been keenly aware, even before the serialization of his novel had run its course, and long before it appeared in book form (1916), that the greatest promoter of his work to date had singled out likeness to Flaubert as his writing's most distinctive and admirable feature. What Joyce thought of Pound's analogies, and whether they led to any changes to the closing chapters of *A Portrait*, is not precisely known. But some of Joyce's unpublished letters to Pound seem to indicate tacit endorsement of the Flaubertian analogies. In a letter of 24 July 1917, Joyce thanks Pound in Shakespearean terms for being the father of his book: 'I enclose some press notices. Yours comes first as only begetter of this book.' The press notice to which Joyce refers consists of excerpts from Pound's review of *A Portrait*. Flaubert's name occurs twice among the selected extracts, and no other author features:

> James Joyce produces the nearest thing to Flaubertian prose that we have now in English [. . .] His novel is very different from *L'Éducation sentimentale* but it would be easier to compare it with that novel of Flaubert's than with anything else.[4]

PLATO AND 'BEAUTY, THE SPLENDOUR OF TRUTH'

The last two of the five chapters of *A Portrait* were sent to London as late as November 1914, which would have allowed Joyce to make corrections or additions inspired by Pound's comments. The hypothesis is appealing, if unverifiable, because the most significant instances of Flaubertian intertextuality in *A Portrait* cluster in the novel's final chapter. These echoes share a source—Flaubert's letters—and occur in close proximity to each other in the midst of Stephen's conversation with his friend Lynch about aesthetics. Firstly, Stephen misattributes the theory that beauty is truth to Plato, exactly as Flaubert had done in a letter of 18 March 1857 to

---

[3] Pound, '*Dubliners* and Mr James Joyce', *P/J*, 27, 30.

[4] Yale University, Beinecke Rare Book and Manuscript Library, YCAL MSS 43, Box 26, Folders 1,112–14 (quotations from Ezra Pound, 'James Joyce: At Last the Novel Appears', *P/J*, 89–90).

his friend Mlle Leroyer de Chantepie. A few pages later, Stephen's disquisition about artistic form culminates in his comparison of the position of the literary author with that of 'the God of the creation' in a sentence which closely resembles one of Flaubert's most famous statements.[5] This chapter looks in detail at these two instances of near-quotation. It goes on to suggest that there is an intertextual connection between Stephen's reaction to the hellfire sermon of the novel's third chapter and Antony's response to the taunting demons of Flaubert's *La Tentation de saint Antoine*. Finally, it looks at ways in which some of the structural features of *L'Éducation sentimentale* may have inspired the contrapuntal structure of *A Portrait* and how Flaubertian techniques for developing strands of narrative in parallel are put to use in Joyce's novel (as they had already been in some of the epiphanies).

The first of *A Portrait*'s allusions to Flaubert differs both from its source and from Joyce's prior uses of that source in his early essay on 'James Clarence Mangan' and in *Stephen Hero*. On 18 March 1857 Flaubert invoked Plato's name in the context of an impassioned letter that called for the application of the scientific method to novelistic writing:

> Art should rise above one's personal attachments and nervous susceptibilities! It is time to give Art—by a pitiless method—all the precision of the physical sciences! The principal difficulty, as I see it, remains none the less the matter of style, of form; indefinable Beauty resulting from the idea itself, which is the radiance of Truth, as Plato said.[6]

In 'James Clarence Mangan' Joyce declares that:

> Beauty, the splendour of truth, is a gracious presence when the imagination contemplates intensely the truth of its own being or the visible world, and the spirit which proceeds out of truth and beauty is the holy spirit of joy.[7]

The grammar of the statement—whereby the opening phrases are apposed, and the verb that follows conjugated in the singular—makes it clear that beauty is being defined as truth. There is no suggestion here that

[5] The likelihood of these connections is noted in *The Critical Writings of James Joyce*, ed. Ellsworth Mason and Richard Ellmann (London: Faber and Faber, 1959), 83, 141–3; *Workshop*, 248; *JJ*, 296; *OCPW*, 301; *P*, 275, 278.

[6] Flaubert to Mlle Leroyer de Chantepie, 18 March 1857, *GW*, 248 ['l'Art doit s'élever au-dessus des affections personnelles et des susceptibilités nerveuses! Il est temps de lui donner, par une méthode impitoyable, la précision des sciences physiques! La difficulté capitale, pour moi, n'en reste pas moins le style, la forme, le Beau indéfinissable *résultant de la conception même* et qui est la splendeur du Vrai, comme disait Platon.' (*C2*, 691)].

[7] 'Mangan', *OCPW*, 60.

the idea is not Joyce's own. In *Stephen Hero* a similar pronouncement, articulated by way of the same apposition, is reiterated; again, there is no suggestion of a borrowing:

> It is time for them [the critics] to acknowledge that here the imagination has contemplated intensely the truth of the being of the visible world and that beauty, the splendour of truth, has been born.[8]

It is only in *A Portrait of the Artist as a Young Man* that the dictum is attributed to Plato. With the attribution comes a significant alteration to Joyce's and Stephen's earlier formulations of the aesthetic equation:

> Plato, I believe, said that beauty is the splendour of truth. I don't think that it has a meaning but the true and the beautiful are akin. Truth is beheld by the intellect which is appeased by the most satisfying relations of the intelligible: beauty is beheld by the imagination which is appeased by the most satisfying relations of the sensible.[9]

Stephen's interpretation modifies the meaning of the statement as it appeared in both antecedent versions. For although Stephen asserts that Plato means that beauty *is* the splendour of truth, he goes on to twist the proposition in such a way that it comes to mean the opposite: that truth and beauty are not one and the same, but parallel phenomena, the one relating to the intellect, the other to the imagination. Beauty no longer 'is' truth, it is merely 'akin to' truth: the terms pertain to the apprehensions of different faculties. By this shift from 'is' to 'akin to', the tenet is transformed in a way that befits Stephen's evasion of realism as a mode of writing.

Indeed, to make psychological sense of Stephen's interest in keeping truth and beauty separate, one need only remember his first narrated attempt at literary creation: the composition of the poem about his encounter with 'E. C.' near the beginning of Chapter II. The episode is revelatory regarding Stephen's conceptions of what writing involves. It is significant, for instance, that Stephen's youthful effort should be marked by a strict adherence to existing models of writing. He writes the letters of the Jesuit motto at the top of the page 'From force of habit' before inscribing his dedication 'To E–C–' because 'He knew it was right to begin so for he had seen similar titles in the collected poems of Lord Byron.'[10] After these overdetermined first few jottings, Stephen comes to a stop, until, slowly, a poem takes shape, which, if it has any beauty, certainly bears very little autobiographical truth:

---

[8] *SH*, 80.   [9] *P*, 174–5.   [10] *P*, 58.

he thought himself into confidence. During this process all those elements which he deemed common and insignificant fell out of the scene. There remained no trace of the tram itself nor of the trammen nor of the horses: nor did he and she appear vividly. The verses told only of the night and the balmy breeze and the maiden lustre of the moon [...] and when the moment of farewell had come the kiss, which had been withheld by one, was given by both.[11]

In other words, all realistic detail 'falls out' of the picture, leaving only a setting made up of worn romantic clichés, and a plotline that stands in ironic and unwittingly humorous contrast to what has actually happened between Stephen and E. C. The ending of the 'story' in Stephen's poem is utterly unfaithful to the reality of his lived experience, with a triumphant kiss, 'given by both', sealing the success of the evening. In transforming the encounter in this fashion Stephen acts on a radically different view of art from that which had prompted Joyce to categorically refuse to 'alter in the presentment, still more to deform, whatever he has seen and heard'.[12] Stephen writes a poem that seems to aspire to emulate symbolist obscurity, but lacking the cerebral force and precision of, say, Mallarméan imagery, it achieves only a vagueness that shrouds all the events described in an affected, hackneyed mist. Beauty, for Stephen, manifestly involves un-truth rather than the splendour of truth. Margot Norris argues that the 'falling out' from Stephen's poem of 'all those elements which he deemed common and insignificant' is representative of the 'aestheticization'—or erasure of material realities—involved in much modernist art. Joyce himself, on Norris's analysis, does not carry out the kind of censorship we see at work in Stephen's writing: rather, Joyce stages and ironizes 'aestheticism's aestheticizing of itself'.[13] Stephen, especially in these early stages of the novel, adheres to a highly idealistic conception of what it means to be a writer, in which the making of literary art requires the elision of realities such as destitution, work (as represented by the tram-men's shift), and sexual frustration. Poverty must be put out of sight to enable the act of writing—thus it is with new writing instruments laid out before him that Stephen sets out to produce a prime example of what Oscar Wilde called the 'art of lying': 'Before him lay a new pen, a new bottle of ink and a new emerald exercise.'[14] The materials Stephen assembles tell a lie about the circumstances in which he writes, a lie

---

[11] *P*, 59.
[12] Joyce to Grant Richards, 5 May 1906, *L2*, 134.
[13] Margot Norris, *Joyce's Web: The Social Unraveling of Modernism* (Austin: University of Texas Press, 1992), 58.
[14] *P*, 58.

betrayed by the impoverished conditions of both his previous and subsequent attempts at writing. It was 'on the back of one of his father's second moiety notices'[15] that Stephen had tried to write his first poem about the death of Parnell, and it is on a cigarette packet that he scribbles the villanelle of Chapter V. Like his childhood poem to E. C., the villanelle provides an extreme example of Stephen's resistance to realistic truth in poetic creation, and of his reliance on veiling and displacement as means of expression. The trigger for Stephen's inspiration, sexual arousal, is completely transfigured in the poem. E. C.'s wilful heart, for instance, becomes Mary's virgin heart.[16] In both these instances, Stephen writes poems that bear little relation to the events from which they spring. His reinterpretation of the 'beauty as truth' theory of art is in keeping with the kind of art he produces.

Given these intratextual connections (connections, that is, which are discernible within a work or body of works), the changes Stephen brings to the aesthetic tenet are ironic even before it is noticed that his attribution of the theory to Plato derives from Flaubert's letter. The discovery of this source multiplies the statement's ironic resonance. For one thing, Stephen, like Flaubert before him, is wrong: for Plato never did define beauty as truth. R. J. Schork provides an illuminating explanation for Flaubert's 'mistake'. It may not, as he explains, have been a mistake at all, but a private reference that most readers naturally miss:

> Flaubert was greatly influenced by the philosophical works of Victor Cousin, one of the premier and most prolific French thinkers of the first half of the nineteenth century. In fact, in a letter of 22 September 1846 to Louise Colet, Flaubert refers to Cousin by the honorary name of 'Plato'—an ironic tribute to a learned mentor whose life has lost its splendor. I suspect that the citation in the 1857 letter, attributed to the ancient Plato and so accepted by scholars of both Flaubert and Joyce, is in fact a paraphrase, an aesthetic statement made by the contemporary French 'Plato', Maître Victor Cousin. [...] Joyce was certainly aware of Victor Cousin's French translation of Aristotle's *Metaphysics*, from which he quotes in his Paris Notebook.[17]

---

[15]   *P*, 58.   [16]   *P*, 183.
[17]   R. J. Schork, *Greek and Hellenic Culture in Joyce* (Gainesville: University Press of Florida, 1998), 150–1. According to Joseph J. Kockelmans, the Latin phrase *splendor veri* was coined by Albert the Great in the thirteenth century in a work entitled 'De Pulchro et Bono' (I, 6, 2)—*Heidegger on Art and Art Works* (Dordrecht and Boston: M. Nijhoff, 1995), 16. The expression subsequently gained currency as an accurate description of St Augustine's position on the relations between truth and beauty. St Augustine's aesthetics were themselves heavily influenced by Plotinus's Neo-Platonist treatise 'On Beauty'. By the nineteenth century, *splendor veri* had become a catchphrase, and it seems likely, as Schork suggests, that Flaubert may have been echoing Victor Cousin, one of the most eminent nineteenth-century authorities on Platonist and Neo-Platonist matters. Joyce may also have

In appropriating Flaubert's phrase, Stephen compounds misinformation (about Plato) with a misreading—or a deliberate distortion—of Flaubert's equation of truth and beauty.

The cautious 'I believe' that Stephen utters in relation to the Plato reference can be read either as a casual, merely rhetorical 'I believe' (meaning not just 'I believe' but 'I know') or as an expression of genuine doubt regarding his source.[18] That Joyce himself was aware of the theory's provenance in Flaubert's letters is clear from the fact that he quotes from the very same letter five pages later, when Stephen likens authorship to godliness. So what motivates Stephen's expletive inclusion of 'I believe'? And how, more broadly, do these quotations from Flaubert's letter inflect our reading of Stephen? Is Stephen circumspect about his mention of Plato because he knows that he has got his quotation from Flaubert rather than from its putative original? Is this a hint to the reader that despite his alleged knowledge of ancient philosophy, Stephen is only familiar with a limited tract of the corpus and in fact relies on mediating texts for many of his opinions? Is Stephen, eager perhaps to live up to his reputation as an original thinker, depending on more recent writers and thinkers, such as Flaubert, and reluctant to admit that his novel ideas are not really his own? On this suspicious view, the withholding of Flaubert's name might indicate a form of anxiety of influence (though not necessarily of the rivalrous Oedipal type depicted by Harold Bloom) on Stephen's part. But Stephen's unease, if unease there is, need not imply disquiet in the author himself. On the contrary, Joyce frames Stephen as he negotiates a borrowing awkwardly underwritten by suggestions of secrecy and plagiarism, using his character's dealings with an influential text to ironize the intertextual situation itself as a given of all artistic endeavour. (The mention of irony here—as in earlier chapters—is not intended to imply negative commentary, but merely to evoke a neutral, lucid, evaluative distance.)[19]

---

come across the phrase in W. H. Hill's *Elements of Philosophy Comprising Logic and Ontology or General Metaphysics* (Baltimore: John Murphy, and London: R. Washburne, 1873). (I am grateful to Geert Lernout for drawing my attention to this book.) This was a widely used Catholic philosophy manual (an eighth edition was issued in 1887), which Joyce may have encountered during his time at University College, Dublin. The Platonic definition of beauty features in the volume in the following terms: 'Intellectual beauty exists in objects of the intelligible order./Plato defines beauty to be the "splendor of truth;" "*splendor veri*"'—174. Such a source may explain Stephen's pedantic insertion of the phrase 'I believe' before his mention of the Platonic catchphrase. However, the numerous echoes of Flaubert's letters in this section of *A Portrait* support the view that the *Correspondance* is the predominant intertext here.

[18] For R. J. Schork 'Stephen Dedalus's modest qualification [. . .] seems more like a signal of documentary hesitation than of genetic coyness.'—*Greek and Hellenic Culture in Joyce*, 151.

[19] As Jonathan Culler writes of Flaubert, 'The irony that interests us here is not a limited negativity, which negates this or that particular in the name of an alternative; it is rather a

THE FLAUBERTIAN INVISIBLE AUTHOR-GOD

The suggestion that Stephen is being cast as a (mis)reader of Flaubert is confirmed by the declaration about the author-God which shortly follows. Stephen tells Lynch that:

> The artist, like the God of creation, remains within or behind or beyond or above his handiwork, invisible, refined out of existence, indifferent, paring his fingernails.[20]

There can be no doubt that the source of Stephen's declaration is in Flaubert:

> I have put nothing of my own feelings or my own life into it. On the contrary, the illusion (if there is one) stems from the *impersonality* of the work. That is one of my principles, you must not *write yourself.* The artist in his work must be like God in creation, invisible and all-powerful; you can sense him everywhere but you cannot see him.[21]

Stephen's words echo this passage even before his own figure of the author-God comes into the picture. In the sentences that lead up to his reformulation of the dictum the use of the verb 'impersonalise' in the reflexive form makes for a rather awkward, conspicuously French-sounding phrase:

> The personality of the artist, at first a cry or a cadence or a mood and then a fluid and lambent narrative, finally refines itself out of existence, *impersonalises itself,* so to speak.[22]

The closing 'so to speak' seems to signal Stephen's awareness of the cumbersomeness of the final verb. It is as though Stephen, his reading

---

sense that the author is distanced from his language, which is proffered as if by citation, but that one does not know where he stands.'—*Flaubert: The Uses of Uncertainty*, 202.

[20] *P*, 181. David Hayman uses this sentence to demonstrate the existence of a Mallarméan influence in Joyce's works. Although he makes a strong case for the influence of Mallarmé's aesthetics on *Finnegans Wake*, Hayman's argument seems forced as regards *A Portrait*, and is undermined by his failure to identify the source of Stephen's borrowing in Flaubert. The obfuscation is baffling, especially as mentions of Flaubert in footnotes and endnotes seem to stop just short of volunteering the information. See *Joyce et Mallarmé*, vol. 1, footnote on page 117 and endnote 54 on pages 193–4.

[21] Flaubert to Mlle Leroyer de Chantepie, 18 March 1857, *GW*, 247–8 ['je n'y ai rien mis ni de mes sentiments ni de mon existence. L'illusion (s'il y en a une) vient au contraire de *l'impersonnalité* de l'oeuvre. C'est un de mes principes, qu'il ne faut pas *s'écrire*. L'auteur doit être dans son oeuvre comme Dieu dans la création, invisible et tout-puissant; qu'on le sente partout, mais qu'on ne le voie pas.' (*C2*, 691)].

[22] *P*, 180–1 (my emphasis).

of Flaubert fresh in his mind, had tried to find an adequate translation for the words of the letter (for Flaubert's emphasis on 'impersonnalité' in particular), and failed to discover a felicitous turn of phrase. The verbal locution, 'refines itself out of existence', with which 'impersonalises itself' features in apposition, constitutes a more natural-sounding approximation and echoes Flaubert's own use of the word 'existence' ('je n'y ai rien mis ni de mes sentiments ni de mon existence'). But the French verb endures, providing another hint of Stephen's source.

Moreover, it seems likely that Joyce drew on more than one Flaubertian letter in composing Stephen's disquisition about literary genres. Stephen's account of 'the epical form', which emphasizes the correlation between authorial 'impersonalization' and authorial immanence, strongly recalls another Flaubertian letter. Stephen explains to Lynch that:

> The narrative is no longer purely personal. The personality of the artist passes into the narration itself, flowing round and round the persons and the action like a vital sea.[23]

This description of the author's personality as 'a vital sea' 'flowing round and round' fictional characters and events vividly echoes an image used by Flaubert in a letter of 1853. The sentence in question refers to a created world in which the disseminated author freely and delightedly circulates:

> it is a delectable thing, writing! Not having to be *yourself*, being able to circulate in amongst the whole creation that you are describing.[24]

It is worth noting that this cluster of intertextual echoes is not drawn from Flaubert's fictional works but from his vast collection of reflections on the craft of literature: the *Correspondance*. By delegating to one of his characters the near-reiteration of views first expressed in the intimate context of Flaubert's letters, by dramatizing those most private elements of Flaubert's writing, Joyce in effect impersonalizes his predecessor's most personal statements. In this sense, he does not contravene Flaubert's frequently uttered wish that his life be forgotten as irrelevant to his art ('The man is nothing, the work is everything!'[25]), so much as act in a fashion Flaubert himself would have advocated: impersonalizing the personality of the artist, refining him out of existence, rendering him

---

[23] *P*, 180.
[24] Flaubert to Louise Colet, 23 December 1853, *GW*, 233 ['c'est une chose délicieuse que d'écrire! que de ne plus être *soi*, mais de circuler dans toute la création dont on parle.' (*C2*, 483)].
[25] Flaubert to George Sand, late December 1875, *GW*, 401 ['L'homme n'est rien, l'oeuvre tout!' (*C4*, 1,000)].

invisible, 'so to speak'. Joyce may have seen added benefits in such a use of source: not merely the subtly ambivalent ironization of Stephen Dedalus within *A Portrait*, but also detachment from Flaubert on his own part. To objectify Flaubert by way of a silent act of quotation, itself performed by a deputee, is to assert a knowing distance, and through that distance, control—to turn what might have been an influence into an intertextual engagement.

Stephen's rephrasing of Flaubert's theory of impersonality is deeply paradoxical. The connection it forges between impersonality and intertextuality is in itself unproblematic. Intertextuality can certainly involve the disappearance of the author's voice behind the veils of other voices: such a view is, in fact, fundamental to intertextual theory, as it is to much modernist practice. But paradox arises because Stephen's borrowed declaration consists of a denial of intertextuality as a modus operandi of literary creation. Indeed, no position could stand in starker opposition to the intertextual author or Barthesian 'scriptor'[26] than the figure of God at the origin of creation, creating out of nothing. In this latter view of authorship, creation is carried out in a void in which all models vanish. Ahistorical and unreferential, the work of art is portrayed as the very first of literary acts, in contrast to all the other works of art that follow the original creative moment.

Stephen's declaration lends itself to ironic readings even if his Flaubertian subtext goes unnoticed: for previous chapters, and previous depictions of his attempts to create art, have portrayed a young man steeped in prior example, more reliant on precedent than he is original. Like Emma Bovary, Stephen lives by the book, mapping his attitudes and writing onto the models of eminent precursors.[27] Such a 'bovariste' pattern of behaviour is obvious from as early as Stephen's schooldays. Out on the sports pitch at Clongowes, he reflects to himself that 'It was nice and warm to see the lights in the castle. It was like something in a book.'[28] He

---

[26] 'Having buried the Author, the modern scriptor [. . .] traces a field without origin—or which, at least, has no other origin than language itself, language which ceaselessly calls into question all origins.'—Barthes, 'The Death of the Author', 146 ['le scripteur moderne, ayant enterré l'Auteur [. . .] trace un champ sans origine—ou qui, du moins, n'a d'autre origine que le langage lui-même, c'est-à-dire cela même qui sans cesse remet en cause toute origine.' ('La Mort de l'auteur', 67)].

[27] André Topia devotes Part II ('*A Portrait of the Artist as a Young Man*: la grille et le rite') of his *doctorat d'état* to the importance to Stephen of established rites—'Modèles et écarts: scénarios d'écriture de *Dubliners* à *Ulysses*', unpublished doctoral thesis, University of Paris (VIII), 1995.

[28] *P*, 7.

musters the courage to complain to the rector about his unjust pandying by thinking of those great men in whose footsteps he treads:

> A thing like that had been done before by somebody in history, by some great person whose head was in the books of history.[29]

Reading *The Count of Monte-Cristo*, he imagines for himself 'a long train of adventures, marvellous as the book itself'.[30] Stephen acts and writes as though everything were determined by a matrix of prior writing and event. His fantasy of an act of creation ex nihilo is, therefore, starkly at odds with what we know of his fascination with previous example— except, of course, that in uttering those words to Lynch, Stephen is in fact acting as a 'bovariste' once more, reiterating Flaubert's words even as those would seem to call for radical originality.

Ironies spiral into each other as the reader realizes that Stephen's theory of creation in a vacuum, in denial of the literary past and of all artistic civilization, is articulated by way of a quotation, and an unacknowledged one at that. This complex intertextual moment brings issues of borrowing, forgery, and plagiarism to the forefront of the text. Stephen's protracted and unresolved hesitation as to where to place the author in his work (should the author remain 'within or behind or beyond or above his handiwork'?) is also related to these issues. The second of these terms, 'behind', constitutes a particularly interesting variation on the Flaubertian quotation. The preposition is used several times in *A Portrait* to connote secrecy; a secrecy that is at times serious, as when the image of an 'arras'[31] conjures Hamlet's murder, committed by 'thrust[ing] his rapier through the arras' to kill Polonius who hides 'behind';[32] and at times mischievous or ridiculous, as when Stephen, sitting in the physics amphitheatre, imagines the Jesuit community 'whispering two and two behind their hands'.[33] The preposition evokes what lies behind, such as a sentence borrowed from Flaubert and passed off by Stephen as his own. It also (however shadowily) refers to the position of the impersonal author who writes concealed behind his handiwork,[34] and of the author who cites as

---

[29] *P*, 44.   [30] *P*, 52.

[31] *P*, 141.

[32] William Shakespeare, *Hamlet*, Act III, scene 4, line 6. The Shakespearean intertext is shadowily present again in Stephen's musings about Danish ghosts on the following page: 'A moment before the ghost of the ancient kingdom of the Danes had looked forth through the vesture of the hazewrapped city—*P*, 142.

[33] *P*, 161.

[34] Barthes emphasizes the same preposition in discussing Flaubert's shadowy presence *behind* the veils of his impersonal, citational writing: '*one never knows if he is responsible for what he writes* (whether there is an individual subject *behind* his language); for the very being of writing (the meaning of the labor that constitutes it) is to keep the question *Who is*

that of one who comes behind his predecessors. The text itself draws attention to this interpretation just a few pages later, when Stephen no less grandiosely announces that he will no longer 'serve':

> – I will not serve, answered Stephen.
> – That remark was made *before*, Cranly said calmly.
> – It is made *behind* now, said Stephen hotly.[35]

Stephen's anger at being reminded that his statement is not original but merely the latest in a long series of biblical and non-biblical 'non serviams' (including his own), and the use of the word 'behind' in his quick repartee, refer back to that position with which Stephen toys in his contradictory depiction of the author-God.

Other intratextual hints shed light on Stephen's paradoxical statement. His earlier thoughts about the experience of reading, for instance, are pertinent to the interpretation of the author-God passage. The reader knows, from the beginning of Chapter IV, that when Stephen reads he:

> retain[s] nothing of all he read save that which seemed to him an echo or prophecy of his own state.[36]

It seems safe to deduce, therefore, that Stephen has appropriated Flaubert's words because they have special resonance for him. This raises a question as to the object of Stephen's identification: what is it about Flaubert's statement that rings to him as 'an echo or prophecy of his own state'? Although identification with Flaubert and with God are not to be ruled out, given Stephen's egotism and ambition, the psychological appeal of Flaubert's theory of impersonality seems the most likely reason for its impact on Stephen. Indeed, the theory could not be better suited to Stephen's strange capacity for emotional detachment. This natural Flaubertian impassibility (after the author-God passage Stephen is described as 'bright, agile, impassible and, above all, subtle'[37]) is in evidence throughout the novel and is related to Stephen's sense of isolation ('he was different from others'[38]). One of the first instances of this detachment occurs after the Dedalus family's removal from 'the comfort and revery of Blackrock'.[39] Like the ideal author figure he later describes in Chapter V, Stephen keeps his 'vision' impermeable to adulteration by emotion:

---

speaking? from ever being answered.'—*S/Z*, trans. Richard Miller (London: Jonathan Cape, 1975), 140 ['*on ne sait jamais s'il est responsable de ce qu'il écrit* (s'il y a un sujet *derrière* son langage); car l'être de l'écriture (le sens du travail qui la constitue) est d'empêcher de jamais répondre à cette question: *Qui parle?*' (*S/Z* [Paris: Éditions du Seuil, 1970], 146)].

[35] *P*, 201 (my emphases).
[36] *P*, 131.   [37] *P*, 202.   [38] *P*, 54.   [39] *P*, 55.

his anger lent nothing to the vision. He chronicled with patience what he saw, *detaching himself from it* and tasting its mortifying flavour in secret.[40]

Stephen's impassibility is mobilized again on the evening of the Whitsuntide play. Heron's words that night summon back the memory of Stephen's humiliating childhood beating. But in the present as in the past, the event is free of emotional charge:

> the memory of it called forth no anger from him. All the descriptions of fierce love and hatred which he had met in books had seemed to him therefore unreal. Even that night as he stumbled homewards [...] he had felt that some power was divesting him of that suddenwoven anger as easily as a fruit is divested of its soft ripe peel.[41]

It is the same power that intervenes just a few pages later to dispel Stephen's frustration when E. C., of whom he has been thinking throughout the day, remains absent from the performance:

> A film still veiled his eyes but they burned no longer. A power, akin to that which had often made anger or resentment fall from him, brought his steps to rest.[42]

A touching version of this strange self-alienation unfolds when a younger Stephen tries to recall his childhood, only to find that it has vanished irretrievably:

> He had not died but he had faded out like a film in the sun. He had been lost or had wandered out of existence for he no longer existed. How strange to think of him passing out of existence in such a way, not by death but by fading out in the sun or by being lost and forgotten somewhere in the universe![43]

The passage, which evidently foreshadows Stephen's later statement about the figure of the invisible author-God, also echoes the earlier death fantasy, which, shaped by what he knows of the demise of Parnell, takes hold in the midst of his spell in the Clongowes infirmary:

> There was cold sunlight outside the window. He wondered if he would die. You could die just the same on a sunny day.[44]

As a boy, Stephen already imagines a world from which he seems to have somehow absconded. At this early stage on the path to authorship (and in the formation of his own personality), Stephen's detachment is an entirely passive phenomenon. It is not a willed aloofness but a

---

[40] *P*, 56 (my emphasis).   [41] *P*, 69.   [42] *P*, 72.
[43] *P*, 78.   [44] *P*, 19.

sensation of fading, of 'passing out of existence'. Stephen's sensation is described as an experience of loss: the loss of previous versions of himself.[45] The striking image of Stephen's self as a reel of photographic film should not be read as representing a mere 'fading' or loss: from the negative of a personality 'passing out of existence' may come the positive of authorial detachment.[46] Until the last chapter, however, this 'positive' is not in view, and we can only witness, with Stephen, the fact that 'A cold lucid indifference reigned in his soul'.[47] That the process of loss is also one of growth and maturation is aptly conveyed by the image of a fruit divested of its soft ripe peel, which returns in Chapter IV:

> A brief anger had often invested him but he had never been able to make it an abiding passion and had always felt himself passing out of it as if his very body were being divested with ease of some outer skin or peel.[48]

With such predispositions for detachment, it is not surprising that Stephen should find Flaubert's theory of impersonality so appealing.

The verbs 'invest' and 'divest' that appear in the last quotation are two of a large number of allusions to clothing and attire in *A Portrait*. These motifs have bearing on literary matters, and in particular on the novel's self-conscious intertextual relationship to the body of works that precedes it. This connection is apparent when Stephen describes lyrical form as 'the simplest verbal vesture of an instant of emotion'.[49] The act of writing is presented as a twofold process requiring, firstly, that the author be divested of emotion, and secondly, that the experienced but discarded emotion be re-embodied in the 'vesture' of a literary form. This association between clothing and writing is complicated by the book's many references to costume. Stephen, for instance, finds it difficult to differentiate people from the clothes that they wear. 'You could always tell a Jesuit by the style of his clothes',[50] remembers Stephen in the vestry before the Whitsuntide

---

[45] Stephen's vision of irretrievable former selves bears affinities to Flaubert's sense of his personality as the surviving self among many possible, but ultimately discarded, earlier selves: 'I can see myself very clearly at different moments of history, following different trades, according to my luck. My present self is the outcome of all my extinct selves.'— Flaubert to George Sand, 29 September 1866, *GW*, 312 ['Je me vois à différents âges de l'histoire très nettement, exerçant des métiers différents et dans des fortunes multiples. Mon individu actuel est le résultat de mes individualités disparues.' (*C3*, 536)].

[46] The photographic analogy returns in *Finnegans Wake*: 'if a negative of a horse happens to melt enough while drying, well, what you get is, well, a positively grotesquely distorted macromass of all sorts of horsehappy values and masses of meltwhile horse'—*FW* 111: 27–30.

[47] *P*, 87.   [48] *P*, 126.   [49] *P*, 180.   [50] *P*, 71.

play begins. Accordingly, he finds himself bewildered by the sight of his friends swimming naked in the sea:

> How characterless they looked: Shuley without his deep unbuttoned collar, Ennis without his scarlet belt with the snaky clasp and Connolly without his Norfolk coat with the flapless side-pockets![51]

In these examples Stephen reads items of attire as indicators of essence, treating clothes as legible and reliable signs of character. He himself, by contrast, seems quite comfortable with the prospect of adopting a set of 'new secondhand clothes'[52] on the eve of his departure for Paris. This detail acts as more than a reflection of the poverty of Stephen's family; it is a reminder of all those roles we have seen him adopt over the course of the novel, of his capacity to imitate and appropriate, to slip himself into other people's clothes, or other authors' words, and 'take [them] off rippingly',[53] with all the potential for forgery, plagiarism, and literary talent that those words imply. With his skill for imitation and natural ability to 'divest' himself of his emotions, Stephen has the versatility of a chameleon. His metamorphoses are complete: previous selves are 'lost' for good, and 'no longer exist', leaving the artist-in-the-making free not just to 'impersonalise [him]self' but also to impersonate others, including Flaubert.

The second half of Stephen's Flaubertian sentence about the figure of the artist-God diverges significantly from its original. These variations turn Stephen's appropriation into a creative act in its own right. The first difference, discussed above, resides in the prepositional hesitation that characterizes the sentence's central verbal clause. Stephen's faltering progression from one preposition to another as he fails to decide whether the author remains 'within or behind or beyond or above his handiwork' institutes an increasing distance between his version and the Flaubertian source. The most striking of Stephen's additions to Flaubert's dictum is the closing expression, 'paring his fingernails', the foppish connotations of which ring in tune with the second occurrence in the paragraph of the adjectival phrase 'refined out of existence', which also bears mildly dandyish undertones. The connection between the two phrases is confirmed by Lynch's immediate repartee to the mention of these fingernails: 'Trying to refine them also out of existence.'[54] Like most of the items of Stephen's comparison, the phrase about the paring of the fingernails stands in an intratextual relationship to other parts of the book, and specifically, to a network of homoerotic suggestion that meshes right across the novel, beginning with the punning

---

[51] *P*, 142.   [52] *P*, 213.   [53] *P*, 63.   [54] *P*, 181.

allusions to Oscar Wilde ('O, the wild rose blossoms'[55]) on the first page, and centring around the first occurrence of the phrase 'paring his fingernails' in Chapter I. When five Clongowes boys are caught 'smugging' in the school square, Stephen tries to make sense of the confused situation by summoning what he knows about the boys involved. Tusker Boyle stands out for his nickname and for his fingernails:

> And one day Boyle had said that an elephant had two tuskers instead of two tusks and that was why he was called Tusker Boyle but some fellows called him Lady Boyle because he was always at his nails, paring them.[56]

All the way through *A Portrait of the Artist*, Stephen seems faintly conscious of, as well as faintly troubled by, the homoerotic implications of other people's behaviour and of his own responses to events. Stephen's thoughts about Tusker Boyle and the punishment his behaviour will entail conjure the image of Mr Gleeson's hands, whose task it will be to flog Corrigan (another of the five 'smuggers'). Again Stephen's memory and imagination involve nails, 'cruel nails', the thought of which arouses a 'feeling of queer quiet pleasure inside him':

> But Mr Gleeson had round shiny cuffs and clean white wrists and fattish white hands and the nails of them were long and pointed. Perhaps he pared them too like Lady Boyle. [. . .] And though he trembled with cold and fright to think of the cruel long nails and of the high whistling sound of the cane and of the chill you felt at the end of your shirt when you undressed yourself yet he felt a feeling of queer quiet pleasure inside him to think of the white fattish hands, clean and strong and gentle.[57]

Even after his pandying, Stephen's mind returns repeatedly to the 'touch of the prefect's fingers as they had steadied his hand': 'he had steadied the hand first with his firm soft fingers'.[58]

Stephen's ambivalent 'homosexual panic'[59] returns later when he spends hours walking through the streets of Dublin with male university friends such as Davin, Lynch, and Cranly. The nature of his relationship with Cranly is particularly ambiguous. Whereas the section devoted to Stephen's time with Davin is mostly given over to the latter's report of an encounter with a woman in the countryside, and whereas heterosexual banter constitutes a constant strand of his relationship with Lynch, Stephen's conversations with Cranly tend to strike more personal notes,

---

[55] *P*, 5.   [56] *P*, 35.   [57] *P*, 38.   [58] *P*, 43.

[59] Tim Dean uses the phrase coined by Eve Kosofsky Sedgwick in *Epistemology of the Closet* (Berkeley: University of California Press, 1990) to describe Stephen's reaction to events in 'Paring His Fingernails: Homosexuality and Joyce's Impersonalist Aesthetic', in *Quare Joyce*, ed. Joseph Valente (Ann Arbor: University of Michigan Press, 1998), 251.

which sometimes seem tinged with homoerotic suggestion. Stephen, for instance, asks Cranly whether he is 'trying to make a convert of me or a pervert of yourself'.[60] The words stand out in Ireland's Catholic context, as does Stephen's excitement—in a book that so insists on his indifference to those around him—when Cranly presses his arm: Stephen, as we read, is 'thrilled by his touch'.[61] It is, finally, in the ambivalent terms of friendship that Cranly and Stephen discuss their parting ('And not to have any one person, Cranly said, who would be more than a friend, more even than the noblest and truest friend a man ever had'), and it is by means of a question that Stephen, finally, declines to answer Cranly's question: 'Of whom are you speaking?'[62]

The relevance of the novel's numerous homoerotic undertones to the Flaubertian quotation consists in the very strong connections that obtained, at the turn of the century, between homosexuality and aestheticism, and between homosexuality and secrecy. Although the pressure for homosexuality to be invisible had run high before the Oscar Wilde trial of 1895, the publicity with which the case was surrounded accentuated a pervasive sense of the necessity for the 'love that dare not speak its name' to remain both unseen and unspoken. Commenting on the references to Wilde and his green carnation in *A Portrait* ('But you could not have a green rose. But perhaps somewhere in the world you could.'),[63] and on the phrase 'paring his fingernails', Tim Dean argues that instances of this 'homosexual code' should be interpreted:

> as a sign of Joyce's familiarity with a set of mainstream cultural conceptions of homosexuality, including the idea that the association with concealment means that homosexuality is most effectively, albeit paradoxically, denoted by means of connotation.[64]

In *Epistemology of the Closet* (1990), Eve Sedgwick argues that homosexuality was actually constituted *as* secrecy at the close of the nineteenth century. Dean adduces this fact to suggest that Joyce saw in homosexuality an apt and contemporary thematic illustration of his (Flaubertian) impersonalist aesthetic:

---

[60] *P*, 204.   [61] *P*, 208.

[62] *P*, 208–9. For a discussion of the homoerotic undertones of Stephen's friendship with Cranly, see Joseph Valente, 'Thrilled by His Touch', in *Quare Joyce*. For a discussion of the 'Friendship Tradition' that preceded the emergence of the discourses of homosexuality in the nineteenth century, see Michael Lynch, '"Here is Adhesiveness": From Friendship to Homosexuality', *Victorian Studies*, vol. 29, no. 1 (Autumn, 1985).

[63] *P*, 9. See Richard Ellmann, *Oscar Wilde* (New York: Alfred A. Knopf, 1988), 365.

[64] Dean, 'Paring His Fingernails', 249.

by the end of the nineteenth century, when it had become fully current—as obvious to Queen Victoria as to Freud—that knowledge meant sexual knowledge, and secrets sexual secrets, there had in fact developed one particular sexuality that was distinctively constituted *as* secrecy: the perfect object for the insatiably exacerbated epistemological/sexual anxiety of the turn-of-the-century subject.[65]

In this perspective, the hint of homosexual implication that attaches to Stephen's enunciation of Flaubert's aesthetic necessarily carries sugges-tions of illicit activity, with writing connoted as a pursuit involving concealment. This is a suggestion made available by the word 'smugging' from as early as Chapter I. The term's exact meaning has baffled readers and annotators, but its original meanings relate to plagiarism, theft, and forgery.[66] Indeed, the *OED* lists its first meaning as: 'steal, filch, run away with'. (This definition may explain some of the Clongowes' boys' confusion as to the nature of the smuggers' offence and their initial hypothesis that they might have been 'feck[ing] cash'.[67]) The verb's second meaning—'copy surreptitiously', 'crib'—is directly related to the act of writing. Its third meaning, 'hush up', specifically involves secrecy. These definitions prefigure Stephen's resolution at the end of the book to express himself by means of what are, in effect, three different kinds of 'smugging': 'silence, exile, and cunning'.[68] Stephen's vision of authorship as an activity conceptually related to homosexuality is thus at the fulcrum of Joyce's treatment of the theme of intertextuality and its illicit counter-parts, forgery and plagiarism.

The uses of the word 'forgery' in the novel are emblematic of this hesitation. Given that Stephen spends his days absorbed in 'a garner of slender sentences from Aristotle's poetics and psychology and a *Synopsis Philosophiæ Scholasticæ ad mentem divi Thomæ*',[69] the subsequent mention of the 'monkish learning, *in terms of which* he was striving to *forge out* an esthetic philosophy'[70] is perhaps intended to hint that Stephen's apparently painstakingly elaborated philosophy is more indebted to the very 'terms' of the texts on which he draws than he would be willing to admit. Furthermore, although Stephen seems content to acknowledge the influ-ence of Aquinas and Aristotle, he shows none of this readiness about his

[65] Dean, 'Paring His Fingernails', 250.
[66] Dean, 'Paring His Fingernails', 250.
[67] *P*, 33.
[68] *P*, 208.
[69] *P*, 148.
[70] *P*, 151 (my emphasis).

readings of Flaubert. His silent borrowings from the latter insinuate a subtle shade of irony into the phrasing of his penultimate diary entry:

> Welcome, O life! I go to encounter for the millionth time the reality of experience and to *forge* in the smithy of my soul the uncreated conscience of my race.[71]

It is possible that Stephen's language here (his use of the verb 'to forge') is not so much a betrayal of his own consciousness—an unexpected and undesired verbal slip—as a deliberate expression of commitment to intertextuality as a literary project. But this is almost certainly to grant Stephen a more modernist mindset than the rest of the novel suggests he has.

LA TENTATION DE SAINT ANTOINE AND STEPHEN'S VISION OF HELL

The *Correspondance* is not the only Flaubertian text to which Joyce's novel responds. Indeed Stephen's hallucinated experience of hell in the third chapter of *A Portrait* strongly recalls Flaubert's representation of Antony's turmoil in *La Tentation de saint Antoine*. The fact that Joyce purchased a copy of *La Tentation* sometime between October 1913 and May 1914 provides a solid bibliographical foundation for an intertextual reading of this passage.[72] Joyce had already alluded to the pictorial subject of *The Temptation of Saint Antony* in *Stephen Hero*. In Chapter XVII of the draft novel, Stephen and Maurice contemplate a representation of those trials:

> One evening during the retreat he asked his brother what kind of sermons the priest was giving. The two were standing together looking into the window of a stationer's shop and it was a picture of S. Anthony in the window which led to the question. Maurice smiled broadly as he answered: – Hell today.[73]

It was the viewing of a pictorial treatment of the saint's life that first kindled Flaubert's interest in writing his own *Tentation*. In 1845 he had written from Genoa to his friend Alfred Le Poittevin to tell him about an experience that would inspire him for the rest of his life:

---

[71] *P*, 213 (my emphasis).
[72] In addition to *La Tentation de saint Antoine*, Joyce bought two volumes of Flaubert's *Premières Oeuvres* during this period—*JJ*, 779. Joyce's Triestine library in 1920 included two other books by Flaubert: *Madame Bovary*, trans. Henry Blanchamp (London: Greening, [n.d.]), which according to Richard Ellmann was probably sent to Joyce by Nora Barnacle's uncle, Michael Healy, at some point after their first meeting in 1909; and *Salammbô* (Paris: Bibliothèque Charpentier, 1914)—*CJ*, 6, 108–9.
[73] *SH*, 57.

I saw a picture by Brueghel, *The Temptation of Saint Antony*, which made me think of arranging *The Temptation of Saint Antony* for the theatre.[74]

In Brueghel's medieval painting, as in Flaubert's nineteenth-century retelling, Saint Antony crouches over an open Bible, seeking courage and comfort from the terrifying hybrid demons that threateningly and overwhelmingly surround him. Joyce's interest in the kinds of haunted, tortured turmoil the scene encapsulates was to be granted its fullest enactment in the 'Circe' episode of *Ulysses*. But it is already discernible in *A Portrait*.[75] On returning to his room after the hellfire sermon delivered during Clongowes's religious retreat, Stephen fears 'the fiends that inhabit darkness'.[76] As in Flaubert's *Tentation*, devilish forms are everywhere: 'Faces were there; eyes: they waited and watched.'[77] The description of Stephen crouching in prayer as his sins crowd around ('The leprous company of his sins closed about him'[78]) echoes Antony's predicament in *La Tentation* when 'all the heretics [*heresiarchs*] encircle Antony, who is crying, his head in his hands'.[79] Stephen's panic-stricken vision of hell ('That was his hell!'[80]) features the kind of grotesque, hybrid creatures ('Goatish creatures with human faces, hornybrowed, lightly bearded and grey as indiarubber'[81]) that also populate Antony's hallucinations. For both Antony and Stephen, seeing is a treacherous perceptual act: 'Antony closes his eyes [*eyelids*]'; Stephen 'bind[s] down his eyelids'.[82] Both collapse under the strain of the hellish visions that assail them: Antony suffers 'a burning contraction [*violent convulsion*] in the pit of his stomach', and 'a convulsion seized [Stephen] within'.[83] Stephen's crisis of faith is thus infused with the graphic and visceral intensity of Antony's

---

[74] Flaubert to Alfred Le Poittevin, 13 May 1845, *GW*, 25 ['J'ai vu un tableau de Breughel représentant *La Tentation de saint Antoine*, qui m'a fait penser à arranger pour le théâtre *La Tentation de saint Antoine*.' (*C1*, 230)].

[75] Commenting on the reference to 'S. Anthony' in *Stephen Hero*, R. J. Schork notes that in *A Portrait* 'a reformed Stephen reflects on this sort of spiritual assault'—*Joyce and Hagiography: Saints Above* (Gainesville: University Press of Florida, 2000), 75.

[76] *P*, 114.

[77] *P*, 114–15.

[78] *P*, 115.

[79] *TAE*, 118 ['tous les hérésiarques font un cercle autour d'Antoine, qui pleure, la tête dans ses mains' (*TA*, 88)].

[80] *P*, 116.

[81] *P*, 116. These sentences are clearly adapted from one of Joyce's epiphanies: 'A small field of still weeds and thistles alive with confused forms, half-men, half-goats. Dragging their great tails they move hither and thither, aggressively. Their faces are lightly bearded, pointed and grey as india-rubber.'—*Workshop*, 16.

[82] *TAE*, 72 ['Antoine ferme ses paupières.' (*TA*, 39)]; *P*, 116.

[83] *TAE*, 72 ['une convulsion violente à l'épigastre' (*TA*, 39)]; *P*, 116.

trials. The parallel between the two characters is a vector of irony as well as of similarity. At the end of *A Portrait*'s Chapter III a serious, quietly exalted Stephen prepares to take communion: 'The ciborium had come to him.'[84] This conclusion to the religious travails of the episode is arguably undercut by the ambiguity that characterizes Antony's own mystifying reconciliation with the Christian God whose existence and goodness he has so violently doubted. 'Antony makes the sign of the cross and returns to his prayers.'[85] Antony's spiritual future remains unknown, but the weakness of Stephen's resolve—as intertextually adumbrated by his affinity with *La Tentation*'s eponymous saint—is promptly confirmed by the following chapter of *A Portrait*, which sees him choose to devote himself to the priesthood 'of the eternal imagination' instead.[86]

STRUCTURAL AND TECHNICAL PARALLELS: IRONIES OF CONTRAST

Precise intertextual echoes of this kind are compounded by structural and technical correspondences to Flaubert. As was mentioned in Chapter 1, David Hayman has highlighted a likely connection between the structures of *L'Éducation sentimentale* and *A Portrait of the Artist as a Young Man*, suggesting that Joyce derived the contrapuntal rhythm of his novel—which alternates between phases of exhilaration and disillusionment—from the Flaubertian precedent. He describes the architecture of Joyce's novel as:

> a framework composed of systematically paired antithetical sequences, that is, lyrical moments (epiphanies) followed in due time by lucid ones (anti-epiphanies).[87]

Hayman's contention about the Flaubertian connection can seem strained because the neat structural stylization of *A Portrait*, wherein the novel's ironic focus is primarily trained on a single character, does not so evidently obtain in *L'Éducation*, which charts the sentimental education of an entire nation over several decades. Hayman's main point, however, is valid. Like *L'Éducation*, *A Portrait* is structured by way of contrasts. Both novels follow 'the curve of an emotion'[88] (whether of a nation or of a central protagonist) as it

---

[84] *P*, 123.
[85] *TAE*, 232 ['Antoine fait le signe de croix et se remet à ses prières.' (*TA*, 200)].
[86] *P*, 186.
[87] Hayman, '*A Portrait of the Artist as a Young Man* and *L'Éducation sentimentale*', 163.
[88] *APA*, 211.

crests and falls, letting the mere fact of juxtaposition generate impersonal ironies that substitute for the commentary the invisible narrator withholds.

Many of the techniques Joyce develops from Flaubert involve effects of contrast. The first of these techniques is the procedure of the cinematographic cut, that technique which Proust, commenting on the sudden narrative silence that follows Dussardier's death in L'Éducation, so admired, and which Joyce, as was seen in Chapters 1 and 2, already mobilizes in Dubliners and Stephen Hero. Like some of the Dubliners stories, A Portrait draws attention to these cuts, using asterisks to emphasize abrupt spatial and temporal leaps. The opening vignette of Stephen's very early childhood, which ends with the taunting 'Apologise/Pull out his eyes' refrain, is cut off in this way from the following scene, a game of school rugby or Gaelic football, which takes place when Stephen is presumably considerably older.[89] The novel is punctuated by visible interruptions of this kind. Asterisks follow Stephen's momentary flash of rage after the Whitsuntide play and his subsequent dissatisfaction with his father during the trip to Cork. They precede and follow the religious sermons that form the core of Chapter III. In the final chapter, they separate the villanelle from Stephen's preceding discussion with Lynch, and the end of Stephen's conversation with Cranly from the beginning of the diary entries.[90] There are many other examples. These frequent cinematographic cuts effect a myriad of montage-like juxtapositions that maximize effects of contrast and irony even within the novel's overarching structure of rise and fall.

Contrasts are also cultivated on a smaller scale by Joyce's adoption and adaptation of Flaubertian simultaneity. As was discussed in Chapter 1, the 'comices agricoles' episode of Madame Bovary is the canonical example of Flaubert's separation of the narrative into two separate but simultaneous strands. Joyce tailors this conceptual breakthrough to different ends in A Portrait, in keeping with the predominantly psychological concerns of the novel. Instead of mapping two external events against each other, Joyce establishes simultaneity between the visions that unfold in Stephen's mind and the events from the 'outside world' which continue to occur around him (the technique had already been essayed in parts of Joyce's early writing, as for instance in the 'ship' epiphany discussed in Chapter 1). This interweaving of the novel's inner and outer worlds constitutes an all-pervasive feature of Joyce's novel. Stephen's conversation with Heron and Wallis before the Whitsuntide play in Chapter II is typical in this

---

[89] P, 6. See the note on the sport in question—P, 225.
[90] P, 72, 80, 182, 188, 209.

respect. Enjoined by his schoolmates to 'Admit!', Stephen recites the *Confiteor* while his mind transports him to an entirely different place:

> The confession came only from Stephen's lips and, while they spoke the words, a sudden memory had carried him to another scene called up, as if by magic, at the moment when he had noted the faint cruel dimples at the corners of Heron's smiling lips.[91]

Stephen's memory of his childhood beating unfolds for a full four pages before the simultaneity established at the opening is reasserted ('While he was still repeating the *Confiteor* [. . .] and while the scenes of that malignant episode were still passing sharply and swiftly before his mind'[92]), condensing swathes of text back into the few seconds during which the vision has filled Stephen's consciousness. Such vivid mental excursions trick the reader into thinking that he is 'suddenly'[93] somewhere else entirely. In this respect also, *A Portrait* harks back to Flaubert's *Tentation*: in their clarity and intensity, Stephen's visions conjure worlds that, for their entire duration, entirely supplant the circumstances from which they have arisen, only to be abruptly synchronized with them again once the visions recede.

Pound was adamant that Joyce's style, in *A Portrait* as in *Dubliners*, was laudably Flaubertian. But Joyce's engagement with Flaubert in his first novel is about more than the 'clarity', 'hardness', and 'metallic exactitude'[94] that so impressed Pound. It ranges from precise echoes of phrases borrowed from specific passages in Flaubert's works and letters to the use of broader Flaubertian structures and techniques. The use of literary references—such as those to *La Tentation*—as a mode of ironic counterpoint forms an important strand of Joyce's engagement with his predecessor in *A Portrait*. As in *Dubliners*, Joyce's dealings with Flaubert betray no anxiety of influence. On the contrary, by delegating acts of quotation bordering on plagiarism to Stephen Dedalus, Joyce performs a highly self-conscious *mise en scène* of such an anxiety. Far from dissimulating any unease of his own, Joyce's staging of another writer's failure to move beyond near-quotation ironizes the intertextual situation itself. Indeed, Joyce's *mise en abyme*[95] of Stephen's forgeries bears no hint of

---

[91] *P*, 65.   [92] *P*, 69.

[93] David Weir rightly observes the prevalence of this adverb in *A Portrait* and its use as an indicator that an 'epiphanic moment' is near at hand—*James Joyce and the Art of Mediation*, 23.

[94] Pound to Llewelyn Roberts, 3 August 1915, *P/J*, 39; Pound, 'The Non-Existence of Ireland', in *P/J*, 32; Pound, 'Joyce', in *P/J*, 136.

[95] The phrase, which was coined by André Gide in a diary entry of 1893, denotes the process of 'self-reflection within the structure of a literary work' (*OED*)—André Gide, *Journal, 1889–1939* (Paris: Gallimard, 1948), 41.

condemnation. Rather, it constitutes a recognition that the voices of the dead permeate all creative endeavours. This acknowledgement of the inescapably intertextual make-up of all writing is not conveyed in depressed or defeated tones. Ultimately, the humour of Stephen and Lynch's vision of the author-God refining his fingernails out of existence can only leave the reader with a sense that the author, as so often, is 'laughing in [his] sleeve':[96] not mourning, but lucidly accepting.

[96] *P*, 176.

4

Adultery and Sympathy in
Ulysses and *Exiles*

In 'A Painful Case', one of the later *Dubliners* stories, Joyce writes of James Duffy that he had 'an odd biographical habit which led him to compose in his mind from time to time a short sentence about himself containing a subject in the third person and a predicate in the past tense'.[1] This portrait of man in exile from himself rings in tune with *A Portrait*'s emphasis on Stephen's instinctive talent for impersonality, with Joyce's own sense of writing as 'a form of exile [...] a source of detachment',[2] and with his view of his life in Pola (and then Trieste, Zurich, Paris) as that of a 'voluntary exile'.[3] The title of Joyce's only play, *Exiles*, reflects the theme's importance throughout his life, both as a perpetual mode of being (when they were not travelling from one country to another, the Joyces moved incessantly between apartments[4]) and as a necessary stimulus to his thinking about himself and the world.[5]

Joyce began jotting down notes for *Exiles* in the autumn of 1913, and completed the play on 1 April 1915. Its composition thus straddled the beginnings of Joyce's work on *Ulysses* in March 1914 and the final stages of his work on *A Portrait* (which Joyce was then perfecting for serialization in *The Egoist*). Exile features as a preoccupation in all of these works. At

---

[1] *D*, 104.

[2] *JJ*, 110.

[3] *JJ*, 194.

[4] Seamus Deane notes that the pace of change was particularly hectic during the Joyces' Paris years: 'By the time they left the Hôtel Lutetia on the boulevard Raspail in December 1939 to escape the War, they had had over 120 addresses, less than twenty of them in Paris itself, the others being holiday addresses, staging points on various visits to other parts of France, England, Wales, Germany, Switzerland, Belgium and Denmark—but never Ireland.'—Introduction, *Finnegans Wake* (London: Penguin Classics, 2000), xxiii.

[5] Exile provides Hélène Cixous with the title and one of the main themes of her psychobiographical study, *The Exile of James Joyce*, trans. Sally A. Purcell (London: John Calden, 1976). Part IV, 'Exile as Recovery', and the subsections numbered XVI ('The Choice of Exile'), XVII ('Exile of the Soul'), XVIII ('The Notion of Exile Within'), and XIX ('*Exiles*, or the Discovery of Creative Doubt'), 437–563, are particularly pertinent to this subject.

the end of Joyce's first novel, Stephen prepares for a Parisian adventure undertaken for the sake of artistic fulfilment, nurturing a vocation that seems to require departure more than it depends on arrival at any particular destination. In *Ulysses* Stephen has returned from his exile and roams the streets of Dublin dejectedly, disillusioned by his encounters with the wild geese (or exiled nationalists) of Ireland. The experience of the characters in *Exiles* more closely approximates Joyce's own more permanent exile.

Joyce's perennial interest in the value and difficulty of exile is conjugat-ed in *Exiles* with items of his fascination with the relationship between men and women. The issue of marriage naturally impinges on such musings. One need only recall Joyce's words in a 1906 letter to Stanislaus to be reminded of the strong vein of outrage that underpinned his thinking on the matter:

> I am nauseated by their lying drivel about pure men and pure women and spiritual love and love forever: blatant lying in the face of the truth.[6]

Each of Joyce's works explores the relationship between men and women—a relationship he described to Arthur Power as 'the most impor-tant relationship there is'[7]—probing it in both its sanctioned and its unsanctioned modes. 'Matrimonial situations and, in particular, adulter-ous ones' are, as Richard Brown observes, 'a central focus of interest in Joyce's writing'.[8] Adultery had already featured in Joyce's works in the tragic figure of Mrs Sinico in 'A Painful Case', and the figure of the jealous husband, exiled from his wife by their respective emotions, had featured in 'The Dead'. Given this interest in the marital situation (a framework from which Joyce determinedly exiled himself until 1931, when he and Nora were wedded in London to facilitate his family's 'inheritance under will'[9]), it is gratifying but perhaps unsurprising to find that *Madame Bovary*, that most resonant and emblematic nineteenth-century treatment of the

---

[6] Joyce to Stanislaus Joyce, 13 November 1906, *SL*, 129.
[7] Arthur Power, *Conversations with James Joyce*, ed. Clive Hart (1974) (Chicago: Chicago University Press, 1982), 35.
[8] Brown, 'Shifting Sexual Centres: Joyce and Flaubert', 66.
[9] The phrase is Joyce's in a letter to Stanislaus Joyce of 18 July 1931, *L3*, 222. Ellmann quotes a statement Joyce made on the matter to his solicitor Lionel Munro: 'I cannot explain very clearly why I wish my son and grandson to bear my name. Nevertheless I do wish it.' Further, 'Should their legitimacy ever be questioned, he [Joyce] had a codicil drawn up to specify that they would inherit if they assumed his surname.'—*JJ*, 639. Cixous also asserts the marriage was arranged 'for material rather than for social reasons: there was no longer any risk of being suspected of conformism, but it was necessary to envisage the eventuality of his death and to think about protecting his children. [...] by 1931, Joyce no longer risks being transformed by marriage into a successor of his father; he is no longer afraid of Nora, society, the Church, or public opinion, and his gesture has only the strictly limited value he gives it: that of a "legal fiction."'—*Exile of James Joyce*, 50.

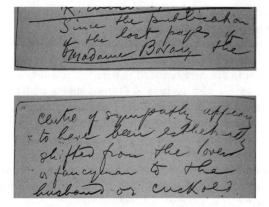

Fig. 15. Joyce's comment about *Madame Bovary* among the preparatory notes for *Exiles*, Buffalo III.A.9 and III.A.10; reproduced from *JJA 11*, 9–10.

theme, should have played a part in shaping his musings on the marriage question in *Exiles* and *Ulysses*.

As was rehearsed in Chapter 1, the existence of a copy of *Madame Bovary* signed and dated in Joyce's hand testifies to his very early acquaintance (June 1901) with Flaubert's novel. Joyce's library in Trieste held an English translation of the work.[10] But it was almost certainly the French edition of *Madame Bovary* published by Louis Conard in 1910 that he had in mind when in November 1913 he jotted down the following observation in a notebook in which he was preparing the composition of *Exiles* (fig. 15):

> Since the publication of the lost pages of *Madame Bovary* the centre of sympathy appears to have been esthetically shifted from the lover or fancy-man to the husband or cuckold.[11]

Joyce's perception of the redistribution of sympathy effected by Flaubert's representation of adultery in *Madame Bovary* yielded puzzling results in *Exiles*, but was put to masterful use in *Ulysses*. This chapter will examine the impact of Joyce's reading of *Madame Bovary* on both these works, focusing on the theme of cuckoldry that lies at the heart of all three. It begins by considering the role played by the Conard edition of *Madame Bovary* in drawing Joyce's attention to the importance of the figure of the

---

[10] For the Flaubertian holdings of Joyce's Triestine library, see Chapter 3, footnote 73. Jane Ford comments on a marking in Joyce's copy of the English translation in 'James Joyce's Trieste Library: Some Notes on its Use', in *Joyce at Texas: Essays on the James Joyce Materials at the Humanities Research Centre*, ed. Dave Oliphant and Thomas Zigal (Austin: The University of Texas at Austin, 1983), 146.

[11] *JJA 11*, 9–10; printed in *E*, 165.

cuckold; it goes on to question Joyce's assertion that the change inaugurated by Flaubert in *Madame Bovary* is 'utilized in *Exiles*';[12] it then looks
at how the technical innovations Joyce brought to bear on his writing in
Ulysses facilitate reader sympathy; and finally considers ways in which
Joyce's interest in Flaubert extended to paratextual details—as evidenced,
for instance, by his wish to have *A Portrait* appear under a publishing
imprint that was also issuing Flaubert's works, and by arrangements he
made for the first American edition of *Ulysses* to replicate the format of the
édition définitive of *Madame Bovary*.

Joyce's cryptic allusion to the 'lost pages' of *Madame Bovary* in the
Flaubert-centred *Exiles* note has never been properly linked to the 1910
Louis Conard edition of Flaubert's text.[13] Michael Mason dismisses the
edition's likely role as a trigger to Joyce's thinking:

> By the publication of the lost pages of *Madame Bovary* he [Joyce] almost
> certainly means simply the restoration in the 1857 edition of the deletions
> Flaubert had been forced to make for the novel's publication in serial form
> the previous year in the *Revue de Paris*. There is plenty of manuscript
> material for *Madame Bovary* in existence, some of it in the form of rejected
> sections of the novel, but none of these were printed until 1936.[14]

Mason is mistaken in stating that none of Flaubert's manuscripts for *Madame
Bovary* were printed before 1936. The 1910 Conard edition of the text
compiled a very substantial dossier of materials concerning the novel's genesis
and reception. Among these documents were transcriptions of Flaubert's
scénarios for the novel (fragmentary vignettes outlining a skeleton plot) and
five facsimile reproductions of manuscript pages from the *Bovary* archive,
including a topographical map of one of the novel's main settings (Yonville
l'Abbaye) drawn in Flaubert's hand. These reproductions constitute the most
eye-catching feature of the Conard edition, and the novelty of such material
may well have inspired Joyce's reference to 'lost pages' restored.

[12] *E*, 165.
[13] One reason for this, though surely not a sufficient reason, may be that the book does
not feature in catalogues of Joyce's Triestine library. For a list of these catalogues, see
Chapter 1, footnote 12. There are a couple of exceptions to the generalized critical blindspot concerning the importance of *MB 1910*. Jacques Aubert suggests a connection
between Joyce's *Bovary* note and the Conard edition, James Joyce, *Oeuvres*, ed. Jacques
Aubert, 2 vols (Paris: Gallimard, 1982–95), vol. 1 (1982), 1,774. Jean-Michel Rabaté and
Pierre-Marc de Biasi suggest a connection between the Flaubertian *scénarios* transcribed in
the Conard edition and Joyce's *Exiles* note—'Joyce, Flaubert et *Exiles*'. This hypothesis is
reiterated by Rabaté in *Joyce upon the Void: The Genesis of Doubt* (Basingstoke: Macmillan,
1991), 23.
[14] Michael Mason, 'Why is Leopold Bloom a Cuckold?', *ELH*, no. 1 (1977), 173.

SYMPATHY AND IMPERSONALITY

Joyce's perception of a sympathetic shift in favour of the figure of the cuckolded husband in *Madame Bovary* is surprising on several counts, and seems related to his acquaintance with the 1910 edition of Flaubert's novel. The comment is intriguing in the first instance because the issue of sympathy is such a convoluted one in Flaubert's works: it is surprising that Joyce should have thought it so succinctly summarizable. Sympathy for one character over another was not a response Flaubert was interested in cultivating. As Paul Bourget noted in a talk given in 1897 (and printed in a volume that had been available to Joyce at the National Library of Ireland—see Chapter 1), Flaubert's aesthetic forbade:

> the use of the sympathetic character, for to prefer one of one's characters to another is still to reveal oneself.[15]

In accordance with his own rule of artistic impersonality, Flaubert sought both to distance himself from his characters and to forestall too strong an identification between the reader and his characters. The reader's primary interest should concern the flawless impersonal artistry resulting from the novelist's 'hidden, infinite impassibility'.[16] The reader should be spellbound by the beauty of a book's artistry, rather than by its plot, characterization, or the interest of its relation to the author:

> The effect for the spectator must be a kind of amazement. 'How is all that done?' one must ask.[17]

The very distancing that formed the cornerstone of Flaubert's poetic practice involved an initial stage of extreme identification with the characters he was creating. As Stephen in *A Portrait* is invested with emotions before divesting himself of them, so Flaubert needed to get under his characters' skins before abstracting himself from them and from the narrative in which they are embedded. As he recalled some years after the writing of *Madame Bovary*:

> My imaginary characters overwhelm me, pursue me—or rather it is *I who find myself under their skins*. When I was writing Madame Bovary's poisoning

---

[15] ['Il interdit [...] an romancier l'emploi du personnage sympathique, parce que préférer un de ses personnages à un autre, c'est encore se montrer' (Bourget, 'Gustave Flaubert', 263–4)].

[16] Flaubert to Louise Colet, 9 December 1852, *FS1*, 173 ['une impassibilité cachée et infinie' (*C2*, 204)].

[17] Flaubert to Louise Colet, 9 December 1852, *FS1*, 173 ['L'effet, pour le spectateur, doit être une espèce d'ébahissement. Comment tout cela est-il fait! doit-on se dire!' (*C2*, 204)].

scene I had such a taste of arsenic in my mouth, I was so poisoned myself, that I had two bouts of indigestion one after the other.[18]

These retrospective musings accurately reflect the closeness between the writer and his characters that transpires from letters written during the period of *Madame Bovary*'s composition. In 1852 Flaubert merges with Emma in a symbiotic first-person pronoun: 'I'll go to a Ball and then spend a rainy winter, which I'll end with a pregnancy.'[19] In 1853 he worries about having a nervous attack in sympathy with the heightened emotions he has been ascribing to Emma in the context of her first sexual encounter with Rodolphe:

> at the moment when I wrote the phrase *a nervous attack*, I was so carried away, I was making such a racket, and feeling so intensely what my little woman was feeling, that I began to fear I was about to have one myself.[20]

This intensity of identification was not confined to the eponymous character. In the same letter Flaubert expressed an exhilarating sense of consubstantial connection with every item of his imagined universe:

> as a man and as a woman, as lover and mistress both, I have been out riding in a forest on an autumn afternoon, and I was the horses, the leaves, the wind, the words that they spoke to each other and the red sunlight that made them half-close their eyes, eyes that were brimming with love.[21]

Flaubert occasionally uses the word 'sympathy' to describe this process of identification:

> The poet is now required to have sympathy for *all things* and for *everyone*, in order to understand them and to describe them.[22]

---

[18] Flaubert to Hippolyte Taine, 20 November 1866, *GW*, 316 (my emphasis) ['Les personnages imaginaires m'affolent, me poursuivent,—ou plutôt *c'est moi qui suis dans leur peau.* Quand j'écrivais l'empoisonnement de Mme Bovary j'avais si bien le goût d'arsenic dans la bouche, j'étais si bien empoisonné moi-même que je me suis donné deux indigestions coup sur coup.' (*C3*, 562)].

[19] Flaubert to Louise Colet, 27 March 1852, *FS1*, 157 ['j'irai au Bal, et passerai ensuite un hiver pluvieux, que je clorai par une grossesse' (*C2*, 63)].

[20] Flaubert to Louise Colet, 23 December 1853, *GW*, 233 ['au moment où j'écrivais le mot *attaque de nerfs*, j'étais si emporté, je gueulais si fort, et sentais si profondément ce que ma petite femme éprouvait, que j'ai eu peur moi-même d'en avoir une' (*C2*, 483)].

[21] Flaubert to Louise Colet, 23 December 1853, *GW*, 233 ['homme et femme tout ensemble, amant et maîtresse à la fois, je me suis promené à cheval dans une forêt, par un après-midi d'automne, sous des feuilles jaunes, et j'étais les chevaux, les feuilles, le vent, les paroles qu'ils se disaient et le soleil rouge qui faisait s'entre-fermer leurs paupières noyées d'amour' (*C2*, 483–4)].

[22] Flaubert to Mlle Leroyer de Chantepie, 12 December 1857 ['Le poète est tenu maintenant d'avoir de la sympathie pour *tout* et pour *tous*, afin de les comprendre et de les décrire.' (*C2*, 786)].

In later years George Sand advised Flaubert to inflect his narration with a kind of sympathy that would go beyond imaginative empathy. By this she meant that Flaubert should give explicit expression to his opinions regarding his characters' moral standing and tell his readers about the distribution of his fondness and antipathy:

> To conceal one's own opinion about one's characters, and to thereby leave the reader uncertain as to what he should make of them, is to court misunderstanding.[23]

Flaubert made a vehemently, resolutely principled response to Sand's suggestions, insisting that if the reader failed to see what the inherent moral of a book might be without the author disclosing a personal view:

> this is either because the reader is an imbecile or because the book is *inaccurate* in its details.[24]

Stephen Heath stresses the incompatibility of Sand's demand with Flaubert's understanding of the requirements of art. '[T]o be an artist is to be committed to self-abdication'; impersonality is crucial to Flaubert because it realizes 'a diffuse presence of the artist'; it is 'immersion, *circulation*'; the author must be everywhere equally; 'taking sides is simply to negate the truth by the reiteration of some conventional moral fiction'. Flaubert's novels are not about sympathy for one character over another, but about the broad interrogative vista that they enable by existing side by side. Impersonality, in Heath's words, is a question of 'a play of visions, perspectives, perceptions across the characters and their doings and their world'.[25]

As Flaubert oscillated between identification and distancing in relation to his characters, so he hesitated between the desirability of such reactions in his readers. Towards the beginning of his work on *Madame Bovary*, Flaubert hoped that his portrayal of Emma would make identification with her irresistible to female readers:

> If my book is good, it will gently caress many a feminine wound: more than one woman will smile as she recognizes herself in it.[26]

---

[23] George Sand to Flaubert, 12 January 1876 ['Cacher sa propre opinion sur les personnages que l'on met en scène, laisser par conséquent le lecteur incertain sur l'opinion qu'il doit en avoir, c'est vouloir n'être pas compris.' (*C5*, 7)].

[24] Flaubert to George Sand, 6 February 1876, *GW*, 404 ['c'est que le lecteur est un imbécile ou que le livre est *faux* au point de vue de l'exactitude' (*C5*, 12)].

[25] Stephen Heath, *Madame Bovary* (Cambridge: Cambridge University Press, 1992), 93, 105, 106, 105, 106.

[26] Flaubert to Louise Colet, 1 September 1852, *FS1*, 168 ['Si mon livre est bon, il chatouillera doucement mainte plaie féminine.—Plus d'une sourira en s'y reconnaissant.' (*C2*, 147)].

His response to such identification when it occurred, however, was to dispel it. Mlle Leroyer de Chantepie, who sent her first letter to Flaubert after reading the book in serialized form, expressed complete identification with Emma:

> I identified with her life so much that it seemed to me that I was her and she me![27]

Flaubert's response, in the famous letter of 18 March 1857 from which Stephen misquotes in *A Portrait*, was to assert that 'Art should rise above one's personal attachments'.[28] In his next letter, Flaubert exhorts his correspondent to resist identification with his character, passing judgement on Emma in denigrating terms he would never have allowed himself in fiction:

> don't compare yourself to the Bovary woman. You have little in common with her! She was a lesser person than you as a mind and as a heart; for she is a somewhat perverse nature, a woman of false poetry and false sentiments.[29]

Flaubert's immovable dedication to impersonality did not mean resistance to the idea of the sympathetic character, nor did it in any way represent a commitment to the creation of unsympathetic characters. Rather, his aim was to craft personalities towards whom sympathy would be possible but complicated in both kind and intensity, ideally springing from a balanced evaluation enabled but not constrained by the novel's prose. This is why Mlle Leroyer de Chantepie's fervent identification with Emma Bovary so devastatingly overstepped the mark: the ardency of her identification intimated to Flaubert that his meticulous authorial abstinence had not made his writing proof to such one-dimensional affective reactions. Given the intricacy of Flaubert's sympathetic procedures and effects, and Joyce's familiarity with his poetics, it is somewhat surprising that Joyce should have read *Madame Bovary* as though performing a straightforward 'shift in the centre of sympathy'.

Moreover, it is also intriguing that Joyce's interest in the figure of the sympathetic cuckold should have been fuelled by a novel in which the figure of the wife—rather than those of either her husband or her

---

[27] Mlle Leroyer de Chantepie to Flaubert, 18 December 1856 ['Je me suis identifiée à son existence au point qu'il me semblait que c'était elle et que c'était moi!' (*C2*, 654)].

[28] Flaubert to Mlle Leroyer de Chantepie, 18 March 1857, *GW*, 248 ['l'Art doit s'élever au-dessus des affections personnelles' (*C2*, 691)].

[29] Flaubert to Mlle Leroyer de Chantepie, 30 March 1857 ['ne vous comparez pas à la Bovary. Vous n'y ressemblez guère! Elle valait moins que vous comme tête et comme coeur; car c'est une nature quelque peu perverse, une femme de fausse poésie et de faux sentiments.' (*C2*, 696–7)].

lovers—clearly predominates. '[I]t is she', as Heath notes of Emma, 'who is the central figure of the book and the point of its narration'.[30] She is, as Ronald Bush observes, the 'prime beneficiary' of Flaubert's deployment of *style indirect libre*.[31] Why then does Joyce's note identify the husband as such a pivotal figure? Although Charles is sketched more fully than he might have been in stock treatments of adultery, to describe him as a 'centre of sympathy', as Joyce does, is accurate neither to Flaubert's impersonal portrayal nor to a great many readers' experience. Indeed, a recent issue of the mainstream French *Magazine Littéraire* (2006) emphasized the frustration that Flaubert's neutral treatment of Charles Bovary has caused generations of readers.[32] Dissatisfaction with the inscrutability of Flaubert's ambivalent characterization has, as the *Magazine* articles point out, given rise to a number of books written to rehabilitate Charles. Laura Grimaldi rewrites Charles's story in *Monsieur Bovary*.[33] Jean Améry presents Charles as a lovable man fallen prey to Flaubert's hatred of mediocrity.[34] Antoine Billot draws on Flaubert's manuscripts to 'set the record straight' about Charles, rectifying the silence and absence to which he is reduced in Flaubert's novel.[35] Such confusion about the character is not new: the issue has long perplexed readers, who have, in this case at least, manifested precisely the kind of puzzlement and indecision Flaubert had in mind. The question was in fact at the heart of the *Bovary* court case.

At the time of the trial in 1857, a legal decree forbade the publication of court proceedings.[36] Notwithstanding, Flaubert arranged for a stenographer to transcribe the various speeches. By the time the *édition définitive* of the novel was being prepared for publication by Charpentier in 1874, almost twenty years later, the law had changed, and Flaubert succeeded in having the materials included.[37] The *édition définitive* went through numerous reprints: it was one of these that Joyce purchased in 1901, and also one of these that the National Library of Ireland acquired in

[30] Heath, *Madame Bovary*, 91.

[31] Ronald Bush, 'Joyce's Modernisms', in *Palgrave Advances in James Joyce Studies*, ed. Jean-Michel Rabaté (Basingstoke and New York: Palgrave Macmillan, 2004), 18.

[32] 'Charles Bovary, héros malgré lui', *Magazine Littéraire*, no. 458 (November 2006), 62–3.

[33] Laura Grimaldi, *Monsieur Bovary*, trans. (into French from Italian) Geneviève Leibrich (Paris: Métailié, 1995).

[34] Jean Améry, *Charles Bovary, médecin de campagne: portrait d'un homme simple*, trans. Françoise Wuilmart (Paris: Actes Sud, 1991).

[35] Antoine Billot, *Monsieur Bovary* (Paris: Gallimard, 2006).

[36] Article 17 of the decree of 17 February 1852; see Léon Vingtain, *De la liberté de la presse* (Paris: Michel Lévy, 1860), 145.

[37] Gustave Flaubert, *Madame Bovary* (Paris: Bibliothèque-Charpentier, 1874).

1903. The 1910 Conard edition followed the by then established practice of including the trial materials as an appendix to the reading text.

It is apparent from the court transcripts that sympathy for Charles was deemed a clinching factor in deciding the novel's acceptability, with the prosecution and defence articulating starkly opposed readings of the character. The state prosecutor, Ernest Pinard, condemned Flaubert's portrayal of Charles as a husband whose shortcomings are such as to make his wife's betrayals seem understandable—whose ineptitude comes close to excusing her infidelity. Pinard described Charles as a contemptible character—stupid ('clumsy and shy'), blind ('the blindest of husbands'), naive ('so naive that he believes in his wife's virtue'):[38] all in all, a virtual accomplice in his wife's adultery. Charles's love for Emma was exposed as a weakness aggravated by his wife's hatred,[39] and by the hint of masochistic pleasure that tinges his forgiving response to the discovery of her affairs: 'on the contrary he gets excited, is exalted by this woman that others have possessed'.[40] By contrast, the defence lawyer, Maître Sénard, saw in Charles a man whose unstinting devotion to his wife renders him 'noble, sublime'.[41] In maintaining this view, the lawyers echoed Mlle Leroyer de Chantepie's reaction earlier that year: 'Yes, Monsieur, that is love in its extremest form, love which has reached the sublime state of religion and of martyrdom!'[42]

Mason correctly observes that the deletions performed by La Revue de Paris are listed in the Conard edition of 1910. But he goes on to state that:

> Joyce cannot have meant that these deletions in themselves had encouraged a shift of sympathy to the cuckold since, with a couple of exceptions, they do not at all bear on the estimate of Charles Bovary.[43]

However, the Conard edition specifically draws attention to just such a cut: 'a whole page has been cut, it spelt out the faults and excesses of Charles Bovary'.[44] The comment may in itself have been sufficient to suggest to Joyce that one of the aims of the Revue's deletions had been to minimize

---

[38] ['lourd et timide'; 'le plus aveugle des maris'; 'si naïf qu'il croit à la vertu de sa femme' (MB 1910, 560)].

[39] MB 1910, 566, 564.

[40] ['il s'excite, au contraire, il s'exalte pour cette femme que d'autres ont possédée' (MB 1910, 561)].

[41] ['grand, sublime' (MB 1910, 601)].

[42] Mlle Leroyer de Chantepie to Flaubert, 26 February 1857 ['Oui, Monsieur, c'est là l'extrême limite de l'amour, arrivé à l'état sublime de religion et de martyre!' (C2, 686)].

[43] Michael Mason, 'Why is Leopold Bloom a Cuckold?', 173–4.

[44] ['une page entière a été supprimée, elle détaillait les excès et les désordres de Charles Bovary' (MB 1910, 506)].

Charles's 'blame', thereby maximizing reader sympathy and enhancing perceptions of him as the guiltless victim of a reckless wife.

The 1910 Conard edition featured at least one other strong comment on the issue of reader sympathy for Charles, and this may also have contributed to Joyce's sense of the importance of the debate. In a section of the edition devoted to the contemporary reception of *Madame Bovary*, Edmond Texier remarks upon the absence of any sympathetic character in the novel ('how can he not have thought to create a single truly sympathetic character?'[45]) and deems the book a failure for that reason. Flaubert's treatment of Charles is judged the fatal flaw: 'There however lay all the interest of the situation.'[46] Charles, Texier asserts, should have emerged as 'the martyr of the domestic hearth, as a friend one remembers forever'.[47] The extensive contemporary debate about the fraught issue of sympathy for Charles, reprinted in the Conard edition, was probably at the root of Joyce's aspiration to render Richard Rowan sympathetically in *Exiles*, and of his depiction of Leopold Bloom as a likeable cuckold in *Ulysses*.

Joyce's identification of *Madame Bovary* as a landmark literary event is accompanied by a comment about the role played by the theatre-going public in the shift of sympathy from the lover to the husband:

> This displacement is also rendered more stable by the gradual growth of a collective practical realism due to changed economic conditions in the mass of people who are called to hear a work of art relating to their lives.[48]

Brown comments on the surprising 'element of historical determinism'[49] in Joyce's remark, outlining the modulations that have marked literary treatments of adultery since the Middle Ages:

> The audience and the economic conditions under which they live provide a context in which certain effects are possible, certain impossible. In Mediaeval and Neo-classical literatures [...] adultery is a battle for sexual possession and domination and the comic cuckold or jealous husband are familiar stereotypes; in Romantic literatures the panache of Don Juan, the seducer, or the passions of the adulterous wife are the centre of interest, but in the new democratic, modern, realistic or ironic age aesthetic sympathies need to

---

[45] ['comment n'a-t-il pas songé à en créer un seul qui fût vraiment sympathique?' (Edmond Texier, *L'Illustration*, 9 May 1857, repr. in *MB 1910*, 537)].

[46] ['Là cependant était tout l'interêt du drame.' (*MB 1910*, 537)].

[47] ['le martyr du foyer domestique, comme un ami dont on se souvient toujours' (*MB 1910*, 537)].

[48] *E*, 165.

[49] Brown, 'Shifting Sexual Centres', 66–7.

be trained on what Joyce's note goes on to call 'the delicate, strange and highly sensitive conscience' of the husband.[50]

Giuseppina Restivo glosses Joyce's note with specific reference to the changes brought about by the shift from a predominantly aristocratic to a predominantly bourgeois audience:

> Since Flaubert's *Madame Bovary*, Joyce argues, the new broad middle class literary public, no longer bound by the old aristocratic concepts of 'honour' and of the husband's 'possession' of his wife, has broken the long literary tradition of contempt for the cuckold.[51]

Tony Tanner also provides an illuminating contextual framework by stating that although 'in evidence in literature from the earliest times', 'adultery takes on a very special importance in the late eighteenth- and nineteenth-century novel',[52] when marriage had become the dominant ideology's keystone institution:

> marriage is *the* central subject for the bourgeois novel [...] marriage *is* the mythology [...] a means by which society attempts to bring into harmonious alignment patterns of passion and patterns of property [...] For bourgeois society marriage is the all-subsuming, all-organizing, all-containing contract.[53]

Joyce's note shows him to have been eager to identify and play on the ideological leanings of his work's potential audience. His reflections on these matters are continued in the penultimate *Exiles* note, which evokes Paul de Kock's failure to handle the subject of adultery in the comic mode:

> A striking instance of the changed point of view of literature towards this subject is Paul de Kock—a descendant surely of Rabelais, Molière and the old *Souche Gauloise*. Yet compare *George Dandin* or *Le Cocu imaginaire* of Molière with *Le Cocu* of the later writer. Salacity, humour, indecency, liveliness were certainly not wanting in the writer yet he produces a long, hesitating, painful story—written also in the first person. Evidently that spring is broken somewhere.[54]

---

[50] Brown, 'Shifting Sexual Centres', 67.

[51] Giuseppina Restivo, 'From *Exiles* to *Ulysses*: The Influence of Three Italian Authors on Joyce—Giacosa, Praga, Oriani', in *Anglo-American Modernity and the Mediterranean: Milan, 29–30 September 2005*, ed. Caroline Patey, Giovanni Cianci, and Francesca Cuojati (Milan: Cisalpino, 2006), 135.

[52] Tony Tanner, *Adultery in the Novel: Contract and Transgression* (Baltimore and London: Johns Hopkins University Press, 1979), 12.

[53] Tanner, *Adultery in the Novel*, 15.

[54] *E*, 175.

Joyce, who owned a copy of *Le Cocu* in Trieste,[55] probably knew that a 'long, hesitating, painful story' was not what de Kock had intended to write. The book's preface clearly states its comic aspirations: 'the word *Cuckold* must arouse laughter, and that is all. Isn't that the effect it produces in the theatre?'[56] That Joyce's note was inspired by this preface is apparent from the fact that de Kock also adduces Molière as an example of the salacious approach to cuckoldry in literature. The echo is conspicuous because *Le Cocu imaginaire*—as it appears in both de Kock's preface and Joyce's note—was not the title but merely the subtitle of Molière's play, better known as *Sganarelle* (1660). As *Le Cocu* was written in 1831, Joyce's note about de Kock pushes back by over twenty years the date at which a shift in the centre of sympathy putatively occurred. Also significantly, the last of Joyce's comments on de Kock, which describes *Le Cocu* as a story 'written also in the first person',[57] heralds the technique of interior monologue that was to play such an essential role in making Leopold Bloom a sympathetic character.

In both the notes discussed above, Joyce's interest is in novelistic treatments of adultery—an interest that seems prescient from the perspective of *Ulysses*, but less relevant in the context of Joyce's preparatory notes for *Exiles*. Other notes reflect Joyce's thinking about parallel developments in the dramatic mode. Marco Praga (1862–1943) and Giuseppe Giacosa (1847–1906) are cited immediately after Flaubert as theatrical exemplars of the same kind of shift:[58] 'Praga in *La Crisi* and Giacosa in *Tristi Amori* have understood and profited by this change.'[59] These playwrights were not new-found objects of interest to Joyce (in 'The Day of the Rabblement' Giacosa features as one of a group of 'earnest dramatists of the second rank', and Joyce's Paduan essay of 1912, 'The Universal Literary Influence of the Renaissance', describes Praga as 'simply amoral'[60]), though his interest may have been rekindled by performances of their plays in Trieste.[61] Shakespeare is also mentioned, as are a number of philosophers and artists, among them Wagner, Spinoza, Nietzsche,

---

[55] *CJ*, 116.

[56] ['le mot *Cocu* doit faire rire, et voilà tout. N'est-ce pas l'effet qu'il produit au théâtre?' (de Kock, *Le Cocu* [Paris: Gustave Barba, 1931], x)].

[57] *E*, 175.

[58] For more on Joyce's interest in these playwrights, see Corinna de Greco Lobner, *James Joyce's Italian Connection: The Poetics of the Word* (Iowa City: University of Iowa Press, 1989), 3.

[59] *E*, 165.

[60] 'Rabblement', *OCPW*, 50; James Joyce 'The Universal Literary Influence of the Renaissance', in *OCPW*, 189.

[61] John McCourt, *The Years of Bloom: James Joyce in Trieste 1904–1920* (Dublin: Lilliput Press, 2000), 152.

Schopenhauer, Hume, Berkeley, Balfour, Bergson, Sacher-Masoch. This listing of precursors confirms Joyce's tendency, manifest as early as 1901 in 'The Day of the Rabblement', to think in terms of genealogies—his wish to learn from literary history and from the examples of specific precursors. The author's interest in the devices and techniques used in earlier studies of jealousy combines in the *Exiles* notes with a keen sense of the importance of understanding and addressing an audience's concerns. Drawing on his knowledge of the literary past and the ideological present, Joyce's preparatory jottings manifest an investment in representing adultery in ways that would speak to spectators 'called' to hear *Exiles*.[62]

EXILES

There are a number of differences between the ways in which adultery is treated in *Madame Bovary* and in *Exiles*. While adultery is a reality in *Madame Bovary*, in *Exiles* it features almost solely as a theoretical question far removed from the 'practical realism' mentioned in Joyce's note. In terms of plot, adultery remains confined to the realm of the prospective, the hypothetical, the unknown. As Jean-Michel Rabaté points out, 'the plot leaves us with an open question mark'.[63] Restivo echoes this, noting that '*Exiles* closes on an endless suspension of doubt and impossible catharsis'.[64] To say as much is in fact only to restate Richard Rowan's own reference to his 'deep wound of doubt which can never be healed'.[65] In addition to opting for this lack of resolution, Joyce alters the parameters of the central question by having the possibility of betrayal arise within the framing context of an unmarried relationship. This change (which is biographically related to Joyce's unmarried union of twenty-seven years to Nora Barnacle) is highly significant: the liberal, uncontracted partnership of Richard and Bertha adumbrates a post-matrimonial, post-moral bourgeois order which has little in common with the rigidly regimented ideological world that *Madame Bovary* so radically questions.

This point of difference between the two works is fundamental to an understanding of their vastly discrepant effects and receptions. Tony Tanner describes *Madame Bovary* as 'the most important and far-reaching novel of adultery in Western literature'[66] precisely because it uses its

---

[62] *E*, 165.
[63] Jean-Michel Rabaté, *Joyce upon the Void*, 24.
[64] Restivo, 'From *Exiles* to *Ulysses*', 136.
[65] *E*, 162.
[66] Tanner, *Adultery in the Novel*, 235.

central theme to perform a thoroughgoing interrogation of bourgeois ideology at the height of its power. Flaubert mobilizes the incendiary figure of the adulteress in order to turn the bourgeois novel, which Tanner sees as 'coeval and coterminous with the power concentrated in the central structure of marriage',[67] against the ideology that underpins it. *Madame Bovary* forcefully contests this keystone institution: at the heart of the novel is an unsatisfactory marriage twice betrayed.

Joyce, by contrast, removes the premise of marriage from his play: Richard and Bertha are contractually free. In Restivo's interpretation, this choice reflects Joyce's intent to forge:

> a new ethics for the couple. This implies first of all the right to a free union (as in Joyce's case) rather than a marriage contract, so as to maintain reciprocal constant individual rights to choose one's partner according to actual feelings, rather than to social and religious conventions, in defiance of both Irish Catholicism and common bourgeois rules.[68]

The religious and political ramifications of Richard's and Bertha's contractual freedom are clearly important, but the play's primary preoccupations are with abstruse forms of psychological and philosophical freedom: in Richard Brown's words, 'sexual fidelity has been intellectualized into an investigation of the philosophic possibility of ever knowing another person's desires and motivations'.[69] The sustained discussion of such abstract matters is in fact only possible because both parties' legal and social freedoms are already assured. Although the play evades much discussion of anything so practical as a contract, it is telling, as Rabaté points out, that:

> Bertha is the only character in the cast to be deprived of a family name, as if she was still waiting for a name to be given her by marriage with any one of her possible partners.[70]

Just as Richard and Robert and (though this is more ambiguously suggested) Beatrice avail themselves of their sexual freedom, Bertha is legally free to do as she pleases. Although the play shows this anomalous arrangement to have passed more or less muster in social terms (Richard has been employed in Catholic Rome, and is under consideration for an academic job in Catholic Ireland), neither Richard nor Bertha seem to benefit from their unshackled, uncontracted freedom at this time of crisis.

---

[67] Tanner, *Adultery in the Novel*, 15.
[68] Restivo, 'From *Exiles* to *Ulysses*', 135.
[69] Richard Brown, *James Joyce and Sexuality* (Cambridge: Cambridge University Press, 1985), 18.
[70] Rabaté, *Joyce upon the Void*, 30.

Despite having been forced to accept Richard's philandering as a fait accompli, Bertha does not want the freedom Richard so insistently grants her: it is, in fact, his 'refusal to forbid',[71] as a conventional husband would, that precipitates and stokes the crisis of their relationship. The play is, in this sense, about the psychological fetters that endure even when the obstacle of commitment to a publicly witnessed contract has been removed.

For all its flavour of the daring and the avant-garde, the removal of marriage from the equation of the adulterous plot arguably works to the detriment of dramatic tension. The displacement of the issue from the realm of 'practical realism' to that of abstract philosophical musing (about which Bertha, for one, cares little, and the convolutions of which Pound deemed 'too great for an audience to be able to follow'[72]) takes the bite out of a moral dilemma that Joyce considered to be so difficult and so important. The language of the characters betrays discomfort with a situation that is governed by no established rules. When owning up to Richard about his feelings for Bertha, Robert falters: 'I admire very much the personality of your ... of ... your wife.'[73] As Rabaté explains, Robert's hesitation emphasizes the awkwardness generated by the unconventionality of the scenario in which the characters find themselves. Confusion and embarrassment prompt Robert to conjure the more reassuring, because more familiar, situation of adultery:

> if he also wishes to situate her as Richard's wife, it is because he prefers to place her and himself in the bourgeois situation of adultery, in which stock responses to typical situations allow people to go on playing a game, whilst he feels totally unsure of himself in Richard's mystical and perverse drama.[74]

Both Robert and Bertha miss the clarifying presence of a contract that would draw boundary lines around the central couple, turn Robert's advances into an easily recognizable form of transgression, and elicit predictable patterns of behaviour. As Joyce's notes for the play clearly state, this removal of commonplace safeguards was absolutely intentional:

> Robert wishes Richard to use against him the weapons which social conventions and morals put in the hands of the husband. Richard refuses. Bertha wishes Richard to use these weapons also in her defence. Richard refuses also and for the same reason.[75]

[71] Rabaté, *Joyce upon the Void*, 28.
[72] Ezra Pound, 'Mr James Joyce and the Modern Stage', in *P/J*, 52.
[73] *E*, 83.
[74] Rabaté, *Joyce upon the Void*, 29.
[75] *E*, 163.

Pound intuited that Joyce's aim was to render the adoption of stereotypical behaviour impossible for his characters:

> the author is portraying an intellectual-emotional struggle, because he is dealing with actual thought, actual questioning, not with clichés of thought and emotion.[76]

But Joyce's (and Richard's) predilection for existential doubtfulness arguably goes further than the play's bourgeois domestic setting can accommodate. It is a telling fact that for all his steadfast defence of the play, Joyce elected to factor marriage back into the adulterous scenario in *Ulysses*. His critique of 'the inadequacy of the matrimonial formulation of the sexual relationship and the representation of individuals as fundamentally separate from each other'[77] would gain more leverage, as he realized, by being represented from within the consciousness of his characters and couched in the context of the commonplace difficulties of married life exemplified in the union of Molly and Leopold Bloom.

Joyce thought he had successfully 'shift[ed] the centre of sympathy from the lover or fancyman to the husband or cuckold' in *Exiles*. This is clear from the remainder of the *Madame Bovary* note (presumably Joyce's comment on an extant draft version of the play), which states that 'This change is utilized in *Exiles*'.[78] But sympathy, again, seems too broad and vague a word to convey what Joyce had in mind for Richard's character. As is apparent from another of Joyce's *Exiles* jottings, the author expected a substantially different response from the audience—one involving neither identification nor empathy nor sympathy, but admiration (by contrast Joyce doubts that Beatrice will succeed in arousing even a basic level of interest):

> It will be difficult to recommend Beatrice to the interest of the audience, every man of which is Robert and would like to be Richard—in any case Bertha's.[79]

Such a comment suggests that 'sympathy', in its common acceptation, is something of a red herring as a description of Joyce's aims in *Exiles*—as it also is in relation to *Madame Bovary*. Richard is shaped by Joyce's penchant for the idea of the Nietzschean *Übermensch* and by his reading of Schopenhauer ('His language must at times be nearer to that of Schopenhauer'[80]): he is an incarnation in life of that aesthetic detachment

---

[76] Pound, 'Mr James Joyce and the Modern Stage', *P/J*, 52.
[77] Brown, *Joyce and Sexuality*, 35.
[78] *E*, 165.
[79] *E*, 164.
[80] *E*, 169.

that Flaubert's poetics so insistently call for, and by which the Stephen of *A Portrait* is so fascinated. Joyce wished to make Richard impressive rather than likeable: in this sense Joyce was trying to go further than Flaubert. *Exiles* may 'utilize' Flaubert's shift, but Joyce turns the wheel another quarter, making his own intellectual would-be cuckold an object of awed respect rather than of sympathy. This accords with Joyce's statement to himself, shortly after the mention of *Madame Bovary*, that the change introduced by Flaubert is 'utilized' in *Exiles*:

> as a technical shield for the protection of a delicate, strange, and highly sensitive conscience.[81]

Sympathy, then, is neither a self-evident nor a common response to Richard. For Robert M. Adams, Richard's abstract erudition and articulate 'cruelty' make him 'a narcissistic prig',[82] while for Hélène Cixous he is at least partly 'Richard the sadist, the masochist, and selfish coward'.[83] The situation might have been different if the character had been portrayed 'from the inside', through focalization, rather than from the external perspective imposed by dramatic form. The exigencies of the theatre exile Joyce's characters into a distance that makes their concerns remote and accentuates the opacity of their behaviour. Hugh Kenner suggests that the play was intended precisely as an experiment in absolute impersonality:

> He needed to write something with no point of view, no narrator, whatever: something wholly 'objective': something in which the only point of view would be that of the spectator [. . .] What happens when the storyteller gets as far outside his story as that?
> When the writer is Joyce, what happens is that he loses control; the characters do not reveal themselves sufficiently.[84]

Perhaps Joyce felt as much himself, for in *Ulysses* some of those features which most sharply distinguish *Madame Bovary* from *Exiles*—the novelistic mode, the use of point of view, and a situation revolving around a legally contracted marriage—are reinstated.

For all its many differences from *Madame Bovary*, *Exiles* was certainly shaped by Joyce's thoughts about it. There is at least one explicit trace of *Madame Bovary*'s formative role in the genesis of the play. Perhaps in an attempt to blur the boundaries between husband and lover, Joyce has

[81] *E*, 165.
[82] Robert M. Adams, 'Light on Joyce's *Exiles*? A New MS, a Curious Analogue, and Some Speculations', *Studies in Bibliography*, vol. XVII (1964), 92–3.
[83] Cixous, *Exile of James Joyce*, 555.
[84] Kenner, *Joyce's Voices*, 24.

Robert engage in an act of faux adultery (faux because no contract of any kind is breached), which unmistakably recalls the most iconic sexual encounter in *Madame Bovary*. At the end of the play's third act, Robert reports that after seeing Bertha he 'went to a certain nightclub':

> I saw her home in a cab. She lives in Donnybrook. In the cab took place what the subtle Duns Scotus calls a death of the spirit. Shall I go on?[85]

The cab is peculiar enough of a sexual venue to constitute a clear allusion to the scene in which Emma and Léon consort in a hackney cab that rushes through the streets of Rouen. The intertextual allusion functions ambivalently. Joyce may have meant the *clin d'oeil* as a reminder or confirmation that Robert is a mere 'fancyman', or he may have intended to signpost his play's position within a literary tradition that interrogates marriage. This hypothesis gains some support from the fact that the woman Robert meets in the nightclub is described specifically as a divor-cee: 'She told me she was the divorced wife of a barrister.'[86] In this, *Exiles* again suggests that although marriage compromises freedom, the freedom that lies outside its bounds may not always be happy.

ULYSSES

In *Ulysses* Joyce returns to the question of adultery. Marriage is reinstalled as a source for the social tension that is lacking in *Exiles*. Molly Bloom's planned act of adultery is suspected by various denizens of Dublin whose unwitting or ill-intentioned hints give Bloom cause for upset throughout 16 June 1904. This sets the issue within a social context that has no counterpart in *Exiles*. Although personal hurt is uppermost in Bloom's thoughts about Boylan's tryst with Molly, he is not so romantic as to forget that legal matters may obtain. It is significant, for instance, that Bloom should consider divorce as one of the forms of retribution available to him for Molly's adultery: 'Divorce, not now.'[87] That the word features is important, as a reminder of what—in addition to lovesickness—is at stake: a social contract and a family. In this light, Molly's final 'Yes', as well as resounding with affirmation in the present, recalls the oral contract into which she and Leopold entered years ago on the Hill of Howth, the very same contract that she has broken on 16 June. It is notable that although Bloom considers divorce, violent means of revenge ('Assassination [. . .]

---

[85] *E*, 154–5.   [86] *E*, 155.   [87] *U* 17: 2,202.

Duel by combat'[88]) are dismissed. The very mention of what seem such disproportionate, melodramatic, outmoded practices highlights an important point of difference between *Ulysses* and *Madame Bovary*: although Bloom's is a sad story, it is not, like *Madame Bovary*, a tragedy. The matter is no longer, as in earlier centuries, one of patriarchal honour—to be defended, if necessary, in brutal fashion—but one of private hurt, to be dealt with within the confines of the marriage. Both *Exiles* and *Ulysses* undo the association between adultery and tragedy. The ending of *Exiles* is ambiguous but bears no intimation of death. *Ulysses* is similarly ambivalent, steering a bittersweet course between comedy and tragedy and ultimately settling for neither.

Ulysses and *Madame Bovary* share a concern with the marital framework, yet their treatment of the same core situation differs drastically. Emma Bovary is entrammelled in a deeply restrictive, moralizing bourgeois society. Richard and Bertha, having disregarded social pressures to wed, live in an isolated, liberated, a-matrimonial bubble. The marriage represented in *Ulysses* is neither as radical as the free-love union of Richard and Bertha nor as oppressive as that of Charles and Emma, but Joyce's treatment of the institution is subversive nonetheless. Bloom's decision not to prevent Molly's meeting with Boylan and the uncertainty of the day's ultimate outcome for the central couple's relationship adumbrates the possibility that marriage and adultery may not be mutually exclusive. This provocative implication subtends *Ulysses*, which is in part the story of a couple dealing without sensationalism with an act of adultery of which both are cognizant in advance. For all his suffering and jealousy Bloom understands—recapitulating in his mind the length of time since he and Molly last had satisfactory sexual relations—why Molly may be acting as she is, and privileges generous over angry responses, overcoming envy and jealousy by abnegation, and thereby achieving equanimity. Bloom puts Molly's infidelity into perspective, and in so doing manages to attain 'emotional equilibrium':[89] he realizes that Molly's affair is 'as natural as any and every natural act', 'not so calamitous as a cataclysmic annihilation of the planet', 'less reprehensible' than many crimes, and, in a sad, resigned coda, 'more than inevitable, irreparable'.[90] By making Bloom capable of seeing his wife's adultery for what it is—that is, not solely as an act of betrayal committed against him—Joyce disarms the bombshell of adultery from within the union that it endangers.

In *Stephen Hero* the protagonist condemns marriage as a traffic operation in women's bodies:

---

[88] *U* 17: 2,200–1.   [89] Brown, *Joyce and Sexuality*, 19.
[90] *U* 17: 2,178, 2,180–1, 2,182, 2,194.

A woman's body is a corporal asset of the State: if she traffic with it she must sell it either as a harlot or as a married woman or as a working celibate or as a mistress.[91]

The 'Ithaca' episode in *Ulysses* proffers an echo of this view in describing marriage as an outrage: 'From outrage (matrimony) to outrage (adultery) there arose nought but outrage (copulation).'[92] Yet in the same episode and throughout the book, equanimity emerges as the view that society, following Bloom's example, might most fruitfully adopt towards the institution. Joyce's works, in their decreasingly critical treatment of marriage, chart the curve of his own changing view of such a state of union (as evidenced by his own ultimate willingness to enter into such a contract, if only to legalize his succession).

Ulysses presents infidelity as a matter for private discussion rather than public outcry. The question it asks is not 'why is marriage good and adultery immoral?' but 'to whom do marriage and adultery matter?'. Such an alteration of the terms of the debate accords with the purport of attacks led against marriage by a previous generation of socio-political activists and commentators. As Brown notes:

During the nineteenth century few questions were so high on the agenda for discussion and reform as questions of marriage.[93]

It is a telling fact that while *Madame Bovary* was brought to trial over adultery (though the official charge alleged 'offenses à la morale publique et à la religion' the focus on adultery is clear from the court proceedings), the *Ulysses* trial was precipitated by a general sense (or rumour-fuelled suspicion) of the text's obscenity, and got underway in response to what happens on the beach in 'Nausicaa' rather than to Molly's tryst with Boylan. While concerns were expressed in both cases concerning the potential corruption of female readers, the fulcrum of the outrage triggered by Flaubert's novel indubitably resided in the desecration of the Bovary marriage. The bourgeoisie's capacity to absorb the shock of initially controversial art meant that *Madame Bovary*, which began by causing such a stir, rapidly became a massive *succès de scandale*. In later years Flaubert came to resent the public's unstinting *engouement* for a book which no subsequent work of his could dethrone in his readers' affections and esteem (a state of affairs that has remained unchanged to this day). In 1879 he wrote to his publisher—who had asked for permission to issue yet another reprint of the novel—to bemoan his inextricable association with one work alone:

---

[91] *SH*, 202.   [92] *U* 17: 2,196–7.
[93] Brown, *Joyce and Sexuality*, 12.

I'm fed up with *Bovary*. The constant mention of that book gets on my nerves. Everything I wrote after it doesn't exist.[94]

Yet in his frustration he may have underestimated the nature and extent of his novel's deeper impact on his readers. *Madame Bovary* became one of the iconic texts of its generation. The issues it raised accordingly became household topics. In absorbing a text that questioned one of its ideological pillars, the bourgeoisie left itself open to being changed by it. Habituation got the better of the fever of excitement and disgust that had initially greeted the book's serialization. The actual and symbolic place of marriage in society did begin to change—as *Ulysses*, which asks a different set of questions, duly illustrates.

How did the issues of sympathy that preoccupied Joyce in the preparation of *Exiles* shape *Ulysses*? Principally, those concerns, and their unconvincing realization in the play, seem to have prompted a return to the novel genre and to narrative techniques involving the use of point of view. That Bloom's reaction to the knowledge of his wife's adultery elicits sympathy and even admiration is due in large part to the intimacy which interior monologue establishes between character and reader. At the close of the novel, Molly also becomes one of the beneficiaries of this technique. Yet even as her long continuous interior monologue is privileged by its closing position the sense of belatedness in 'Penelope' also emphasizes Bloom's centrality. These structural choices invert the emphases of *Madame Bovary*. Narrative attention to Charles, as was repeatedly emphasized during the *Bovary* trial, frames the story of Emma's life.[95] The novel opens with a chronicle of Charles's youth, and closes with an account of his life and death after Emma's suicide: in the intervening years, Charles exists only on the fringes of Emma's life, off-centre. In *Ulysses*, by contrast, it is Molly who is relegated offstage for most of the novel. The arrangement fosters sympathy for Bloom, who profits from the reader's greater familiarity with him than with any other character.

Arguably equally decisive in effecting the successful shift of sympathy from the lover to the cuckold is Joyce's denial of interior monologue to the

---

[94] Flaubert to Georges Charpentier, 16 February 1879, *FS2*, 251 ['La *Bovary* m'embête. On me *scie* avec ce livre-là.—Car tout ce que j'ai fait depuis n'existe pas.' (*C5*, 543)].

[95] Pinard noted that 'it's with the husband that the book begins and ends' ['c'est le mari qui commence et qui termine le livre' (*MB 1910*, 559)]. By contrast, Sénard interpreted Charles's return to centrality at the end of the novel as an indication of Flaubert's endorsement: 'M. Flaubert is not only a great artist, but also a man of great heart for having, in the last six pages, poured all horror and contempt on the wife, and invested all interest in the husband.' ['M. Flaubert n'est pas seulement un grand artiste, mais un homme de coeur, pour avoir dans les six dernières pages déversé toute l'horreur et le mépris sur la femme, et tout l'intérêt sur le mari.' (*MB 1910*, 601)].

fancyman in *Ulysses*, Blazes Boylan. Boylan makes few appearances in the novel, and those that he does make unfold in an impressionistic style that reveals little about the man other than the clothes he wears and the formulaic fashion in which he behaves (the jingling refrain—'Jingle jingle jaunted jingling'[96]—that attaches to his every move emphasizes this). Boylan is a mere assemblage of parts ('Straw hat in sunlight. Tan shoes. Turnedup trousers.'[97]), who acts out 'the mere Dublin *idée reçue* of a fancyman or adulterer'.[98] Without interior monologue, Boylan remains a mere montage of adulterous code. He is, in this sense at least, no rival for Bloom. Therein lies one of the keys to the realization in *Ulysses* of the shift of sympathy Joyce had envisaged, with Flaubert in mind, since 1913.

As with so many aspects of Joyce's dealings with Flaubert, specific intertextual details act as signposts to more extensive and thoroughgoing forms of engagement. There are at least two instances in *Ulysses* in which Molly is cast as Emma to Leopold's Charles (in fact these two instances record the same event, twice narrated). When Molly's arm throws a coin out of the window of 7 Eccles Street in 'Wandering Rocks' ('a generous white arm from a window in Eccles street flung forth a coin'; 'A plump bare generous arm shone, was seen, held forth from a white petticoatbodice and taut shiftstraps. A woman's hand flung forth a coin over the area railings.'[99]), the reference is to *Madame Bovary*, which also twice describes an arm flung through a window in like fashion. In the first instance, Emma's naked hand appears through the window of the carriage in which she and Léon are making love (*Exiles*, as was mentioned above, also alludes to this moment):

> a bare hand emerged from between the tiny yellow cloth curtains and flung out some torn scraps of paper, which scattered in the breeze.[100]

The second instance occurs on Emma's last journey from Rouen to Yonville preceding her suicide. Again, the gesture takes place in a carriage, with Emma extending an arm out of the window to toss a coin to 'l'Aveugle' (who seems a likely forerunner to the blind stripling in Joyce's episode).[101] These two instances are paradoxically both telescoped and duplicated in Molly's twice-narrated gesture in 'Wandering Rocks'. The

[96] *U* 11: 15.   [97] *U* 8: 1,168.

[98] Brown, 'Shifting Sexual Centres', 67.

[99] *U* 10: 222–3 and *U* 10: 251–3.

[100] *MBE*, 217 ['une main nue passa sous les petits rideaux de toile jaune et jeta des déchirures de papier qui se dispersèrent au vent' (*MB*, 317)].

[101] 'Filled with disgust, Emma, over her shoulder, flung him a five-franc piece.'—*MBE*, 383 ['Emma, prise de dégoût, lui envoya, par-dessus l'épaule, une pièce de cinq francs.' (*MB*, 383)].

reference to the famous hackney-cab lovemaking scene of Flaubert's novel connects two acts of adultery (Molly is making ready for Boylan's arrival), while the allusion to Emma's gesture of despair reads as a (somewhat unsettling) reminder of difference rather than similarity—that is, of the fact that the danger associated with adultery in Flaubert's novel is eschewed in Joyce's.[102]

Extratextual facts support the suggestion that Joyce's engagement with Flaubert in *Exiles* and *Ulysses* was deliberate and self-conscious. Specifically, Joyce seems to have been interested in aspects of Flaubert's publication history. In suggesting that Joyce was inspired by the 1910 Conard edition of *Madame Bovary* in his *Exiles* note, Jacques Aubert remarks that:

> It was probably his interest in this edition which gave him the idea of offering *A Portrait* to a French publisher.[103]

Joyce's letters on the subject do indeed betray an eagerness to place *A Portrait* with Conard. In October 1915 he wrote to his agent, James Pinker:

> *A Portrait of the Artist as a Young Man*: May I suggest that you withdraw this from Messrs Duckworth and send it to Mr Louis Conard, 17 Boulevard de la Madeleine, Paris? [. . .] if recommendation be needed, besides the press

---

[102] Another echo of this very specific kind may obtain between Bloom's memories of his courtship of Molly in 'Lestrygonians' and Charles's awkward courtship of Emma at the beginning of Flaubert's novel. Bloom's vivid vision of his proposal to Molly on the Hill of Howth is brought on by the sight of buzzing flies: 'Stuck on the pane two flies buzzed, stuck.'—*U* 8: 896. In *Madame Bovary* a similar occurence marks the beginning of Charles's clumsy courtship of Emma: 'On the table, flies were crawling up the used glasses left from the last meal, and buzzing as they drowned in the remaining dregs of cider.' (*MBE*, 21) ['Des mouches, sur la table, montaient le long des verres qui avaient servi, et bourdonnaient en se noyant au fond, dans le cidre resté.' (*MB*, 43)]. Richard Ellmann notices the parallel and remarks that 'what Bloom remembers, as what Charles Bovary perceives, is beyond the flies, who frame and contrast the human scene'—*Ulysses on the Liffey* (London: Faber and Faber, 1972), 79. Following a genetic line of inquiry, Rabaté suspects a connection between the fact that the name of Léon Dupuis (Emma Bovary's second lover) starts off as 'Léopold' in the Flaubertian *scénarios* published in the 1910 Conard edition, speculating that Joyce found in them 'a neglected source of inspiration for the domestic dilemmas of Leopold Bloom' ['une source négligée d'inspiration pour les dilemmes domestiques de Léopold Bloom' (Jean-Michel Rabaté and Pierre-Marc de Biasi, 'Joyce, Flaubert, et *Exiles*', 166)]. As the name shifts from Flaubert's cuckold to Joyce's cuckoldee, Joyce may have seen the transfer of the name as a significant, if private, symbol of the sympathetic shift he hoped to effect. Such onomastic reasoning might also suggest a link (admittedly a highly superficial one) between Madame Bovary and Molly Bloom on the grounds that both abbreviate to the same initials, M. B.: 'M. B. loves a fair gentleman.'—*U* 12: 1,495.

[103] ['Sans doute est-ce son intérêt pour cette publication qui lui donna l'idée de proposer le *Portrait de l'artiste en jeune homme* à l'éditeur français.' (Jacques Aubert in Joyce, *Oeuvres*, vol. 1, 1,774)].

notices of my other books, it might be possible to obtain this from Mr Yeats or Mr Wells or Mr Pound.[104]

Joyce was still hoping for publication by Conard a month later, as is clear from a letter in November to Harriet Shaw Weaver:

> As it seems difficult to persuade London publishers to bring out my novel which appeared in your paper my agent, Mr Pinker, intends to try some firms in Paris: *Mercure de France* or Mr Conard.[105]

This interest in seeing his works published in the same format as Flaubert's was replicated in Joyce's later dealings with the American publisher of *Ulysses*. Flaubert had prefaced the first edition of *Madame Bovary* with a note of thanks to his defence lawyer stating that the trial had granted his novel 'an unexpected authority'.[106] Joyce's awareness of *Madame Bovary*'s tortuous publication history is clear from a letter penned to T. S. Eliot in December 1933:

> Dear Eliot: Thanks for your letter but the U.S. ban does not 'seem' to be lifted. It is lifted. [. . .] The defendant, Cerf, then said he would publish the book with an account of the proceedings (I suppose like the *édition définitive* of *Madame Bovary*) on 19 January next.[107]

The first American edition of *Ulysses* was published on this model, with the text of the novel preceded by preliminary materials documenting its rocky road to publication.[108] These comprised a foreword by the defence lawyer, Morris L. Ernst, the decision of the United States District Court rendered by Judge John M. Woolsey, and 'A Letter from Mr. Joyce to the Publisher'. Joyce's statement in the letter (dated 2 April 1932) recalls Flaubert's address to Maître Sénard. Referring to the 'complications which followed it [*Ulysses*] in America', he claims that 'they have given my book in print a life of its own'.[109]

---

[104] Joyce to James Pinker, 31 October 1915, *L1*, 84.

[105] Joyce to Harriet Shaw Weaver, 22 November 1915, *L3*, 369.

[106] ['une autorité imprévue' (*MB 1910*, iv)].

[107] Joyce to T. S. Eliot, 18 December 1933, *L3*, 295. Joyce was not the first to see a connection between these two highly publicized literary trials. The parallel was first drawn by the Irish critic Ernest Boyd in 'Adult or Infantile Censorship?', *The Dial*, 70:4 (April 1921), 384. As Paul Vanderham reports, 'Boyd complained that the US court lacked the civilized view of art expressed in the French decision that had exonerated Flaubert of corrupting public morals through *Madame Bovary* in 1857.'—*James Joyce and Censorship: The Trials of 'Ulysses'* (London: Macmillan Press, 1998), 55. It is intriguing, in the light of Boyd's comment, that the copies of *Madame Bovary* and *L'Éducation sentimentale* that Joyce bought as a student in 1901 later came into his possession—see Chapter 1, footnote 11.

[108] Joyce, *Ulysses* (New York: Random House, 1934).

[109] Joyce, *Ulysses* (New York: The Modern Library, 1961), xiii.

From the start, *Exiles* met with a more mixed reception than Joyce's previous works. Although he had encountered endless difficulties in finding publishers for *Dubliners* and *A Portrait*, he had at least, from 1914 onwards, seen his work actively championed by Pound. But the poet's response this time was frankly baffled:

> Yes, it is interesting. It won't do for the stage. [. . .]
> [. . .] even read it takes very close attention and concentration. I don't believe an audience could follow it or take it in [. . .]
> Roughly speaking, it takes about all the brains I've got to take in [the] thing, *reading*. And I suppose I've got more intelligence than the normal theatre goer (god save us).[110]

Despite Pound's lukewarm response, *Exiles* was eventually published in England and America in 1918. It soon ran into further difficulties, however, when Aurélien Lugné-Poë—the highly regarded avant-garde theatre director who had agreed to put on the play at his Théâtre de l'Oeuvre—reneged on his commitment at the last minute, explaining that another play involving very similar themes (*Le Cocu magnifique*, by Belgian playwright Fernand Crommelynck) had been a spectacular success, and that in its wake *Exiles* seemed certain to entail substantial financial losses.

Pound later wrote of *Exiles* that it was 'a side-step, necessary katharsis, clearance of mind from continental contemporary thought'.[111] The play has unquestionably struggled to find an audience: it is still, by and large, considered to be an aberration in the Joycean corpus, perhaps his only completed work not to be a masterpiece. But as this chapter has sought to show, there is a sense in which calling *Exiles* a side-step may offer an illuminating way of capturing the play's particular place in the unfolding narrative of Joyce's engagement with Flaubert. *Exiles* and *Ulysses* tell a story of their own when viewed in this context, charting the stages of an evolving, subtle, and self-conscious intertextual response.

---

[110] Pound to Joyce, 6–12 September 1915, *P/J*, 45. Even in his disappointment with Joyce's latest offering, Pound had Flaubert in mind. After expressing his reservations about the theatre in general (presumably to soften the blow of his discontent with Joyce's own efforts in that realm), he alludes to Flaubert's letters to George Sand, which often opened with the salutation, 'Chère maître': 'if I had written this letter last night (2 a.m) just after finishing the "Portrait", I should have addressed you "Cher Maître"./Now what would he want to write for the stage for/?????'—*P/J*, 46. Pound was wrong to assume that Flaubert did not write for the stage—he did (*Le Candidat*, 1874; *Le Château des Coeurs*, 1880), but with even less success than Joyce had with *Exiles*. Pound may also have had in mind Maupassant's addresses to Flaubert as his 'maître', most notably in his dedication to *Des Vers* (1880)—Guy de Maupassant, *Oeuvres poétiques complètes: Des Vers et autres poèmes*, ed. Emmanuel Vincent (Rouen: Publications de l'Université de Rouen, 2001), 33.

[111] Ezra Pound, '*Ulysses*', in *P/J*, 139.

5

Ulysses

ULYSSES AND LA TENTATION DE SAINT ANTOINE

The 'chaffering allincluding most farraginous chronicle'[1] that is *Ulysses* giddies the intertextual mind, resisting exhaustive cataloguing of its relations to other texts even as it seems to invite the endeavour. Nowhere more than in this seemingly all-encompassing work (except, perhaps, in *Finnegans Wake*) is the usefulness and value of the concept of intertextuality, with its defining eschewal of boundaries, more compellingly demonstrated. The following pages are written in recognition of the porosity of textual boundaries in *Ulysses*. They are—to borrow Fritz Senn's felicitous phrases—a highly selective series of 'Ulyssean close-ups' or 'inductive scrutinies'.[2] Concentrating on a number of salient Flaubertian nodes in Joyce's text, they seek to explore some of the ways in which these intertextual moments generate meaning.

Joyce's thoughts about *Ulysses* began to take shape long before work on the text commenced in earnest—long even before *Exiles* came into mental view. It was in September 1906 that Joyce first mentioned, in a letter to Stanislaus, his idea for a new short story about a Dublin-based Jew called Alfred H. Hunter.[3] Even in its most primitive form, Joyce's subject was defined by preoccupations that would remain clearly discernible in the finished novel: his sense of himself as an exile (as Richard Ellmann notes, 'The subject of the Jews had seized upon Joyce's attention as he began to recognize his place in Europe to be as ambiguous as theirs'), and his heightened interest in the theme of adultery ('The rumor of Hunter's unfaithful wife was known to him').[4] Over the years, Joyce's temporarily discarded project became subject to the limning of intertextual exposure. The embryonic idea of an adulterous motif, for instance, became inflected by Joyce's musings about *Madame Bovary*. The long gestation of *Ulysses*

---

[1] *U* 14: 1,412.
[2] Fritz Senn, *Ulyssean Close-ups* (Roma: Bulzoni Editore, 2007); *Inductive Scrutinies: Focus on Joyce*, ed. Christine O'Neill (Dublin: The Lilliput Press, 1995).
[3] Joyce to Stanislaus Joyce, 30 September 1906, *L2*, 168.
[4] *JJ*, 230.

allowed plenty of time for other corners of Flaubert's oeuvre to become relevant to Joyce's new project: one such formative reading encounter involved Flaubert's *La Tentation de saint Antoine*, which had already impinged on *Stephen Hero* and *A Portrait of the Artist* along the way.

Strong bibliographical grounds for an investigation of Joyce's use of *La Tentation* in *Ulysses* are provided by Ellmann, who cites a Triestine bookseller's bill bearing witness to Joyce's purchase of the book sometime between October 1913 and May 1914, along with two volumes of his *Premières Oeuvres* (which betray a marked predilection for the same dark, morbid, supernatural motifs).[5]

La Tentation de saint Antoine held a special place at the heart of Flaubert's creative life. In 1872 (the year in which the book was finally published) Flaubert described it to Mlle Leroyer de Chantepie as a lifetime's companion:

> Amid my sorrows I'm finishing my *Saint Antony*. It is the work of my life, as the idea for it first came to me in 1845, in Genoa, in front of a Brueghel painting and since then I have never left off thinking about it or doing relevant reading.[6]

Flaubert's recollection of the date, twenty-seven years on, is exact. On 13 May 1845 he had written from Genoa to his friend Alfred Le Poittevin to share his new ambition, expressing an excitement that would translate into decades of devotion to the theme:

> I saw a picture by Brueghel, *The Temptation of Saint Antony*, which made me think of arranging *The Temptation of Saint Antony* for the theatre. [...] I would certainly give the entire collection of *Le Moniteur* if I had such a thing

---

[5] *JJ*, 779. For the other Flaubertian items of Joyce's Triestine library, see Chapter 3, footnote 73. It is possible that Joyce's copy of *La Tentation* belonged to the eighteen-volume 1910 Conard edition of Flaubert's *Oeuvres complètes* (Paris: Louis Conard, 1910) which was discussed in Chapter 4 in relation to *Madame Bovary*. Other editions of *La Tentation* available to Joyce at this time were (Paris: Fasquelle, 1913) and (London: J. M. Dent; Paris: G. Crès, 1913). The Conard edition of *La Tentation* stands out as the first edition to include all three versions of *La Tentation*. The 1874 version was given prominence as the main reading text, while the versions of 1849 and 1856 were provided in an appendix. Flaubert's *Premières Oeuvres* (4 vols) were published by Fasquelle in Paris between 1913 and 1919. Volumes 1 and 2 appeared before the end of 1914 (which means that Joyce could have bought them in this edition at the same time as he purchased *La Tentation*). Similar texts had been published as part of Conard's 1910 *Oeuvres complètes* under the title *Oeuvres de jeunesse inédites*.

[6] Flaubert to Leroyer de Chantepie, 5 June 1872 ['Au milieu de mes chagrins, j'achève mon *Saint Antoine*. C'est l'oeuvre de toute ma vie, puisque la première idée m'en est venue en 1845, à Gênes, devant un tableau de Breughel et depuis ce temps-là je n'ai cessé d'y songer et de faire des lectures afférentes.' (*C4*, 531)].

and a hundred thousand francs as well, to buy that picture, which most who look at it certainly regard as inferior.[7]

When Flaubert was not at work on one of the three different versions of his *Tentation* (in 1848–9, 1856, and 1872 respectively), his thoughts about it filtered into other endeavours. Michel Foucault notes that:

> La Tentation runs through the whole of Flaubert's oeuvre. Beside the other texts, behind them, La Tentation forms a prodigious store of violences, of phantasms, chimeras, nightmares, buffoonish silhouettes.[8]

The book is certainly the formal hybrid Flaubert had from the start aspired to create. It is an imaginative recreation of the torment of temptation endured by Saint Antony during his hermitic retreat in a mode that combines decadent symbolism with medieval allegory, interweaving the pathetic and the burlesque. Alone in the wilderness, Antony experiences 'a conjuring up of spectres from the catacombs of consciousness', peering at and participating in 'processions of grotesque symbolic figures streaming across the desert'.[9] It is a highly visual prose rendition of a series of dramatized pageants, a surreal closet drama that constantly undermines its own legibility as either play or novel. It is a blend of the fruits of Flaubert's compulsively detailed research about the ancient world, and of some of his most deep-seated sensual fantasies. Harry Levin observes that:

> Though it does not adapt itself readily to formal classification, it is a philosophic closet-drama, an encyclopaedic prose-poem. Substantially, it is a dream [...] a play about an anchorite, an expressionistic monodrama in which temptation and flagellation were performed by the same actor upon himself.[10]

The work's reception was mixed from the outset. Maxime Du Camp and Louis Bouilhet, two of Flaubert's closest friends, could not abide it when the author first read it out to them, from beginning to end, in 1859.

---

[7] Flaubert to Alfred Le Poittevin, 13 May 1845, *GW*, 25–6 ['J'ai vu un tableau de Breughel [*sic*] représentant *La Tentation de saint Antoine*, qui m'a fait penser à arranger pour le théâtre *La Tentation de saint Antoine*. [...] Je donnerais bien toute la collection du *Moniteur* si je l'avais, et 100 mille francs avec, pour acheter ce tableau-là, que la plupart des personnages qui l'examinent regardent assurément comme mauvais.' (*CI*, 230)].

[8] ['*La Tentation* parcourt toute l'oeuvre de Flaubert. A côté des autres textes, derrière eux, il semble que *La Tentation* forme comme une prodigieuse réserve de violences, de fantasmagories, de chimères, de cauchemars, de profils bouffons.' (Michel Foucault, *La Bibliothèque fantastique: A propos de 'La Tentation de saint Antoine' de Gustave Flaubert* [Bruxelles: La Lettre volée, 1995], 6)].

[9] Stuart Gilbert, *James Joyce's 'Ulysses': A Study* (1930) (New York: Vintage Books, 1955), 320.

[10] Harry Levin, *The Gates of Horn: A Study of Five French Realists* (New York: Oxford University Press, 1966), 241–2.

Henry James's response to the third version was more favourable: on his view, *La Tentation* is 'a medley of wonderful bristling metals and polished agates'.[11] Ezra Pound, on the other hand, disliked the work intensely, and whilst conceding that it played a key role in the moulding of *Ulysses*,[12] dismissed it as 'something which matters now only as archaeology'.[13]

La Tentation in the Ulyssean 'Telemachiad'

Flaubertian reminiscences seem to impact on *Ulysses* from as early as 'Telemachus', wherein they subtend Stephen's thoughts about church heresiarchs. Joyce's interest in heresy is obvious from his earliest publications. 'The Day of the Rabblement' (1901) opens with an obscure allusion to Giordano Bruno, whom Joyce cryptically refers to merely as 'the Nolan'.[14] In 1903 Joyce wrote a review of a biography of Bruno in an article, 'The Bruno Philosophy', which was published in the Dublin *Daily Express*. In *Stephen Hero* and *A Portrait*, Bruno is discussed in the context of Stephen's Italian lesson with Father Artifoni: 'He said Bruno was a terrible heretic. I said he was terribly burned.'[15] In *Ulysses* this concern is still apparent, but Stephen now seems less preoccupied with heretics than with the founders and leaders of heretical schools: heresiarchs. Three figures feature prominently in his thoughts upon such matters: Arius, Valentine, and Sabellius. All three of these third- and fourth-century heresiarchs process through Stephen's mind in 'Telemachus':

> The proud potent titles clanged over Stephen's memory the triumph of their brazen bells: *et unam sanctam catholicam et apostolicam ecclesiam* [. . .] Symbol of the apostles in the mass of pope Marcellus, the voices blended, singing alone in loud affirmation: and behind their chant the vigilant angel of the church militant disarmed and menaced her heresiarchs. A horde of heresies fleeing with mitres awry: Photius and the brood of mockers of whom Mulligan was one, and Arius, warring his life long upon the consubstantiality of the Son with the Father, and Valentine, spurning Christ's terrene body, and the subtle African heresiarch Sabellius who held that the Father was

[11] James, 'Gustave Flaubert', *Macmillan's Magazine*, 339.

[12] Ezra Pound, 'James Joyce et Pécuchet', *P/J*, 207.

[13] Ezra Pound, 'Paris Letter', in *P/J*, 194.

[14] 'Rabblement', *OCPW*, 50.

[15] *P*, 210; the exchange features in the mode of direct speech in *SH*, 170. Joyce's dealings with heresy have been examined in two recently completed doctoral theses: Gareth Downes, 'James Joyce, Catholicism, and Heresy: With Specific Reference to Giordano Bruno', University of St Andrews, 2001; and Steven Morrison, 'Heresy, Heretics, and Heresiarchs in the Work of James Joyce', University of London, 2000. See also Gareth Downes, 'The Heretical *Auctoritas* of Giordano Bruno', *Joyce Studies Annual* (2003).

Himself His own Son. Words Mulligan had spoken a moment since in mockery to the stranger. Idle mockery. The void awaits surely all them that weave the wind.[16]

The passage abounds in connections to Flaubert. To begin with, Stephen's quotation from the Latin, '*et unam sanctam catholicam et apostolicam ecclesiam*' ('and in one holy Catholic and Apostolic Church'), derives from the Nicene Creed. The Creed was composed at the Council of Nicaea in 325, a meeting convened in a bid to curb the Arian and other Trinitarian heresies (the phrase Stephen recites was actually added to the Creed fifty-six years later at the Council of Constantinople, held in 381—twenty-five years after the 'real' Antony's death—to quell troubles and disagreements left unsolved at Nicaea).[17] The phrase echoes Saint Antony's declamation of this particular version of the creed in *La Tentation*:

> he repeats the symbol of Jerusalem [. . .]
>
> I believe in one God, the Father—and in one Lord, Jesus Christ—first-begotten son of God—who was incarnate and was made Man [. . .] and in one baptism of repentance—*and in one holy catholic Church*—and in the resurrection of the flesh—and in life eternal!'[18]

Stephen's Flaubertian musings in 'Telemachus' revolve around a word that is used relatively rarely in English: 'heresiarchs'. The *OED* suggests that the sixteenth-century French term *hérésiarque* is the English word's most immediate antecedent. *La Tentation* makes repeated use of the word. In the section of the text to which Flaubertian criticism habitually refers as *l'épisode des hérésiarques* (Part IV of *La Tentation*), the leaders of various heretical schools enounce their contestant versions of the Holy Trinity. Arius, Sabellius, and Les Valentiniens are the first to speak.[19] When Antony breaks down under the pressure of so much unorthodoxy, the heresiarchs join hands to form a 'horde of heresies' of the kind Stephen imagines: 'And all the heretics [*heresiarchs*] encircle Antony, who is crying,

---

[16] *U* 1: 650–62.

[17] Don Gifford, with Robert J. Seidman, *'Ulysses' Annotated: Notes for James Joyce's 'Ulysses'*, 2nd edn (London: University of California Press, 1989), 25.

[18] *TAE*, 188–9 (my emphasis) ['il répète le symbole de Jérusalem [. . .]/Je crois en un seul Dieu, le Père,—en un seul Seigneur, Jésus-Christ,—fils premier-né de Dieu,—qui s'est incarné et fait homme [. . .] et à un seul baptême de repentance,—*et à une seule sainte Église catholique*,—et à la résurrection de la chair,—et à la vie éternelle!' (*TA*, 157)].

[19] Valentine explains his religious views before the other heresiarchs (*TAE*, 106–7; *TA*, 76–7). In the *épisode des hérésiarques* itself, his followers, 'The Valentinians', enter first (*TAE*, 117; *TA*, 87); Valentine soon reappears, however, to take part in the debate in person (*TAE*, 118; *TA*, 88).

his head in his hands.'[20] The text's typography and layout emphasizes the heresiarchs' new status as a group character. Capitalized at the centre, they become:

THE HERETICS [LES HÉRÉSIARQUES][21]

It is Stephen's choice of heresiarchs and the manner of his swift mental reckoning, however, that most clearly aligns this passage with *La Tentation*. As Senn notes: 'The similarity is mainly in the quick succession of position statements.'[22] *Ulysses* also replicates Flaubert's focus on Arius (who gives the opening speech at the heresiarchs' assembly), with Stephen's mind returning to him in both 'Proteus' and 'Circe'.

While the fit between the heresiarchs in 'Telemachus' and their namesakes in *La Tentation* is so perfect as to make a connection seem indisputable, Joyce's inclusion of Photius unsettles the neat symmetry between the two texts. Photius comes first in Stephen's mental listing, and is aligned with Buck Mulligan as a mocker. Whereas Arius, Sabellius, and Valentine lived in the second, third, and fourth centuries, Photius lived in the ninth century; and although very much at the heart of religious and political controversy, Photius was no heresiarch. The *Catholic Encyclopedia* describes him as 'one of the worst enemies the Church of Christ ever had, and the cause of the greatest calamity that ever befell her'.[23] This refers to the Eastern schism that Photius initiated, and which culminated in the separation of the Eastern Orthodox and Roman Catholic Churches in 1054. Joyce may have associated Photius and Arius because of the extreme divisions both occasioned within the Church. According to Rowan Williams, Arius's questioning of established beliefs was so venomously resented that he was in consequence 'irrevocably cast as the Other in relation to Catholic (and civilized) religion'.[24] But whereas Arius's divisiveness resulted from doctrinal heresy, the fractures caused by Photius were the outcome of political scheming. Photius's career consisted in a series of excommunications from and restorations to the Church (when in power Photius himself excommunicated the Pope). This tendency to veer between opposite positions may explain why Stephen associates Photius with

---

[20]   *TAE*, 118 ['Et tous les hérésiarques font un cercle autour d'Antoine, qui pleure la tête dans ses mains.' (*TA*, 88)].

[21]   *TAE*, 119; *TA*, 88.

[22]   Fritz Senn, 'Trivia Ulysseana IV, Brood of Tempters', *JJQ*, vol. 19, no. 2 (Winter 1982), 152.

[23]   'Photius of Constantinople', in *The Catholic Encyclopedia*, http://www.newadvent.org/cathen/12043b.htm (July 2011).

[24]   Rowan Williams, *Arius: Heresy and Tradition*, 2nd edn (London: scm press, 2001), 1.

Buck Mulligan, whose manipulative ambivalence (especially in his dealings with Haines) so irks Stephen.

Stephen's thoughts imply that Photius and Mulligan are merely 'idle
mockers', and that, by contrast, Arius, Sabellius, and Valentine should be
taken seriously. But Joyce almost certainly knew that Flaubert's Arius has
none of the arch-seriousness with which Stephen's imagination endows
him. In *La Tentation*, Arius writes catchy ditties to disseminate heretical
Trinitarian ideas:

with bursts of laughter—a song rises in which the name of Jesus recurs. [. . .]

ARIUS

[. . .] I've composed some little poems, so funny that people know them off
by heart in the mills and the taverns and the ports.[25]

Such frivolity seems a likely precedent for Mulligan's blasphemous
levity at the beginning of *Ulysses*. The parallel between Arius's mirthful
mocking and Mulligan's religious clowning is striking. Like Arius's songs,
Mulligan's 'Ballad of Joking Jesus' satirizes the Christian doctrine of a
God-begotten, consubstantial Christ:

He [. . .] began to chant in a quiet happy foolish voice:
—*I'm the queerest young fellow that ever you heard.*
My mother's a jew, my father's a bird.
With Joseph the joiner I cannot agree.[26]

Mulligan's behaviour has much in common with that of Flaubert's heresiarchs: indeed his frolicsome larks may well be the trigger to Stephen's
recall of *La Tentation*. Mulligan's 'capering' replicates the taunting, frisky
animation of the heresiarchs. His 'hat quivering in the fresh wind' and
'fluttering [. . .] winglike hands'[27] seem related to Stephen's mental image
of the heresiarchs' flapping headgear ('mitres awry') and 'weav[ing] [of]
the wind'. Similarly, Mulligan's playful tottering above the forty-foot hole
seems to adumbrate Stephen's thoughts about 'the void' that 'awaits surely
all them that weave the wind'.[28]

If Mulligan's Arian antics by the sea play a subliminal part in shaping
the Flaubertian strain of Stephen's thoughts concerning Church history,
one of Haines's questions may also be conducive to such associations:

---

[25] *TAE*, 116–17 ['une chanson s'élève avec des éclats de rire, où le nom de Jésus revient.
[. . .]/ARIUS/[. . .] j'ai composé de petits poèmes tellement drôles, qu'on les sait par coeur
dans les moulins, les tavernes et les ports' (*TA*, 86)].
[26] *U* 1: 581–6.
[27] *U* 1: 600–2.
[28] *U* 1: 661–2.

—You're not a believer, are you? Haines asked. I mean, a believer in the narrow sense of the word. Creation from nothing and miracles and a personal God.[29]

The phrase 'Creation from nothing', like much else in this first episode of *Ulysses*, harks back to the last chapter of *A Portrait of the Artist as a Young Man*, in which Stephen had echoed Flaubert's analogy between the creating artist and the God of creation, thereby effectively making himself a proponent of a poetics of creation from nothing. Stephen's thoughts about heresy in 'Proteus' centre around the same words:

> One of her sisterhood lugged me squealing into life. Creation from nothing. What has she in the bag? A misbirth with a trailing navelcord, hushed in ruddy wool. The cords of all link back, strandentwining cable of all flesh. That is why mystic monks. Will you be as gods?[30]

Stephen's distaste regarding the biological realities of human birthing is clear. The imagined midwives (who are invested with a religious aura by Stephen's mental reference to their 'sisterhood') give rise to thoughts of death rather than of birth: in lieu of the Christ-like image of a child wrapped in swaddling clothes, Stephen's mind conjures the gruesome image of newborn crying silenced, 'hushed in ruddy wool'. Human beginnings, including Stephen's own, are associated with violence ('lugged me into life'), distress ('squealing'), and the possibility of blood and dire failure ('a misbirth'). Stephen's aversion regarding these universal physiological processes recalls the shock that the discovery of the word 'foetus' had caused him in *A Portrait*,[31] and is in keeping with his quest, in both novels, for a mode of spiritual paternity that would circumvent the unpalatable bodily facts of physical reproduction. By contrast, godly creation smacks of absolute simplicity, logical absurdity ('Creation from nothing'), and mathematical clarity: 'Aleph, alpha: nought, nought, one'[32]—all of which Stephen finds formally pleasing. His Flaubertian conception of the artist as an analogue of 'the God of the creation'[33] seems to underpin these thoughts: 'Creation from nothing' and 'Will you be as gods?' (the latter phrase echoing the serpent's words to Eve in Genesis 3:5—'Ye shall be as gods') aptly sum up the earlier formula. As against these thoughts of ex nihilo creation, Stephen's vision of 'trailing navelcords' and of 'the cords of all link[ing] back' provides a stunning image for both human and textual descendency—that is, for intertextuality. Paradoxical ideas of increasing distance from, as well as enduring

---

[29] *U* 1: 611–13.   [30] *U* 3: 35–8.   [31] *P*, 75.
[32] *U* 3: 39–40.   [33] *P*, 181.

continuity with, an original moment of creation combine in Stephen's vision of a 'strandentwining cable of all flesh'. As a noun and as a verb, 'strand' does double duty. As a noun combined with a gerund ('entwining'), it images Joyce's work as a multifarious textual fabric in which strings and yarns and threads and filaments are woven together to form a rope or cord or line or cable. As a verb, the word evokes precarious continuity, combining suggestions of erosion and tearing (the term can denote the breaking of one or more strands of a rope) and of creative meshing. Whichever way the compound is parsed, intertextuality is adumbrated as a cord of connection between 'the now, the here'[34] and their point of origin: as a textual cable stretching across time and space, taut and twisted from the tensions between identity and adaptation. Whereas genealogical and textual descent leave traces on bodily and textual surfaces ('Gaze in your *omphalos*'[35]), the works of a Flaubertian author-God would bear no intertextual markings of any kind, being the equivalent in literature of:

> naked Eve. She had no navel. Gaze. Belly without blemish, bulging big, a buckler of taut vellum.[36]

The word 'vellum' makes explicit the literary analogy subtending Stephen's musings.[37] Like an untouched roll of parchment, Eve's navel-less body is an unmarked page, a text without an intertext: an utterly original text. By contrast, intertextuality—like the human body after Adam and Eve, with its navels and blemishes—is a mark of the human condition, an inescapable fact of literary creation.

A problem emerges here in that Stephen's mental picture of trailing navelcords suggests an adherence to a model of literary relations that is based on influence rather than intertextuality. The cords, despite their unimaginable lengths, ultimately lead back to an origin: Stephen's musings remain encased within a biblical train of thought that involves those origins whose very existence the intertextualists so insistently deny. At this point it is crucial to remember that Stephen has lost faith in the Christian symbolic system from which his mind coins its images: just as he knows that artists cannot be as gods, so does his disbelief in biblical Scripture undercut the truth value of his conjured image of Eve's blank belly as a site

---

[34] *U* 9: 89.

[35] *U* 3: 38.

[36] *U* 3: 41–2.

[37] Maud Ellmann discusses these correspondences between flesh and word, and these oppositions between godly creation and intertextuality, in her essay: 'Polytropic Man: Paternity, Identity, and Naming in *The Odyssey* and *A Portrait of the Artist as a Young Man*', in *James Joyce: New Perspectives*, ed. Colin MacCabe (Brighton: Harvester Press, 1982), 101.

of origin, leaving only a properly intertextual sense of infinite textual and human connectivity.

It is against the backdrop of such musings that Arius re-enters Stephen's interior monologue:

> Wombed in sin darkness I was too, made not begotten. By them, the man with my voice and my eyes and a ghostwoman with ashes on her breath. They clasped and sundered, did the coupler's will. From before the ages He willed me and now may not will me away or ever. A *lex externa* stays about Him. Is that then the divine substance wherein Father and Son are consubstantial? Where is poor dear Arius to try conclusions? Warring his life long on the contransmagnificandjewbangtantiality. Illstarred heresiarch. In a Greek watercloset he breathed his last: euthanasia. With beaded mitre and with crozier, stalled upon his throne, widower of a widowed see, with upstiffed omophorion, with clotted hinderparts.[38]

Stephen tries to make sense of 'consubstantiality'—a dogma first asserted at Nicaea, according to which Christ was 'begotten, not made'. Contra this, Arius claimed, as he does in Flaubert's *Tentation*, that Christ was 'made' (not begotten) and that He was, therefore, God's 'creature'. This echoes Stephen's conviction, expressed as early as *Stephen Hero*, that artists and art are 'made', not 'born':

> He was not convinced of the truth of the saying [*Poeta nascitur, non fit*] 'The poet is born not made' but he was quite sure of the truth of this at least: [*Poema fit, non nascitur*] 'The poem is made not born.'[39]

In 'Proteus' Stephen thinks of himself as 'made not begotten' and of his own birth as having been 'willed' 'From before the ages'. In this way, he establishes a rapprochement between himself and Arius, and distance between himself and his biological parents who, in doing 'the coupler's will', were also, unwittingly, doing God's will, abiding by His '*lex externa*'. According to this *lex externa* (as defined by Thomas Aquinas):

> While not as yet existing in themselves things nevertheless exist in God in so far as they are foreseen and preordained by Him.[40]

This explains how Christ can have been begotten by God while also being consubstantial—that is co-eternal—with Him. Having stated the orthodox view about God's *lex externa* and questioned the orthodox view about Christ's begetting, Stephen suddenly turns the tables on his own tentative

---

[38] *U* 3: 45–54.
[39] *SH*, 33.
[40] Thomas Aquinas, *Summa Theologica*, Prima Secundae, Query 91, article 1, 'Varieties of Law', quoted in Gifford, *'Ulysses' Annotated*, 47.

musings, wishing Arius were at hand to be his theological whetstone: 'Where is poor Arius to try conclusions?'

Senn's survey of Joyce's invocation of the Flaubertian heresiarchs in *Ulysses* ends by suggesting that:

> While Stephen is fretting publicly against three masters, perhaps his creator is silently acknowledging a master of his own choice, one, curiously, that is never mentioned at all and remains mostly invisible, but is recognizable at times within the handiwork.[41]

If Joyce is 'silently acknowledging a master' in Flaubert, the densely textured opening of 'Proteus' subtly hints at Stephen's growing awareness that all texts are connected by 'strandentwining cables'—that all texts are, in fact, 'strandentwining cables'. Nothing, he realizes, is created out of nothing: 'nothing', as Leopold Bloom realizes later in the day, is 'new under the sun'.[42]

La Tentation in 'Circe'

There is a long-standing critical tradition of adducing *La Tentation de saint Antoine* as a source for the 'Circe' episode of *Ulysses*. The idea was first emitted by Pound in his 'Paris Letter' of June 1922: Joyce, he stated, 'has swallowed the Tentation de St Antoine [*sic*] whole, it serves as a comparison for a single episode in *Ulysses*'.[43] In asserting as much, Pound knowingly or unknowingly echoed a phrase used by James in his 1893 review of Flaubert's letters. There James stated that the best way to appreciate Flaubert would be to 'swallow him whole'. To do this, as James advocated, would be 'the best way to appreciate him', to 'cherish him as a perfect example'—thus would 'his weaknesses fall into their place'.[44] James's sense of the Flaubertian oeuvre as a luminous, nourishing feast for future generations of writers is transformed by Pound's act of critical misprision. For Pound, Joyce's incorporation of *La Tentation* is understood as cathartic, purgative—an act of denigration rather than a tribute, an improvement involving annihilation. As much is clear from 'James Joyce et Pécuchet', Pound's next essay on Joyce's connection to Flaubert, and that in which he most openly expresses his view of literary history as a violent, murderous battle of the titans. Arguing that Jules Laforgue dealt Flaubert's 'romans historiques' (presumably *La Tentation* and *Salammbô*) their death blows, Pound declares that:

---

[41] Senn, 'Trivia Ulysseana', 153.   [42] *U* 13: 1,104–5.
[43] Pound, 'Paris Letter', *P/J*, 194.   [44] James, 'Gustave Flaubert', 339.

The efficient critic is the artist who comes after, to kill or to inherit; to surpass, to augment, or to diminish and bury a form.[45]

In Pound's view, Joyce follows James's instruction, absorbing Flaubert but discarding his work's failings and weaknesses: whether his writing 'overcomes and augments' or 'buries' Flaubert's form is not spelt out. But the understanding of literary relations encapsulated in Pound's phrases sits uncomfortably with the outlook shadowed forth in *Ulysses*, which strongly contradicts Pound's aggressive images of authors feeding off each other's corpuses, annihilating each other's example by ingurgitation. Indeed Joyce's writing delineates a peaceful vision of inevitable, mutually inform-ing and enriching textual coexistence. Whereas Pound sees literary evolu-tion as a matter of usurpation, a cultural analogue of the Darwinian idea of the survival of the fittest, Joyce's conception reiterates Darwin's emphasis on connection: the textual world, on this view, is, like the natural world, an 'inextricable web of affinities', a mesh of verbal threads and filaments vitally connecting texts to each other, performing those life-giving, nur-turing functions that umbilical cords fulfil for human beings.[46] Joyce's version of incorporation prefers collaboration over competition, commu-nion over cannibalism.

Whereas Pound states that 'Circe' 'correspond[s] to' and improves on *La Tentation*,[47] Wyndham Lewis, in his notoriously scathing 'Analysis of the Mind of James Joyce' (1927), adopted the parallel only to emphasize the inferiority of 'Circe':

> Nor really can the admirable Goya-like fantasia in the middle of the book, in which all the characters enjoy a free metaphysical existence [...] be com-pared for original power of conception with the *Tentation*.[48]

In *James Joyce and the Making of 'Ulysses'* (1934), Frank Budgen, placing Flaubert within a wider intertextual network, more neutrally listed *La Tentation* as one of the works with which 'Circe' is most often aligned. Joyce's Nighttown episode, he noted:

---

[45] ['Le critique efficace est l'artiste qui vient après, pour tuer ou pour hériter; pour dépasser, pour augmenter, pour diminuer et enterrer une forme.' (Pound, 'James Joyce et Pécuchet', *P/J*, 203)].

[46] Charles Darwin, *On the Origin of Species*, ed. Gillian Beer (Oxford: Oxford University Press, 2008), 319.

[47] 'A single chapter of *Ulysses* (157 pages) corresponds to the *Tentation de saint Antoine*.' ['Un seul chapitre de *Ulysses* (157 pages) correspond à la *Tentation de saint Antoine*.' (Pound, 'James Joyce et Pécuchet', *P/J*, 207)].

[48] Wyndham Lewis, 'An Analysis of the Mind of James Joyce', in *Time and Western Man* (London: Chatto & Windus, 1927), 91–130 (121).

has justly been compared with the Walpurgisnacht in Goethe's *Faust*, to Flaubert's *La Tentation de saint Antoine* and to Strindberg's *Dream Play*.[49]

Occasional mentions of Flaubert's text have remained an enduring feature of critical writing on 'Circe'. Such intimations have occasionally been expanded into broader comparative investigations. In *Flaubert and Joyce*, Richard Cross devotes Chapter VII to 'Expressionism in *La Tentation de saint Antoine* and "Circe"'.[50] In 1988 Elizabeth Brunazzi wrote a doctoral thesis on 'The Autogenetic Text in Flaubert's *La Tentation de saint Antoine* and Joyce's *Ulysses*'.[51] In 1990 Richard Brown examined 'an aspect of *The Temptation of Saint Anthony* in his essay on 'Shifting Sexual Centres'.[52] Although these provide valuable expansions of the habitual mode of laconic academic allusion to Flaubert as a forerunner to Joyce, each contribution remains focused on a discrete set of resemblances. As a result, critical understanding of the relationship between these two works remains splintered and fragmentary. The following pages seek to remedy some of these lacunae by addressing a range of different forms of intertextual connection that obtain between 'Circe' and *La Tentation*. These include structural and technical parallels, major correspondences in character, plot, and theme, and localized linguistic echoes.

Structural and Technical Parallels

While writing the 'Circe' episode of *Ulysses*, Joyce confessed to Harriet Shaw Weaver that 'Like its fellows it presents for me great technical difficulties'.[53] Flaubert's three different versions of *La Tentation* powerfully illustrate his perfectionism in the quest for the ideal form for his dark imaginings; Joyce was similarly uncompromising in his Circean labours, famously asserting in a letter to John Quinn that he had written the text 'nine times from first to last'.[54] Might some of Joyce's 'great technical difficulties' have sprung from his engagement with Flaubert's own tortured text? At all events, the recognition of Joyce's use of structures and techniques deployed by Flaubert in *La Tentation* explains many of the more peculiar and arresting features of the make-up of 'Circe'.

[49] Budgen, *James Joyce and the Making of 'Ulysses'*, 252.

[50] 'The Nethermost Abyss: Expressionism in *La Tentation de saint Antoine* and "*Circe*"'— *F&J*, 125–49.

[51] Elizabeth Brunazzi, 'The Autogenetic Text in Flaubert's *La Tentation de saint Antoine* and Joyce's *Ulysses*', Ph.D, Princeton University (Ann Arbor: U.M.I. Research Press, 1988).

[52] Brown, subsection entitled 'an aspect of *The Temptation of Saint Anthony*' in 'Shifting Sexual Centres' (77–83).

[53] Joyce to Harriet Shaw Weaver, 12 July 1920, *SL*, 266.

[54] Joyce to John Quinn, 7 January 1921, *L1*, 156.

The basic structure of *La Tentation* and 'Circe' is identical: from a book (the Bible in one case, the preceding episodes of *Ulysses* in the other) emerges a long series of hallucinations. This conceit is explicit in *La Tentation*.[55] At the book's opening Antony turns to the Bible to combat his mounting despair, nervously flicking through its pages at random.[56] There is a clear relationship between the biblical passages Antony reads out and his subsequent hallucinations: the former unmistakably sow the seeds of the latter. Antony's Queen of Sheba hallucination, for instance, stems directly from a sentence encountered on one of the pages he peruses:

> *Now when the queen of Sheba heard of the fame of Solomon, she came to tempt him with hard questions.*[57]

The whole of *La Tentation* functions as an intratextual enactment of the original matrix of Antony's biblical reading. To be more precise: this enactment is intertextual in the sense that its scenes clearly derive from the Bible, but intratextual in the sense that Antony's hallucinations spring exclusively from those biblical passages that are interpolated in the opening pages of the book—those that are integral to the make-up of *La Tentation* from the very beginning.

Likewise, intratextuality is one of the governing principles in 'Circe', to the point that it can seem as though everything in 'Circe' is connected by a 'strandentwining cable' to other parts of *Ulysses*. Stuart Gilbert aptly sums up this creative dynamic by stating that in 'Circe': '*Ex nihilo nihil fit*; even the magician Circe could only transform, not create.'[58] In his discussion of the episode, Hugh Kenner compares *Ulysses* to a linguistic system or 'collective vocabulary', which 'Circe' plunders for its textual elements. According to this argument, the recycling of details from earlier episodes in 'Circe' enacts and creates an intratextual grammar of borrowing and transformation, conflation and dissemination:

---

[55] Gilbert initiated a misunderstanding regarding the 'Circe'-*Tentation* connection by arguing that Antoine's hallucinations arise randomly, rather than being subject to the intratextual logic that governs the episode: 'Generally, however, in the *Tentation*, the phantoms arise automatically, as it were, out of the inane, whereas "Circe"'s "temptations" are always prepared, the logical amplification of some real object, glosses of some silent or uttered thought.'—*James Joyce's 'Ulysses'*, 320. Cross restates Gilbert's view of Antoine's hallucinations as free-floating visions bearing no connection to any other part of the text: 'The fact that the hallucinations in "Circe" are carefully prepared for gives them a resonance generally lacking in the *Tentation* [...] Antoine waits passively in the empty desert night while scenes randomly appear and vanish.'—*F&J*, 128. Brown takes this view on board without question—'Shifting Sexual Centres', 80.

[56] *TAE*, 66–8; *TA*, 33–5.

[57] *TAE*, 68 ['*La Reine de Saba, connaissant la gloire de Salomon, vint le tenter, en lui proposant des énigmes.*' (*TA*, 35)].

[58] Gilbert, *James Joyce's 'Ulysses'*, 319.

As for the so-called hallucinations [. . .] All we can safely say of their detail is that it tends to come from earlier in the book, a sort of collective vocabulary out of which, it seems, anything at all can now be composed.[59]

Brown even wonders whether:

we might discover that there is nothing in 'Circe' that is not a recapitulation of something occurring in the earlier parts of the book or even that there is nothing in the earlier parts of the book that does not get, in some way, re-cycled or re-cannibalised here.[60]

Joyce's self-consciousness regarding the intra- and intertextual dimensions of 'Circe' is adumbrated by a cryptic exchange between Bloom and his father concerning Virag's roll of parchment. 'Mnemo?', asks Bloom. To which Virag 'excitedly' answers: 'I say so. I say so. E'en so. Technic.'[61] The passage refers to memory ('mnemotechnic'), upon which both intra- and intertextuality depend, but also to 'Circe''s 'technic', named as 'hallucination' in the 'Gilbert schema' (produced in 1921 to help Stuart Gilbert make sense of *Ulysses*).[62] The word is eminently relevant to Flaubert's role in the shaping of this episode. Indeed, hallucination was a bewildering, distressing, and recurring feature of the author's life. Flaubert's first experience of hallucination, widely believed to have marked the onset of epilepsy, took place in 1844, when he was twenty-two years old. Many violent fits followed. Amid serious worries that he might die, the aspiring author was freed from parental pressure to continue his (disastrously unsuccessful) studies in law: out of hallucination sprang a lifetime of freedom to pursue his artistic vocation. In the 1860s Flaubert wrote an account of his experience of such crises in a letter to his friend Hippolyte Taine, who was then at work on a treatise on the workings of the human mind.[63] Flaubert's description of the sensations that hallucination provoked in him involve lightning, memory, fireworks, and blood loss:

Then, as sudden as lightning, a seizure, or rather an instantaneous irruption of *memory*, for hallucination properly speaking is precisely that, at least in my case. It is a malady of the memory, a letting go of its entire contents. You feel the images pouring out of you like a stream of blood. It seems as if everything in your

[59] Hugh Kenner, *Ulysses* (London: George Allen & Unwin, 1980), 123.

[60] Richard Brown, '"Everything" in "Circe"', in *Reading Joyce's 'Circe'*, ed. Andrew Gibson, *European Joyce Studies* 3 (Amsterdam: Rodopi, 1994), 233.

[61] *U* 15: 2,390–2.

[62] The slightly different schema produced for Carlo Linati in 1920 (known as the 'Linati schema') lists the 'technic' of 'Circe' as 'vision animated to bursting point'. The Gilbert and Linati schemas are reproduced in James Joyce, *Ulysses*, ed. Jeri Johnson (Oxford: Oxford University Press, 1993), 734–5 and 736–9 respectively.

[63] Hippolyte Taine, *De l'intelligence*, 2 vols (Paris: Hachette, 1870).

head is going off at once like the thousand pieces of a firework, and there's no time to look at these internal images that go marching past at a furious pace.[64]

The dreadful uncontrollability of the occurrence is suggested by Flaubert's use of the word in *La Tentation* to describe Antony's incapacity to oppose any resistance to its enthralling force: 'hallucination again grips him'.[65] 'Circe' seems to draw attention to its adoption of hallucination as a 'technic' by referring to the phenomenon. J. J. O'Molloy, for instance, defends Bloom's behaviour by invoking 'a momentary aberration of heredity, brought on by hallucination'.[66]

There is an important difference, however, in the ways hallucination operates in these two texts. *La Tentation* clearly establishes the status of Antony's visions as hallucinations. The hallucinations in 'Circe' do not conform to this model. As Charles Peake explains:

> The technique of the 'Circe' chapter is 'Hallucination', but this does not refer to hallucinations experienced by the characters. The technique is operative in the descriptions of the Mabbot street entrance of Nighttown before Stephen and Bloom arrive there and in the interval between Stephen's departure to the brothel and Bloom's entry. 'Hallucination' is the mode of the chapter.[67]

'Hallucination' in 'Circe', in other words, is a 'technic' or mode of writing rather than a perceptual experience. Flaubert's *Tentation* anticipates expressionist drama in endowing the figments of Antony's mind with the status of characters; Joyce retains this mode of writing but takes it further, because many of the objects and persons granted character status in 'Circe' have no 'real' existence in terms of either plot, or perception, or conscious thought (no character, that is, is actually bearing them in mind at the point at which they make their 'appearance' in 'Circe'). Antony is at least intermittently conscious that he is hallucinating. The same is not true of Bloom and Stephen in 'Circe'. Peake observes that 'Bloom is clearly not in a hallucinated state'[68] and that, unlike Stephen, he is not even drunk.

---

[64] Flaubert to Hippolyte Taine, 1 December 1866, *GW*, 318 ['Puis, tout à coup, comme la foudre, un envahissement ou plutôt irruption instantanée *de la mémoire* car l'hallucination proprement dite n'est pas autre chose,—pour moi, du moins. C'est une maladie de la mémoire, une relâchement de ce qu'elle recèle. On sent les images s'échapper de vous comme des flots de sang. Il vous semble que tout ce qu'on a dans la tête éclate à la fois comme les mille pièces d'un feu d'artifice, et on n'a pas le temps de regarder ces images internes qui défilent avec furie.' (*C3*, 572)].

[65] *TAE*, 125 ['l'hallucination le reprenant' (*TA*, 95)].

[66] *U* 15: 944–5.

[67] Charles Peake, *James Joyce: The Citizen and the Artist* (London: Edward and Arnold, 1977), 263.

[68] Peake, *James Joyce*, 265.

Furthermore, his mind, insofar as its contents are revealed in subsequent episodes, registers no memory of the vast majority of the hallucinations in which he is involved in the Nighttown episode: 'The only inference is that his conscious mind is totally unaware of them.'[69] Kenner, who argues the same point, interprets the Messianic episode of Bloom's rise and fall as a sequence that:

> articulates and extends a transient Bloomish feeling of which his observable behaviour displays no trace, and there is no later sign that he remembers it or has even been aware of it.[70]

These observations open up a rift between *La Tentation* and 'Circe'. Antony's hallucinations are always Antony's at the same time as we are privy to them. In 'Circe', on the other hand, the 'so-called hallucinations appear [...] primarily to the mind of the text'[71]—by which Kenner means, of course, that it is to us, the text's readers, that the hallucinations appear as such:

> The 'hallucinations' exist almost wholly for us. We, if not Bloom, see many strange things in this long episode.[72]

The hallucinatory mode of 'Circe', then, differs significantly from the hallucinations represented in *La Tentation*: too literal a reading of Joyce's stated 'technic' risks occluding what is really going on in the episode. That said, at least one of the 'hallucinations' in 'Circe', involving the appearance of Stephen's mother, is a 'real hallucination': a vision that *can* be attributed to Stephen. At the climax of the episode, the circumstances required to make such a vision credible are brought together. Peake notes that:

> as he grows progressively drunker, the boundary between his consciousness and his unconscious becomes confused and uncertain, until, in the giddiness following his whirling and frenzied dance, his conscious mind loses control. His dialogue with his mother's corpse differs from the other 'hallucinatory' episodes because Stephen does not know where he is or what he is doing: this is real hallucination.[73]

The genuinely hallucinatory quality of this vision adds to the likeliness of an intertextual connection to Antony's vision of his own mother at the end of *La Tentation* (this is discussed in detail below). The vision's status as a 'real hallucination' acts as a reminder of the role played by the subconscious in this episode. Like Antony, Joyce's characters are enthralled to their hidden drives. This explains why the dream analogy has become such

---

[69] Peake, *James Joyce*, 265.   [70] Kenner, *Ulysses*, 120.
[71] Kenner, *Ulysses*, 120.   [72] Kenner, *Ulysses*, 121.   [73] Peake, *James Joyce*, 273.

a staple of critical commentary on 'Circe': 'like dreams', 'Circe' is taken to be 'symbolically representative of the climate of the unconscious'.[74] Such discussions often register the likelihood of Joyce's indebtedness to August Strindberg's *A Dream Play*: and indeed, dreamlike, hallucinatory, and theatrical elements combine in 'Circe'—as in Flaubert's closet drama and as in Strindberg's expressionist theatre—'to create a symbolic drama of the unconscious'.[75]

In discussing the hallucinatory quality of 'Circe', Fredric Jameson refers to the dramatic framework adopted in the episode as a means of 'bind[ing] [. . .] discontinuous images' imported from other parts of *Ulysses*.[76] Kenner refers to the playscript format as a means of blurring the boundaries between the realms of the actual and the hallucinated, the public and the private:

> Nothing, in 'Circe', distinguishes 'real' from 'hallucinatory', nor any part of the episode from any other. Format and idiom are homogenous throughout: speakers' names in CAPITALS, spoken words in Roman type, narration and description in the *italics* of stage-directions.[77]

These comments are accurate to *La Tentation* as well as to 'Circe': the playscript layout constitutes the most prominent area of similarity between the two texts. Both texts are poised between theatrical and novelistic writing. A reader flicking through the pages of either text might think a traditional stage play at hand, but such misapprehensions are rapidly dispelled: the illusion of stageable drama cannot survive the briefest of investigations.

This faux theatricality is a deliberate and important characteristic of these texts. Each includes a number of self-conscious *clins d'oeil* to the conventions of staged theatre. *La Tentation*, for instance, is divided into seven parts, each of which starts on a new page beneath a Roman numeral. The change from one section to the next often corresponds to a change of scene, as it might in the theatre—but these section breaks are merely mock-theatrical 'Acts', and that word is never used in its theatrical sense between the covers of the book. Moreover, Flaubert cultivates a sense of scenographic space by setting his character on a stage-like platform. Benoît Tadié likens the form of *La Tentation* and of 'Circe' to that of the nineteenth-century panorama, which would condense 'historical and allegorical scenes into continuous spectacles apprehended by the gaze of the

[74] Peake, *James Joyce*, 265.
[75] Peake, *James Joyce*, 269.
[76] Fredric Jameson, '*Ulysses* in History', in *James Joyce and Modern Literature*, ed. W. J. McCormack and Alistair Stead (London: Routledge and Kegan Paul, 1982), 137.
[77] Kenner, *Ulysses*, 123.

spectator' seated at the centre of the structure.[78] The analogy is partly accurate to *La Tentation*, which installs its principal character within just such a circular stage-like structure, inviting the reader to identify with Antony and visualize the scenes he hallucinates (whilst at the same time enjoining us, through the book's mock-dramatic form, to apprehend Antony and his visions from a reflective distance). The space in which 'Circe' unfolds is more complex and more fluid: the episode's 'events' occur in a context that seems unbounded and immaterial. This is not to say that there are no elements of 'imitation theatre' in 'Circe' (indeed, there are many), but Joyce's allusions to the practicalities of theatrical staging betray a heightened degree of tongue-in-cheek self-consciousness regarding the impossibility of his 'dreadful performance'[79] ever being staged. Early on in the episode, Joyce uses Bloom's encounter with a ragman to maximize the reader's awareness of this unfeasability:

> (*He steps forward. A sackshouldered ragman bars his path. He steps left, ragsackman left.*)

BLOOM

I beg.

> (*He leaps right, sackragman right.*)[80]

These right-left stage directions create an illusion that they simultaneously highlight as fake. 'Left' and 'right' are indications that only have meaning in relation to each other, and only make sense in a context in which it is clear whether they invoke the character's or the audience's point of view. In 'Circe' no such point of view is explicit. Likewise, the humour of the stage direction which states that '(*A panel of fog rolls back rapidly*)'[81] derives from its reference to the material paraphernalia of a non-existent theatrical illusion. Another instance of faux theatricality occurs when Joyce writes '(*Exeunt severally*)' just after '*Virag unscrews his head in a trice and holds it under his arm*', implying that Virag's head and body can now act only 'severally'.[82] As there is no implied theatrical space in 'Circe', there can be no such thing as a character entrance or exit. Joyce's 'Exeunt' merely emphasizes the status of theatrical layout as a sham in 'Circe': a novelistic hoax.

Joyce's use of the hallucination technique within a faux theatrical framework enables him to play extensively with the boundaries that

---

[78] Benoît Tadié, 'The Room of Infinite Possibilities: Joyce, Flaubert, and the Historical Imagination', *Études anglaises*, vol. 58, no. 2 (April–June 2005), 138.

[79] Joyce to Frank Budgen, Michaelmas 1920, *SL*, 271.

[80] *U* 15: 222–6.

[81] *U* 15: 1,139.   [82] *U* 15: 2,639, 2,636.

traditionally distinguish the representation of inner and outer worlds in literature. Daniel Ferrer summarizes the tension between these contending perspectives:

> The narrative set-up of the episode [...] combines both a theatrical form (which normally implies an external mode of focalization) and a radically internal focalization (whereby the subjective experience of hallucination is objectivized on the stage).[83]

This paradoxical combination provides the context for a curious technical anomaly in the episode, featured at the point at which Bloom is brought to trial. In this section, Joyce introduces a twist that goes against the grain of two of the tacit rules of 'Circe'. One of these is the dramatic convention according to which stage directions provide indications about the manner of a character's speech and behaviour. The second is Joyce's practice, in 'Circe', of presenting what the reader recognizes as private thought in the form of dramatic speech. In a doubly paradoxical moment, 'Circe' turns the tables on both of these rules by having Bloom speak in his own defence *within* a stage direction, and in free indirect style. Bloom's faux speech is fittingly introduced by George Fottrell as the trick that it is: 'The accused will now make a bogus statement.'[84] The stage direction begins straightforwardly as third-person narration in the present tense. But within a sentence Bloom's name is replaced by the third-person pronoun and the verbs switch from present to past tense:

> *Bloom, pleading not guilty and holding a fullblown waterlily, begins a long unintelligible speech. They would hear what counsel had to say in his stirring address to the grand jury. He was down and out but, though branded as a black sheep, if he might say so, he meant to reform, to retrieve the memory of the past in a purely sisterly way and return to nature as a purely domestic animal.*[85]

The reported speech stretches over more than twenty lines, at which point a more familiar narrative voice returns: '*He mumbles incoherently. Reporters complain that they cannot hear.*'[86] Joyce uses Flaubert's hallmark technique of *style indirect libre* to play with the conventions of theatrical writing,

---

[83] ['Le dispositif narratif de l'épisode [...] combine à la fois une forme théâtrale (impliquant normalement une focalisation externe) et une focalisation interne radicale (la subjectivité de l'hallucination objectivée sur la scène).' (Daniel Ferrer, 'Peut-on parler de métalepse génétique?' in *Métalepses: Entorses au pacte de la représentation*, ed. John Pier et Jean-Marie Schaffer [Paris: Éditions de l'EHESS, 2005], 114)].

[84] *U* 15: 896–7.

[85] *U* 15: 898–906.

[86] *U* 15: 898–924.

internalizing what should be external, and rendering indirectly what would usually be rendered directly. By using free indirect style in a manner which conflicts with readerly expectations, Joyce shows again that:

'outer' and 'inner' alike are neither reportage nor science, but ways of rehandling the conventions of writing a novel.[87]

The passage raises fundamental questions about the hybrid form of 'Circe', highlighting the ways in which generic doubt is used to accentuate the many other kinds of doubt fostered by Joyce's and Flaubert's texts.

In both 'Circe' and *La Tentation*, the impression of hallucination is conveyed by verbs that produce strong effects of visual immediacy. The most common of these verbs are 'paraître', 'apparaître', and 'disparaître' in French, and 'to appear' and 'to disappear' in English. In French even more than in English, the 'paraît' root of these verbs suggests falsehood—the fact of merely *seeming* that defines hallucination. These verbs proliferate in both texts, often signalling a shift to the next scene or figure. They perform diegetically what much of the text effects without recourse to diegesis by simply having characters appear on the page, capitalized at centre. In the first example of Flaubert's use of such verbs, the narrator of *La Tentation* laconically notes of a table that 'It disappears.'[88] The self-containment of the sentence, pared down to pronoun and intransitive verb, emphasizes the seemingly impossible change from being to non-being that it states, and intimates Antony's incredulity in the face of such an inexplicable occurrence. The absence of modifying adverbs accentuates the suddenness such verbs imply, thereby participating in the breathless rhythm of hallucination. Throughout Flaubert's text, shadows, objects, and people appear, reappear, or disappear: 'The shadow of the Devil's horns reappears', 'Between their shoulders appears the head of a negro', 'They disappear', 'The vision dims, disappears', 'all at once the Sphinx appears', 'he [. . .] disappears into the sand', 'a forest appears'.[89]

'Circe' manifests the same predilection for these forms: variants of the verb 'to appear' feature twenty-nine times in the episode. Bloom's entrance into Nighttown mobilizes such locutions four times in rapid succession: '*Bloom appears, flushed, panting* [. . .] *He disappears. In a moment he reappears and hurries on* [. . .] *He disappears into Olhausen's,*

---

[87] Kenner, *Ulysses*, 125.

[88] *TAE*, 75 ['Elle disparaît.' (*TA*, 42)].

[89] *TAE*, 83, 114, 161, 220, 221, 224, 226 ['L'ombre des cornes du Diable reparaît', 'Entre leurs épaules paraît la tête d'un nègre', 'Ils disparaissent', 'La vision s'atténue, disparaît', 'voilà que le Sphinx apparaît', 'il [. . .] disparaît dans le sable', 'une forêt paraît' (*TA*, 51, 83, 128, 188, 189, 192, 194)].

the porkbutcher's'.[90] Hélène Cixous evocatively describes the effects of startling instantaneousness such verbs produce:

> The scene gives a start. All at once someone is there. At that very instant an object is no longer there. The approach no longer exists. But the sudden appearance, the brutal reversal: there/not-there, without transition, without withdrawal.[91]

These ceaseless appearing and disappearing acts go hand in hand with another key process: transformation. Metamorphosis rules the figments of Antony's frenzied imagination. Such transformations are completely naturalized in Flaubert's text, as though they were the least surprising process in the world: 'Objects are meanwhile transformed', 'The rocks facing Antony have become a mountain.'[92] Like the sudden appearances and disappearances that punctuate the text, the effect of such transformations is cinematographic. As Senn states:

> the only medium that might be remotely adequate to express its antics [those of 'Circe'] would be obviously neither the stage nor the ballet, nor even moving pictures but cinematographic (or nowadays) computerized animation.[93]

To discover cinematographic effects in 'Circe' is less surprising than to experience such sensations in La Tentation, which was written decades before the invention of the cinematograph in 1895. It was none other than Joyce, after all, who set up the first cinema in Ireland in 1909; even had this not been the case, 'Circe' was written at a time when the cinema had become an established form of popular entertainment.[94] But—as was discussed in earlier chapters—Flaubert's inauguration of proto-cinematographic writing techniques is discernible from as early as Madame Bovary, and cinematographic tricks are everywhere in La Tentation (not for nothing was one of the earliest films ever made an adaptation of La Tentation de saint Antoine by George Méliès in 1898).[95] The verbs

[90] U 15: 142–55.
[91] Hélène Cixous in 'At Circe's, or the Self-Opener', boundary 2, vol. 3, no. 2 (Winter 1975), 387.
[92] TAE, 72, 186 ['les objets se transforment'; 'Les rochers en face d'Antoine sont devenus une montagne.' (TA, 39, 154)].
[93] Fritz Senn, '"Circe" as Harking Back in Provective Arrangement', in Reading Joyce's 'Circe', ed. Andrew Gibson, European Joyce Studies 3 (Amsterdam: Rodopi, 1994), 79.
[94] JJ, 300–3.
[95] In Méliès's film as in Flaubert's work, Antoine's temptations appear in the strangest of places and the strangest of guises. Marco Camerani makes a strong case for the likely influence of George Méliès's works on 'Circe' in Joyce e il cinema delle origini: Circe (Firenze: Cadmo, 2008).

Flaubert uses to conjure *La Tentation*'s first pageant of hallucinated images constitute a notable anticipation of cinematographic language:

> They gather speed. They *wheel past* at a dizzy pace. At other times, they *halt* and gradually *fade*, or *merge*.[96]

Similarly, the narrator's description of the basilica in which Antony suddenly finds himself at the beginning of the *épisode des hérésiarques* arrestingly prefigures cinematographic lighting: 'Light is projected from the far end, as if from a marvellous multi-coloured sun.'[97]

Images of cinematographic projection read more self-consciously in 'Circe'. For all these surrounding contexts, Joyce's specific literary legacy is clearly discernible. The key verbal phrase in the following example, 'is projected', is exactly the same (albeit in the passive voice) as Flaubert's 'se projette':

> *The image of the lake of Kinnereth with blurred cattle cropping in silver haze is projected on the wall.*[98]

Joyce's mock playwright makes use of the effects of cinematographic fade-in and fade-out. One stage direction announces that '*All recedes.*'[99] A technical *clin d'oeil* to the new medium also seems likely in the statement that Mrs Breen '*fades from his [Bloom's] side*'.[100] At the close of the episode, Rudy appears as if by fade-in: '*Against the dark wall a figure appears slowly*'. As in silent cinema, he '*reads* [...] *inaudibly*'.[101]

Echoes in Characterization, Plot, and Theme

These extensive intertextual connections between 'Circe' and *La Tentation* at the level of structure and technique are confirmed and compounded by an array of echoes at the level of characterization, plot, and theme.

Early on in 'Circe', Molly appears to Bloom. Like the Queen of Sheba in Flaubert's *Tentation*, she is an oriental apparition:[102]

[96] *TAE*, 72 (my emphasis) ['Leur mouvement s'accélère. Elles *défilent* d'une façon vertigineuse. D'autres fois, elles *s'arrêtent* et *pâlissent* par degrés, se *fondent*' (*TA*, 39)].

[97] *TAE*, 101 ['La lumière se projette du fond, merveilleuse comme serait un soleil multicolore.' (*TA*, 71)].

[98] *U* 15: 976–7.

[99] *U* 15: 1,266.

[100] *U* 15: 577.

[101] *U* 15: 4,956–7, 4,959.

[102] This parallel is noted by Block, 'Théorie et Technique', 230; Gilbert, *James Joyce's 'Ulysses'*, 321; Cross, *F&J*, 139; Brunazzi, 'Autogenetic Text', 5; and Brown, 'Shifting Sexual Centres', 78–9. The Queen of Sheba makes (very brief) earlier appearances in *Ulysses*, in 'Scylla and Charybdis' and 'Cyclops'—*U* 9: 630–1 and *U* 12: 198.

Beside her mirage of datepalms a handsome woman in Turkish costume stands before him. Opulent curves fill out her scarlet trousers and jacket, slashed with gold. A wide yellow cummerbund girdles her. A white yashmak, violet in the night, covers her face, leaving free only her large dark eyes and raven hair. [. . .] A coin gleams on her forehead. On her feet are jewelled toerings. Her ankles are linked by a slender fetterchain. Beside her a camel, hooded with a turreting turban, waits. A silk ladder of innumerable rungs climbs to his bobbing howdah. He ambles near with disgruntled hindquarters. Fiercely she slaps his haunch, her goldcurb wristbangles angriling, scolding him in Moorish.[103]

There is a parallel between Molly's jacket and yellow cummerbund and the Queen of Sheba's tight corset ('as if her corset restricted her') and restricting dress ('Her gown of golden brocade [. . .] pinches her waist in a tight bodice'). Like Molly, the Queen of Sheba wears a wristbangle ('her little round arm, ornamented at the wrist by an ebony bracelet'), and a multitude of rings, though in moving from one text to the other these have migrated from the Queen's fingers ('her ring-laden hands') to Molly's toes ('*On her feet are jewelled toerings.*'). The spectacular headgear of the Queen of Sheba's white elephant ('the bouquet of ostrich feathers attached to its head-piece')[104] has a counterpart in the 'turreting turban' of Molly's camel. Similarly, the 'slender fetterchain' that links Molly's ankles recalls the alluring gold chain worn by the Queen:

A flat golden chain passing under her chin runs along her cheeks, spirals around her blue-powdered hair, and then dropping down grazes past her shoulder and clinches over her chest on to a diamond scorpion, which sticks out its tongue between her breasts.[105]

Moreover, Molly's fetterchain also becomes intertwined, in the process of intertextual absorption and transformation, with another Flaubertian ornament. Indeed, a similar fetterchain features in *Salammbô* (of which Joyce owned an original French copy in Trieste),[106] in which ankle chains

---

[103] *U* 15: 297–302 and 312–17.

[104] *TAE*, 83–4 ['comme si son corset la gênait'; 'Sa robe en brocart d'or [. . .] lui serre la taille dans un corsage étroit'; 'son petit bras nu, orné au poignet d'un bracelet d'ébène'; 'ses mains chargées de bagues'; 'le bouquet de plumes d'autruche attaché à son frontal' (*TA*, 52)].

[105] *TAE*, 84 ['Une chaine d'or plate, lui passant sous le menton, monte le long de ses joues, s'enroule en spirale autour de sa coiffure, poudrée de poudre bleue; puis, redescendant, lui effleure les épaules et vient s'attacher sur sa poitrine à un scorpion de diamant, qui allonge la langue entre ses seins.' (*TA*, 52)].

[106] Gustave Flaubert, *Salammbô* (Paris: Bibliothèque Charpentier, 1914)—*CJ*, 6, 108–9. Joyce's familiarity with the volume is also intimated by his reference in a letter to the 'manteau de Tanit', a phrase which Flaubert uses in *Salammbô* to designate the sacred veil around which much of the book's action revolves. In a letter written to Budgen by Paul Léon on Joyce's behalf on 7 May 1933, the phrase refers to a book about women's

form part of the traditional attire of 'Canaanite virgins', acting as visible testimony to their chastity. Salammbo (who also resembles the Queen of Sheba by virtue of her hair—'powdered with mauve sand'—and spectacular jewellery) abides by the customs of the land so that 'Between her ankles she wore a golden chain to control her pace'.[107] During the eponymous princess's encounter with her irresistible suitor and dangerous nemesis, Mâtho, Salammbo's fetterchain is broken, leaving the reader to infer what the narrator merely suggests: 'Mâtho seized her heels, the golden chain snapped.'[108] Thus do Molly's gold-bound feet recall details from both *Salammbô* and *La Tentation*. The layering of two or more separate sources within a single Circean sentence, by a process that could be termed intertextual conflation, represents one of the distinctive ways in which Joyce handles Flaubertian echoes.

'Circe''s subtle invocation of *Salammbô* at this point is significant in a wider sense as well. For Flaubert's literary reconstruction of the Carthaginian wars was, like *Ulysses*, conceived as an attempt to write a modern epic, an epic novel. Flaubert had had in mind the composition of such a generic hybrid from as early as 1853, while still in the early stages of his work on *Madame Bovary*: 'I want to write two or three long epic books, novels set in a grand context.'[109] The urge to write such books sprang partly from Flaubert's passion for the grandeur of antiquity, but it was also motivated by his dedication to the quest for a truly modern form. To try to wed the epic and the novel was in some ways to seek to overcome an oxymoron. To Flaubert's mind the prose and prosaic plots and settings of contemporary novels stood in sharp contrast to the metrical verse and heroic purport of the ancient epics. Although he loved the beauties of the older mode, Flaubert saw the novel, with all its mundanities of language and content, as the more lucid form—the more suited to a democratic, bourgeois age peopled by the likes of Emma Bovary and Frédéric Moreau—and also the

---

underwear (such, at least, is Ellmann's explanation): 'As regards the "Nausicaa" chapter you will receive a ponderous volume of some six hundred large pages on the origin and history of what he chooses to call "Le Manteau de Tanit". He believes that this subject should be treated by you with IMMENSE seriousness, respect, circumspection, historical sense, critical acumen, documentary accuracy, citational erudition and sweet reasonableness.'— *L3*, 279–80. Brown also reads this allusion to 'Le Manteau de Tanit' as a Flaubertian reference—'Shifting Sexual Centres', 80.

[107] *SALE*, 25 ['Sa chevelure, poudrée de sable violet [...] selon la mode des vierges chananéennes [...] Elle portait entre les chevilles une chaînette d'or pour régler sa marche' (*SAL*, 36)].

[108] *SALE*, 187 ['Mâtho lui saisit les talons, la chaînette d'or éclata' (*SAL*, 211)].

[109] Flaubert to Louise Colet, 7 September 1853 ['Je veux faire deux ou trois longs bouquins épiques, des romans dans un milieu grandiose' (*C2*, 428)].

more fertile in the breadth of its unsounded potentialities. The novel meant authorial freedom from the constraints of earlier genres:

> Form, as it becomes ever more adroit, is progressively attenuated; it relinquishes all liturgy, rule and measure; it abandons the epic for the novel, verse for prose; it no longer acknowledges any form of orthodoxy, it is free, it takes the impress of the creator's will.[110]

Prose could both enable and register new insights about human nature:

> Classic form is insufficient for our needs, and our voices are not created to sing those simple tunes. Let us, if we can, be as dedicated to art as they were, but differently. The human consciousness has broadened since Homer. Sancho Panza's belly has burst the seams of Venus's girdle.[111]

It is clear from Flaubert's letters that his thoughts about the epic form came to impinge on his *romans de moeurs* as well as on his 'bouquins épiques', and that his *Bildungsromanen* gradually took on some of the characteristics of epic in his mind, despite their unheroic subjects. Even when his subjects demanded that his writing be most firmly rooted in the particulars of daily life in nineteenth-century France, Flaubert wanted:

> to impart to prose the rhythm of verse (leaving it still prose and very prosey) [...] to write about ordinary life just as we write history or epic (without distorting the subject).[112]

In *Salammbô*, however, which was written between the contemporary panoramas of *Madame Bovary* and *L'Éducation sentimentale*, Flaubert acted fully on his initial dream of a symbiotic union of genres by resurrecting the ancient world in the medium of modern prose.

Flaubert's statements fascinatingly foreshadow Joyce's own interest in composing an epic of modern life, an *Odyssey* for modern times. The connection between these shared aspirations is remarkable, but also fits into a general pattern of generic correspondences between the two

---

[110] Flaubert to Louise Colet, 16 January 1852, *GW*, 170 ['La forme, en devenant habile, s'atténue; elle quitte toute liturgie, toute règle, toute mesure; elle abandonne l'épique pour le roman, le vers pour la prose; elle ne se connaît plus d'orthodoxie et est libre comme chaque volonté qui la produit.' (*C2*, 31)].

[111] Flaubert to Louise Colet, 15 July 1853, *FSI*, 193 ['La forme antique est insuffisante à nos besoins et notre voix n'est pas faite pour chanter ces airs simples. Soyons aussi artistes qu'eux, si nous le pouvons, mais autrement qu'eux. La conscience du genre humain s'est élargie depuis Homère. Le ventre de Sancho Pança fait craquer la ceinture de Vénus.' (*C2*, 384–5)].

[112] Flaubert to Louise Colet, 27 March 1853, *GW*, 203 ['donner à la prose le rythme du vers (en la laissant prose et très prose) et écrire la vie ordinaire comme on écrit l'histoire ou l'épopée (sans dénaturer le sujet)' (*C2*, 287)].

authors. *Dubliners* builds on the meticulous architectural substructures of *Trois Contes*. *A Portrait* and *L'Éducation* lend themselves to analogy by virtue of their use of focalization, their structural patterning, and their affinities as *Bildungsromanen*. *Madame Bovary* and *Ulysses* are related by their complex treatment of adultery. In 'Circe', Joyce's wild experimentation with dramatic form responds to Flaubert's own exploration of the possibilities of the closet drama in *La Tentation*. Within this tight nexus of formal and thematic intersections, Joyce includes a reference to *Salammbô*, that other generically baffling prose epic.

To return to 'Circe': Flaubert's Queen of Sheba impacts on the episode at many other points. Although Molly's exotic oriental image disappears, Bloom comments to Mrs Breen:

> She often said she'd like to visit. Slumming. The exotic, you see. Negro servants in livery too if she had the money.[113]

This echoes Flaubert's description of the Queen's Negro slaves:

> twelve frizzy little negroes carry the long tail of her gown, held at the very end by a monkey who lifts it up from time to time.[114]

Joyce's predilection for a procedure whereby elements that are grouped together in the source text are scattered in his own—a technique which one might, by opposition to intertextual conflation, call intertextual dissemination—is apparent when Flaubert's voyeuristic trainbearers make a second appearance in 'Circe' as escorts to Stephen.[115] The twelve trainbearing slaves are replaced by seven monkeys (in lieu of Flaubert's single monkey), all of them peeping unrestrainedly beneath his priestly robes:

> *His Eminence Simon Stephen cardinal Dedalus, primate of all Ireland, appears in the doorway, dressed in red soutane, sandals and socks. Seven dwarf simian acolytes, also in red, cardinal sins, uphold his train, peeping under it.*[116]

This 'stage direction' punningly interweaves the simian and the religious: as 'primate of all Ireland' Stephen holds the most prestigious religious office in the land while also being a mere primate, different from his 'dwarf simian acolytes' only in that he is, apparently, of normal human size. This wordplay is primarily comic, but also underscores the perceptual

---

[113] *U* 15: 408–9.

[114] *TAE*, 84 ['douze négrillons crépus portent la longue queue de sa robe, dont un singe tient l'extrémité qu'il soulève de temps à autre' (*TA*, 53)].

[115] Block and Gilbert note this correspondence—'Théorie et technique', 230, and *James Joyce's 'Ulysses'*, 322.

[116] *U* 15: 2,654–7.

and epistemological problems 'Circe' continually raises: in the episode's hallucinatory context, it is fundamentally unclear whether Stephen and his aids are primates, or whether they are merely like primates. Similarly, doubt obtains as to whether the cardinal is Simon or Stephen Dedalus, or a surreal merger of both into one (the possibility foreshadows the fusion of Stephen and Bloom in the mirrored face of Shakespeare towards the end of the episode).[117] But the confusion is short-lived: on the following page, Stephen 'shrink[s] quickly to the size of his trainbearers'.[118]

Next in line to make an appearance in the partial guise of the Queen of Sheba is Bloom, who during his time as a popular leader appears 'seated on a milkwhite horse with long flowing crimson tail, richly *caparisoned*, with golden headstall',[119] much as the Queen of Sheba arrives to meet Antony on 'A white elephant *caparisoned* with cloth and gold' with a 'bouquet of ostrich feathers attached to its head-piece'.[120]

Joyce's use of salient details of the Queen of Sheba's appearance does not stop here; as 'Circe' unfolds, more and more characters take on Flaubertian hues. When Bloom goes from civic glory to sexual ridicule, some of the Queen's characteristics are transferred to his entourage. Joyce's portrayal of Bella Cohen is a case in point. Bella's eyes 'are deeply carboned',[121] like those of the Queen: 'The edges of her eyelids are painted black.'[122] Similarly, Bella's 'large pendant beryl eardrops'[123] mirror the Queen's richly jewelled ears: 'Two large blonde pearls pull at here ears.'[124] Bloom addresses Bello as 'Empress',[125] perhaps with reference to the royal lineage of her Flaubertian antecedent. 'Circe' reinforces this mapping of Bella-Bello against the model of the Queen of Sheba by replicating the gender dynamic of Flaubert's text. The Queen attempts to seduce Antony by inverting traditional gender roles: 'Ah! When you become my husband, I'll dress you, I'll perfume you, I'll depilate you', 'I've brought you my wedding presents', 'I'll have it made into robes for

---

[117] '(Stephen and Bloom gaze in the mirror. The face of William Shakespeare, beardless, appears there, rigid in facial paralysis, crowned by the reflection of the reindeer antlered hatrack in the hall.)'—U 15: 3,821–4.

[118] U 15: 2,684–5.

[119] U 15: 1,444–5 (my emphasis).

[120] TAE, 83 (my emphasis) ['Un éléphant blanc, *caparaçonné* d'un filet d'or [. . .] le bouquet de plumes d'autruche attaché à son frontal' (TA, 52)].

[121] U 15: 2,746.

[122] TAE, 84 ['Le bord de ses paupières est peint en noir.' (TA, 53)].

[123] U 15: 2,748.

[124] TAE, 84 ['Deux grosses perles blondes tirent ses oreilles.' (TA, 52–3)].

[125] U 15: 2,838.

you, which you can wear at home.'[126] Bello is none so subtle, and a reference to Bloom's 'womanish care'[127] is followed by a rather less delicate demonstration of Bloom's femininity: '*(he bares his arm and plunges it elbowdeep in Bloom's vulva)*'.[128]

Finally, Rudy's apparition at the close of the episode is not without its own possible connections to Flaubert's Queen of Sheba.[129] His diamond and ruby-studded buttons recall the 'pearl, jet, and sapphire'[130] of the Queen's costume, while his 'slim ivory cane'[131] may be related to her 'green parasol with an ivory handle'.[132]

From all this it is apparent that the Queen of Sheba is a multifarious presence in 'Circe'. Her short, self-contained appearance in Flaubert's text is disseminated throughout Joyce's episode (as well as conflated with the bejewelled eponymous protagonist of *Salammbô*), shaping the fantastical portrayal of characters in 'Circe' as various as Molly, Stephen, Bloom, Bella-Bello, and Rudy.

The same is true, albeit on a lesser scale, of the character of Hilarion, Antony's disciple of many years past—a spiritual son who returns to taunt him with the temptations of philosophical relativism (Christianity's superiority over other religions, for instance, is questioned, and all religions are depicted as sublime and grotesque in equal measure, depending on point of view). It is under the appearance of a child that Hilarion makes his first appearance in *La Tentation*:

> This child is as small as a dwarf and yet as stocky as a Cabirus, misshapen, miserable-looking. White hairs cover his prodigiously large head; and he shivers under a mean tunic, while clasping in his hand a roll of papyrus.[133]

---

[126] *TAE*, 85–6 ['Ah! quand tu seras mon mari, je t'habillerai, je te parfumerai, je t'épilerai'; 'Je t'ai apporté des cadeaux de noces'; 'Je t'en ferai des robes, que tu mettras à la maison.' (*TA*, 54–5)].

[127] *U* 15: 3,016.

[128] *U* 15: 3,088–9.

[129] Rudy's appearance at the end of 'Circe' is a veritable patchwork of intertextual allusions, and references to Flaubert are just one strand of the web. Gifford notes connections to Celtic folklore, Cinderella, Hermes/Mercury, ancient Rome, and a cluster of passages from the Old Testament that seem to designate Rudy as a sacrificial lamb— '*Ulysses' Annotated*, 529. The passage also alludes to *A Portrait*, in which Stephen himself appears dressed in an Eton suit, and to *The Tempest*, in which 'to kiss the book' means to drink alcohol—*P*, 24 and *The Tempest*, II.2.127.

[130] *TAE*, 84 ['de perles, de jais et de saphirs' (*TA*, 52)].

[131] *U* 15: 4,966.

[132] *TAE*, 84 ['parasol vert à manche d'ivoire' (*TA*, 53)].

[133] *TAE*, 90 ['Cet enfant est petit comme un nain, et pourtant trapu comme un Cabire, contourné, d'aspect misérable. Des cheveux blancs couvrent sa tête prodigieusement grosse; et il grelotte sous une méchante tunique, tout en gardant à sa main un rouleau de papyrus.' (*TA*, 60)].

When Rudy becomes mysteriously present at the very end of 'Circe', the similarities between the two mystifying events are patent:

> *Against the dark wall a figure appears slowly, a fairy boy of eleven, a changeling, kidnapped, dressed in an Eton suit with glass shoes and a little bronze helmet, holding a book in his hand. He reads from right to left inaudibly, smiling, kissing the page* [...] *gazes, unseeing, into Bloom's eyes and goes on reading, kissing, smiling. He has a delicate mauve face. On his suit he has diamond and ruby buttons. In his free left hand he holds a slim ivory cane with a violet bowknot. A white lambkin peeps out of his waistcoat pocket.*[134]

Like Hilarion in the first of his several guises, Rudy is strange and otherworldly, 'a fairy boy of eleven, a changeling'.[135] Celtic folklore typically described changelings as stupid or ugly, which accords with Hilarion's physical oddities: his dwarfness, his white hair, his peculiarly large head.[136] Both characters appear bearing a text: Rudy 'hold[s] a book in his hand',[137] while Hilarion 'clasp[s] in his hand a roll of papyrus'.[138] Even the cinematographic effect achieved by Joyce's introductory phrase—'Against a dark wall a figure appears'[139]—recalls Flaubert's use of an eerily focused moonbeam as a spotlight shining down upon Hilarion: 'The light of the moon, grazed by a passing cloud, falls on him.'[140]

For Frank Budgen however, Bloom's grandfather, Lipoti Virag, constitutes a more obvious intertextual reference to Hilarion in 'Circe'.[141] As Hilarion bears 'a roll of papyrus' and Rudy his book, so Lipoti Virag 'holds a roll of parchment'.[142] A certain comic, surreal logic pertains to Joyce's depiction of Virag and Rudy as presenting a family resemblance to the same character in Flaubert's closet drama.

Finally, another instance of intertextual conflation Stephen's sudden 'shrinking [...] to the size of his trainbearers',[143] seems inversely related to Hilarion's spurts of growth throughout *La Tentation*. As early on as in

---

[134] *U* 15: 4,956–67.
[135] *U* 15: 4,957.
[136] Gifford, *'Ulysses' Annotated*, 529.
[137] *U* 15: 4,958.
[138] *TAE*, 90 ['gardant à sa main un rouleau de papyrus' (*TA*, 60)].
[139] *U* 15: 4,956.
[140] *TAE*, 90 ['La lumière de la lune, que traverse un nuage, tombe sur lui.' (*TA*, 60)].
[141] 'An evident parallel to this apparition of Bloom's long since dead relative is Hilarion in *La Tentation de Saint Antoine*, only the doubts of the believer, personified in the pupil of Flaubert's tortured saint, is, in Joyce's *Circe*, a mocking old man, surveying, without illusion of sex, the physical defects of the singularly unattractive whores.'—Budgen, *James Joyce and the Making of 'Ulysses'*, 245–6. Cross and Brown also make this connection—*F&J*, 146, and 'Shifting Sexual Centres', 79.
[142] *TAE*, 90 ['un rouleau de papyrus' (*TA*, 60)]; *U* 15: 2,307.
[143] *U* 15: 2,684–5.

Part II, a dumbfounded Antony comments on the incipience of change in Hilarion: 'It seems to me that you're growing...'.[144] The following 'stage direction' validates the impression: 'Hilarion's height has indeed progressively increased.'[145] By the beginning of Part V, Hilarion has assumed supernatural height: 'Hilarion presents himself—dressed as a hermit, very much larger than before, colossal.'[146] Towards the end of Flaubert's book, the change in Hilarion is so great that Antony can scarcely recognize him:

> in front of him is Hilarion—but transfigured, lovely as an archangel, luminous as a sun—and so tall that to see him

> ANTONY

> tilts his head back.[147]

Correspondences of this kind at the level of characterization are compounded by parallels between some of the plot motifs discernible across both texts. The Messianic scene in 'Circe', for instance, in which Bloom is promoted to the highest honours only to find himself subsequently demoted and degraded, constitutes a notable counterpart to a sequence of scenes in *La Tentation*. In two consecutive vignettes, Antony encounters and finds favour with men of great power: first, the Roman Emperor Constantine (AD c.274–337), then King Nebuchadnezzar of Babylon (634–562 BC). The rhythm of Antony's rise to power, like Bloom's sudden good fortune in 'Circe', is breathless. On meeting Constantine, Antony is promptly elevated to the Emperor's inner circle and invested with enormous political power:

> So here he is, a magnate of the Court, the Emperor's confidant, the prime minister! Constantine places his diadem on Antony's forehead. And Antony keeps it, treating the honour as a matter of course.[148]

At this point Antony's hallucination dissolves. It gives way to a second vision, set in Babylon centuries before. This time, Antony does not meet the king, nor does any official appointment take place. Antony simply

---

[144] *TAE*, 96 ['Il me semble que tu grandis...' (*TA*, 66)].

[145] *TAE*, 96 ['En effet, la taille d'Hilarion s'est progressivement élevée' (*TA*, 66)].

[146] *TAE*, 163 ['Hilarion se présente—habillé en ermite, beaucoup plus grand que tout à l'heure, colossal.' (*TA*, 130)].

[147] *TAE*, 203 ['Hilarion est devant lui,—mais transfiguré, beau comme un archange, lumineux comme un soleil,—et tellement grand, que pour le voir/ANTOINE/se renverse la tête.' (*TA*, 171–2)].

[148] *TAE*, 81 ['Le voilà devenu un des grands de la Cour, confident de l'Empereur, premier ministre! Constantin lui pose son diadème sur le front. Antoine le garde, trouvant cet honneur tout simple.' (*TA*, 49)].

becomes Nebuchadnazzar: 'he becomes Nebuchadnezzar'.[149] On this occasion, however, power and glory arouse disgust rather than delight. To remedy his acute and instantaneous revulsion at his position, Antony immediately seeks experience of the opposite order in extreme degradation:

> since nothing is more vile than a brute beast, Antony drops down on all fours on the table and bellows like a bull.[150]

Bloom's rise to power is more democratic. It is initiated by Zoe's suggestion, in response to a lewd comment by Bloom about a cigar, that he 'Make a stump speech out of it.'[151] Bloom does so, accoutred *in workman's corduroy overalls*.[152] Unanimous approval follows, and Bloom becomes a hero:

> *Under an arch of triumph Bloom appears, bareheaded, in a crimson velvet mantle trimmed with ermine, bearing Saint Edward's staff, the orb and sceptre with the dove, the curtana. He is seated on a milkwhite horse with long flowing crimson tail, richly caparisoned, with golden headstall. Wild excitement.*[153]

Bloom is declared 'emperor-president and king-chairman, the most serene and potent and very puissant ruler of this realm'.[154] Like Antony, who responded without bashfulness to the great honours unexpectedly bestowed upon him, Bloom assumes his role without surprise, lacing his thanks to the Bishop with royal condescension: 'Thanks, somewhat eminent sir.'[155] Although both Antony and Bloom relapse into a state of abjection almost as fast as they rise to glory, Bloom's return to humble status is not volitional: he is dragged down by the mob, his rise and fall arranging themselves symmetrically around his moment of glory. Thus does the diptych of Antony's ascent and descent find a structural echo in the diptych of Bloom's ascent and descent. In this respect, Bloom's version of Antony's meteoric worldly trajectory constitutes yet another instance of the procedure of intertextual conflation.

As is the case in *Dubliners*, *A Portrait*, and *Exiles*, Joyce's intertextual engagement with Flaubert is signposted by an overlay of more specific, localized allusion. When Bloom, then at the height of his powers, is

---

[149] *TAE*, 82 ['il devient Nabuchodonosor' (*TA*, 50)].

[150] *TAE*, 82 ['comme rien n'est plus vil qu'une bête brute, Antoine se met à quatre pattes sur la table, et beugle comme un taureau' (*TA*, 50)].

[151] *U* 15: 1,353.

[152] *U* 15: 1,355.

[153] *U* 15:1,441–6.

[154] *U* 15: 1,471–2.

[155] *U* 15: 1,478.

interrogated by members of the public, the question and answer session rapidly turns into a quiz that anticipates the catechistic mode of the 'Ithaca' episode and vividly recalls Flaubert's *Dictionnaire des Idées Reçues*. The brevity of the exchanges enhances their formulaic absurdity:

> BEN DOLLARD
>
> Pansies?
>
> BLOOM
>
> Embellish (beautify) suburban gardens.
>
> BEN DOLLARD
>
> When twins arrive?
>
> BLOOM
>
> Father (pater, dad) starts thinking.[156]

Bloom's first response, which answers a nominal query ('pansies?') with a defining verbal object phrase, is exactly analogous to one of the typical structures of Flaubert's dictionary entries, as evidenced in the following examples:

> CIRCUS TRAINERS: Use obscene practices.
> HYDROTHERAPY: Cure and cause of all illnesses.
> ORGAN MUSIC: Lifts the soul up to God.
> SLEEP: Thickens the blood.[157]

That Bloom is behaving like a dictionary or thesaurus is comically emphasized by his provision of additional, self-evident definitions within his replies to Dollard's questions: 'beautify' is given as a synonym for 'embellish', 'pater' and 'dad' as alternatives for 'father'. As another instance of intertextual conflation, the allusion to the *Dictionnaire* exemplifies both the breadth and detail of Joyce's response to Flaubert in 'Circe'.

A further example of Joyce's intertextual engagement with *La Tentation* at the level of plot can be found in his deployment of the Flaubertian motif of the return of the mother. Antony is haunted by his mother from the opening of Flaubert's book. His thoughts turn to her even before his visions first take hold. He is plagued by a deep sense of guilt at having acted against her dying wishes by leaving home to pursue his religious calling: 'They all blamed me when I left home. My mother collapsed, dying.'[158] This anguish

---

[156] *U* 15: 1,664–71.
[157] *DIRE*, 298, 311, 320, 326 ['DOMPTEURS DE BÊTES FÉROCES: Emploient des pratiques obscènes./DORMIR (trop): Épaissit le sang./HYDROTHÉRAPIE: Enlève toutes les maladies et les procure./ORGUE: Élève l'âme vers Dieu.' (*DIR*, 415, 416, 424, 431)].
[158] *TAE*, 62 ['Tous me blâmaient lorsque j'ai quitté la maison. Ma mère s'affaissa mourante' (*TA*, 28)].

returns at the end of Flaubert's phantasmagoria, with conscious memories developing into a vivid, nightmarish vision:

> She must have cursed me for abandoning her, must have torn her white hair out by the handful. And her corpse has been left lying in the middle of the hut, under the roof of reeds, between the tumbledown walls. A hyena snuffles through a hole, nosing forward! . . . Horrible! horrible![159]

At this point, imagination (as Antony is conjuring a scene he never witnessed) turns to hallucination. An old woman ('une vieille femme') appears, and 'He thinks he sees his mother come back to life.'[160] Antony's vision of his mother's physical decrepitude is extremely detailed:

> A shroud knotted around her head hangs with her white hair all the way down her legs, which are lean as two crutches. The brilliance of her ivory-coloured teeth makes her earthy skin duller still. The orbs of her eyes are full of darkness, and in their depths flicker two flames, like grave-lamps.[161]

Likewise, Stephen is haunted by the memory of his mother and of her final illness throughout 16 June 1904. His unsummoned visions of her are gripping, terrifying occurences. In 'Telemachus' Stephen's interior monologue recalls such a moment:

> In a dream, silently, she had come to him, her wasted body within its loose graveclothes giving off an odour of wax and rosewood, her breath, bent over him with mute secret words, a faint odour of wetted ashes.
>
> Her glazing eyes, staring out of death, to shake and bend my soul. On me alone. The ghostcandle to light her agony. Ghostly light on the tortured face. Her hoarse loud breath rattling in horror, while all prayed on their knees. Her eyes on me to strike me down. [. . .]
>
> Ghoul! Chewer of corpses!
>
> No, mother! Let me be and let me live.[162]

The 'return' of Stephen's mother in 'Circe' constitutes one of the episode's most emotionally charged hallucinations. Like Antony at the end of *La Tentation*, Stephen visualizes his mother's disease-ridden body with arresting precision:

---

[159] *TAE*, 214 ['Elle m'aura maudit pour mon abandon, en arrachant à pleines mains ses cheveux blancs. Et son cadavre est resté étendu au milieu de la cabane, sous le toit de roseaux, entre les murs qui tombent. Par un trou, une hyène en reniflant, avance la gueule! . . . Horreur! horreur!' (*TA*, 182)].

[160] *TAE*, 215 ['Il croit voir sa mère ressuscitée.' (*TA*, 183)].

[161] *TAE*, 215 ['Un linceul, noué autour de sa tête, pend avec ses cheveux blancs jusqu'au bas de ses deux jambes, minces comme des béquilles. L'éclat de ses dents, couleur d'ivoire, rend plus sombre sa peau terreuse. Les orbites de ses yeux sont pleins de ténèbres, et au fond deux flammes vacillent, comme des lampes de sépulcre.' (*TA*, 183)].

[162] *U* 1: 270–9.

Stephen's mother, emaciated, rises stark through the floor, in leper grey with a wreath of faded orangeblossoms and a torn bridal veil, her face worn and noseless, green with gravemould. Her hair is scant and lank. She fixes her bluecircled hollow eyesockets on Stephen and opens her toothless mouth uttering a silent word.[163]

The correspondences between these two apparitions are salient. Stephen's mother wears a wreath; a 'shroud' hangs from the head of Antony's mother. The face 'green with gravemould' mirrors 'her earthy skin'. The 'bluecircled hollow eyesockets' echo 'The orbs of her eyes are full of darkness'. Antony and Stephen have similar reactions. Antony 'leaps up with a terrified start'[164] while Stephen '*chok[es] with fright, remorse and horror*'.[165] Antony sees a hyena advancing to devour his mother's corpse; Stephen screams 'The ghoul! Hyena!' and 'The corpsechewer!' when his mother appears to him.[166] The connection between the two texts is further strengthened by the fact that in both cases the figure of the mother represents and heralds death. The old woman whom Antony mistakes for his mother in *La Tentation* in fact turns out to be Death itself, an allegorical temptress (modelled on the template of her forerunners in medieval morality plays) who enjoins him to commit suicide.[167] Similarly, Stephen's mother warns him of his own inevitable demise: 'All must go through it, Stephen. [. . .] You too. Time will come.'[168] The relationship between these two dark, emotive moments is reinforced by analogies of structure. In both *La Tentation* and *Ulysses* the figure of the hallucinated mother makes a first appearance in the opening few pages and is resurrected towards the end in more elaborate detail.

Thematically, Joyce's intertextual engagement with Flaubert's phantasmagoria is discernible in both texts' obsessive preoccupation with the void.[169] In *Ulysses* the word makes its first appearance in 'Telemachus' when Stephen speculates, with Arius, Sabellius, and Valentine in mind, that 'The void awaits surely all them that weave the wind'.[170] Fear of the void (of Christian doubt and of the unknown in general) crescendoes in both texts. From the opening page of *La Tentation*, Antony's existential

---

[163] *U* 15: 4,157–61.
[164] *TAE*, 215 ['se relève dans un sursaut d'épouvante' (*TA*, 183)].
[165] *U* 15: 4,185.
[166] *U* 15: 4,200, 4,214.
[167] *TAE*, 215–18; *TA*, 183–6.
[168] *U* 15: 4,182–4.
[169] Cross entitles his chapter on the parallels between *La Tentation* and 'Circe' 'The Nethermost Abyss: Expressionism in *La Tentation de saint Antoine* and "*Circe*"', but no mention is made of these texts' preoccupation with the void—*F&J*, 125–49.
[170] *U* 1: 661–2.

doubt is starkly literalized: the protagonist is placed, together with his hut and Bible, on the very edge of a precipice, 'high on a mountain'.[171] Thus are the theoretical and theological abstractions of the Void and Fall provided with a visual objective correlative. Antony and others repeatedly approach the literal void to express their fear, or putative fearlessness, of a more threatening, existential void. The literal and spiritual senses of the word are compounded when Antony, overcome by his relentless visions, gropes for his bearings in the darkness of night, fearful of a fall into 'the abyss'.[172] A few pages later, Apollonius (a first-century Greek Neopythagorean philosopher and orator) and Damis (his disciple), who have been trying to tempt Antony away from Christianity in favour of Platonism, prove their indifference to the threat of the void by walking backwards over the edge of the cliff. In a moment that combines the qualities of Christian miracle and supernatural grotesque, the two men remain surreally suspended over the void: 'He [Appolonius] backs away towards the edge of the cliff, overshoots its, and stays suspended.'[173] Not all are so fortunate—in a later section of La Tentation, the Roman gods, facing their twilight, tumble into the abyss in a long, lemming-like pageant, enacting the end of their era in a series of extravagantly stylized falls: Apollo 'falls head first into the abyss';[174] Venus falls 'describing an immense parabola';[175] as for Cérès, 'The abyss swallows her.'[176] Anxieties about the void reach a climax during Antony's encounter with the devil. Having climbed onto the devil's back to take an exploratory flight through space, Antony reiterates his terror of both a literal and a spiritual faux pas: 'Enough! enough! I'm frightened! I shall fall into empty space [the abyss].'[177] The devil (like Apollonius and Damis before him) denies the very existence of any kind of literal void: 'There is no emptiness! there is no void!'[178] It is at the end of this dialogue with the devil that the meaning of 'the void' comes into focus. The word denotes both nothingness per se, and the psychological and spiritual void that follows from Antony's incapacity to adhere to

---

[171]   TAE, 61 ['au haut d'une montagne' (TA, 27)].

[172]   TAE, 140 ['l'abîme' (TA, 110)].

[173]   TAE, 160 ['Il s'approche à reculons du bord de la falaise, la dépasse et reste suspendu.' (TA, 128)].

[174]   TAE, 195 ['tombe vers l'abîme, la tête en bas' (TA, 163)].

[175]   TAE, 195 ['décrivant une immense parabole' (TA, 164)].

[176]   TAE, 194 ['L'abîme l'engouffre.' (TA, 162)].

[177]   TAE, 209 ['Assez! assez! J'ai peur! Je vais tomber dans l'abîme.' (TA, 177)].

[178]   TAE, 209 ['Le néant n'est pas! le vide n'est pas!' (TA, 177)].

Christian faith without doubt. By extension, and more radically, it signifies absolute epistemological doubt, 'the impossibility of ever knowing anything!',[179] the realization that there are no grounds for believing in anything at all. In the devil's words: 'But are you sure of seeing? Are you even sure of being alive? Perhaps there is nothing!'[180] The spiritual, existential, and epistemological blindness evoked by the devil (in a complete turn-around from his previously stated position about the non-existence of the void) is literalized for Antony: 'ANTONY/cannot see a thing. He feels faint.'[181] Doubt—'le néant'—enters his consciousness like an experience more absolute than death itself:

> It's like a death deeper than death. I'm spinning in vast darkness. It's inside me. My conscious self shatters under this dilating void.[182]

Words used to describe the void ('abyss', 'pitch dark', 'pit', 'black hole', 'emptiness', 'void')[183] recur with increasing frequency as the book unfolds, often juxtaposed within a single phrase ('your mind [. . .] vanished into the void'),[184] as if to underscore the inescapability of the problem and the mounting psychological pressure it exerts on Antony.

In 'Circe' the 'void' becomes a similarly obsessive concern. The parallels begin with a passage that recalls Antony's vision of the Milky Way 'suspended' (like Apollonius and Damis earlier on in *La Tentation*) over the void:

> He watches how they [the planets] come from far off—balanced like stones in a sling—to describe their orbits and draw out their hyperbolas.[185]

This planetary scene features in 'Circe' in the mode of miniaturized farce. A hobgoblin gambles. The universe is at stake. Governed by chance, game and world degenerate into chaos:

> *Sieurs et dames, faites vos jeux!* (He crouches juggling. Tiny roulette planets fly from his hands). *Les jeux sont faits!* (the planets rush together, uttering crepitant

---

[179] *TAE*, 213 ['l'impossibilité de rien connaître!' (*TA*, 181)].

[180] *TAE*, 212 ['Mais es-tu sûr de voir? es-tu même sûr de vivre? Peut-être qu'il n'y a rien!' (*TA*, 180)].

[181] *TAE*, 212 ['ANTOINE/n'y voit plus. Il défaille.' (*TA*, 179)].

[182] *TAE*, 212 ['C'est comme une mort plus profonde que la mort. Je roule dans l'immensité des ténèbres. Elles entrent en moi. Ma conscience éclate sous cette dilatation du néant!' (*TA*, 179–80)].

[183] *TAE*, 194–6, 209 [('abîme', 'ténèbres', 'gouffre', 'trou noir', 'néant', 'vide' (*TA*, 162–4, 177)].

[184] *TAE*, 219 ['ta pensée [. . .] s'abîmait dans le néant' (*TA*, 187)].

[185] *TAE*, 207 ['Il les [ces globes lumineux] voit venir de loin,—et suspendus comme des pierres dans une fronde, décrire leurs orbites, pousser leurs hyperboles.' (*TA*, 175)].

cracks) *Rien va plus! (The planets, buoyant balloons, sail up and away. He springs off into vacuum.)*[186]

This anticipates Stephen's own Wagnerian 'ruin of all space' towards the end of the episode:

STEPHEN

Nothung!

> (He lifts his ashplant high with both hands and smashes the chandelier. Time's livid final flame leaps and, in the following darkness, ruin of all space, shattered glass and toppling masonry.)[187]

At the end of 'Circe' all hell breaks loose: unaccountable changes come over sun and earth, fires burn, chasms open. In a clear *clin d'oeil* to *La Tentation*, Tom Rochford and a crowd of others dive into the void in fantastical poses, re-enacting the suicidal procession of Flaubert's gods:

> *Brimstone fires spring up. Dense clouds roll past.* [...] *Pandemonium* [...] *The midnight sun is darkened. The earth trembles.* [...] *A chasm opens with a noiseless yawn. Tom Rochford, winner, in athlete's singlet and breeches, arrives at the head of the national hurdle handicap and leaps into the void. He is followed by a race of runners and leapers. In wild attitudes they spring from the brink. Their bodies plunge.*[188]

In both 'Circe''s and *La Tentation*'s treatments of the theme of the void, serious concerns lurk barely concealed beneath the veneer of pantomimic cheer and music-hall merriment.

Localized Linguistic Echoes

Major echoes of plot and theme (such as those considered above) are accompanied by a large number of localized echoes, sometimes consisting of a single word or phrase. A few pages into the episode, Bloom notices a 'composite portrait' of himself in a shop window. What he sees is in fact his own reflection as refracted and distorted by a montage of mirrors:

> *A concave mirror at the side presents to him lovelorn longlost lugubru Booloohoom. Grave Gladstone sees him level, Bloom for Bloom.* [...] *in the convex mirror grin unstruck the bonham eyes and fatchuck cheekchops of jollypoldy the rixdix doldy.*[189]

In *La Tentation* the devil uses the image of a concave mirror to bring into question Antony's beliefs. Antony's consciousness, he argues, deforms the

---

186   *U* 15: 2,161–4.   187   *U* 15: 4,241–5.
188   *U* 15: 4,661–76.   189   *U* 15: 145–9.

truths of the visible world: 'things reach you only through the medium of your mind. Like a concave mirror it distorts objects.'[190] By saying this, the devil in effect suggests that the hallucinations which make up *La Tentation* are just as likely to be the creatures of Antony's mind as to have any substantial reality. The reader of 'Circe' is confronted with similar uncertainties, though the question has less to do with any single character's psychic responsibility for the episode's unfathomable happenings than with the identity of the narrative agency that appears to be doing the subconscious dream-work in *Ulysses*. Is anything happening in 'Circe', and, if so, how might one accurately describe the strange events that unfold over its pages? The image of the 'concave mirror', imported from *La Tentation* draws attention to both texts' cultivation of existential and epistemological doubt. Bloom's contemplation of his various mirrored reflections produces an optical triptych that underscores the unreliability of sensual perception as a way of attaining truth. No Bloom, be he '*lovelorn longlost lugubru Booloohoom*', '*Bloom for Bloom*', or '*jollypoldy the rixdix doldy*',[191] is truer than the others.

One of the most striking direct echoes between 'Circe' and *La Tentation* occurs when:

> *A cake of new clean lemon soap arises, diffusing light and perfume.*

and a few lines later:

> *The freckled face of Sweny, the druggist, appears in the disc of the soapsun.*[192]

An unmistakably analogous sequence of events unfolds at the end of *La Tentation*. Dawn breaks, heralding the end of Antony's temptations. The sun rises ('Day at last dawns'), and 'There in the middle, inside the very disc of the sun, radiates the face of Jesus Christ.'[193] Despite the language difference, the words are the same: 'face', 'disc/disque', 'soapsun/soleil'. Joyce's rewriting highlights the element of grotesque that pertains to Jesus's apparition in the sun at the close of Flaubert's book. The soap's ditty makes the buffoonery of the scene unmistakable:

> We're a capital couple are Bloom and I.
> He brightens the earth. I polish the sky.[194]

---

[190] *TAE*, 212 ['les choses ne t'arrivent que par l'intermédiaire de ton esprit. Tel qu'un miroir concave il déforme les objets' (*TA*, 180)].

[191] *U* 15: 145–9.

[192] *U* 15: 335–6, 340–1.

[193] *TAE*, 232 ['Le jour enfin paraît'; 'Tout au milieu, et dans le disque même du soleil, rayonne la face de Jésus-Christ.' (*TA*, 200)].

[194] *U* 15: 338–9.

Flaubert's ending is itself already charged with irony, mingling pagan and Christian elements in a moment that all too ambiguously seems to intimate Antony's victory over his heathen temptations. The solemness of his reaction ('Antony makes the sign of the cross and returns to his prayers') is undercut by the narrator's emphasis on the event's resemblance to a theatrical performance involving stage curtains and other dramatic props and effects:

> like the raised curtains of a tabernacle, golden clouds furling into large scrolls uncover the sky.[195]

Joyce's adaptation of Flaubert's motif, combining change and recognizability, exemplifies his ability to telescope echo and commentary. Joyce grasps the ambivalence of *La Tentation*'s ending and responds by grafting Flaubertian elements into his own text to comic effect and in ways that enhance the reader's awareness of the tensions inherent in the original.

A number of the more specific intertextual connections between Joyce's and Flaubert's works relate to their treatment of sexuality. Bloom's enjoyment of spanking ('A warm tingling glow without effusion. Refined birching to stimulate circulation.')[196] is in line with the unexpected pleasure Antony experiences from self-flagellation.[197] Mrs Bellingham's injunction to mutilate Bloom sexually ('Geld him')[198] mirrors the self-mutilation enacted by the Greek god Atys in *La Tentation* ('With a sharp stone he emasculates himself, then starts to run around furiously, waving in the air his severed organ.').[199] Antony seeks degradation after experiencing wealth and power and 'drops down on all fours'[200] in order to fulfil his need for bestial humiliation. Bloom (as Bella) re-enacts Antony's gesture exactly: '*With a piercing epileptic cry she sinks on all fours, grunting, snuffling, rooting at his feet.*'[201]

A few final examples of the innumerable Flaubertian echoes to be found in 'Circe' will demonstrate the use made by Joyce of even the most minute borrowings. In one of his incoherent, drunken speeches, Stephen makes mention of Ceres:

---

[195] *TAE*, 232 ['comme les rideaux d'un tabernacle qu'on relève, des nuages d'or en s'enroulant à larges volutes découvrent le ciel' (*TA*, 200)].

[196] *U* 15: 1,095–6.

[197] This is noted by Cross—*F&J*, 136.

[198] *U* 15: 1,105.

[199] *TAE*, 180 ['Avec une pierre tranchante il s'émascule, puis se met à courir furieux, en levant dans l'air son membre coupé.' (*TA*, 147)].

[200] *TAE*, 82 ['se met à quatre pattes' (*TA*, 50)].

[201] *U* 15: 2,852–3.

of texts so divergent as priests haihooping round David's that is Circe's or what am I saying Ceres' altar.[202]

In Flaubert's text the ancient deity makes a fuller appearance, giving voice to virulent xenophobic views ('How wise it was to debar strangers, atheists, epicureans and christians!')[203] before tumbling into the void. In *La Tentation* the god Crépitus features shortly after Cérès in the pageant of the ancient gods;[204] accordingly, planets 'utter *crepitant* cracks' just after Stephen's evocation of Ceres.[205] The neat sequential parallel between the two texts here is representative of both the subtlety and the playfulness of Joyce's response to Flaubert.

Joyce's personified description of the hours of the day at the end of 'Circe'

> *From a corner the morning hours run out, goldhaired, slimsandalled, in girlish blue, waspwaisted, with innocent hands. Nimbly they dance, twirling their skipping ropes. The hours of noon follow in amber gold.*[206]

has a precedent in *La Tentation* when a stage description in Part V nonchalantly notes that 'Equal in build, the Hours hold each other by the hand'.[207] The vast number of such precise, localized echoes makes it difficult not to hear *La Tentation* ringing in one's ears when Bloom uses the words 'tempt', 'saint', and 'demon' in close proximity to each other:

> She rolled downhill at Rialto bridge to tempt me with her flow of animal spirits. [...] A saint couldn't resist it. The demon possessed me.[208]

The 'Circe' Notesheets and La Tentation

Although more has been written about the likelihood of a connection between 'Circe' and *La Tentation* than about any other aspect of *Ulysses*'s relations to Flaubert, these discussions have not so far been tested against the relevant genetic material. The notesheets Joyce compiled in preparation for the composition of *Ulysses*, transcribed and edited by Philip Herring in 1972, do not constitute the first but 'the second stage in the

[202] *U* 15: 2,090–2.
[203] *TAE*, 193 ['On avait bien raison d'exclure les étrangers, les athées, les épicuriens et les chrétiens!' (*TA*, 162)].
[204] *TAE*, 201; *TA*, 169.
[205] *U* 15: 2,163 (my emphasis).
[206] *U* 15: 4,054–7.
[207] *TAE*, 187 ['Les Heures, de taille égale, se tiennent par la main' (*TA*, 155)].
[208] *U* 15: 3,357–9.

creative process'.[209] Herring speculates that a first set of notes or primitive drafts was produced around 1914, at the beginning of Joyce's work on *Ulysses* (and at around the time of his purchase of *La Tentation*), and that those notes not used at that time were subsequently entered on the notesheets now kept at the British Library.[210] Internal evidence indicates that the 'Circe' notesheets were compiled 'shortly after Joyce and his family arrived in Paris (8 July 1920) from Trieste'[211]—that is, at around the same time as Joyce set to work on the episode itself.[212]

A number of notes scattered across the notesheets testify to Joyce's reading of *La Tentation de saint Antoine*. The discovery of these Flaubertian reading notes provides an extremely strong foundation for an intertextual reading of *Ulysses*—especially of 'Circe'—and *La Tentation*.[213] There are too many potentially relevant notes on these sheets for a comprehensive analysis to be provided here (a longer listing—which does not, however, claim to be exhaustive—may be found in the Appendix). The following pages will focus on a few of the most indubitable traces of Joyce's reading of Flaubert.

On the eighth of the 'Circe' notesheets one note simply reads:

S. Anthony[214]

Notes from the sixth of the notesheets put this saint's Flaubertian origins beyond doubt. The clinching notes read as follows:

Jesus, S of Pantherus & parfumeuse
fille d'Israel qui se donna aux porcs
quel homme [?]juste, hein?[215]
Agamemnon du ciel
Anthony says creed[216]

---

[209] Philip Herring, *Joyce's 'Ulysses' Notesheets in the British Museum* (Charlottesville: University Press of Virginia, 1972), 523. The 1972 British Library Act made that library independent of the British Museum, thereby rendering the title of Herring's study inaccurate. Accordingly, the repository of Joyce's *Ulysses* notesheets is here referred to as 'the British Library'.

[210] Herring, *Notesheets*, 6.

[211] Herring, *Notesheets*, 526–7.

[212] Herring, drawing on Ellmann and others, dates Joyce's work on 'Circe' to the period between June and December 1920—*Notesheets*, 526.

[213] I am grateful to Ronan Crowley for drawing my attention to a clutch of 'Flaubert' jottings he had identified in the *Ulysses* notesheets at the British Library—a discovery that in time led to many more.

[214] 'Circe' notesheet 8, line 105; Herring, *Notesheets*, 310.

[215] I have corrected an error in Herring's transcription of this jotting: Joyce wrote 'hein' (in keeping with French usage), not 'hien'.

[216] 'Circe' notesheet 6, lines 20, 21, 26, 82, 83; Herring, *Notesheets*, 297, 299. The first four of these jottings could be translated as follows: 'Jesus, S[on] of Pantherus & parfumeuse'; 'daughter of Israel who gave herself to pigs'; 'what a just man, eh?'; 'Agamemnon of the sky'.

Two of the jottings listed above—'quel homme [?]juste, hein?' and 'Agamemnon du ciel'—constitute straightforward extractions, presenting no deviation (except for punctuation: Joyce changes the exclamation mark that features after 'juste' to a comma) from the text of *La Tentation*.[217] Their exact conformity to the Flaubertian original suggests that Joyce had a copy of the book before him as he took these notes (or the earlier notes from which these may have been cribbed). Despite being crossed out (Joyce's habitual way of indicating to himself that notesheet material had been used), neither of these jottings made its way into 'Circe'.

There is a close similarity between the third note listed above—'fille d'Israel qui se donna aux porcs'—and a phrase from *La Tentation* in which Simon Magus describes a woman named Helen—who represents all female prostitutes—as 'that daughter of Israel who gave herself to goats'.[218] The sentence is clearly recognizable, but the changes effected in Joyce's version are intriguing.[219] He may have wanted to exacerbate the outrageousness of the woman's behaviour by having her consort with an animal her race and religion deem particularly unclean.

In 'Jesus, S of Pantherus & parfumeuse', Joyce uses Franglais to summarize one of *La Tentation*'s many blasphemies. The snippet derives from a passage in the *épisode des hérésiarques* in which a leprous Jew says of Jesus that:

> his mother, the perfume-seller, gave herself to Pantherus, a Roman soldier, on some sheaves of maize, one evening in harvest-time.[220]

This jotting (which is crossed out) travels into 'Circe' in modified form. Virag, an 'agueshaken' Jew with 'profuse yellow spawn foaming over his epileptic lips' states that:

> She sold lovephiltres, whitewax, orangeflower. Panther, the Roman centurion, polluted her with his genitories.[221]

---

[217] *TA*, 112 and 158 ['What a just man! eh?'; 'Agamemnon of the sky!' (*TAE*, 143 and 189)].

[218] *TAE*, 137 ['cette fille d'Israël qui s'abandonnait aux boucs' (*TA*, 107)].

[219] These differences are not attributable to Joyce's possible reading of the earlier versions of Flaubert's text (dated 1849 and 1856), which were included in an appendix to the 1910 Conard edition. In both its antecedent forms the phrase reads: 'she was the daughter of Jews who wandered away from the camp to give herself to goats'—*La Tentation de saint Antoine* (Paris: Louis Conard, 1910), 266 and 527 ['elle a été cette fille des Juifs qui s'écartait du camp pour se livrer aux boucs'].

[220] *TAE*, 119 ['sa mère, la parfumeuse, s'est livrée à Pantherus, un soldat romain, sur des gerbes de maïs, un soir de moisson' (*TA*, 88)].

[221] *U* 15: 2,599–600. Senn noted the link between these two passages in 1982 in 'Trivia Ulysseana IV', 152.

The sixth jotting reads: 'Anthony says creed'. This note manifests the same summarizing strategy as 'Jesus, S of Pantherus & parfumeuse'. In *La Tentation*, Saint Antony does indeed say the creed, and that creed in turn crosses Stephen's mind in 'Telemachus' (as was discussed earlier in this chapter).

Other jottings in the notesheets relate specifically to Flaubert's treatment of heresy: 'heretic catechism', 'Arius', 'heresiarchus'.[222] The latter two entries, 'Arius' and 'heresiarchus', though separate on the notesheets, are brought together in 'Circe' when Arius's name appears in Latinate pomp as 'Arius Heresiarchus'.[223]

'Circe' constitutes a concentrated Flaubertian 'echoland'[224] at the heart of *Ulysses*. But Joyce's intertextuality does not, as Pound suggested, convey the impression that Joyce 'swallowed *La Tentation* whole'.[225] Certainly *La Tentation* stands as a stepping stone in relation to the generic revolution enacted in 'Circe'. But the episode's response to Flaubertian precedent is far more complex than Pound's image of wholesale absorption can convey: Joyce's use of Flaubert in 'Circe' is both wildly creative and textually tethered to its source.

For all their precision Joyce's intertextual procedures are not intended to function as annotation: the reader is not required or enjoined to recapitulate and analyze the nuts and bolts of Flaubert's erudition, or decipher symbols that would have been obscure even to the author's contemporaries (he or she may, however, spontaneously derive from the text that pleasure of recognition which a mode of intertextuality as punctilious and creative as Joyce's so satisfyingly affords). *Ulysses*'s recall of Flaubert's text is exact and focuses around particular nodes, but the meaning of this intertextuality is general and extends beyond binary correspondences. The effect of Joyce's telescoping of intertexts within his works is to open up an imaginary space behind the episode—a textual matrix of prior writings from which its elements are derived and rearranged into a series of carefully calibrated echoes. This effect almost exactly corresponds to Foucault's account of *La Tentation*'s dizzyingly complex relations to other books:

> it opens up the space of a literature that exists only within and through the network of the already written: it is a book in which the fiction of books is played out. It is not so much a new book, to be placed alongside the others, as it is a work which spreads itself out over the space of existing books. It

---

[222] 'Circe' notesheet 8, line 109; 'Circe' notesheet 10, line 69; 'Circe' notesheet 13, line 23; Herring, *Notesheets*, 310, 322, 333.
[223] *U* 15: 2,643.
[224] *FW* 13: 5.
[225] Pound, 'Paris Letter', *P/J*, 194.

covers them, conceals them, reveals them, in a single movement makes them sparkle and disappear [...] it is the dream of the other books: all the other books, dreaming books, dreamed books,—taken up again, fragmented, displaced, combined.[226]

One of the key characteristics of Joyce's intertextuality is that it is, like Flaubert's, self-referential: it seems, by its very prevalence, to draw attention to itself. As adumbrated by Stephen's thoughts in 'Proteus', *Ulysses*—and especially 'Circe', which in this respect constitutes a tipping point in Joyce's oeuvre—turns intra- and intertextuality into compositional principles (as they are in *La Tentation*, *Bouvard et Pécuchet*, and the *Dictionnaire des Idées Reçues*), thereby emphasizing the importance of those procedures of stranding and twining that enable writers to take their place within vast literary systems of connectivity without forfeiting their aspirations to originality.

CITIZENS IN *ULYSSES* AND *L'ÉDUCATION SENTIMENTALE*

'Circe' is by no means the only nexus of Flaubertian intertextuality in *Ulysses*. 'Cyclops' is another distinctly Flaubertian 'echoland'[227] within the novel. In that episode Joyce makes one character, designated as 'the citizen', the mouthpiece of the most fiercely nationalistic and anti-Semitic diatribe in the novel. The character, who remains as nameless as the narrator[228] who bears witness to the events that take place in Barney Kiernan's on the afternoon of 16 June 1904, is widely believed to have been inspired by the biographical model of Michael Cusack. Indeed, according to a very prevalent academic *idée reçue*, the citizen was fashioned directly from the stuff of Joyce's own encounters with the famous nationalist.[229] Yet this widespread view of the character as a realistic rendering of

---

[226] ['elle ouvre l'espace d'une littérature qui n'existe que dans et par le réseau du déjà écrit: livre où se joue la fiction des livres. [...] C'est moins un livre nouveau, à placer à côté des autres, qu'une oeuvre qui s'étend sur l'espace des livres existants. Elle les recouvre, les cache, les manifeste, d'un seul mouvement les fait étinceler et disparaître. [...] elle est le rêve des autres livres: tous les autres livres, rêvants, rêvés,—repris, fragmentés, déplacés, combinés' (Foucault, *La Bibliothèque fantastique*, 10)].

[227] *FW* 13: 5.

[228] In the 'Circe' episode, the narrator of 'Cyclops' reappears as 'the nameless one'— *U* 15: 1,143–9.

[229] Gifford states that 'the citizen' is 'Modeled on Michael Cusack (1847–1907), founder of the Gaelic Athletic Association (1884) [...] Cusack styled himself "Citizen Cusack"'—'*Ulysses' Annotated*, 316. Gifford refers the reader to Ellmann, who also writes of Cusack as a 'model': 'He [Clancy] brought Joyce to meet Cusack a few times, and Joyce

the founder of the Gaelic Athletic Association occludes other significant readings. The problem with this commonplace assumption of an equation between fact and fiction is not that it is untrue, but that it is only partially true, and that it has created and fostered a detrimental critical blindspot. That is to say: the inferred connection between 'the citizen' of 'Cyclops' and his putative real-life counterpart hinders a comprehensive grasp of the intertextual and semantic complexity of Joyce's chosen naming device. The supposition that Cusack's nickname is straightforwardly imported into the book detracts readers from sounding the word for other potential resonances: 'the citizen', as a name, has remained remarkably impermeable to scholarly investigation.

In Flaubert's *L'Éducation sentimentale* a vehemently chauvinistic character goes by the name of 'le Citoyen'.[230] The correspondences between Joyce's and Flaubert's citizens are numerous and compelling, strongly suggesting that Joyce's nameless citizen was at least partly forged in response to Flaubert's depiction of post-revolutionary France. Such an intertwining of realistic and literary elements in Joyce's works is not unusual: the incorporation of details taken from documented 'real life' is a constant feature of his writing; but just as crucial as the 'real-life' facts are the artistic procedures—techniques, structures, and devices—by which realistic elements are moulded into aesthetic form. The Ovidian and Apuleian *Metamorphoses* in *A Portrait of the Artist as a Young Man* and the Homeric *Odyssey* in *Ulysses* are the most obvious examples of Joyce's use of pre-existing formal literary structures to subtend narratives of life in contemporary Ireland. In analogous (but less overt) fashion, Joyce draws on the gnomonic architecture of Flaubert's *Trois Contes* to shape the stories of *Dubliners*. The adoption of Flaubert's 'Citoyen' represents

---

liked him little enough to make him model the narrow-minded and rhetorical Cyclops in *Ulysses*'—*JJ*, 61. Jeri Johnson annotates the first appearance of the citizen in the following terms: 'modelled on Michael Cusack (1847–1907) (as Joyce names him in an early draft of this episode)'—*Ulysses*, ed. Jeri Johnson, 885. The association is so widely accepted that a certain circularity prevails: Irish historians refer to Joyce's rendering of Cusack before (or instead of) providing independently discovered biographical facts. W. F. Mandle, for instance, introduces Cusack by invoking Joyce's character: 'Cusack was by all accounts a man of expansive gestures, fiery temperament and romantic aspiration. He has been immortalized as the Citizen in *Ulysses*, complete with knee breeches, a large hat, an even larger dog and a blackthorn stick—a massive figure who quaffed porter by the pint and hailed scabrously against English "syphilisation's" influence on Ireland. [. . .] The evidence from the real Cusack's letters and speeches and from what we know of his career, suggest that Joyce's parody was only slightly exaggerated.'—W. F. Mandle, *The Gaelic Athletic Association and Irish Nationalist Politics 1884–1924* (London: Christopher Helm, 1987), 2.

[230] The sobriquet of Joyce's citizen is never capitalized. That of Flaubert's 'Citoyen' almost always is, after some inconsistency of spelling in the character's first appearances.

another striking instance of Joyce's willingness to appropriate and adapt devices that Flaubert elaborated before him.

Although this section argues for the formative and hermeneutic importance of the antecedent of Flaubert's 'le Citoyen', the intention is not to deny the existence of biographical links to Cusack. The evidence that Joyce did have Michael Cusack in mind when he wrote the 'Cyclops' episode is strong enough; but it is worth stressing that it is evidence of a connection which Joyce chose to efface and destabilize. Indeed, the stages of the episode's composition show Joyce's decision to problematize the association. In the first drafted segments of the episode, inscribed in Buffalo notebook V.A.8, Joyce does not name any of his characters: instead, snippets of dialogue are preceded by symbols—such as dashes, *á*, or Z. By the end of the fourth of these drafted segments, the aggressive nationalist character has become 'Cusack'.[231] The next relevant genetic document—which probably came into existence before the drafting of this fourth fragment—consists of a letter Joyce received from Henry Davray around 28 June 1919, and on the back of which he compiled a list of characters under the heading 'Cyclops': 'Citizen Cusack' features as one of these.[232] In the later 'Cyclops' draft acquired by the National Library of Ireland in 2002, the 'Cusack' character is returned to anonymity as 'the citizen'.[233] These shifts from anonymity to onymity ('Cusack') and back to anonymity ('the citizen') through the successive stages of the episode's composition show Joyce's elaboration of the 'citizen' tag to have been a gradual, oscillating process, and highlight the importance he came to attach to anonymity as one of his character's defining features.

And indeed the body of Joyce's prior works suggests a long-standing investment in the evocative power of anonymity in fictional renderings of Cusack. 'The citizen' is anonymous in *Stephen Hero*, in which he is lampooned as the exponent of a kind of nationalism Stephen holds in contempt. The omission of Cusack's name in this instance is noteworthy because *Stephen Hero* in general is considerably more explicit in its political allusions than Joyce's later works. The word 'citizen' is already in place in the early draft novel, but its significance as a *clin d'oeil* to Cusack is even more veiled than in *Ulysses*. Featuring as a standard common noun, the term bears no hint of its referential implications:

---

[231] *JJA 13*, 109.

[232] *JJA 13*, 137. The letter belongs to the Cornell Joyce Collection and is listed in *The Cornell Joyce Collection: A Catalogue*, ed. Robert Scholes (Ithaca: Cornell University Press, 1961), 25. The description given here of the genetic stages of Joyce's portrayal of Cusack is indebted to Michael Groden's article, 'Cyclops in Progress, 1919', *JJQ*, vol. 12, nos 1 and 2 (Fall 1974 and Winter 1975), 125–6.

[233] 'Joyce Papers 2002', II.ii.4. 'Cyclops': Partial Draft', Dublin, National Library of Ireland, NLI MS 36,639/10, 11r.

A very stout black-bearded citizen who always wore a wideawake hat and a long bright green muffler was a constant figure at these meetings. When the company was going home he was usually to be seen surrounded by a circle of young men who looked very meagre about his bulk. He had the voice of an ox and he could be heard at a great distance, criticising, denouncing and scoffing. His circle was the separatist centre and in it reigned the irreconcilable temper.[234]

For all the grammatical simplicity by which it is effected, the withholding of the citizen's name does not entirely forestall attention: it seems rather odd, in fact, that a character especially singled out among the separatist crowd should be identified by neither name nor status. In *A Portrait of the Artist as a Young Man* the word 'citizen' disappears altogether, with Stephen pointedly steering clear of any reference to the Irish 'nation'—mention of which would suggest allegiance to those nationalist groups from which he seeks to distance himself—in favour of a reference to his mission as the forger of 'the consciousness of [his] race'.[235] Michael Cusack makes a cameo appearance in the novel as a spur to Davin's 'delight in rude bodily skill' ('for Davin had sat at the feet of Michael Cusack, the Gael'), but Joyce avoids overly explicit an emphasis on his practical involvement in political militancy by dubbing him 'the Gael' rather than 'the citizen' (the chosen epithet befitting Stephen's interest in 'race' over 'nation' in *A Portrait* but also ensuring that Cusack's predominant association at this point is with the Gaelic Athletic Association and with that sporting enthusiasm it sought to promote in the likes of Davin).[236]

This section of Chapter 5 will argue that Joyce's reading of *L'Éducation sentimentale* was crucial to the moulding of 'the citizen'. But even before the close parallels to Flaubert's novel are noted, the term's deployment in 'Cyclops' rings as an intentional invocation of the connotations attaching to ideas of 'citizenship' in revolutionary and post-revolutionary France. In particular, the word summons the spirit of egalitarian struggle that led to the overturning of the French Ancien Régime in 1789, to the July Revolution of 1848, and to the other democratic overhauls that rippled across Europe during the Spring of Nations. The fact that the combative, anti-imperialistic connotations of the French word were still present to Irish minds at the turn of the twentieth century is to be understood in the context of Ireland's continuing sense of a prospective alliance with France,

---

[234] *SH*, 61.
[235] *P*, 213.
[236] *P*, 151. Stephen's distrust of the ideology of nationhood is evident in his conversation with Davin in Chapter V: 'You talk to me of nationality, language, religion. I shall try to fly by those nets.'—*P*, 171.

a country that had been considered a source of potential military assistance since the late eighteenth century—particularly during and in the aftermath of the French Revolution, and subsequently in 1796 and 1798 (with Wolfe Tone at the Irish helm).[237] Separatist hope in nineteenth-century Ireland was intertwined with this legacy of expectation. Towards the end of the nineteenth century a new Anglo-French war was considered by some Irishmen to represent the country's best hope for freedom. The centenary of the 1798 uprising reignited a wistful sense of connection with France and rekindled hopes of a political alliance.[238] In the context of this historical perspective, Cusack's nicknaming as 'the citizen' comes to look less like the idiosyncratic gesture of a group of backward-looking, chauvinistic eccentrics and more like a symptom of widespread nostalgic separatist Francophilia.

Joyce's awareness of such political attitudes is clear from a passage in *Stephen Hero* in which Stephen mentally derides what he considers to be a form of naive and outdated optimism on the part of his countrymen. The nationalist fervour unduly fuelled by reports of insignificant gestures across the Channel is dismissed as laughable overexcitement:

> The orators of this patriotic party were not ashamed to cite the precedents of Switzerland and France. The intelligent centres of the movement were so scantily supplied that the analogies they gave out as exact and potent were really analogies built haphazard upon very inexact knowledge. The cry of a solitary Frenchman (A bas l'Angleterre!) at a Celtic re-union in Paris would be made by these enthusiasts the subject of a leading article in which would be shown the imminence of aid for Ireland from the French Government.[239]

The futility of Ireland's hopes regarding French assistance is highlighted again in *A Portrait of the Artist as a Young Man*. Walking through the streets of Dublin, Stephen is reminded of a ceremony he witnessed some years previously:

> In the roadway at the head of the street a slab was set to the memory of Wolfe Tone and he remembered having been present with his father at its laying. He remembered with bitterness that scene of tawdry tribute. There were four French delegates in a brake and one, a plump smiling young man, held, wedged on a stick, a card on which were printed the words: *Vive l'Irlande!*[240]

[237] R. F. Foster, *Modern Ireland: 1600–1972* (Harmondsworth: Penguin Press, 1988), 314n, 259–80.
[238] Patrick Maume, *The Long Gestation: Irish Nationalist Life 1891–1918* (Dublin: Gill and Macmillan, 1999), 27–8.
[239] *SH*, 62.
[240] *P*, 154. The passage evokes a real event: 'In Dublin, separatists raised funds for a Wolfe Tone monument in Stephen's Green, while Redmond planned a Parnell monument

Stephen considers his countrymen's deluded Francophile hopefulness with cynicism and discouragement. In *Ulysses* Stephen's disenchanted recollections of his encounters with Kevin Egan[241] in Paris act as a restatement of his disillusionment regarding a French connection that endured in the popular consciousness but had in reality long been extinct. In 'Cyclops' even the citizen has lost all faith in the possibility of assistance from abroad, the signature of the Entente Cordiale between France and England on 8 April 1904 having marked the definitive breach of trust on that score:

> –The French! says the citizen. Set of dancing masters? Do you know what it is? They were never worth a roasted fart to Ireland. Aren't they trying to make an entente cordial [*sic*] now at Tay Pay's dinnerparty with perfidious Albion? Firebrands of Europe and they always were.
> –*Conspuez les français*, says Lenehan, nobbling his beer.[242]

Like *Ulysses*, *L'Éducation sentimentale* is much concerned with prevalent contemporary discourses of nationalism and citizenship. And Flaubert's treatment of post-revolutionary France in the novel can be seen as a springboard to many of the attitudes embodied in Joyce's modern-day Cyclops. The book spans at least three of France's numerous nineteenth-century political regimes: the July Monarchy (1830–48), the Second Republic (1848–52), and the Second Empire (1852–70). There are some arresting connections to the reflections on empire that are to be found in *Ulysses*. Thus, *L'Éducation* stages precisely the kind of empty gesture that inspires Stephen's disheartened detachment concerning the prospect of political and military aid from France. In the middle of his doctoral examination, Deslauriers (who plays the part of friend and foil to the novel's protagonist Frédéric Moreau), overcome by a sense of the world's injustice, exclaims against all forms of tyrannical oppression, envisioning a world free of colonial domination. Specific mention is made of Ireland's predicament:

---

at the top of O'Connell Street.'—Maume, *The Long Gestation*, 28. The slab is also mentioned in 'Wandering Rocks'—*U* 10: 378.

[241] Stephen and 'the citizen' have encounters with Kevin Egan in common. 'The citizen' mentions his meetings with the Parisian wild goose in a tirade against the English and their putative belonging to the 'European family': 'They're not European, says the citizen. I was in Europe with Kevin Egan of Paris. You wouldn't see a trace of them or their language anywhere in Europe except in a *cabinet d'aisance*.'—*U* 12: 1,202–5.

[242] *U* 12: 1,385–9.

and then the Franks will no longer oppress the Gauls, *the English the Irish*, the Yanks the Red Indians, the Turks the Arabs, the whites the blacks, Poland...[243]

Joyce may also have noted with interest the vehement hatred Flaubert's 'Citoyen' expresses for England:

The stars were not guiding things in accordance with his ideas. He was becoming a hypochondriac, wouldn't even read the papers, and bellowed with rage at the mere mention of England.[244]

The first appearance of Flaubert's 'Citoyen' is silent and anonymous. Frédéric barely notices him when he first sees him reading in a corner of Mr Arnoux' art shop:

In an armchair on the right next to a filing cabinet a man sat reading a paper, still with his hat on.[245]

It is only by way of an animal-like grunt that the man reclaims narrative attention:

But a sort of growl was coming from the corner of the fireplace; it was the newspaper reader in his armchair. He was five feet nine inches tall, had slightly drooping eyelids, grey hair and a majestic look. His name was Regimbart.
'What's the matter, Citizen?' enquired Arnoux.
'Another bit of skulduggery by the government!'[246]

Unlike Joyce's citizen, Flaubert's character is given a proper name even though both the narrator and his acquaintances in the novel more often address him by his sobriquet. The surname Flaubert chooses for him is not innocent, however: it adds to the reader's sense of 'le Citoyen' as a brutish character, whose outlandish behaviour pertains more to the animal than to the human. The French verb 'régimber' refers to the kicking action of

---

[243] *ESE*, 121 (my emphasis) ['et les Franks ne pèseront plus sur les Gaulois, *les Anglais sur les Irlandais*, les Yankees sur les Peaux-Rouges, les Turcs sur les Arabes, les blancs sur les nègres, la Pologne...' (*ES*, 130)].

[244] *ESE*, 187 ['La Providence ne gouvernant point les choses selon ses idées, il tournait à l'hypocondriaque, ne voulait même plus lire les journaux, et poussait des rugissements au seul nom de l'Angleterre.' (*ES*, 194)].

[245] *ESE*, 37 ['À droite, près d'un cartonnier, un homme dans un fauteuil lisait le journal, en gardant son chapeau sur sa tête' (*ES*, 52)].

[246] *ESE*, 38 ['Mais une sorte de grommellement sortit du coin de la cheminée; c'était le personnage qui lisait son journal, dans le fauteuil. Il avait cinq pieds neuf pouces, les paupières un peu tombantes, la chevelure grise, l'air majestueux,—et s'appelait Régimbart./–Qu'est-ce donc, citoyen? dit Arnoux./–Encore une nouvelle canaillerie du Gouvernement!' (*ES*, 53)].

an animal—usually a horse or mule—when it refuses to move forward. Used figuratively, the verb means to act in a recalcitrant manner, to complain, protest, or resist. The normal form of the word is 'régimbeur/euse'; so that 'Régimbart' reads as a common variation on the proper adjectival form (though the correct spelling would be 'régimbard'). In French the practice of coining new words by the addition of an -*ard* suffix is well established ('pleurnichard' describes a person prone to complaining, 'vantard' describes a person prone to boastfulness). The suffix's meaning is immediately recognizable: its value is augmentative and pejorative. To a French ear, the word combines allusions to unsubmissive animals, politics (the adjunction of the '–ard' suffix can denote belonging to a political group, as in 'soixante-huitard'), with the ring of insult. 'Le Citoyen', as Flaubert's onomastic choice suggests, is a rather contemptible, recalcitrant, conservative animal.[247]

We soon hear more about 'le citoyen Régimbart'. Like 'the citizen' of 'Cyclops', he sits in corners reading nationalistic and republican newspapers:

> Every day the latter [Regimbart] would settle down in his armchair by the fireside, pick up *Le National*, and monopolize it, expressing his reactions by exclaiming out loud or merely shrugging his shoulders.[248]

As in *Stephen Hero*, in which Joyce painted a picture of the citizen as a man 'who always wore a wideawake hat',[249] 'le Citoyen' has a 'hat with a turned-up brim'[250] that never fails to mark him out in a crowd. Like

---

[247] In keeping with the animal connotations of his surname (Régimbart), Flaubert's 'Citoyen' behaves like an animal. He emits 'a sort of growl' in lieu of words and 'bellowed with rage'—*ESE*, 38, 187 ['une sorte de grommellement'; 'poussait des rugissements' (*ES*, 53, 194)]. This may have inspired Joyce's emphasis on the citizen's canine features. When he is found in Barney Kiernan's, 'the citizen claps his paw on his knee'—*U* 12: 137. He later demonstrates his remarkable ability to engage in extensive conversations with his dog Garryowen: 'Then he starts hauling and mauling and talking to him in Irish and the old towser growling, letting on to answer, like a duet in the opera. Such growling you never heard as they let off between them.'—*U* 12: 705–7. This spectacular form of interaction is immediately parodied in one of the episode's 'gigantic' passages, which makes mention of a 'really marvellous exhibition of cynanthropy' (which the *OED* defines as 'species of madness in which a man imagines himself to be a dog')—*U* 12: 714. Joyce makes witty, typically punning use of the word in this passage: the context makes it clear that the narrator refers to Garryowen's special ability to impersonate human behaviour.

[248] *ESE*, 42 ['Tous les jours, Régimbart s'asseyait au coin du feu, dans son fauteuil, s'emparait du *National*, ne le quittait plus, et exprimait sa pensée par des exclamations ou de simples haussements d'épaules.' (*ES*, 57)]. *Le National* had a republican bias—*ES*, editorial note to page 57, 480.

[249] *SH*, 61.

[250] *ESE*, 42 ['chapeau à bords retroussés' (*ES*, 57)].

'the citizen' of 'Cyclops', whose handkerchief gives rise to a 'gigantic' parody ('The muchtreasured and intricately embroidered ancient Irish facecloth'),[251] 'le Citoyen' has a distinctive handkerchief:

> From time to time he'd wipe his forehead with a handkerchief which he kept tightly rolled and stuffed between the two top buttons of his green frock-coat.[252]

Régimbart's daily routine involves ceaseless moves from one drinking hole to the next. As the narrator explains, it is not merely the craving for alcoholic beverages that impels Regimbart to traipse from bar to bar. The mix of politics and alcohol is as central to the life of Flaubert's 'Citoyen' as it is to that of Joyce's 'citizen':

> it was not his fondness for drink that attracted Citizen Regimbart to these haunts but his ingrained habit of talking politics in such places.[253]

Like 'the citizen', 'le Citoyen' has a predilection for bars that recall dark and distant caves (not least because the French word 'caves' can mean both 'caves' and 'wine cellars'). Frédéric rushes around Paris 'grimly determined to dig him out of his wine-cellar, however remote',[254] foreshadowing Joyce's mock-ironic portrayal of the citizen as a 'broadshouldered deep-chested stronglimbed [. . .] hero' whose breathing causes the 'walls of the cave to vibrate and tremble'.[255] When Frédéric finally finds him, 'le Citoyen' is at the back of a bar on his own, much as 'the citizen' is discovered 'up in the corner' of Barney Kiernan's:[256]

> And at last, through the pipe smoke, he sighted him at the back of the room beyond the bar, sitting by himself behind the billiard table with his chin sunk on his chest meditating in front of a mug of beer.[257]

Like Joyce's 'citizen', Flaubert's 'Citoyen' is at once ridiculous and obscurely threatening—so much so in fact that he is described as 'haunting'

---

[251] *U* 12: 1,438–64.

[252] *ESE*, 42 ['De temps en temps, il s'essuyait le front avec son mouchoir de poche roulé en boudin, et qu'il portait sur sa poitrine, entre deux boutons de sa redingote verte.' (*ES*, 57)].

[253] *ESE*, 43 ['ce n'était pas l'amour des boissons qui attirait dans ces endroits le citoyen Régimbart, mais l'habitude ancienne d'y causer politique' (*ES*, 57–8)].

[254] *ESE*, 117 ['bien résolu à l'extraire des caves les plus lointaines' (*ES*, 127)].

[255] *U* 12: 152–5, 167.

[256] *U* 12: 119.

[257] *ESE*, 117–18 ['Enfin, il l'aperçut à travers la fumée des pipes, seul, au fond de l'arrière-buvette après le billard, une chope devant lui, le menton baissé et dans une attitude méditative.' (*ES*, 127)].

the cafés he patronizes.[258] Again, the details are conspicuously similar to their later Joycean counterparts:

> It was a small one in the place de la Bastille where he'd spend all day, in the corner on the right at the back, more or less part of the furniture.[259]

The political opinions of Flaubert's 'Citoyen' also read as antecedents to those of Joyce's 'citizen'. One of 'le Citoyen''s greatest grievances is against the French monarchy, much as the citizen's venom is both implicitly and explicitly directed at the English Crown: 'The Citizen would start by voicing fresh grievances against the Crown.'[260] His republican views, like those of 'the citizen', are nationalistic to the point of xenophobia. His understanding of international relations is bitter ('Haven't we been insulted enough by bloody foreigners?'[261]) and bellicose, and his views are especially passionate regarding the need to regain lost territories:

> He was unhappy about everything and especially that 'we hadn't got back our national frontiers'.[262]

He is also ridden with class hatred, and these aggressive tendencies are confirmed when Frédéric appeals to 'le Citoyen' to act as a witness to his duel with Cisy. Republicanism turns to homicidal glee when 'le Citoyen' gathers that Cisy is a gentleman of rank: 'And when he heard that the opponent was a viscount, his face lit up with a murderous grin.'[263] His attitude throughout the build-up to the duel is vicious. His advice is dealt out 'brutally'.[264] His shadow, projected onto the wall as he imparts his fencing knowledge to Frédéric, is both literally gigantic and 'gigantic' in a way that anticipates Joyce's use of the word ('gigantism') to describe the 'technic' in 'Cyclops'.[265] All at once terrifying and grotesque,

---

[258] *ESE*, 428 ['il [. . .] connut ainsi le café que hantait maintenant le Citoyen' (*ES*, 425)].

[259] *ESE*, 428 ['C'était un petit café sur la place de la Bastille, où il se tenait toute la journée, dans le coin de droite, au fond, ne bougeant pas plus que s'il avait fait partie de l'immeuble.' (*ES*, 425)].

[260] *ESE*, 187 ['Le Citoyen commençait par articuler contre la Couronne quelque nouveau grief.' (*ES*, 194)].

[261] *ESE*, 188 ['Est-ce que nous n'avons pas assez des affronts de l'étranger!' (*ES*, 195)].

[262] *ESE*, 321 ['Il était mécontent de tout, et particulièrement de ce que nous n'avions pas repris nos frontières naturelles.' (*ES*, 323–4); Parmée takes a liberty in placing the last seven words in inverted commas: they are not thus framed in the original text.].

[263] *ESE*, 243 ['Et un sourire homicide le dérida, en apprenant que l'adversaire était un noble.' (*ES*, 248)].

[264] My translation; *ESE*, 243 ('curtly') ['brutalement' (ES, 248)].

[265] Gilbert, *James Joyce's 'Ulysses'*, 30.

his enormous figure was silhouetted on the wall and his hat seemed to be touching the ceiling.[266]

L'Éducation portrays the beginnings of the Second Republic in 1848 as completely chaotic. Flaubert's parody of the meaning of the word 'citoyen' takes on a new dimension with this change of political regime. Indeed, whereas Régimbart was at first the only character in the book to be referred to as a 'citoyen', the return to a republican mode of government after the fall of the July Monarchy leads to a generalization of the appellation: suddenly the book resonates with the cries of innumerable 'citoyens' intent upon reliving 1789 en masse. When elections are called, Frédéric decides to stand for a seat at the Assemblée Nationale. The first gathering to which he proposes to give a speech is opened by a reading of 'the Declaration of the Rights of Man and of the Citizen, the usual act of faith'.[267] From this moment on, the proliferation of the word becomes a measure of Flaubert's barely impersonalized, deeply cynical view of France's hopelessly sentimental attempt to recapture the spirit of the earlier revolution: 'The Citizen Jean Jacques Langreneux', 'Oh, I'm sorry, citizens, so sorry!', 'citizens seeking a mandate from the people', 'Citizens! said Compain, Citizens!'[268] The narrator emphasizes the era's obsession with the term: 'And having by continual repetition of "Citizens!" obtained relative silence'.[269] Notions of citizenship are linked to ideas of purity and renewal ('We need new blood, citizens whose hearts are pure, whose hands are clean! Would anyone like to come forward?'[270]). Such aspirations are systematically undercut by the staleness of the clichés with which the new system is already riddled:

> To be accepted you always had to speak disparagingly of lawyers and trot out expressions like 'grist to the mill', 'social problem', and 'workshop' as often as possible.[271]

---

[266] ESE, 243 ['sa silhouette énorme se projetait sur la muraille, avec son chapeau qui semblait toucher au plafond' (ES, 249)].

[267] ESE, 329 ['la déclaration des Droits de l'homme et du citoyen, acte de foi habituel'. (ES, 331)].

[268] ESE, 329–32 ['Le citoyen Jean-Jacques Langreneux'; 'Pardon! citoyens! pardon!'; 'les citoyens qui briguaient le mandat populaire'; 'Citoyens! dit alors Compain, citoyens!' (ES, 332, 334)].

[269] ESE, 332 ['Et, à force de répéter: "Citoyens", ayant obtenu un peu de silence' (ES, 334)].

[270] ESE, 334 ['Il nous faut des citoyens purs, des hommes entièrement neufs! Quelqu'un se présente-t-il?' (ES, 336)].

[271] ESE, 327 ['On devait, par affectation de bon sens, dénigrer toujours les avocats, et servir le plus souvent possible de ces locutions: 'apporter sa pierre à l'édifice,—problème social,—atelier.' (ES, 330)].

In keeping with the demands of his poetics, Flaubert's fiction impersonalizes the acerbically angry political positions articulated in his letters. In the *Correspondance*, he sometimes refers to friends or respected acquaintances as 'citizen X' or 'citizen Y': 'I have seen citizen Bouilhet, who has had a real triumph in his glorious birthplace';[272] 'enormous success of *L'Assommoir* by citizen Zola'.[273] In such phrases Flaubert's usage is clearly tongue-in-cheek. The impression conveyed is of an in-joke about the current political order and its efforts to instil through language (the dissemination of the word 'citoyen') a sense of equality that Flaubert perceived as a reprehensible legitimization of mediocrity. The jocose treatment of the new social and political regime where mentions of friends are concerned is counterpointed by numerous allusions to other 'citoyens' whose names are associated with denigration or disgust. There is outrage in Flaubert's mention of the man who called for the execution of Louis-Philippe without trial:

> Fangeat, who's lately reappeared, is the citizen who, on 24 February 1848, requested the execution of Louis-Philippe, 'without trial'. That's the way to promote Progress.[274]

Flaubert uses the word to revel in the misfortunes of those he despises: 'Delighted to see citizen Méry in such a fiasco!'[275] Incensed by the automatic equation of citizenship with progress and enlightenment, and deeply distrustful of the linguistic glorification of the masses[276] and of a sense of belonging that he did not feel and did not want to feel, Flaubert vigorously asserted that:

---

[272] Flaubert to George Sand, 15 December 1866, *GW*, 319 ['J'ai vu le citoyen Bouilhet, qui a eu dans sa belle patrie un vrai triomphe.' (*C3*, 578)].

[273] Flaubert to Léonie Brainne, 15–16 February 1877 ['succès fou de *L'Assommoir* du citoyen Zola' (*C5*, 188)].

[274] Flaubert to George Sand, 24 June 1869 ['Fangeat, reparu ces jours derniers, est le citoyen qui, le 25 février 1848, a demandé la mort de Louis-Philippe, "sans jugement". C'est comme ça qu'on sert la cause du Progrès.' (*C4*, 61)].

[275] Flaubert to Louise Colet, 26 September 1853 ['Enchanté du fiasco du citoyen Méry!' (*C2*, 441)]. Joseph Méry (1798–1866) was a poet, novelist, and journalist of Flaubert's acquaintance. The low esteem in which Flaubert held him—chiefly for his treatment of art as a money-making pursuit—is obvious from the rest of the letter.

[276] In *L'Éducation* 'le peuple' gradually becomes the object of what appears to be fanatical adulation by the narrator (with the admixture of Flaubert's hallmark ambiguous irony) and characters alike. There are suggestions of enormous power in the narrator's laconic observation: 'It was the Paris People.' Indications of the people's new status abound: '"What a myth!" said Hussonet. "Behold the sovereign people!"'; 'there were too many people about'; 'a platoon of Municipal Guards [...] made a deep bow to the People'; '*I* think the People are terrific [*sublime*]!'—*ESE*, 314–16 ['C'était le peuple.'; 'Quel mythe! dit Hussonet. Voilà le peuple souverain!'; 'la multitude était trop nombreuse'; 'un peloton de gardes municipaux [...] saluèrent le peuple très bas'; 'moi, je trouve le peuple sublime' (*ES*, 317–19)].

I want not to belong to anything, to be a member of no academy, no corporation, no association whatsover. I hate the herd, the norm and the leveller. Bedouin all you please; citizen, never.[277]

Flaubert's fury is a rage against cliché, against the mould, the mob, and against linguistic and ideological forces that he saw as a threat to individual thought, to art, to truth. The Second Republic (like its eighteenth-century predecessor) aspired to act as a social leveller. But in Flaubert's view 'le niveau' threatened to destroy everything—insight, beauty, excellence—that rose above the norm. Towards the end of his life, when France seemed about to fall to Prussia, Flaubert blamed the idealization of citizenship for the country's decline:

> My dream is to live elsewhere than in France, in a country where one would not be obliged to be a citizen, to hear the beating of drums, to vote, to be part of a commission or jury. Ugh! Ugh![278]

It is ironic that 'le Citoyen' should share this cynical view of egalitarianism. When Pellerin (failed painter turned photographer) and other aspiring artists solicit government funding to fulfil their farcical clichéridden dreams, it is 'le Citoyen' who exclaims:

> 'How stupid!' grumbled a voice in the crowd. 'Nothing but humbug all the time! Never any real action!'
> It was Regimbart.[279]

One of Flaubert's most heartfelt opinions is thus introduced into the text by way of one of the book's most obviously caricatural characters. Moments such as these, in which a knowing reader may recognize the author's own views, are a feature of Flaubert's and Joyce's writing. Flaubert's personal opinions are systematically dispersed among his characters, effecting a discursive diffusion that deprives the reader of any firm interpretative footholds. Early on in the novel Deslauriers, another of the novel's most dislikeable characters, becomes the mouthpiece of Flaubert's thoughts concerning the illusory nature of the difference between monarchical and republican modes of government:

---

[277] Flaubert to Louise Colet, 23 January 1854 ['Je veux ne faire partie de rien, n'être membre d'aucune académie, d'aucune corporation ni association quelconque. Je hais le troupeau, la règle et le niveau. Bédouin, tant qu'il vous plaira; citoyen, jamais.' (C2, 515)].

[278] Flaubert to Claudius Popelin, 28 October 1870 ['Mon rêve est de m'en aller vivre ailleurs qu'en France, dans un pays où l'on ne soit pas obligé d'être citoyen, d'entendre le tambour, de voter, de faire partie d'une commission ou d'un jury. Pouah! Pouah!' (C4, 257)].

[279] ESE, 321 ['"Quelle bêtise!" grommela une voix dans la foule. "Toujours des blagues! Rien de fort!"'/C'était Régimbart.' (ES, 323)].

But why should the sovereignty of the people be more sacred than the divine right of kings? They're both fictions![280]

This dissemination of contestant views regarding republicanism and citizenship is compounded by the fact that when the Second Republic is proclaimed and the streets ring with hopeful rallying cries of 'citoyen' once more, nothing changes noticeably for the better. *L'Éducation sentimentale* surveys decades of French history and closes on a note of blank dissatisfaction. Frédéric, previously an enthusiastic republican and a believer in 'le peuple' ('*I* think the People are terrific [*sublime*]!'),[281] loses these faiths:

the Republic seems to me to have run out of steam. Who knows, perhaps Progress can only be achieved by an artistocracy—or by one man? Initiative always comes from above! The masses aren't yet grown up, whatever people claim.[282]

Analogously Dussardier, working man, ardent revolutionary, and one of the very few straightforwardly likeable characters in the book, is driven to despair by the Republic's failure to deliver on its promises:

When the Revolution came I thought we'd be happy. Can you remember how wonderful it all was, how we all felt free to breathe? But now we've sunk even lower than before! [...] you can see the workers are as bad as the middle classes! [...] If it goes on like this, it'll drive me mad. I'd like to get killed![283]

Within the space of twenty pages, Dussardier is shot dead with the lost cause upon his lips: 'Long live the Republic!'[284] In the novel's closing scene, Frédéric and Deslauriers remember an unsuccessful adolescent excursion to a provincial brothel as the highlight of their lives. No mention is made of the (distinctly inglorious) part each has played in the politics of the day, as though recent history were a nightmare from which each were trying to forget. Their silences and recollections confirm that in private as in public, little if anything has been learnt, little if anything has turned out well. The novel comes to a close on this vignette,

---

[280] *ESE*, 194 ['Mais en quoi la souveraineté du peuple serait-elle plus sacrée que le droit divin? L'un et l'autre sont deux fictions!' (*ES*, 201)].

[281] *ESE*, 316 ['moi, je trouve le peuple sublime' (*ES*, 319)].

[282] *ESE*, 402 ['la République me paraît vieille. Qui sait? Le Progrès, peut-être, n'est réalisable que par une aristocratie ou par un homme? L'initiative vient toujours d'en haut! Le peuple est mineur, quoi qu'on prétende.' (*ES*, 400)].

[283] *ESE*, 433–4 ['J'avais cru, quand la révolution est arrivée, qu'on serait heureux. Vous rappelez-vous comme c'était beau! comme on respirait bien! Mais nous voilà retombés pire que jamais. [...] les ouvriers ne valent pas mieux que les bourgeois, voyez-vous! [...] J'en deviendrai fou, si ça continue. J'ai envie de me faire tuer.' (*ES*, 430)].

[284] *ESE*, 455 ['Vive la République!' (*ES*, 450)].

the nation's sentimental hopes of ideal citizenry punctured by the wistful backward glances of two of its once buoyant, now disappointed children.

In the 'Eumaeus' episode of *Ulysses*, the narrative voice (as though rehearsing one of the lessons of Flaubert's novel) reflects that 'history repeat[s] itself with a difference'.[285] In 'Cyclops', Joyce repeats Flaubert with a difference, personifying the concept of citizenship to probe the darker resonances of one of the Enlightenment's most central aspirations. In both *L'Éducation* and *Ulysses* citizenship proves to be 'one of those big words which make us so unhappy'.[286] As such, it forms part of each writer's interrogation of the legacy of the Enlightenment. As Ronald Bush has argued, two strands of modernist thinking coexist in each author's works, and this duality applies to the issue of citizenship. In each, the idea evokes both the anticipation and reality of progress, and the farcical, destructive extremism to which uncritical adherence to the term can potentially give rise. Joyce's and Flaubert's citizens reflect their authors' shared determination 'to expose rather than advance the pretence of Western rational conviction'.[287] Flaubert, as Bush advances, 'skewers modernizing cant' by personifying catchwords such as citizenship to satirize 'not just superstitious traditional culture nor a caricatured version of rational modernity, but the Enlightenment itself'[288] in its buoyantly optimistic attitude to progress. In Flaubert's own words:

> The human race is not doing anything unexpected. Ever since my youth its hopeless miseries have filled me with bitterness. Therefore I feel no sense of disillusion at all. I believe that the crowd, the herd, will always be odious. [. . .] We are blundering about with the fag-end [*afterbirth*] of the French Revolution, which has been an abortion, a failure, a flop, 'whatever people may say'.[289]

Without carrying over Flaubert's despair, Joyce's intertextual response mobilizes his knowledge of *L'Éducation* in the service of his own impersonalized, intellectual scepticism regarding the assumptions inherent in the social and political heritage of the Enlightenment.

---

[285] *U* 16: 1,525–6.
[286] Joyce, 'An Irish Poet', *OCPW*, 62.
[287] Bush, 'Joyce's Modernisms', 13.
[288] Bush, 'Joyce's Modernisms', 16.
[289] Flaubert to George Sand, 8 September 1871, *GW*, 362 ['L'humanité n'offre rien de nouveau. Son irrémédiable misère m'a empli d'amertume, dès ma jeunesse. Aussi, maintenant, n'ai-je aucune désillusion. Je crois que la foule, le nombre, le troupeau sera toujours haïssable. [. . .] Nous pataugeons dans l'arrière-faix de la Révolution, qui a été un avortement, une chose ratée, un four "quoi qu'on dise"' (*C4*, 375–6)].

ULYSSES, BOUVARD ET PÉCUCHET, AND THE DICTIONNAIRE DES IDÉES REÇUES

Like *La Tentation de saint Antoine*, *Bouvard et Pécuchet* has long been credited with having sown the seeds of some of the experimental writing deployed in Joyce's *Ulysses*. Flaubert's last, unfinished, posthumously published novel tells the story of two Parisian copying clerks who leave the capital on their retirement to set up house in the Norman countryside and devote themselves to the acquisition of knowledge. Branch after branch of learning is assayed, field after field of scholarship—whether theoretical or practical, scientific or literary—is tackled in turn, until the two, full of goodwill and bonhomie though they are, renounce their aims, finding the task more intractable, and truth fundamentally more elusive, than they had anticipated. In the sketchily drafted ending of the book, Bouvard and Pécuchet return to the simple unthinking pleasure of handwritten copying. Guy de Maupassant refers to 'this strange and encyclopaedic book' as 'a philosophical novel and the most prodigious ever written'.[290] Mario Vargas Llosa describes Flaubert's prose in *Bouvard* as 'erudite, scientific and full of irony or sarcasm, with flashes of humour'.[291] Henry James sees in it 'the intended epos of the blatancy, the comprehensive bêtise of mankind'. With chagrin he calls the book 'as sad as something perverse and puerile done for a wager'; and with typical bafflement remarks that 'it had literally been his [Flaubert's] life-long dream to crown his career with a panorama of human ineptitude'.[292] James also notes that *Bouvard* is:

> the cream of that *Dictionnaire des idées reçues* for which all his life he had taken notes, and which eventually resolved itself into the encylopaedic exactitude and the lugubrious humour of the novel.[293]

James is accurate in his observation that the conception of the *Dictionnaire* predated that of *Bouvard*: it was indeed from the germ of that original project that the 'bouvard-et-pécuchetian' scheme emerged.[294] As early as

---

[290] ['ce livre étrange et encyclopédique'; 'un roman philosophique, et le plus prodigieux qu'on ait jamais écrit' (Guy de Maupassant, review of *Bouvard et Pécuchet*, *Le Gaulois*, 6 April 1881, in *BP*, 445–6)].

[291] Llosa, 'Flaubert, Our Contemporary', 223.

[292] James, 'Gustave Flaubert', 339, 335.

[293] James, 'Gustave Flaubert', 342.

[294] The coinage is Roland Barthes': 'what I would very much like to call (but I see storm-clouds on the horizon): bouvard-and-pécuchet-ity', *Mythologies*, trans. Annette Lavers (London: Jonathan Cape, 1972), 136 ['ce que je voudrais bien pouvoir appeler (mais je sens des foudres à l'horizon): la bouvard-et-pécuchéité' (*Mythologies* [Paris: Flammarion, 1992], 27)].

September 1850 Flaubert sketched out his fiercely ironic plan for the dictionary in a letter to Louis Bouilhet:

> Such a book, done thoroughly, with a good preface explaining that the aim of the book is to wed the public to tradition, order and general orthodoxy, yet with the materials arranged so that the reader has no idea whether or not we're taking the piss, it might be a rather strange book, and even a successful one, for it would be intensely topical.[295]

Thoughts of the *Dictionnaire* and of novelistic fury were intertwined in a letter penned to Louise Colet two years later:

> Sometimes I have an atrocious urge to shower insults all over the human race and one day I shall do so, in another ten years, with a long novel done on a grand scale; meanwhile an old idea has come back to me, I mean my *Dictionnaire des idées reçues*.[296]

Twenty years later, with the Prussian invasion and the reviled confusion of the Commune at the forefront of his mind, a furious Flaubert ('The enormity of modern stupidity makes me furious')[297] finally got started on these twinned endeavours. The two-pronged project was a vast one, and it was not until he was nearing its end that Flaubert decided that the *Dictionnaire*, whence his thoughts of *Bouvard* had sprung, was to become subsumed to the novel and 'placed in the second volume'.[298]

As is the case with many of the relationships that have been discovered between Joyce's and Flaubert's writing, the analogy between *Ulysses* and *Bouvard et Pécuchet* was first articulated by Ezra Pound in reviews of *Ulysses* written during its serialization in *The Little Review* and following its subsequent publication in book form. Pound's analysis of Joyce's debt to Flaubert in this area has exerted a strong influence on subsequent critical thinking. Richard Cross, for instance, devotes a chapter of *Flaubert and Joyce* to the connections between

---

[295] Flaubert to Louis Bouilhet, 4 September 1850, *GW*, 155 ['Ce livre *complètement* fait et précédé d'une bonne préface où l'on indiquerait comme quoi l'ouvrage a été fait dans le but de rattacher le public à la tradition, à l'ordre, à la convention générale, et arrangée de telle manière que le lecteur ne sache pas si on se fout de lui, oui ou non, ce serait peut-être une oeuvre étrange, et capable de réussir, car elle serait toute d'actualité.' (*C1*, 678–9)].

[296] Flaubert to Louise Colet, 16 December 1852, *GW*, 196 ['J'ai quelquefois des prurits atroces d'engueuler les humains et je le ferai à quelque jour, dans dix ans d'ici, dans quelque long roman à cadre large; en attendant, une vieille idée m'est revenue, à savoir celle de mon *Dictionnaire des idées reçues*' (C2, 208)].

[297] Flaubert to Léonie Brainne, 14[?] June 1872 ['L'immense bêtise moderne me donne la rage.' (*C4*, 536)].

[298] Flaubert to Edma Roger des Genettes, 7 April 1879 ['placé dans le second volume' (*C5*, 599)].

'Ithaca' and *Bouvard*.[299] The most significant offshoot of Pound's idea is incontestably Hugh Kenner's book, *Flaubert, Joyce, and Beckett: The Stoic Comedians*, in which *Bouvard et Pécuchet* and the *Dictionnaire* play a prominent role.

It was in a letter written to Joyce in November 1918 that Pound first adduced *Bouvard et Pécuchet* as an element in his continuing evaluation of *Ulysses* in terms of Flaubert:

> I looked back over *Bouvard et Pécuchet* last week. Bloom certainly does all Flaubert set out to do and does it in one tenth of the space.[300]

The idea took root[301] and by the time 'James Joyce et Pécuchet' was published in June 1922, Pound had come to see *Bouvard* as the most crucial strand of Joyce's response to Flaubert. Pound's article, which appeared in the Parisian *Mercure de France*, opens with a reminder of what he takes to be a symbolic conjunction of dates. *Ulysses*—as Joyce, living in Paris as he then was, and given his notorious preoccupation with anniversary dates, was probably aware—came out in the centenary of Flaubert's birth (12 December 1821):

> Flaubert's centenary year, the first of a new era, also sees the publication of a new volume by Joyce, *Ulysses*, which, in some respects, may be considered the first which, by inheriting from Flaubert, continues the development of Flaubertian art, such as he left it in his last unfinished work.[302]

For Pound, *Bouvard et Pécuchet* differs from Flaubert's earlier novels and short stories in that it does not merely constitute a superlative example of an existing genre, but marks the 'inauguration of a new form, a form which had no precedent'.[303] That form, according to Pound, is best

---

[299] Cross, 'Impassive Stars: The Vision of Fact in *Bouvard et Pécuchet* and 'Ithaca'", *F&J*, 153–77.

[300] Pound to Joyce, 22 November 1918, *P/J*, 145.

[301] In another letter to the editor of *The Little Review*, dated 1919, Pound stated that 'I am not a[n] excitable critic but I believe that he is doing in this work what Flaubert attempted but did not quite bring off in *Bouvard et Pécuchet*.'—*P/J*, 153. In 'Joyce', an essay written in 1920, Pound declared that Joyce's work was an 'epitome' of *Bouvard et Pécuchet*—*P/J*, 139. In 'Paris Letter', his first essay on Joyce to be written after the publication of *Ulysses* in book form, Pound reiterated the view that the book 'does complete something begun in Bouvard' – *P/J*, 196.

[302] ['L'année du centenaire de Flaubert, première d'une ère nouvelle, voit aussi l'édition d'un nouveau volume de Joyce, *Ulysses*, qui, à certains points de vue, peut être considéré comme le premier qui, en héritant de Flaubert, continue le développement de l'art flaubertien, tel qu'il l'a laissé dans son dernier livre inachevé.' (Pound, 'James Joyce et Pécuchet', *P/J*, 201)].

[303] ['inauguration d'une forme nouvelle, une forme qui n'avait pas son précédent' (Pound, 'James Joyce et Pécuchet', *P/J*, 201)].

described in Flaubert's own words about *Bouvard*, as that of a 'farcical Encylopedia'.[304]

Pound's understanding of *Bouvard* and of its relations to *Ulysses* is confessedly indebted to a critical study entitled *Autour de Bouvard et Pécuchet*, which was published by René Descharmes in 1921.[305] Pound draws on Descharmes' analysis of the role played by cliché in Flaubert's final work, identifying the treatment of received ideas as the most important point of convergence between *Ulysses* and *Bouvard*:

> this is where one sees a connection between Flaubert and Joyce. Between 1880 and the year in which *Ulysses* was begun no one had had the courage to write the gigantic sottisier.[306]

In *Ulysses*, however, Joyce 'completed the great sottisier'.[307] For Pound, *Ulysses* realizes a seamless artistic transition between Flaubert and Joyce: in 1922, a year rich in Flaubertian centennial celebrations, Joyce seized the baton extended by Flaubert in his unfinished final work. This view of literature as a collaborative, genealogical relay race features explicitly or implicitly as a template for all of Pound's statements about Joyce's relations to Flaubert. To an extent, Pound's idiosyncratic *idée fixe* registers an awareness of Joyce's own interest in questions of literary influence. In 1933 Pound would 'Tell us in plain words'[308] what is more subtly intimated in his earlier essays, invoking the model of paternity as the most accurate description of the literary relationship he placed at the heart of modernist experimentation and achievement in prose: 'Joyce', he maintained, 'went back to Papa Flaubert'.[309] There is much to comfort Harold Bloom in Pound's bizarrely infantilizing application of Stephen Dedalus's musings about spiritual paternity to Joyce's own artistic relations. Indeed, the comment, which came more than ten years after the first publication of *Ulysses*, seems a kind of response to the theory of aesthetic

---

[304] ['Encyclopédie mise en farce' (Pound, 'James Joyce et Pécuchet', *P/J*, 203]. It was in a letter of 19 August 1872 to Edma Roger des Genettes that Flaubert used the expression Pound paraphrases here: 'It's the story of two chaps who copy, a kind of farcical critical encyclopaedia' ['C'est l'histoire de ces deux bonshommes qui copient, une espèce d'encyclopédie critique en farce.' (*C4*, 559)].

[305] René Descharmes, *Autour de 'Bouvard et Pécuchet'* (Paris: Librairie de France, 1921). The book was part of a series entitled 'Le Centenaire de Gustave Flaubert'. In 'James Joyce et Pécuchet', Pound lauds Descharmes as 'your most solid Flaubertian' ['votre plus solide flaubertien' (*P/J*, 203)].

[306] ['c'est par là qu'on voit un rapport entre Flaubert et Joyce. Entre 1880 et l'année où fut commencé *Ulysses* personne n'a eu le courage de faire le sottisier gigantesque' (Pound, 'James Joyce et Pécuchet', *P/J*, 205)].

[307] ['a complété le grand sottisier' (Pound, 'James Joyce et Pécuchet', *P/J*, 206)].

[308] *U* 4: 343.

[309] Pound, 'Past History', *P/J*, 248.

reproduction expounded in 'Scylla and Charybdis'. At all events, to refer to Joyce as Flaubert's literary son is to articulate a view of the relationship that is substantially different from that which Pound had previously formulated in stating that in 'Circe' the author had 'swallowed the *Tentation de saint Antoine* whole'.[310] While the latter comment implies a determined, even aggressive drive to improve on the predecessor's work, to overcome his example, and demote his text by rendering it obsolete, the familial model deployed in Pound's later analogy outlines a peaceful coexistence, and sees the father as a source of desired and actively sought-out instruction. Pound leaves behind his earlier preoccupation with necessary usurpation—in 1922 he had declared that artists come after each other in order either 'to kill or to inherit'[311]—in favour of an image of fruitful consensual collaboration.

Friendship Couples

In what ways, then, is *Bouvard et Pécuchet* the 'immediate forerunner'[312] to *Ulysses*? One of the most striking intertextual connections between these works (and a parallel not mentioned by Pound, who focuses on Bloom alone) consists of the friendship couples that form such an integral part of both (fig. 16). To call Stephen Dedalus and Leopold Bloom a friendship couple *à la Bouvard et Pécuchet* is admittedly to overstate the case, but in formal terms the pairing—which only reaches full prominence in the last three chapters—is significant irrespective of the sentiments that the characters themselves attach to the relationship.

The works' respective narrators put these 'duumvirate' relationships[313] to analogous uses: in both cases the pairings emphasize difference and similarity, with each binomial unit providing the material for countless comparisons. This comparing frenzy is especially pronounced at the beginning of *Bouvard*—immediately after Flaubert's *bonshommes* first meet—and at the end of 'Eumaeus' and beginning of 'Ithaca'—wherein the rapprochement between Stephen and Bloom, which has been waiting in the wings throughout the long peregrinations of 'Oxen' and 'Circe', finally takes place (only to be dissolved again on Stephen's departure from 7 Eccles Street in the morning hours of 17 June).

---

[310] Pound, 'Paris Letter', *P/J*, 194.
[311] Pound, 'Paris Letter', *P/J*, 203.
[312] Pound, 'Past History', *P/J*, 250.
[313] 'Of what did the duumvirates deliberate during their itinerary?'—*U* 17: 11.

Fig. 16. Cover illustration of the first English translation of *Bouvard et Pécuchet* emphasizing the centrality of the friendship between the two protagonists—*Bouvard and Pécuchet*, trans. D. F. Hannigan (London: Nichols, 1896).

The opening of *Bouvard* is almost entirely comparative. Bouvard and Pécuchet are described in relation to each other, whether the point of the comparison be difference ('The taller of the two [...] The smaller one'),[314] or identity ('they were both copy-clerks').[315] The differences are emphasized by a narrative pendulum movement, which divides the text into consecutive vignettes. Symmetry prevails, whether performed by way of chiasmus:

---

[314] *BPE*, 21 ['Le plus grand [...] Le plus petit' (*BP*, 47)].
[315] *BPE*, 24 ['ils étaient tous les deux copistes' (*BP*, 50)].

> Bouvard's likeable appearance charmed Pécuchet at once. [. . .]
> Pécuchet's serious appearance struck Bouvard[316]

or by the apposition of carefully ordered parallel (in this case, ternary) structures:

> Bouvard smoked a pipe, liked cheese, regularly took his cup of black coffee. Pécuchet took snuff, ate nothing but preserves for dessert and dipped a lump of sugar in his coffee. One was confident, thoughtless, generous; the other discreet, thoughtful, thrifty.[317]

By contrast, the comparisons made between Stephen and Bloom in 'Eumaeus' are disorderly, repetitive, and more blatantly subjective, for reasons that follow logically from the episode's distinctively rambling, clumsy, Bloom-inflected point of view. (According to Hugh Kenner, 'Eumaeus', 'Copious in its fecund awfulness [. . .] is Joyce's return to the tonic of his method: the Uncle Charles Principle *in excelsis*, a stylistic homage in Bloom's style to Bloom.')[318] The comparisons consistently stress difference rather than similarity. They express Bloom's admiration for Stephen, his eagerness to 'cultivate the acquaintance of someone of no uncommon calibre',[319] his desire to strike up a good rapport with one 'blessed with brains':[320]

> The vicinity of the young man he certainly relished, educated, *distingué* and impulsive into the bargain, far and away the pick of the bunch.[321]

Bloom thinks of himself as 'the elder man who was several years the other's senior or like his father',[322] and 'the more experienced of the two',[323] but this in no way detracts from his excitement at finding himself in Stephen's company. Stephen, however, cuts a gloomy figure:

> The guarded glance of half solicitude half curiosity augmented by friendliness which he gave Stephen's at present morose expression of features.[324]

---

[316] *BPE*, 21, 22 ['L'aspect aimable de Bouvard charma de suite Pécuchet./[. . .] L'air sérieux de Pécuchet frappa Bouvard.' (*BP*, 48)].

[317] *BPE*, 27 ['Bouvard fumait la pipe, aimait le fromage, prenait régulièrement sa demitasse. Pécuchet prisait, ne mangeait au dessert que des confitures et trempait un morceau de sucre dans le café. L'un était confiant, étourdi, généreux; l'autre discret, méditatif, économe.' (*BP*, 55)].

[318] Kenner, *Joyce's Voices*, 38.

[319] *U* 16: 1,219–20.

[320] *U* 16: 1,829.

[321] *U* 16: 1,476–8.

[322] *U* 16: 1,568–9.

[323] *U* 16: 777.

[324] *U* 16: 300–2.

The confusion characteristic of the narrator's Bloom-like idiom and syntax magnifies the reader's sense of the differences between the two men:

> On this knotty point however the views of the pair, poles apart as they were both in schooling and everything else with the marked difference in their respective ages, clashed.[325]

The end of 'Eumaeus' brings about a physical closeness between the two figures that recalls the opening of *Bouvard et Pécuchet*, in which Flaubert's two *bonshommes*, having arrived from opposite directions, meet by chance on a Parisian bench. Bloom emits an invitation: 'Come. It's not far. Lean on me',[326] and so 'they made tracks arm in arm across Beresford place'.[327]. On the way to Eccles Street, Bloom 'pluck[s] the other's sleeve gently',[328] and 'look[s] sideways in a friendly fashion at the sideface of Stephen'.[329] The episode's last paragraph somewhat paradoxically seals this new physical proximity by using the cinematographic technique of 'caméra objective'—which involves the distancing of the narrator's gaze—to recount the moment from an external point of view. As the two men walk 'Side by side'[330] into the cab driver's field of vision, the narrative point of view is suddenly delegated to him so as to afford the reader a vision of Bloom and Stephen through third-party eyes (although the fact that the style, if not the point of view, remains 'Bloomian', suggests that Bloom may in fact be imagining what the driver is seeing). So closeness is paradoxically conveyed from afar, the outsider's visual perspective revealing Bloom and Stephen to be as dissimilar in their shapes and sizes as they are in their temperaments and intellects:

> The driver [...] merely watched the two figures [...] both black, one full, one lean, walk towards the railway bridge [...] As they walked they at times stopped and walked again continuing their *tête à tête*.[331]

In 'Ithaca' comparison remains a crucial means of characterization. The catechistic style adopted in the episode clearly recalls, even as it accentuates, the neat, symmetrical, syntactical structures mobilized in *Bouvard et Pécuchet*. The episode's opening is devoted to the enumeration of some of the differences and similarities between Bloom and Stephen. The self-consciously oxymoronic juxtaposition of words expressive of difference and similarity within each question focuses attention on the comparative pattern:

> Did Bloom discover common factors of similarity between their respective like and unlike reactions to experience?

---

[325] *U* 16: 774–6. [326] *U* 16: 1,719–20.
[327] *U* 16: 1,734–5. [328] *U* 16: 1,778–9.
[329] *U* 16: 1,803. [330] *U* 16: 1,880. [331] *U* 16: 1,885–9.

Why similarly, why differently?
In other respects were their differences similar?[332]

The answers also make ostentatious use of the vocabulary and syntax of
likeness and difference:

> *Both* were sensitive to artistic impressions [...] *Both* preferred a continental
> to an insular manner of life [...] *Both* admitted the alternately stimulating
> and obtunding influence of heterosexual magnetism.[333]

Layout and punctuation accentuate the visibility of the narration's swift
oscillation between the two characters:

> What two temperaments did they individually represent?
> The scientific. The artistic.

> What were Stephen's and Bloom's quasisimultaneous volitional quasisensa-
> tions of concealed identities?
> Visually, Stephen's
> Auditively, Bloom's[334]

The prominence of comparison is the key intertextual feature here: it
matters little what the specific differences and similarities are, or that the
analogies and contrasts indicate substantive differences between Bloom
and Stephen and only trivial differences between Bouvard and Pécuchet. It
is in the likeness of the comparative probing brought to bear on these two
'duumvirates' that a significant intertextual connection resides—a connection that uses the process of comparison to underscore both the fundamental sameness of human nature (this point is reinforced by the fact that
Bouvard and Pécuchet are, at times, almost indistinguishable) and the
variety of human character, the infinity of human non-identity. In
Bloom's 'Eumaean' formula, the Joycean and Flaubertian pairings constitute 'a miniature cameo of the world we live in'.[335]

Infinity and Uncertainty

'The world we live in', as *Ulysses* and *Bouvard et Pécuchet* repeatedly
intimate, is infinitely large. A preoccupation with infinity is evident at
many points in *Bouvard* and 'Ithaca'. On a thematic level this concern
is reflected in both texts' allusions to astronomy and outer space.[336]

---

[332] *U* 17: 18–19, 889, 893.   [333] *U* 17: 20–6 (my emphasis).
[334] *U* 17: 559–60, 781–6.   [335] *U* 16: 1,225.
[336] The title of Cross's chapter on the 'Ithaca'-*Bouvard* connection emphasizes this
correspondence—'Impassive Stars: The Vision of Fact in *Bouvard et Pécuchet* and "Ithaca"',
F&J, 155–73. Cross's chapter itself, however, does not.

Pécuchet looks up at the night sky and marvels at 'a vast [infinite] number of lights twinkling against the dark blue sky';[337] Bloom thinks of 'the infinite lattiginous scintillating uncondensed milky way'.[338] In 'Ithaca' this interest in unfathomably large and infinitely distant macrocosms is counterpointed by its 'obverse',[339] a fascination with infinitely tiny microcosms. In a moment that recalls the microscopic vision of atom-sized units of life granted Antony at the end of *La Tentation*, Bloom considers:

> the incalculable trillions of billions of millions of imperceptible molecules contained by cohesion of molecular affinity in a single pinhead.[340]

The mention of a 'pinhead' unmistakably echoes Antony's ecstatic understanding of the complex make-up of matter at the end of *La Tentation*, an understanding derived from the vision of minuscule living organisms no larger than pinheads:

> he sees little globular masses, no bigger than pin-heads and garnished with hairs all round. [. . .] I'd like to [. . .] divide myself up, to be inside everything [. . .] to penetrate each atom, to get down to the depth of matter—to be matter![341]

Antony's exhilarated intuition of the complexity of life at even the smallest, barely detectable levels comes shortly after his vision of the Milky Way and other distant worlds from atop the devil's back:

> The stars multiply and glitter. The Milky Way unravels on high like an enormous belt, set with holes at intervals; within these rents in its clarity, dark tracts reach out.[342]

Similarly, 'Ithaca' moves from a consideration of the inestimable immensity of space surrounding the earth's circumference to the immeasurable realms of minute space contained within the human body. 'Ithaca' conflates the two realms—the immense and the infinitesimal—by deploying the language of astronomy in its description of the human body. Thus, 'the *universe* of human serum' is '*constellated* with red and white bodies', which are:

---

[337] *BPE*, 262 ['sur le bleu noir du ciel, une infinité de lumières scintillaient' (*BP*, 355)].
[338] *U* 17: 1,043–4.
[339] *U* 17: 1,057.
[340] *U* 17: 1,061–3.
[341] *TAE*, 232 ['il aperçoit des masses globuleuses, grosses comme des têtes d'épingles et garnies de cils tout autour [. . .] Je voudrais [. . .] me diviser partout, être en tout [. . .] pénétrer chaque atome, descendre jusqu'au fond de la matière,—être la matière!' (*TA*, 200)].
[342] *TAE*, 207 ['Les astres se multiplient, scintillent. La Voie lactée au zénith se développe comme une immense ceinture, ayant des trous par intervalles; dans ces fentes de sa clarté, s'allongent des espaces de ténèbres.' (*TA*, 175)].

themselves *universes* of *void space constellated* with other bodies, each, in continuity, its *universe* of divisible component bodies of which each was again divisible in divisions of redivisible component bodies, dividends and divisors ever diminishing without actual division till, if the progress were carried far enough, nought nowhere was never reached.[343]

As such meditations intimate, Bloom and Stephen share an awareness of the basic identity of microcosms and macrocosms, all of which have at their core the same epistemological 'incertitude of the void'[344] (a concern that recalls *La Tentation*'s preoccupation with existential doubt). Behind the veil of abstruse language in 'Ithaca', Stephen and Bloom can be 'overheard' engaging in a debate about the theoretically closed field of 'the known' and the theoretically infinite field of 'the unknown'. While Stephen prides himself on being:

a conscious rational animal proceeding syllogistically from the known to the unknown and a conscious rational reagent between a micro and a macro-cosm ineluctably constructed upon the incertitude of the void.[345]

Bloom derives satisfaction from the thought:

That as a competent keyless citizen he had proceeded energetically from the unknown to the known through the incertitude of the void.[346]

Both characters share an investment in the desirability of escaping the unknown, of acceding to the known. Their concern, however veiled and comic the mock-scientific language, is with knowledge. The question of the possibility of improving on current knowledge by obtaining a

---

[343] *U* 17: 1,064–9 (my emphases).

[344] *U* 17: 1,015.

[345] *U* 17: 1,012–15. Stephen's commitment to the idea of a rational progression from the known to the unknown, conveyed in the scientific style of 'Ithaca', echoes Émile Zola's statements in *Le Roman expérimental* (1880) concerning the task of the experimental writer— a task that Zola envisaged as involving just such a gradual advance from the known to the unknown (Zola opposes this way of working to the procedures of less scrupulous authors who write from within a realm of pure fabulation): 'The real task that falls to us experimental novelists is to proceed from *the known to the unknown*, to make ourselves masters of nature while idealist novelists stick to the status quo of the unknown, out of adherence to all sorts of religious and philosophical prejudices' (my emphasis) ['Notre vrai besogne est là, à nous romanciers expérimentateurs, *aller du connu à l'inconnu*, pour nous rendre maîtres de la nature tandis que les romanciers idéalistes restent de parti pris dans l'inconnu, par toutes sortes de préjugés religieux et philosophiques'—*Le Roman expérimental* (Paris: Flammarion, 2006), 67]. The phrase also occurs in a book that fascinates Stephen Dedalus in *A Portrait of the Artist as a Young Man*: in *The Count of Monte Cristo* (1844–5) the protagonist tells Villefort that 'There is an axiom in algebra that requires us to proceed from the known to the unknown, and not the contrary'—Alexandre Dumas, *The Count of Monte Cristo*, trans. Robin Buss (London: Penguin Classics, 2003), 550.

[346] *U* 17: 1,019–20.

gradually more complete, more truthful understanding of the world runs as a thematic thread throughout *Bouvard* and 'Ithaca'.

The key way in which such an improvement might be achieved, the texts suggest, involves the discovery of a greater number of relationships between things rather than the accumulation of facts about them. In a letter written to Maupassant during the composition of *Bouvard*, Flaubert asserts that 'Only so-called relations—that is, our ways of perceiving objects—are true',[347] and the inadequacy of fact runs as a leitmotif throughout Flaubert's 'encyclopaedia of human Stupidity'.[348] Indeed the protagonists repeatedly come up against the impossibility of establishing trustworthy rules and reliable facts. Contradiction permeates human knowledge; systems of thoughts flounder under investigation; in the face of repeated disappointments, the two can only shrug their shoulders and ask: 'What is the rule then [...]?'[349] Similarly, Karen Lawrence argues that 'Ithaca' is less about facts than about 'the *relationship* between events or objects'.[350] Bloom's and Stephen's discussion about infinity is apt in an episode whose mimicry of encyclopaedic form raises questions about the limits of even the most comprehensive and realistic of literary works. Lawrence quotes from Henry James's preface to the 1907 New York Edition of *Roderick Hudson* (1875):

> Really, universally, relations stop nowhere and the exquisite problem of the artist is eternally but to draw, by a geometry of his own, a circle within which they shall happily appear to do so.[351]

Stephen Dedalus may have been responding to this observation in that passage of *A Portrait of the Artist as a Young Man* in which he envisages doing exactly as James recommends—drawing a 'geometry of his own' that hones in on one object at the expense of all other objects to which it is related. In the example Stephen gives his friend Lynch, a basket is isolated

---

[347] Flaubert to Guy de Maupassant, 9 August 1878, *FS2*, 243 ['il n'y a de vrais que les "rapports"' (*C5*, 416)].

[348] Flaubert to Edgard Raoul-Duval, 13 February 1879 ['encyclopédie de la Bêtise humaine' (*C5*, 535)].

[349] *BPE*, 56 ['Où est la règle alors?' (*BP*, 90)]. Bouvard and Pécuchet's study of linguistic systems is a representative instance. Even language, as they discover, is full of holes, and the idea of a clear and consistent language system is a mere illusion: 'they began to study grammar. [...] Whence they concluded that syntax is a fantasy and grammar an illusion.'—*BPE*, 141–2 ['ils se mirent à étudier la grammaire. [...] Ils en conclurent que la syntaxe est une fantasie et la grammaire une illusion.' (*BP*, 203–4)].

[350] Karen Lawrence, 'Style and Narrative in the *Ithaca* Chapter of Joyce's *Ulysses*', *ELH*, vol. 47, no. 3 (Autumn 1980), 567.

[351] Henry James, Preface to *Roderick Hudson*, quoted in Lawrence, 'Style and Narrative', 566.

for artistic treatment while the butcher boy on whose shoulders it rests is elided:

> –In order to see that basket, said Stephen, your mind first of all separates the basket from the rest of the visible universe which is not the basket. The first phase of apprehension is a bounding line drawn about the object to be apprehended.[352]

Joyce's attitude to Stephen, in this as in so many respects, is at least partly ironic.[353] 'Ithaca', as

> a demonstration that 'relations stop nowhere' and a refusal to limit the representation of experience in a personal 'geometry'[354]

seems to confirm this.

There can be no question of a 'personal geometry' in either 'Ithaca' or *Bouvard*. The analogies between the 'Ithacan' and 'bouvard-et-pécuche-tian' styles in this respect are evident. Impersonal, anonymous questions punctuate the adventures of Flaubert's protagonists: 'What experiments?', 'but how are the species to be established?', 'Why bad? What is abuse? How can one know whether something agrees with one?', 'What then is hygiene?'[355] This pattern is replicated in 'Ithaca', although the narrative voice in Joyce's episode is arguably even more unfathomable—its interests more wildly versatile, its selection procedures more elusive. Moreover, more than *Bouvard*, 'Ithaca' conveys a strong impression of surplus. The excess of information it provides transgresses 'the threshold of functional relevance'[356] and has the narration constantly veering off in unexpected directions, 'spin[ning] a web of actions and reactions, antecedents and causes'[357] that appears to be potentially infinite. In this way:

> the idea of plot, based on the concepts of relevance and closure, are [*sic*] parodied, as the surplus of data makes the separation of the relevant from the irrelevant more problematical.[358]

---

[352] *P*, 178.

[353] The full extent of the difference between Stephen's and Joyce's aesthetic and poetic stances is clear from the 'allincluding' (*U* 14: 1412) make-up of *Ulysses* and *Finnegans Wake* (though even in these vast heterogenous works Joyce is at pains to emphasize all that is inevitably left by the wayside).

[354] Lawrence, 'Style and Narrative', 566.

[355] *BPE*, 76, 78, 82, 83 ['Quelles expériences?'; 'mais comment établir les espèces?'; 'Pourquoi mauvais? Où est l'abus? Comment savoir si telle chose vous convient?'; 'Qu'est-ce donc que l'hygiène?' (*BP*, 115, 119, 125, 126)].

[356] Stephen Heath (under the pseudonym 'Cleanth Peters'), 'Structuration of the Novel-Text', in *Signs of the Times: Introductory Readings in Textual Semiotics*, ed. Stephen Heath, Colin MacCabe, and Christopher Prendergast (Cambridge: Granta, 1971), 75, quoted in Lawrence, 565.

[357] Lawrence, 'Style and Narrative', 566.

[358] Lawrence, 'Style and Narrative', 566.

The sudden deviations and unpredictable tangents in 'Ithaca' highlight the relations that can be established between all things and the concomitant selection involved in all narrative processes.

Closed Systems, Facts, Phenomena

This conclusion rejoins Kenner's contention in *The Stoic Comedians* that Joyce's predilection for 'closed systems' pertains to a mode of irony that draws attention to those assumptions of realism, omniscience, comprehensiveness, and closure which underpin traditional nineteenth-century novel-writing. Kenner echoes Pound's claim that Joyce, like Flaubert and Rabelais before him, uses fiction to interrogate the encylopaedia, one of the Enlightenment's most powerful symbols of investment in knowledge.[359] For Kenner, Flaubert 'is busily reproducing in a fabulous narrative the inanity of the Encyclopaedia'.[360] In the wake of *Bouvard* and the *Dictionnaire*, 'Ithaca' uses encylopaedic form to show up the encyclopaedia's absurdity as a closed system, deriding its ambition to make all known facts available to the reader under neat alphabetical headings. Kenner argues that Joyce and Flaubert see encyclopaedias as hubristic and self-defeating projects because they aspire to exhaustiveness in the description of an infinitely complex universe—a universe that lends itself to cataloguing and categorization only at the expense of selection and simplification. Furthermore, encyclopaedias are doubly ridiculous because facts—those units of knowledge upon which they are built—are themselves inherently absurd:

> It is facts that are absurd; nothing is more absurd than the very conception of a *fact*, an isolated datum of experience, something to find out, isolated from all other things that there are to be found out.[361]

A fact, as described by Kenner, is a microcosmic closed system, an item of experience severed from the contextual network of related facts without which all meaning is lost. If a fact is an absurdity, then it follows that an encyclopaedia, as a compendium of such absurdities, is an enterprise run through and through with unfounded intellectual assumptions. For Kenner, 'Ithaca' is 'the point of growth where Joyce explicitly tackles and

---

[359] 'Only Rabelais and Flaubert attack an entire century, taking a stand against a whole idiotic encyclopaedia—in the form of fiction' ['Seuls Rabelais et Flaubert attaquent tout un siècle, s'opposent à toute une encyclopédie imbécile,—sous la forme de fiction.' (Pound, 'James Joyce et Pécuchet', *P/J*, 208)].

[360] *Stoics*, 25.

[361] *Stoics*, 24.

develops the encyclopaedism of Flaubert'.[362] It is certainly true that even at its most seemingly encyclopaedic, 'Ithaca' twists the premises of the encyclopaedic project. Thus, the episode's long enumeration of the qualities of water is not exhaustive—nor does it pretend to be. In fact, the question that prompts the list is couched in carefully subjectivized terms:

> What in water did Bloom, waterlover, drawer of water, watercarrier, returning to the range, admire?[363]

Kenner's identification of the distrust of fact implied in Flaubert's *Bouvard et Pécuchet* and Joyce's *Ulysses* gains corroboration from both works' predilection for the word 'phenomenon'. It is in the context of frustration with misguided inferences of causality (the 'post hoc ergo propter hoc' fallacy according to which an event that follows another must have been caused by it) that the word 'phenomenon' makes its Flaubertian entrée. Bouvard 'was doubtful about causes':

> From the fact that one phenomenon succeeds another, you conclude that it derives from it. Prove it![364]

In one of the novel's drafted closing sentences, Bouvard and Pécuchet—or a narrator summarizing their speech or thoughts—arrive at the conclusion that:

> There is no truth only phenomena.[365]

The word proliferates in 'Ithaca'. We read of a 'concomitant phenomenon', 'the phenomenon of ebullition', 'any cognate phenomenon', 'a natural phenomenon', 'the diurnal phenomenon', 'other more acceptable phenomena', 'attendant phenomena of eclipses, solar and lunar', 'initial paraphenomena', 'phenomena of senescence'.[366] This predilection for phenomena seems related to Joyce's and Flaubert's distrust of fact as an epistemological category.

Indeed since the late eighteenth century, when Immanuel Kant distinguished 'phenomena' and 'noumena' in his *Critique of Pure Reason* (1781), the former has been one of the flagship terms for a philosophical

---

[362] *Stoics*, 78.
[363] *U* 17: 183–4.
[364] *BPE*, 204 ['doutait des causes'; 'De ce qu'un phénomène succède à un phénomène, on conclut qu'il en dérive. Prouvez-le!' (*BP*, 281)].
[365] Passage not featured in *BPE*. ['Il n'y a pas de vrai que les phénomènes.' (*BP*, 390)]. Awkward syntax and lack of punctuation leave this sentence open to conflicting interpretations. The first (more likely) reading yields the translation given above: 'There is no truth only phenomena.' The second interpretation would translate the sentence (roughly) as: 'There are things other than phenomena that are true.'
[366] *U* 17: 255, 257, 858, 925, 1,262, 1,008–9, 1,132, 1,264, 1,927.

scepticism that places the full knowledge of things ineluctably beyond human reach. The word 'noumenon' designates the unknowable 'thing-in-itself' (*Ding an sich*). 'Phenomenon' (or '*Erscheinung*'), by contrast, is Kant's term for the kind of immediate, perceptual, sensory knowledge that is available to us; it denotes the experience or perception of objects and events.[367] A fact, which is the verbal articulation of a phenomenon, installs a further degree of mediation between the mind and the noumenal realm. Language seeks to objectify phenomena (which are subjective experiences): as such the process involves distortion even before the assumptions and connotations that characterize all linguistic systems are taken into account. It is a credit to Bloom, Bouvard, and Pécuchet, in the light of Kant's distinctions, that they should privilege phenomena over facts, thereby registering implicit wariness of linguistic 'truths' and recognition of the fundamental unknowability of things-in-themselves. In this the characters (albeit to a large extent unknowingly) participate in the kind of scepticism exemplified by the encyclopaedic forms of *Bouvard* and *Ulysses*, which ironize (not by chastising, but by revealing the limitations of) the Enlightenment's encyclopaedic project and its dream of encompassing all known facts.[368]

These works' interrogation of the Enlightenment ideal of manageable knowledge is paradoxically carried out by way of characters whose world

---

[367] That Flaubert had Kant's definition of phenomena in mind during the writing of *Bouvard et Pécuchet* is clear from an entry in one of the notebooks he was using in 1878 and 1879: 'If, as Kant instructs, the things we recognize are merely *phenomena* whose forms and laws do not extend to *things themselves*, then we should not too hastily reject the supernatural.' ['Si, comme Kant l'enseigne, les choses que nous reconnaissons ne sont que des *phénomènes* dont les formes et les lois ne s'étendent pas sur *les choses elles-mêmes*, il ne faut pas se hâter de rejeter le surnaturel.' (Gustave Flaubert, *Carnets de Travail*, ed. Pierre-Marc de Biasi [Paris: Balland, 1988], 937)].

[368] Even the word 'phenomenon', however, carries some ironic charge in *Ulysses*. In the mock-scientific context of 'Ithaca' especially, Joyce's use of the word echoes Zola's calls for a science of literature that would emulate the experimental method set out by Claude Bernard in his *Introduction à l'étude de la médecine expérimentale* (1865). 'Ithaca' seems to allude to Zola's manifesto in evoking a progression 'from the unknown to the known' (*U* 17: 1,012–15 and 1,019–20; see footnote 347), so there is reason to think that Joyce also had *Le Roman expérimental* (1880) in mind when including such numerous references to 'phenomena' in 'Ithaca'. Indeed, the word abounds in Zola's statements about the applicability of the experimental method to literature. His conception of phenomena accords great importance to observation—in this sense, it is (distantly) Kantian—but Zola also makes grand assertions regarding humanity's capacity to master all phenomena ('we make ourselves the masters of phenomena'; 'we too want to be masters of phenomena'), and in so doing implicitly denies the existence of a noumenal realm inaccessible to investigation by science and novelistic writing ('To our mind there are only phenomena to study') ['on se rend maître des phénomènes'; 'nous voulons, nous aussi, être les maîtres des phénomènes'; 'Il n'y a pour nous que des phénomènes à étudier' (*Le Roman expérimental* [Paris: Flammarion, 2006], 58–9, 66, 82)]. These latter positions clearly differentiate Zola from the attitudes of 'absolute doubt' favoured by Joyce and Flaubert.

views have been thoroughly shaped by the Enlightenment project. Bouvard, Pécuchet, and Bloom are all, in Pound's words, avatars of the *homme moyen sensuel*—symptoms, representatives, and beneficiaries of a democratic era:

> Bloom, advertisement canvasser, the Ulysses of the novel, the Everyman, the basis, as are Bouvard and Pécuchet, of democracy, the man who believes what he reads in the papers.[369]

Politics aside, *Ulysses* promotes this view of Bloom's role and position (Joyce's depiction of the 'homme moyen sensuel', however, is not intended to be derogative). It is no coincidence that the word 'everyman' should occur twice in 'Eumaeus'. Coming down on the side of science over religion, Bloom responds to Stephen's invocation of proofs from Holy Writ with diplomacy, acknowledging that: 'That's a matter for everyman's [*sic*] opinion.'[370] The shelter's keeper shows the same willingness to allow for other people's views: 'While allowing him his individual opinions as everyman the keeper added he cared nothing for any empire.'[371] It is telling that in both cases the locution ('every man') is contracted to a single word ('everyman') in a curtailment that acts as an ironic corrective to each speaker's meaning. That is: although neither Bloom nor the keeper really think of their opinions as merely as good as an 'everyman's', the text's spelling works against them, suggesting just such an equivalence.

Utopian Plans, Bourgeois Dreams

Bouvard and Pécuchet's thirst for knowledge and aspirations to self-improvement bear the stamp of bourgeois ideology. Their valuation of knowledge for its own sake is a nineteenth-century offshoot of the Enlightenment dream of social egalitarianism. Bouvard and Pécuchet, as Flaubert indicates by their dates of birth (1791), are children of the Revolution. Both are forty-seven years old at the opening of the narrative, which is set in the summer of 1838: they are, as such authorial choices make clear, beneficiaries of the educational and financial possibilities made available to a fast-growing middle class by the legacies of the Enlightenment and of the Revolution.[372]

---

[369] ['Bloom, commis de publicité, l'Ulysse du roman, l'homme moyen sensuel, la base, comme le sont Bouvard et Pécuchet, de la démocratie, l'homme qui croit ce qu'il lit dans les journaux' (Pound, 'James Joyce et Pécuchet', *PJJ*, 206)].

[370] *U* 16: 778–9.

[371] *U* 16: 1,023–4.

[372] Yvan Leclerc, *La Spirale et le Monument: Essai sur 'Bouvard et Pécuchet'* (Paris: SEDES, 1988), 108.

Money, to choose a single marker of these books' engagement with bourgeois concerns, plays an important part in these narratives of hope and opportunity. At the opening of Flaubert's novel, Bouvard and Pécuchet are both copying clerks, leading simple but comfortable lives. Even when Bouvard inherits a substantial sum of money, the two *bonshommes'* long desired and carefully planned move to the countryside is postponed by a couple of years so that Bouvard and Pécuchet may continue to build up their capital until they reach retirement age. Flaubert's narrative dwells repeatedly on the material conditions that enable the fulfilment of the two men's dream. Similarly, references to money punctuate the 'action' of *Ulysses*. Stephen receives payment for his teaching from Deasy in 'Nestor'; Simon Dedalus hands over a shilling and twopence to his pleading daughter Dilly in 'Wandering Rocks'; Stephen spends his earnings on drink in 'Oxen' and 'Circe'. Other examples abound. Such allusions cannot really be assimilated to Joyce's treatment of bourgeois living, however, as it is clear that even Stephen, despite his youth and education, treads a very fine line between lower middle-class poverty and bourgeois possibility. As such, his limited means, and the poverty highlighted by his encounter with his sister, act as counterpoints to Bloom's savings and expenditures, to which *Ulysses* several times refers. Stephen Heath describes the theme of *Madame Bovary* as 'money on the move',[373] and the statement also holds true of Flaubert's other *romans de moeurs*, *L'Éducation sentimentale* and *Bouvard et Pécuchet*. As Mark Osteen has shown, this financial dimension also impinges on the narrative of *Ulysses* at many points, and the account sheet printed in 'Ithaca'[374] confirms the theme's importance in a novel that reflects the socio-economic realities of early twentieth-century Dublin.[375]

Bouvard, Pécuchet, and Bloom have more than money in common. They also share bourgeois attitudes and beliefs, and enjoy bourgeois activities. All three, for instance, have an interest in physical fitness. While Bloom has in the past followed the prescriptions of Eugen Sandow in *Physical Strength and How to Obtain It*,[376] Bouvard and Pécuchet seek moral improvement through exercise: 'Satisfied with their regime, they tried to improve their condition with gymnastics.'[377] Similarly, Bloom's dream of retirement to the countryside replicates Bouvard and Pécuchet's rural idyll. Bloom aspires to the same kind of peaceful, quietly constructive

---

[373] Heath, *Madame Bovary*, 56.
[374] *U* 17: 1,455–78.
[375] Mark Osteen, *The Economy of 'Ulysses'* (New York: Syracuse University Press, 1995).
[376] *U* 17: 512–14.
[377] *BPE*, 183 ['Satisfaits de leur régime, ils voulurent s'améliorer le tempérament par la gymnastique.' (*BP*, 255)].

retreat as they undertake. His 'ultimate ambition'[378] crystallizes in the vision of:

> a thatched bungalowshaped 2 storey dwellinghouse [. . .] rising, if possible, upon a gentle eminence [. . .] and standing in 5 or 6 acres of its own ground.[379]

Bloom's gardening dreams are a perfect match for Bouvard and Pécuchet's bucolic fantasies. Before their move to Normandy they:

> already saw themselves in shirt sleeves, beside a flowerbed, pruning roses, and digging, hoeing, handling the soil, transplanting things [*tulips*].[380]

Bloom's own pastoral daydreams involve:

> a shrubbery, a glass summerhouse with tropical palms, equipped in the best botanical manner, a rockery with waterspray, a beehive arranged on humane principles, oval flowerbeds.[381]

A footnote to Lawrence's article relates these two country-house dreams. 'The passages on Bloom's dream house', she suggests:

> are reminiscent of Bouvard et Pécuchet's exhaustive efforts to improve their lot, to live out the Utopian bourgeois dream.[382]

Lawrence's choice of the word 'Utopian' echoes Bloom, who in thinking of a possible future mentoring relationship to Stephen finds that:

> All kinds of Utopian plans were flashing through his (B's) busy brain, education (the genuine article), literature, journalism, prize titbits, up to date billing, concert tours in English watering resorts.[383]

For Flaubert, the inimical figure of the bourgeois was characterized by his or her crimes against language—the slothful, unthinking repetition of stale formulae. And although aspects of Bouvard and Pécuchet's aspirations are endearingly portrayed, there is also venom in Flaubert's awkwardly disguised aversion for the middle-class mind. In a contemporary review of *Bouvard*, Jules Barbey d'Aurevilly called the book a 'steam-engine of hatred', observing that 'the hatred of the bourgeois was with him [Flaubert] a kind of madness, shrill and sonorous', and that with *Bouvard* Flaubert had

---

[378]   *U* 17: 1,497.

[379]   *U* 17: 504–5, 1,504–12.

[380]   *BPE*, 32 ['se voyaient en manches de chemise, au bord d'une plate-bande émondant des rosiers, et bêchant, binant, maniant de la terre, dépotant des tulipes' (*BP*, 60)].

[381]   *U* 17: 1,552–4.

[382]   Lawrence, 'Style and Narrative', 574.

[383]   *U* 16: 1,652–4.

hoped to 'cleanse the earth of bourgeoisism and bourgeois people'.[384] Pound contends that in *Bouvard* and *Ulysses*, Flaubert and Joyce set out to 'present all sorts of things that the average man of the period would have had in his head',[385] by which he specifically means the received ideas that they automatically adopt and disseminate. Commenting on this strand of analysis in Descharmes' *Autour de 'Bouvard et Pécuchet'*, Pound's review states, clearly with 'Eumaeus' in mind, that:

> In a single chapter he unloads all the clichés of the English language, in an uninterrupted stream.[386]

The article goes on to describe Bloom as a typical sponge for the hundreds of clichés that litter middle-class life:

> he is the much quicker literary 'means', much more apt to pick up what is said and thought everywhere, what people say and rehash a hundred times a week.[387]

Bouvard et Pécuchet and the *Dictionnaire des Idées Reçues* are what the second title promises: dictionaries of received ideas, lists of recycled wisdoms—the emphasis being on the content of the thought, rather than on the word that summons it. In slight contrast, the emphasis in 'Eumaeus' (as in 'Nausicaa' and 'Aeolus', amongst other places) seems to be with blocks of language per se, rather than with the content of the parroted ideas. Stock turns of phrase are imbricated together to form a continuous weave of linguistic cliché, a veritable concatenation of idiomatic phrases and conversational malapropisms. While Flaubert sought to show how words trigger automatic associations, tapping directly into an infinite fount of interconnected prejudices and inherited opinions, Joyce highlights the petrifaction of language into set phrases. In 'Eumaeus' his concern seems less with the ideological thought patterns such fixed locutions imply (though these are certainly adumbrated) than with the very fact of immobilization as a feature of language.

The phenomenon is not treated as a cause for despair, as is the staleness of received ideas in Flaubert's chastising *Dictionnaire*. This is partly

---

[384] ['locomotive de haine'; 'la haine du bourgeois était chez lui [Flaubert] une espèce de folie, clabaudante et sonore'; 'nettoyer la terre du bourgeoisisme et des bourgeois' ('Jules Barbey d'Aurevilly, review of *Bouvard et Pécuchet*, *Le Constitutionnel*, 10 May 1881, in *BP*, 454)].

[385] Pound, 'Paris Letter', *P/J*, 194.

[386] ['Dans un seul chapitre il décharge tous les clichés de la langue anglaise, comme un fleuve ininterrompu.' (Pound, 'James Joyce et Pécuchet', *P/J*, 206)].

[387] ['il est un "moyen" littéraire beaucoup plus rapide, beaucoup plus apte à ramasser ce qu'on dit et pense partout, ce que les gens disent et ramâchent cent fois par semaine' (Pound, 'James Joyce et Pécuchet', *P/J*, 206)].

because there is an explanation—exhaustion—for the extreme clumsiness of Bloom's language, as there cannot be for the commonplaces of an entire culture. Another reason for the marked difference in the tone of the implied commentary derives from the related fact that in 'Eumaeus' received phrases are embedded into the fabric of a character's thoughts and language. This vitalizes idioms that would have seemed inert if presented in the manner of Flaubert's *Dictionnaire*. 'Eumaeus' imparts a very playful feel to the procession of clichés that it stages. This effect has to do with the sheer surfeit of cliché in the episode, but also with the tenderly hilarious infelicity of its malapropisms and collocations. As Christine O'Neill notes, the text, although it appears to be mostly focalized through a consciousness bearing some relation to Bloom's, does not for all that constitute an attack on Bloom: ' "Eumaeus" is dominated not so much by Bloom's voice as by a Bloomian voice, an exaggerated and partly distorted writing effort of the type Bloom would admire and aspire to if he were wielding the pen. It is a voice which strives for an elevated style; the driving desire is to please and impress Stephen.'[388] In its endearing and comic gaucheness, 'Eumaeus' is not an indictment. It is, in fact, as Kenner has argued, a tribute to Bloom, who, having been 'snubbed, thwarted, cuckolded, ignored, jeered at, slandered, put upon', finally feels 'like the hero of a novel, which for Joyce in fiction after fiction is the apotheosis to which fictional beings aspire'.[389]

Yet Bouvard, Pécuchet, and Bloom are more than stereotypical bourgeois everymen. Or rather, all three demonstrate that such a status does not preclude the possibility of genuinely intellectual impulses and curiosities. Indeed, the kinds of inquiry conducted by Joyce's and Flaubert's everymen, and the insights they reach, however intuitively ('phenomenon' being the best shared example), are central to both texts. Through reading, study, and experimentation on the one hand, and enthusiasm and wide-ranging curiosity on the other, all three reach positions of scepticism and doubt (Bloom smiles with 'unbelief')[390] that appear as valid as the concentrated, private, often self-defeating reflections of 'Stephen Dedalus, B. A'.[391]

The means by which Joyce's and Flaubert's everymen arrive at their insights are not all that different from the way Stephen has amassed his erudition. Books provide the bridge between these two kinds of know-

[388] Christine O'Neill, *Too Fine a Point: A Stylistic Analysis of the 'Eumaeus' Episode in James Joyce's 'Ulysses'* (Trier: Wissenschaftlicher Verlag, 1996), 102.
[389] Kenner, *Joyce's Voices*, 35.
[390] *U* 16: 778.
[391] *U* 16: 1,264.

ledge. For all their amateurishness, Bouvard, Pécuchet, and Bloom value books as gateways to knowledge, and books and libraries provide some of the most significant connections between Bloom and his nineteenth-century French counterparts. Pécuchet's extensive, sprawling book collection is described in *Bouvard*'s first chapter:

> all round, on shelves, on the three chairs, on the ancient armchair and in the corners, were heaped pell-mell several volumes of Roret's *Encyclopaedia, The Magnetist's Manual*, a Fénelon, other books.[392]

Bloom's dream library manifests the same taste for reference manuals. In an ideal world his bungalow would accommodate an 'oak sectional bookcase containing the Encyclopaedia Britannica and New Century Dictionary' as well as a 'vulcanite automatic telephone with adjacent directory'.[393] Bloom's actual library, of which 'Ithaca' provides a catalogue,[394] betrays a predilection for primers and other repertories of easily accessible knowledge, and it features, among other factual tomes, such items as *Thom's Dublin Post Office Directory* (1886), *The Child's Guide, Thoughts from Spinoza, Philosophy of the Talmud, Soll und Haben, A Handbook of Astronomy, Physical Strength and How to Obtain It, Short but yet Plain Elements of Geometry*.[395]

Pécuchet's and Bloom's libraries hint at some degree of identification between the authors and their characters. Indeed, the enumerations of the titles each character possesses perform a small-scale autobiographical *mise en abyme*, with each author listing books he himself used in the making of *Bouvard* and *Ulysses*. Flaubert depended on Roret's *Encyclopaedia*, for instance, to write *Bouvard*. And just as *Ulysses*, published in 1922, was composed with an eighteen-year-old edition of *Thom's Directory* open at Joyce's side, so Leopold Bloom, in 1904, owns an eighteen-year-old

---

[392] *BPE*, 24–5 ['tout autour, sur des planchettes, sur les trois chaises, sur le vieux fauteuil et dans les coins se trouvaient pêle-mêle plusieurs volumes de l'encyclopédie Roret, le *Manuel du magnétiseur*, un Fénelon, d'autres bouquins' (*BP*, 52)].

[393] *U* 17: 1,523–6.

[394] *U* 17: 1,361–407.

[395] Various intriguing parallels emerge between Flaubert's *roman philosophique* and salient aspects of Joyce's writing. Pécuchet, for instance, becomes a passionate advocate of the work of Giambattista Vico: 'What matters is the philosophy of history! [. . .] Pécuchet tried to explain myths, and lost himself in the *Scienza nuova*' (*BPE*, 122–3) ['Ce qu'il y a d'important, c'est la philosophie de l'histoire! [. . .] Pécuchet tâcha d'expliquer les mythes, se perdait dans la *Scienza nuova*' (*BP*, 177)]. Paul de Kock, whose books Molly enjoys reading, and whose treatment of adultery Joyce ponders in his preparatory notes for *Exiles*, also features among the authors on the *bonshommes*' extensive reading list: 'He wanted to learn, deepen his knowledge of human ways. He re-read Paul de Kock' (*BPE*, 133) ['Il [Bouvard] voulait s'instruire, descendre plus avant dans la connaissance des moeurs. Il relut Paul de Kock.' (*BP*, 191)].

edition (1886) of the same book. This *mise en abyme* has a bearing on the reading of these texts. In Flaubert's case in particular, the choice to place one of his own research resources in the hands of his *bonshommes* can be read in a way that tempers what is often perceived as visceral disgust for his protagonists. The love of books that he imparts to them, and the titles on which he and they both depend, suggest a less satirical interpretation of the characters than other aspects of the book might suggest.

Such a reading flies against many of the known facts about *Bouvard*—most notably that the book was conceived as a work of retribution, a literary whip with which to punish the French people for its intolerable *bêtise*. Long before the book's composition actually got underway, Flaubert referred to his protagonists as 'deux cloportes' ('two woodlice'). Indeed, the first known manuscript scenario for *Bouvard* (written in late 1862 or early 1863) bore the title: 'Story of Two Woodlice—The two clerks'.[396] Yet in spite of this, and in spite of Flaubert's frequently vitriolic denigration of his characters in letters written while the opus was taking shape, moments of autobiographical *mise en abyme* suggest at least some degree of personal identification with his protagonists. The key moment in this regard occurs in Chapter VIII, in which Bouvard and Pécuchet themselves come to resent the *bêtise* they see everywhere around them (much as Regimbart, the *bête* nationalist of *L'Éducation*, comes to exclaim against the *bêtise* of his countrymen):

> Then a lamentable faculty developed in their minds, that of noticing stupidity and finding it intolerable.[397]

Even Pound—for all his own reservations about bourgeois culture—noted Flaubert's 'sympathy for his *bonshommes*' and observed that:

> the vanity of his own struggle against generalized stupidity lends energy to his portrayal of those other victims of circumstances.[398]

The identification that occasionally filters through Flaubert's largely neutral characterization paves the way for Joyce's less ambiguous treatment of *Ulysses*'s bourgeois hero as a sympathetic 'all-round character'.[399]

---

[396] ['Histoire de Deux Cloportes—Les deux commis' (*Carnets de Travail*, ed. de Biasi, 297)].

[397] *BPE*, 217 ['Alors une faculté pitoyable se développa dans leur esprit, celle de voir la bêtise et de ne plus la tolérer.' (*BP*, 298)].

[398] ['sympathie pour ses bonshommes'; 'la vanité de sa propre lutte contre l'imbecillité générale donne de l'énergie au portrait de ces autres victimes des circonstances' (Pound, 'James Joyce et Pécuchet', *P/J*, 205)].

[399] Budgen, *James Joyce and the Making of 'Ulysses'*, 15.

As Ronald Bush points out, the combination of optimism and doubt, identification and satire, sympathy and impersonality, exemplified by Joyce's and Flaubert's bourgeois characters is representative of each author's thoroughgoing engagement with two strands of modernism, which reflect two distinct aspects of the Enlightenment's thinking about itself. Summarizing Robert Pippin's argument in *Modernism as a Philosophical Problem*,[400] Bush outlines a progression in which:

> The Enlightenment, which vested authority in the discourses of science, philosophy, and history and produced two centuries of mechanistic explanations of man and nature, also provoked, as early as the Romantic philosophy of the late eighteenth and early nineteenth centuries, a revisionary version of itself, no less rooted in skepticism toward authority.[401]

Flaubert is identified as one of the spearheads of this sceptical *seconde vague*:

> The great figures in this revisionary Enlightenment tradition often sound like reactionaries because of their dissatisfaction with an incomplete modernity, and this is if anything more true for literary figures like Baudelaire or Flaubert, whose modernity involves not only the revolutionary gesture of resisting the authority of classical and neoclassical literary convention, but also horror of the intellectual and social hypocrisies of 'bourgeois' society. Though propelled by the great wave of Enlightenment skepticism, such figures focused their energies primarily not on the old regime but on modernity's optimistic and insufficiently grounded belief in the progress of science and the forms of modern capitalism. These attitudes and systems, they concluded, blind to their own contradictions and irrationalities, continue (no less than more traditional institutions like the Church) to obstruct true human self-understanding.[402]

The tensions between denigration and endorsement in Flaubert's depiction of Bouvard and Pécuchet, and between irony and comedy in Joyce's treatment of Bloom, replicate the propensity for self-questioning characteristic of the most vigilant Enlightenment and modernist thinking.

Whereas Flaubert wrote to punish (whether the target be taken to be his *bonshommes*, or the bourgeoisie, or his readers), if only by impersonal implication, Joyce's fictional assessment of human foibles, linguistic and otherwise, is suffused with a more neutral outlook. The closing episodes of *Ulysses* betray an effort to proffer a level-headed evaluation of such matters

---

[400] Robert Pippin, *Modernism as a Philosophical Problem: On the Dissatisfactions of European High Culture* (Oxford: Blackwell, 1991).
[401] Bush, 'Joyce's Modernisms', 10.
[402] Bush, 'Joyce's Modernisms', 11.

rather than to rebuke his characters or his readers. Joyce more effectively realizes the impassibility Flaubert so passionately advocated, achieving a consistency and sophistication in impartial detachment that eluded his precursor in the unfinished *Bouvard et Pécuchet* and long-gestated *Dictionnaire*. 'Eumaeus' and 'Ithaca' variously demonstrate the omnipresence of cliché; the fact that 'relations stop nowhere'; the faux grandeur of which bourgeois dreams are made; the limitations of encyclopaedic form; the overly hopeful expectations of progress inherent in nineteenth-century post-Enlightenment optimism. 'Eumaeus' and 'Ithaca' do this, as Leopold Bloom responds to his wife's adultery, with 'equanimity'.[403] Mobilizing Flaubertian themes to different ends, they formulate a lucid, amoral statement—rather than an indictment—of how things are. This commitment to non-judgemental, serene composure carries over into *Finnegans Wake*, which marks the apotheosis of Joyce's response to Flaubert.

---

[403] *U* 17: 2,155.

6

Finnegans Wake

TRAVELS IN NORMANDY: JOYCE'S FLAUBERTIAN 'HOLIDAY WISDOM'

In 1978 David Hayman made public his discovery of three 'Flaubert' jottings in *Finnegans Wake* notebook VI.B.8.[1] On non-consecutive pages, they read (figs. 17, 18, 19):

> Flaub. treatment
> of language is a kind
> of despair
> J.J contrary
>
> J.S.J can rest having made me
> G.F—— —— ——
>
> Larbaud result of
> JJ. + G.F.[2]

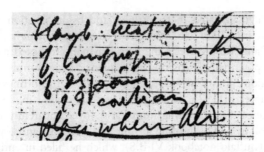

Fig. 17. 'Flaub. treatment/of language is a kind/of despair/J.J contrary', *Finnegans Wake* notebook VI.B.8, 42, *JJA 30*, 315. Because of the ambiguity of Joyce's handwriting, I and others (including David Hayman) have sometimes transcribed the first of these jottings as 'Flaub. treatment/of language *as* a kind/of despair/J.J contrary'.

---

[1] Hayman, Preface *JJA 30*, xviii.
[2] James Joyce, *Finnegans Wake* notebook VI.B.8, 42, 71, 88; *JJA 30*, 315, 329, 338.

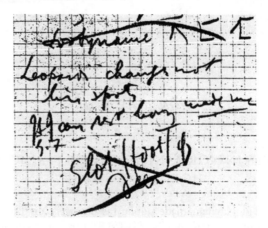

Fig. 18. 'J.S.J can rest having made me/G. F – – — ——', *Finnegans Wake* notebook VI.B.8, 71; reproduced from *JJA 30*, 329.

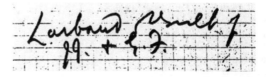

Fig. 19. 'Larbaud result of/JJ. + G.F', *Finnegans Wake* notebook VI.B.8, 88; reproduced from *JJA 30*, 338.

In 1990 Hayman dated these jottings (and by implication, the whole notebook) to mid-1924.[3] In *The Textual Diaries of James Joyce*,[4] published in 1995, Danis Rose corrects the date Hayman attributed to the notebook, with potentially fascinating consequences for our understanding of Joyce's relationship to Flaubert. According to Rose, the jottings were made in the summer of 1925, while Joyce was holidaying in northern and western France. On departing from Paris, Joyce apparently left behind the notebook he had been using in June and early July and began using a new jotter (Buffalo notebook VI.B.8), which he filled in entirely before returning to the only partially filled Parisian notebook.[5] Rose uses a

---

[3] David Hayman, 'Toward a Postflaubertian Joyce'.

[4] Danis Rose, *The Textual Diaries of James Joyce* (Dublin: Lilliput Press, 1995), 82–3.

[5] In *The Textual Diaries* Rose uses a different classification for the *Finnegans Wake* notebooks from the one established by the library of the State University of New York at Buffalo. In Rose's scheme, the notebook Joyce left in Paris in July 1925 is called N19 (rather than VI.B.19), and the notebook he used during his travels is referred to as N18 (rather than VI.B.8).

reference in Joyce's hand to the coastal town of Saint-Valery-en-Caux to establish the probable dates of his use of VI.B.8. Rose conjectures that the place name's appearance in the notebook coincides with Joyce's mention of an excursion to Saint-Valery-en-Caux in a letter to Harriet Shaw Weaver: 'While I was returning from an excursion to S. Valéry the idea for the last watch of Shaun came into my head.'[6] For Rose, the holiday notebook reflects:

> Joyce's immediate concerns: gathering ideas for the fourth episode or 'watch' of Shaun, and the further development of *Anna Livia* for publication.[7]

While the Wakean sigla that are used throughout the jotter act as a constant reminder of these preoccupations, Joyce's notes in VI.B.8 also bear testimony to thoughts that arose specifically from his tourist excursions in Normandy, through that 'pays de Caux', which provided the setting for Flaubert's *Madame Bovary*.[8]

Joyce's travels in the summer of 1925 suggest a motivated quest for exposure to a particular kind of literary inspiration. The dates and provenance of his letters during this period reveal an itinerary intriguingly evocative of a Flaubertian pilgrimage. Joyce's first stop was in Fécamp, where he stayed for a week at the Grand Hôtel des Bains et de Londres. From Fécamp, Joyce travelled to Rouen, where he spent almost two weeks at the Grand Hôtel de la Poste. This sojourn was interrupted by an excursion to the village of Les Andelys, where a single night was spent at the Hôtel du Grand Cerf. From Rouen, Joyce made his way to Arcachon for a longer spell via Niort and Bordeaux.[9] The first few stops on this journey all bear some relation to Flaubert: indeed, it seems likely that Joyce's holidaying destinations were chosen specifically for their Flaubertian connections.

---

[6] Joyce to Harriet Shaw Weaver, 27 July 1925, *L1*, 230.

[7] Rose, *Textual Diaries*, 82–3.

[8] The phrase 'pays de Caux' occurs several times in *Madame Bovary*. The location prompts poetic description: 'Occasionally, squalls would blow up, winds from the sea [...] that whipped right across the plains of the Pays de Caux' (*MBE*, 41) ['Il arrivait parfois des rafales de vent, brises de la mer [...] roulant d'un bond sur tout le plateau du pays de Caux' (*MB*, 77)].

[9] Joyce stayed in Fécamp between 21 and 28 July, in Rouen between 28 July and 9 August, in the village of Les Andelys on the night of 6 August, in Arcachon between 11 August and 3 September, in Niort between 9 and 10 August, and in Bordeaux between 10 and 11 August – Rose, *Textual Diaries*, 185–6.

Fécamp: Flaubert as Literary Father

Fécamp, the Joyces' first port of call on the Norman tour, is mentioned several times in Flaubert's correspondence in relation to the author's dealings with two related families. The first was the Le Poittevin family, the second the Maupassant family.[10] The bonds between the Le Poittevins (who were based in Fécamp) and the Flauberts were close—Flaubert's father was godfather to Alfred, one of Flaubert's closest childhood friends, while Le Poittevin *père* was godfather to Gustave. In 1848 Alfred Le Poittevin died at the age of thirty-two. Flaubert mourned solemnly and passionately, watching over the corpse for two consecutive nights. He often wrote of his friend in subsequent years. In 1860, for instance, he recalls memories of childhood days spent in Fécamp and evokes his enduring sense of loss:

> I stayed with Mme Le Poittevin in Fecamp, where I had not been for 18 years! How I thought about that poor dear Alfred![11]

As is obvious from this account, Flaubert's links with the Le Poittevins were not severed by his friend's death. Indeed, his relations with the family remained, in different ways, almost as intense as they had ever been. In 1846, Alfred's sister, Laure Le Poittevin—who had been a childhood acquaintance, if only by association—married Gustave de Maupassant, a union that led to the birth of Guy de Maupassant, in Fécamp, in 1850. On separating from her husband in 1861, Laure turned to Flaubert—that other Gustave—as a potential substitute for the father her son now lacked. Flaubert, in taking on the role she proposed, engaged willingly in a kind of role-play that the memory of his dead friend urged upon him as more than a favour: a duty, a pleasure. In time, Flaubert introduced Maupassant to the literary luminaries of the day, obtained positions for him, promoted his works, and imparted an intensive literary education. Maupassant's tribute to Flaubert in the preface to *Pierre et Jean* (1888) sketches the outlines of the relationship:

> Flaubert, whom I used to see occasionally, took a liking to me. I took the risk of sending him some of my literary efforts. He was good enough to read

---

[10] The connections between these three families were explored in detail at a conference held in Fécamp in 2000. The proceedings have been published in *Flaubert, Le Poittevin, Maupassant: une affaire de famille littéraire: Actes du Colloque de Fécamp, 27–28 octobre 2000*, ed. Yvan Leclerc and others (Rouen: Publications de l'Université de Rouen, 2002).

[11] Flaubert to Louis Bouilhet, 1 October 1860 ['j'ai couché à Fécamp chez Mme Le Poittevin, où je n'étais pas venu depuis 18 ans! Ai-je pensé à ce pauvre bougre d'Alfred!' (*C3*, 117)].

them [...] I did work, and I often returned to him, realizing that he was fond of me, because he jokingly took to calling me his disciple. [...] The master read it all, then [...] elaborated on his criticisms and gradually drove home to me two or three principles which summarize his long and patient teachings.[12]

The development of the relationship is obvious from letters sent by the 'master' to his 'disciple' over the last decade of his life. In 1875 the tone of Flaubert's letters to his protégé is already warmly affectionate. One letter opens by addressing Maupassant as 'My good chap' and closes with the same tender suggestions of intimacy—'Your old man sends you his love'[13]—as fill Flaubert's letters to George Sand. A progression towards a fatherly relationship is adumbrated by Flaubert's inverted and oxymoronic address to Maupassant as 'My old fellow' later that same year.[14] Shortly before his death in May 1880, Flaubert addresses his disciple as 'My dear good chap',[15] 'My dear friend',[16] and 'My dearest',[17] often signing off as 'Your old man'.[18] On 21 April, Flaubert complimented Maupassant on his latest published work: 'I've re-read *Boule-de-Suif* and maintain that it is a masterpiece.'[19] Maupassant's dedication to *Des Vers*, in the same year, expressed gratitude for the roles—of friend, father, and master—taken on by Flaubert in their crucial, many-sided relationship:

TO
GUSTAVE FLAUBERT
TO THE ILLUSTRIOUS AND FATHERLY FRIEND

---

[12] Guy de Maupassant, in 'Le Roman', Preface to *Pierre et Jean*, trans. Julie Mead (Oxford: Oxford University Press, 2001), 12 ['Flaubert, que je voyais quelquefois, se prit d'affection pour moi. J'osai lui soumettre quelques essais. Il les lut avec bonté [...] Je travaillai, et je revins souvent chez lui, comprenant que je lui plaisais, car il s'était mis à m'appeler, en riant, son disciple. [...] Le maître lisait tout, puis [...] développait ses critiques et enfonçait en moi, peu à peu, deux ou trois principes qui sont le résumé de ses longs et patients enseignements.' (*Pierre et Jean* [Paris: Flammarion, 1992], 27)].

[13] Flaubert to Guy de Maupassant, 15 April 1875, *C4*, 921 ['Mon Bon'; 'Votre vieux vous embrasse'].

[14] Flaubert to Guy de Maupassant, 4 November 1875, *C4*, 989 ['Mon petit Père'].

[15] Flaubert to Guy de Maupassant, 24–25 March 1880, *C5*, 867 ['Mon cher bon-homme'].

[16] Flaubert to Guy de Maupassant, 8 April 1880, *C5*, 880 ['Mon cher ami'].

[17] Flaubert to Guy de Maupassant, 16 April 1880, *C5*, 883 ['Mon chéri'].

[18] ['Ton vieux']. The use of the second-person pronoun is more significant than the 'vieux', which Flaubert uses to denote himself in letters to many friends. However, these other friends were by and large Flaubert's contemporaries. In Maupassant's case, the years between them make paternal connotations inevitable.

[19] Flaubert to Guy de Maupassant, 20–21 April 1880 ['J'ai relu *Boule-de-Suif* et je maintiens que c'est un chef d'oeuvre.' (*C5*, 887)].

Whom I love with all my heart,
TO THE IRREPROACHABLE MASTER
Whom I admire above all others.[20]

Flaubert's response, in one of his very last letters to Maupassant, fully reciprocates the sentiments expressed in this public tribute. The letter's tone is paternal, loving. Recognizing the literary achievement his fathering has made possible, Flaubert remembers Le Poittevin, the long-lost friend whose death had forged the original bond:

My young man,
  You are right to love me, for this old man cherishes you. [. . .]
  Your dedication stirred up in me a whole world of memories: your uncle Alfred, your grandmother, your mother; and for a while this old man's heart was full, and there were tears in his eyes.[21]

It is easy to see how this relationship—of the non-biological father to his spiritual son—would have appealed to Joyce, whose works betray an enduring fascination with just such a mode of paternity. For Stephen Dedalus, whose mind returns obsessively to the problems of fatherhood on 16 June 1904, 'Paternity may be a legal fiction.'[22] But paternity may not be a fiction for fiction: in Flaubert's correspondence Joyce would have found a perfect example of spiritual fatherhood actualized in real life. Flaubert's relationship to Maupassant is ideal fatherhood come true: paternity, in this case, is no longer a fiction but the paternity by one author of the fiction of another. It even seems possible, in the light of the evidence of Joyce's early acquaintance with Flaubert's correspondence, that his knowledge of the relationship between the two French writers may have been at the origin, or at least helped sustain, his lifelong preoccupation with non-biological fatherhood. That preoccupation had other important models (not least that of Jesus Christ, son to God the Father more than to 'Joseph the Joiner'[23]), but the 'master' and his 'disciple' offered an example of a successful and almost contemporary enactment of spiritual, and specifically literary, fatherhood. It is worth

---

[20] ['À/GUSTAVE FLAUBERT/À L'ILLUSTRE ET PATERNEL AMI/Que j'aime de toute ma tendresse,/À L'IRRÉPROCHABLE MAÎTRE/Que j'admire avant tous.' (Guy de Maupassant, *Oeuvres poétiques complètes: Des Vers et autres poèmes*, ed. Emmanuel Vincent [Rouen: Publications de l'Université de Rouen, 2001], 33)]. The capitalization is Maupassant's.

[21] Flaubert to Guy de Maupassant, 25 April 1880, *FS2*, 274 ['Mon jeune homme,/Tu as raison de m'aimer, car ton vieux te chérit. [. . .]/Ta dédicace a remué en moi tout un monde de souvenirs: ton oncle Alfred, ta grand-mère, ta mère, et le bonhomme, pendant quelque temps, a eu le coeur gros et une larme aux paupières.' (*C5*, 890)].

[22] *U* 9: 844.

[23] *U* 1: 586, 607.

noting (at the beginning of a chapter that will be much concerned with Joyce's evolving conception of literary relations) that the Flaubert-Maupassant connection is both a literalization and a contradiction of Harold Bloom's theory in *The Anxiety of Influence*. The relationship constitutes a literalization of that theory insofar as it concerns a strong, formative, productive relationship between a younger and an older author. It contradicts the theory because the reciprocal bond between two adults entailed none of the violent agonistic drives that Bloom considers to be the mainspring of fruitful misprision.

Notebook VI.B.8 bears traces of Joyce's interest in Fécamp. The first of these occurs on page 17 of the notebook, and reads:

[HCE sigla] stone fall
(Fécamp)

On page 22 Joyce noted:

A fig for Fecamp
Fec—4 star brandy
     4 priest mass[24]

It is clear from an explicit reference in a letter (which conspicuously avoids mention of a father) that Joyce had Maupassant in mind during his stay in the town: 'Maupassant was born here but his mother concealed the fact.'[25]

Saint-Valery: Joyce as Literary Father

It is in the same letter that Joyce makes mention of his excursion to Saint-Valery. In the notebook the town enters with a namesake, the place name of Saint-Valery-sur-Somme:

S.Valery en Caux/en Somme.[26]

As was suggested above, the place name bears associations relating to Flaubert's life and works—to that 'pays de Caux' which provided the setting for *Madame Bovary* and *Bouvard et Pécuchet* and was home to the writer for much of his life. The place name also resonates with other notes in VI.B.8: those that refer, explicitly or cryptically, to Valery Larbaud. In the last of the three unequivocally Flaubertian jottings in the notebook, Larbaud's name is closely linked to Flaubert's:

[24] VI.B.8, 17, 22; *JJA*, 302, 305.
[25] Joyce to Harriet Shaw Weaver, 27 July 1925, *L1*, 230.
[26] VI.B.8, 5; *JJA 30*, 296.

Larbaud result of
J[ames]. J[oyce] + G[ustave]. F[laubert].[27]

This delineation of a line of descent running from Flaubert and Joyce to
Larbaud is fascinating in its minimalist neatness and indicative of Joyce's
intense preoccupation with literary influence in the summer of 1925. This
pattern of thinking was not new: indeed, it is obvious from as early
as 'The Day of the Rabblement', and manifest again in his *Exiles* notes.
In 'The Day of the Rabblement' Joyce outlined two separate artistic family
trees. The first of these genealogies dismissed George Moore as a descendant of Flaubert, intimating that Joyce himself had no interest in such an
affiliation.[28] Joyce's equation in VI.B.8 radically revises this initial position by tacitly re-inscribing Joyce and Flaubert within the same tradition.
Flaubert, who stood, in 'The Day of the Rabblement', at the origin of
a tide from which Joyce took care to distinguish himself, becomes, in VI.
B.8, the co-father, with Joyce, of a new authorial figure. Again, the
template of the family romance subtends Joyce's thoughts about literary
begetting and evolution.

Another change has occurred between the early essay and the notebook
jotting: Joyce has moved from his initial position as the 'third minister' in
a series originating in Ibsen and Hauptmann, to adopt second or first place
in a new series—first in terms of importance (for such, perhaps, is the
implication of his own name appearing before Flaubert's), and second in
chronological terms. That said, part of the effect of the jotting's equation
format is to annihilate the sense of chronology that constituted such a clear
feature of the chains of influence outlined in 'The Day of the Rabblement'. A three-term succession is flattened out into two short lines, and JJ.
and G.F., in sharing the second, appear as equal and simultaneous in their
influential force. On such a reading, which privileges the synchrony rather
than the consecutiveness of Joyce's and Flaubert's combined impact, the
diachronic image of the genealogical tree is conjugated with an intertextual
emphasis on the concurrent effects of past literary events.

The 'S. Valery' and 'Larbaud' jottings are symptomatic of Joyce's
intense preoccupation with issues of intertextuality in the summer of
1925. Such a contention is supported by facts extraneous to the notebook
as well as by other manuscript scribblings. There are several reasons why
Joyce may have felt very positively inclined towards Larbaud in the
summer of 1925,[29] and thus enjoyed finding a place name that cast him

---

[27] VI.B.8, 88; *JJA 30*, 338.
[28] 'Rabblement', *OCPW*, 51.
[29] Larbaud had done much for Joyce in previous years. In May 1921 he offered the
Joyces his flat at 71 rue Cardinal Lemoine rent-free. On 7 December 1921 he gave the first

as a saint. In 1922 Larbaud's *Amants, heureux amants* was published with a dedication that bears noticeable affinities to Maupassant's emotional homage to Flaubert in *Des Vers*:

> To
> *James Joyce*
> *my friend, and the only begetter*
> *of the form I have adopted*
> *in this piece of writing.*
> V. L
> Paris, novembre 1921[30]

Larbaud's homage was repeated and extended in his preface to the new edition of Édouard Dujardin's *Les Lauriers sont coupés*[31] which was published in 1925—the very year in which Joyce was using notebook VI.B.8 on his journey through northwestern France. The thrust of Larbaud's preface is twofold. On the one hand, it aims to draw attention to the influence exerted on *Ulysses* by Dujardin's invention of interior monologue; on the other, it seeks to measure the effect of Joyce's use of the technique on contemporary novelists and to forecast his impact on new generations of writers. In effect, Larbaud traces a line of descent that originates in Dujardin and runs through Joyce, the focal point of the entire preface, towards 'the literary history of the future'.[32] Stating from the outset that his intent is not to dwell on Dujardin's book itself, Larbaud launches into an account of the publication of *Ulysses* in *The Little Review*. The question of the book's influence is immediately brought into focus:

> the book's influence soon became discernible in the writings of the young writers of English-speaking countries, who began, even before Joyce had finished and published his work as a bound volume (Paris, Shakespeare & Cie, February 1922), to imitate, or more accurately to make use of, some of the forms deployed in *Ulysses*.[33]

public lecture on *Ulysses* in Adrienne Monnier's bookshop. The text of this lecture was published in the *Nouvelle Revue Française* on 1 April 1922. Larbaud had been involved in the translation of passages from *Ulysses* into French for the purposes of his lecture, and in 1924 Joyce enlisted his help for further work on a full-length translation. – *JJ*, 512, 500, 520–3, 530.

[30] Valery Larbaud, *Oeuvres*, ed. Jean-Aubry and Robert Mallet (Paris: Gallimard, 1957), 615. The italics are Larbaud's.

[31] Édouard Dujardin, *Les Lauriers sont coupés* (1888) (Paris: Albert Messein, 1925).

[32] ['l'histoire littéraire du lendemain' (Valery Larbaud, Preface to Édouard Dujardin, *Les Lauriers sont coupés* [Paris: Albert Messein, 1925], 14)].

[33] ['l'influence de ce livre se fit bientôt sentir dans les écrits des jeunes hommes de lettres des pays de langue anglaise, qui commencèrent, avant même que l'ouvrage de James Joyce eût été terminé et publié en volume (Paris, Shakespeare & Cie, février 1922), à imiter, ou plus exactement à utiliser certaines des formes employées dans *Ulysses*' (Larbaud, *Lauriers*, 6)].

Having read Dujardin's novel on Joyce's recommendation, Larbaud can confirm that *Les Lauriers* must be considered 'one of the formal sources for *Ulysses*'.[34] He laments the fact that Dujardin's novel is still:

> unknown to those able imitators and vulgarizers who might have been able to grasp the new formula, adapt it to popular taste, make it fashionable.[35]

Had it been more widely known, the book 'might have had a fertile influence'.[36] Larbaud's statements are remarkable for the absolute serenity with which they discuss literary influence, which is extolled both as the mark of a successful writer—when the effect of his work manifests itself in the writing of others—and as a phenomenon to which an author may fruitfully be subject himself. Like Joyce's 'Flaubert' jottings (including the one about Larbaud himself), the preface runs counter to Harold Bloom's thesis in the *Anxiety of Influence* by discussing the phenomena that take place at both ends of the literary influence spectrum as wholly desirable and beneficial. Central to Larbaud's argument is the fact that Joyce himself identified and acknowledged Dujardin's influence:

> he told me that this form had already been used, and in a continous fashion, in a book by Edouard Dujardin.[37]

Larbaud's ease with the idea of literary indebtedness reflects Joyce's own: as Larbaud makes clear, Joyce's appropriation of Dujardin's technique would probably have gone entirely unnoticed if Joyce had not drawn attention to it.

The issue of the adoption of forms used by others recurs in many of Larbaud's comments about Joyce. In the dedication to *Amants, heureux amants*, Larbaud writes of Joyce as 'the only begetter of the form I have *adopted* in this piece of writing'.[38] In the preface to *Les Lauriers sont coupés*, he refers to interior monologue as a form 'invented by a French novelist,

---

[34] ['une des sources formelles de *Ulysses*' (Larbaud, *Lauriers*, 7)].

[35] ['inconnu des imitateurs habiles et des vulgarisateurs qui auraient pu s'emparer de la formule nouvelle, l'adapter aux goûts du public, la mettre à la mode' (Larbaud, *Lauriers*, 8)].

[36] ['aurait pu avoir une influence féconde' (Larbaud, *Lauriers*, 8)].

[37] ['il me dit que cette forme avait déjà été employée, et d'une manière continue, dans un livre d'Édouard Dujardin' (Larbaud, *Lauriers*, 6)].

[38] Larbaud, *Oeuvres*, (my emphasis). The words echo the dedication of Shakespeare's sonnets to 'Mr. W. H', 'THE. ONLIE. BEGETTER. OF/THESE. INSUING. SONNETS.' Larbaud dedicated his next work, *Mon plus secret conseil* (1923), to Édouard Dujardin: '*A/Édouard Dujardin/auteur de/*Les Lauriers sont coupés (1887)/*a quo* . . .'— Larbaud, *Oeuvres*, 647.

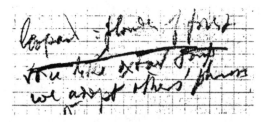

Fig. 20. 'we adopt others' phrases', *Finnegans Wake* notebook VI.B.8, 72; reproduced from *JJA 30*, 330.

adopted in a famous work by an Irish novelist.'[39] That the word struck a chord with Joyce is strongly suggested by his own use of the term in VI.B.8. Almost immediately after the jotting that reads 'G.F [can rest having made me]', Joyce wrote: 'we adopt others' phrases' (fig. 20).[40] This ties in with the theme of literary fatherhood to which Joyce's works so often return. Larbaud must have been aware (from his reading of *Ulysses*, if nothing else) of the importance Joyce attached to this theme when he referred to him as the 'begetter' of the form used in *Amants, heureux amants*. (Joyce had made almost identical use of the word in a 1917 letter to Pound in which he addressed the poet as the 'only begetter' of *A Portrait*.[41])

Dujardin does not feature in notebook VI.B.8. Flaubert completes the series instead, providing the third corner of Joyce's triangular equation. Dujardin's absence suggests where the author's real allegiances lay. Joyce's private admissions of a Flaubertian influence in VI.B.8 confirm what his works repeatedly show: that he was under no illusion as to Flaubert's formative role in his endeavours, and the relationship was one that he embraced without angst. Indeed, the tone of the jottings is anything but anguished: it is laconic, serene, possibly even jocular.

From Fécamp, Joyce moved inland to Rouen, where he settled for just under two weeks (by far his longest stay in any northwestern town that year). Joyce's letters make no mention of the motivations behind the choice of Rouen as a holiday destination, nor do they make reference to

---

[39] ['inventée par un romancier français, *adoptée* dans un ouvrage célèbre par un écrivain irlandais' (Larbaud, Lauriers, 14 [my emphasis])].

[40] VI.B.8, 72; *JJA 30*, 330.

[41] 'I enclose some press notices. Yours comes first as only begetter of this book.'—Joyce to Pound, 24 July 1917, unpublished letter, Yale University, Beinecke Rare Book and Manuscript Library, YCAL MSS 43, box 26, ff. 1,112–14.

the town's greatest cultural attraction: Gustave Flaubert. But the three
'Flaubert' jottings in VI.B.8, if they cannot provide evidence that Flaubert
was the reason for Joyce's trip, suggest that Rouen did not fail to nurture
Flaubertian thoughts in him. The notebook, for instance, contains recognizable references to Rouen Cathedral, which played an important role
in Flaubert's writing. It is in the cathedral that one of *Madame Bovary*'s
best-known scenes is set. Immediately before their erotic journey through
Rouen in a hackney cab, Léon and Emma are given a tour of that
edifice by a Swiss guard eager to awe the couple with the monument's
'curiosités'.[42] The cathedral is also home to the famous Saint Julien
stained-glass window—Flaubert's inspiration for 'La Légende de saint
Julien l'Hospitalier'—and to a tympanum representing the dance of
Salome, which features prominently in 'Hérodias'. On page 25 of VI.
B.8[43] Joyce wrote 'apple sugar candy', the name of a Rouen specialty, and
'Butter Tower', which denotes the famous 'Tour de Beurre' of Rouen
Cathedral (so named because its construction was funded by the sale of
dispensations to eat butter during Lent). On the next page, the following
references also seem to relate to the cathedral:

> decorated (style)
> flamboyant
> = E perpendicular
> [?]. Walsh II
> porte S. Stephen
>   (of a church)
> [Shem sigla] roturier can't
>   sign (face or
>   mark)
>   (except vitriers).[44]
> [HCE sigla] cardinal's hat aloft[45]

Although the source of these jottings has yet to be identified, 'porte
S. Stephen (of a church)' almost certainly refers to the cathedral's 'chapelle
Saint Étienne la Grande Église'. The first jotting lists various architectural
styles (including the 'flamboyant' gothic style in which the Butter Tower
was built), while allusions to Archbishop 'Walsh II', a 'cardinal's hat', and
'glaziers' fit in with the cathedral theme of the surrounding material.

---

[42] *MB*, 311–15.
[43] VI.B.8, 25; *JJA 30*, 306.
[44] [translation of lines 7 to 10: 'commoner can't/sign (face or/mark)/(except glaziers)'].
[45] VI.B.8, 26; *JJA 30*, 307.

Les Andelys: Treading in Flaubert's Footsteps

During his stay in Rouen, Joyce opted to take a trip for a single night to a tiny village situated forty kilometres away: Les Andelys. The address of the hamlet's Grand Cerf hotel appears on the cover verso of VI.B.8, below the address of Shakespeare & Company (the address to which the notebook owner appealed for its return, were it to be lost and found):

> Grand Cerf
> Les Andelys
> 94 [bld ?][46]

Joyce often used notebook covers to jot down addresses. In this case the Grand Cerf stands out as the only hotel address in the notebook. The motivations for the note (prospective? retrospective? practical? literary?) are unknowable, yet connections to Flaubert (concerning Les Andelys and Le Grand Cerf) strongly suggest intertextual affiliations.

Like Fécamp, Les Andelys features frequently in Flaubert's early correspondence. The village was home to another of Flaubert's closest childhood friends, Ernest Chevalier. In 1844 Flaubert urged Chevalier to visit him in Rouen on the occasion of his next return to Les Andelys.[47] A letter of 1846, also to Chevalier, evoked the pleasures of bygone days spent in the village:

> How wonderful they were, my Easter trips to Les Andelys and the extraordinary gusto for larks I had back then! What pipes we smoked! How free we were in our conversations! Such pleasure.[48]

The name of the hotel at which Joyce stayed in Les Andelys, the Hôtel du Grand Cerf, has Flaubertian resonance of its own. In 1846 Flaubert was trying to see Louise Colet without arousing his mother's suspicions about their relationship. Accordingly he planned to feign a trip to Les Andelys and its landmark, Château-Gaillard, to enable a lovers' secret rendez-vous in Mantes (which lies halfway between Rouen and Paris):

---

[46] VI.B.8, cover verso; *JJA 30*, 293.

[47] 'When you come to Les Andelys don't forget to push on as far as Rouen.' – Flaubert to Ernest Chevalier, 1 February 1844 ['Quand tu viendras aux Andelys n'oublie pas de pousser jusqu'à Rouen.' (*C1*, 203)].

[48] Flaubert to Ernest Chevalier, 15 June 1845 ['sais-tu que c'était beau, mes voyages de Pâques aux Andelys et la prodigieuse vigueur de blague que j'avais alors! Quelles pipes! Comme nous avions peu de retenue dans nos propos! C'était plaisir.' (*C1*, 239)].

It is arranged that I shall take this little trip to Les Andelys (read Mantes). [...] We'll go to some nice quiet hostelry.[49]

Flaubert's first letter to Colet on his return from the trip recalls with satisfaction 'ce bon hôtel de Mantes' and thanks her for the poem ('Souvenirs') she has already sent him to immortalize their time there. Colet's verses give a name to 'ce bon hôtel de Mantes'. It was the Hôtel du Grand Cerf: 'We run to the Grand-Cerf, arm in arm'.[50] Either by choice or by chance or by a strange conjunction of mental association and conducive circumstance, Joyce found himself staying in a hotel which bore an identical name to that which had been the site of Flaubert's romantic tryst, and within a village that had also been the scene to a number of his youthful jaunts.

Joyce did not need to be so intimately acquainted with Flaubert's amorous arrangements to make a connection between the Hôtel du Grand Cerf and Flaubert. Indeed, the 'grand cerf' of 'La Légende de saint Julien l'Hospitalier' is arguably one of Flaubert's most memorable fictional characters. Joyce might have been reminded of this fact in Rouen Cathedral where Flaubert, as is emphasized by the closing sentence of 'La Légende', found stained-glass inspiration for his tale. But if the window did remind Joyce of Flaubert's 'grand cerf', it would have done so by association only, because no stag or deer actually appears on the cathedral window. Indeed, the 'cerf' is entirely Flaubert's invention. Flaubert revelled in such departures from the stained-glass tale, gleefully anticipating the reader's confusion at the discrepancies he was insinuating between text and window:

Comparing the image to the text, the reader would say to himself: 'I don't understand. How has he drawn this from that?'[51]

It is especially tantalizing to find the words 'grand cerf' on the inside cover of Joyce's Norman notebook because few stories deal with issues of influence and paternity so strikingly and so enigmatically as 'La Légende de saint Julien l'Hospitalier'. The word 'cerf' features many times in the story, accruing new layers of meaning on each occasion. At first, the 'cerf' is just one of the species of animal Julian must learn to track ('recognizing

---

[49] Flaubert to Louise Colet, 4–5 September 1846 ['Il est arrangé que je ferai ce petit voyage aux Andelys (lisez Mantes). [...] Nous irons dans quelque bonne auberge bien tranquille.' (*C1*, 327)].

[50] ['Nous courons au Grand-Cerf, bras dessus, bras dessous' (Louise Colet to Flaubert, 'Souvenirs', 9-10 November 1846, http://flaubert.univ-rouen.fr./correspondance/conard/autour/mantes.html [July 2011])].

[51] Flaubert to Georges Charpentier, 16 February 1879 ['En comparant l'image au texte on se serait dit: "Je n'y comprends rien. Comment a-t-il tiré ceci de cela?"' (*C5*, 543)].

a stag from its fumets').[52] But the animal soon becomes linked with the very acme of murderous pleasure in the protagonist's mind, so that the mere mention of deer ushers in connotations relating to murder, pain (the animal's), and pleasure (Julian's), the latter two being tightly interwoven by Flaubert's use of the verb 'gémir', which can denote either. In the following quotation, the deer's death moans bring on Julian's delectation:

> when the stag began to moan from the pain of their bites, he would swiftly despatch it, and then delight in the frenzy of the hounds as they devoured their prey.[53]

When the deer next appear, the narration begins to take a more anthropo-morphic view of their activities. A large group of deer are seen gathered closely together ('they warmed each other with their breath')[54] and tacit parallels are established between one particular 'family' of deer and Julian's own family:

> The stag, which was black and of monstrous size, carried sixteen antlers, and had a white tuft of beard. The doe, as light in colour as dead leaves, was grazing the turf; and the dappled fawn clung to her teat without interrupting her progress.[55]

When Julian embarks upon his slaughter of the deer, human terms are used to describe the animals' agony: 'its mother, head raised towards the heavens, let out a harsh cry, deep, heart-rending, human'.[56] The 'cerf' of the family now becomes 'le grand cerf'. With an arrow planted between its enormous antlers, the stag utters the prophecy that will shape the rest of Julian's life:

> The monstrous beast stopped; then with blazing eyes, solemn as a patriarch or a judge, to the sound of a bell ringing in the distance, he repeated three times:
>   'Cursed! Cursed! Cursed! One day, savage heart, you will murder your father and your mother!'[57]

---

[52] *TCE*, 46 ['reconnaître le cerf à ses fumées' (*TC*, 92)].

[53] *TCE*, 48 ['quand le cerf commençait à gémir sous les morsures, il l'abattait preste-ment, puis se délectait à la furie de ses mâtins qui le dévoraient' (*TC*, 95)].

[54] *TCE*, 50 ['ils se réchauffaient avec leurs haleines' (*TC*, 98)].

[55] *TCE*, 51 ['Le cerf, qui était noir et monstrueux de taille, portait seize andouillers avec une barbe blanche. La biche, blonde comme les feuilles mortes, broutait le gazon; et le faon tacheté, sans l'interrompre dans sa marche, lui tétait la mamelle.' (*TC*, 99)].

[56] *TCE*, 51 ['sa mère, en regardant le ciel, brama d'une voix profonde, déchirante, humaine' (*TC*, 99–100)].

[57] *TCE*, 51 ['Le prodigieux animal s'arrêta; et les yeux flamboyants, solennel comme un patriarche et comme un justicier, pendant qu'une cloche au loin tintait, il répéta trois fois:/– "Maudit! maudit! maudit! Un jour, coeur féroce, tu assassineras ton père et ta mère!"' (*TC*, 100)].

The prophecy and its bearer obsess Julian: 'he kept seeing the great black stag'.[58] Much later in the story, when Julian's parents reach the threshold of his distant castle at precisely the time Julian has chosen to go hunting again for the first time in years, the narrator dwells on those of his father's physical features—'his tall figure and long beard'[59]—that recall 'le grand cerf'. Having returned to the castle, Julian bends to kiss his wife, only to feel 'his lips touch what seemed to be a beard'.[60] Julian's homicidal wrath in the darkened bedroom is triggered by an attribute that father and stag—and the adulterer Julian's conscious mind suspects—have in common. Julian's murder, in other words, has a triple target in the signifying economy of the text. But the stag outlives its murder to return as a witness to the fulfilment of its prophecy. As the violent bloodshed unfolds, the moans of Julian's dying parents modulate into the vengeful tones of the 'grand cerf noir':

> He listened intently to the death rattle coming from the two of them almost as one, and as it began to fade away, another, far off, prolonged it. At first hesitant, this long-drawn-out cry of pain came ever nearer, swelled, became cruel; and terror-struck he recognized the belling of the great black stag.[61]

The verb 'recognized [reconnut]'—the same as had been used to describe Julian's mastery of the art of hunting (when he was taught how to 'recogniz[e] a stag from its fumets')[62]—closes the episode and acts as a reminder that Julian's story is a quest for recognition, knowledge, understanding. This quest is, paradoxically, both accomplished and faulted by the parricide: in a tale in which all hints of motivation have been removed,[63] it is impossible for the reader to know whether Julian kills because he recognizes, or fails to recognize, his father, and whether the

---

[58] *TCE*, 52 ['il revoyait toujours le grand cerf noir' (*TC*, 100–1)].

[59] *TCE*, 58 ['sa taille haute et sa grande barbe' (*TC*, 112)].

[60] *TCE*, 62 ['contre sa bouche l'impression d'une barbe' (*TC*, 116)].

[61] *TCE*, 62 ['Il écoutait attentivement leurs deux râles presque égaux, et, à mesure qu'ils s'affaiblissaient, un autre, tout au loin les continuait. Incertaine d'abord, cette voix plaintive longuement poussée, se rapprochait, s'enfla, devint cruelle; et il reconnut, terrifié, le bramement du grand cerf noir.' (*TC*, 117)].

[62] *TCE*, 46 ['reconnaître le cerf à ses fumées' (*TC*, 92)].

[63] Pierre-Marc de Biasi evokes Flaubert's 'elaboration of the undecidable' ['l'élaboration de l'indécidable'] in 'La Légende': 'Between two elements A and B, which follow chronologically from each other and whose adjacency is strategic, a narrative interval is absent or blurred, so that the relation between A and B is ultimately undecidable and unassignable.' ['Entre deux éléments A et B, qui s'enchaînent chronologiquement mais dont la contiguïté textuelle est stratégique, un intervalle narratif manque ou se brouille, de telle façon qu'entre A et B, la relation est finalement indécidable et inassignable.' ('L'élaboration du problématique dans "La Légende de saint Julien l'Hospitalier"', in *Flaubert à l'oeuvre* [Paris: Flammarion, 1980], 72)].

tragic outcome is providentially fated, psychologically determined, or simply coincidental.

The Oedipal shape of the narrative—a fate of inexpiable parricidal guilt sealed by prophecy, a father killed for being found in bed with a mother confused for a wife[64]—seems to invite readings which privilege the theme of influence. A son turns against his father with those skills his father inculcated and prized. Only after his father's death can Julian's life deviate from the trajectory his father's early decision ('his father declared that his son was now of an age when he ought to learn the art of venery')[65] had decreed. And yet the death of the father is not the end of the story for Julian. Like the grand cerf, Julian's father returns to haunt Julian at a crucial moment. Devastated with remorse, Julian, gazing into a pond, considers death by drowning. Peering into his reflection, Julian sees only his father's face, and it is this realization, this final act of both misrecognition and delayed recognition, that forbids suicide:

> Without recognizing his own image, Julian vaguely remembered a face rather like it. He cried out—it was his father; and he thought no more of killing himself.[66]

Julian has become his own father; his father lives in him. To commit suicide would be to commit murder again. The hunt-themed jotting that immediately follows 'G.F [can rest having made me]' in VI.B.8 seems to confirm connections between Flaubert's tale and Joyce's other reflections in the notebook. Crossed out in blue, it reads:

> Slot (foot) of
>   deer[67]

In *Finnegans Wake* the jotting has grown into a fully-fledged hunting scene:

> The cry of the roedeer it is! The white hind. Their slots, linklink, the hound hunthorning![68]

---

[64] Jean-Paul Sartre proposed a psychobiographical reading of 'La Légende' in his *L'Idiot de la famille: Gustave Flaubert de 1821 à 1857*, 3 vols (Paris: Gallimard, 1971–2), vol. 2. An English translation of the most relevant passages (pages 1,897–1,907 and 2,106–17) is provided by William J. Berg in 'The Family Idiot: Julian and Gustave', in *Saint/Oedipus: Psychocritical Approaches to Flaubert's Art*, ed. William J. Berg, Michel Grimaud, and George Moskos (Ithaca and London: Cornell University Press, 1982).

[65] *TCE*, 46 ['son père déclara que l'on devait à son âge apprendre la vénerie' (*TC*, 91)].

[66] *TCE*, 65 ['Sans reconnaître son image, Julien se rappelait confusément une figure ressemblant à celle-là. Il poussa un cri; c'était son père; et il ne pensa plus à se tuer.' (*TC*, 122)].

[67] VI.B.8, 71; *JJA 30*, 229.

[68] *FW* 500: 12–13.

For all these apparent convergences, Joyce's attitude to influence diverges from that which emerges from Flaubert's anxiety-ridden 'Légende'. Joyce's notebook betrays no anxiety of influence. Indeed, the difference between Flaubertian anxiety (as featured in 'La Légende') and Joycean serenity (as expressed in VI.B.8's acknowledgement of Flaubert's paternity) may explain another of the notebook's 'Flaubert jottings':

> Flaub. treatment
> of language is a kind
> of despair
> J.J contrary[69]

The jotting tantalizes by its aphoristic concision, seeming to invite interpretation as a flash of personal discovery on Joyce's part or as a snippet from a private manifesto. The fact of opposition is crucial: whatever the (evolving) tenor of Joyce's thoughts about Flaubert over the years, the purport of this assertion is one of stark differentiation. The note registers the greatest possible disparity between himself and Flaubert. Here the two, far from being aligned, are deemed to be 'contrary' to each other. At this point in VI.B.8, Joyce seems to have been intent on distinguishing himself from the very same figure whom he would acknowledge as a literary father thirty pages later.

These jottings are fascinating in themselves, but their proximity to each other within the same notebook holds additional interest. A relationship first invoked in terms of radical contrast returns to the pages of the jotter in terms of filiation. In what might seem like an intellectual about-turn, a forthright statement of difference modulates into a recognition of descent. It is tempting to speculate whether Joyce's conviction of his disagreement with Flaubert—the realization that his attitude to language is the very opposite of despair—may in fact have been what rendered him able and willing to name him as a father: to identify and claim him as a point of origin, a seed of growth, and object of dissent. In Harold Bloom's terms (though Joyce's thinking processes in VI.B.8 are far too conscious for the analogy to be more than suggestive), one might say that Joyce's assumption of a position of misprision in relation to Flaubert enables, leads to, and ushers forth his declaration of that other author's fathering role. Joyce's attitude to 'Papa Flaubert'[70] in the summer of 1925 bears no trace of anguish or despondency: defining his own outlook and compositional practices as the opposite of Flaubertian 'despair', the notebook is evocative, rather, of an

---

[69] VI.B.8, 42; *JJA 30*, 315.
[70] Pound, 'Past History', *P/J*, 248.

author confidently taking stock of both the importance of, and his own dissimilarity from, a key precursor.

Bearing Pound's striking 'Papa Flaubert' comment in mind makes present another possible interpretation of these 'Flaubert' jottings. Although that particular remark was made eight years after Joyce's Norman tour, it seems possible that Joyce may have found his holiday context conducive to reflection concerning Pound's regular comments on his relations to Flaubert. In a sense, his jottings lend themselves to a comic reading, as a kind of ironic parrotry of Pound's patrilineal conception of literary history and of his *idée fixe* of Joyce as being first and foremost an Irish Flaubert. If Joyce was indeed taking the jocoserious[71] measure of Pound's responses to his work, then his ear proved near-perfect: his echo of the Poundian refrain reads as an almost verbatim anticipation of the critic's later, even more simplified characterization of the relation in 1933. If he was recapitulating one of the most frequently voiced strands of engagement with his work, such an attitude would fittingly adumbrate (if only by inferred contrast) the greater complexity of Joyce's own evolving, ever more intertextual understanding of literary relations.

Another speculative interpretation made available by the consideration of these jottings as witty, playful, private asides—as a joke the author might have been having with himself—arises from the semantic multiplicity of the word 'contrary'. Although the most prominent meaning of the word in this context naturally pertains to Joyce's move to distance himself from Flaubert's world view, or from his treatment of language, the term also resonates with connotations that it carries elsewhere in Joyce's oeuvre. Indeed, the author's interest in contraries, often ascribed to his admiration for Giordano Bruno's doctrine of the identity of opposites or coincidence of contraries ('the maximum and the minimum come together into one existence'),[72] amounted to a belief in their virtue as vectors of revelatory tension and as symptoms of a fundamental subtending unity. In this light, Joyce's view of himself as 'contrary' to Flaubert could be seen as an insistence on a deeper relatedness that would subsume the contrary forms by which likeness expresses itself.

Finally, an even more light-hearted take on Joyce's droll phrase might allow for the possibility that Joyce could here be confessing to his pleasure in adopting a position of contrariness, emphasizing his relish in playing the part of the awkward or recalcitrant follower, refusing to fall in line with

---

[71] *U* 17: 369.
[72] McIntyre, J. Lewis, *Giordano Bruno* (London: Macmillan, 1903), quoted in Weir, 'Gnomon is an Island', 348. Joyce's essay, 'The Bruno Philosophy', was a review of McIntyre's book.

Flaubert's despair. Although the jotting may seem to be expressing a straightforward opposition between Flaubert's perceived hopelessness and Joyce's own comparative optimism, his assertion of contrariness may be more general than personal. Instead of being a statement of opposition to Flaubert or to despair—instead, that is, of expounding an affirmative or celebratory stance—the jotting may be seeking to formulate a different attitude: a determination to be 'contrary' with language. Joyce may, in other words, be expressing a willingness to be rough with words, antagonistic to language, to literature, and conceivably to the world they represent. Such an interpretation accords with his sense, as announced in a letter from 1926 to Harriet Shaw Weaver, that 'wideawake language, cuttandry grammar and goahead plot' leave in the dark a 'great part of human existence'.[73] In VI.B.8, under the guise of a seemingly polar opposition, Joyce articulates what retrospectively reads as an epigrammatic manifesto for the *Wake*, encapsulating a determination to be contrary with language—to break its rules, ignore its etiquette, overturn its decorum, ruffle its feathers, jumble its words. Even at this early stage in its composition, Joyce may have intuited how utterly central a principle the idea of contradiction would become to his *Work in Progress*.

Just above the claim of Flaubert as a literary father, another uncrossed note has bearing on the issue of intertextuality. It reads:

> Leopardi changes not
>   his spots[74]

This allusion to the Italian poet Giacomo Leopardi is framed within a variation on a biblical idiom. The original expression occurs in Jeremiah 13 (22–3) in the form of a question: 'Can the Ethiopian change his skin, or the leopard his spots?' Joyce's inclusion of Leopardi's name in his own version of the biblical sentence reinforces the suggestion that his concern, at this point in the notebook, is with writing processes and specifically with intertextuality. Giacomo Leopardi (with whose writing Joyce was familiar from at least as early as 1901,[75] and with whom, from the

---

[73] Joyce to Harriet Shaw Weaver, 24 November 1926, *SL*, 318.

[74] VI.B.8, 71; *JJA 30*, 329.

[75] Giacomo Leopardi (1798–1837) was, like Flaubert, among the very first authors whom Joyce is known to have read. Curran states that Joyce read Leopardi as part of his Italian course at university from as early as 1901—*James Joyce Remembered*, 14, 26, 120. Evidence of Joyce's acquaintance with the Italian poet may be found in his essay on 'James Clarence Mangan' (May 1902), in which Mangan is declared 'Weaker than Leopardi, for he has not the courage of his own despair'—'Mangan', *OCPW*, 58. It may not be entirely coincidental that the 'despair' Joyce associated with Leopardi also constitutes a strand of his thinking on Flaubert in VI.B.8. This connection may explain the near juxtaposition of both authors' names in the notebook. Joyce's interest in Leopardi continued in later years: his

Triestine years onwards, he happily shared a first name[76]) was himself an artist preoccupied with the relations between imitation and originality, so that Joyce's mention of the poet adds to the likelihood that he was pondering such matters in the summer of 1925.[77] Joyce's jotting provides an answer to the biblical question that twists its original syntax (which invites a choice between two opposites: the possibility or impossibility of change) in order to assert *both* fixity *and* change. The new version of the idiom implies that the permanence of indicative markings—the signs of one's origins and formative influences—does not preclude change. This position constitutes no departure in Joyce's thinking. Indeed, such musings are very much at the forefront of Stephen's mind in *Ulysses*. At the beginning of 'Scylla and Charybdis', Stephen thinks of himself as a being characterized by constant flux, crystallized into selfhood by memory alone: 'Molecules all change. I am other I now.'[78] Yet a few pages later, Stephen

---

Triestine library held a copy of Leopardi's *Poesie* (Milan: Sonzogno, 1910)—*CJ*, 116. In 'Giacomo of Trieste: James Joyce on the Adriatic', John McCourt mentions the large notebook Joyce used for his Italian lessons with Francini Bruni during the Triestine years—http://www.istrianet.org/istria/illustri/non-istrian/joyce/mccourt_giacomo.htm (July 2011). The notebook contains passages from the works of various Italian authors. One of these passages is drawn from Leopardi's *Pensieri* (section XXIV)—see *JJA 2*, 16–18. The thoughts expressed by Leopardi in the extract would undoubtedly have appealed to Joyce as he raged against refusals to publish *Dubliners*: 'Don't expect the public to stir themselves of their own accord out of regard for your personal excellence, or because the things you make are beautiful. They will look on and remain eternally silent; and when they can, they will prevent others from seeing it.'—*Pensieri*, trans. W. S. di Piero (New York: Oxford University Press, 1984), 65.

[76] Commenting on the title *Giacomo Joyce*, John McCourt remarks that it signals a writer 'steeped in Italian culture, literature and language', 'a continental Joyce, happy to wallow in the glow of various Giacomos, including Giacomo Leopardi, one of the few Italian poets Joyce had any time for'—*The Years of Bloom: James Joyce in Trieste 1904–1920* (Dublin: Lilliput Press, 2000), 197. These identical first names add weight to a reading of the manuscript jotting as a comment on Joycean intertextuality: the note summons Giacomo Leopardi, but may also refer to Giacomo Joyce and his own immovable spots.

[77] In January 1816, Madame de Staël published an article in the first issue of the Italian periodical *Biblioteca Italiana* advising Italian writers to relinquish their habit of steeping themselves in their classical past, and to look to contemporary foreign literature for guidance as to how to achieve originality—'De l'esprit des traductions', in *Oeuvres complètes de Madame la baronne de Staël-Holstein*, 2 vols (Paris: F. Didot, and Strasbourg: Treuttel et Würtz, 1836), vol. 2. Leopardi responded in an unpublished letter to the editors, defending the study of the classics by demonstrating the inevitability of imitation. He argues, for instance, that the greatest poets are the most ancient, and that only the first poet in the history of the world can ever have been truly original, uninfluenced by pre-existing models of writing: 'the greatest of all poets is the most ancient, he who had no models' ['il più grande di tutti i poeti è il più antico, il quale non ha avuto modelli'—'Lettera ai Sigg. Compilatori della Biblioteca Italiana in Riposta a quella di Mad. La Baronessa di Staël Holstein ai Medesimi', in *Poesie e Prose*, ed. Rolando Damiani and Mario Andrea Rigoni, 2 vols (Milan: Arnoldo Mondadori, 1987–8), vol. 2, 437.

[78] *U* 9: 205.

gives voice to ideas of permanence within change that aptly foreshadow Joyce's musings in VI.B.8:

> as the mole on my right breast is where it was when I was born, though all my body has been woven of new stuff time after time, so through the ghost of the unquiet father the image of the unliving son looks forth.[79]

Moments later Stephen thinks: 'He is in my father. I am in his son.'[80] This leads (along with further references to moles,[81] and to 'the birthmark of genius'[82]) to Stephen's thoughts regarding the consubstantiality (or not) of the Son and the Father in Catholic belief, and to those reflections about fatherhood that are echoed in VI.B.8:

> He [John Shakespeare] *rests*, disarmed of fatherhood, having devised that mystical estate upon his son. [...] Fatherhood, in the sense of conscious begetting, is unknown to man. It is a mystical estate, an apostolic succession, from only begetter to only begotten. [...]
>   Am I a father? If I were?[83]

Stephen's thoughts on begetting, in a passage about the author of *Hamlet*, are reprised in VI.B.8 by Joyce's references to Valery Larbaud, who employed the verb 'to beget' (with reference, perhaps, to this passage of *Ulysses* as well as to Shakespeare's gratitude to the 'onlie begetter' of his sonnets) in his dedication to *Amants, heureux amants*. The notebook answers Stephen's question about his own fatherhood: in the intervening years, Joyce himself has fathered a son in Valery Larbaud.[84] There is yet another way in which VI.B.8 revisits Stephen's thinking. The same verb, 'he rests', enacts in personal terms the peaceful demotion of the fathers—John Shakespeare, John Stanislaus Joyce, and Gustave Flaubert—who have played their part by passing on their respectively biological and artistic estates:

> J.S.J can rest having made me
> G.F—— — ———

(To read 'Joyce's handwritten 'G.F' as designating Gustave Flaubert is, strictly, a matter of conjecture: but it is an inference that seems amply

---

[79] *U* 9: 378–81.

[80] *U* 9: 390.

[81] *U* 9: 391. The word also features in Joyce's travel notebook, just a few lines below 'we adopt others' phrases' – VI.B.8, 72; *JJA 30*, 330.

[82] *U* 9: 393.

[83] *U* 9: 835–9, 860 (my emphasis).

[84] Of course that 'son' also acted as a 'father' to Joyce in a number of ways: Larbaud's public comments about Joyce, not least in the preface to *Les Lauriers sont coupés*, betray an unwavering dedication to the task of bringing the younger author into the limelight.

justified by the other 'Flaubert' notes in VI.B.8, as well as by related
surrounding materials.) What does this 'rest'—the rest of John Joyce, the
rest of Gustave Flaubert—mean? It is rest as withdrawal, rest as the
cessation of interference, the termination of fatherly presence. It is, if
only symbolically (for John Joyce was alive and well in 1925, and would
die only six years later, in 1931), the rest of the dead, as Stephen's talk of
legacies, estates, and the rotting corpse of that other John, John Shakespeare, suggests. The rest of that father, Stephen contends, enabled the
writing of *Hamlet*:

> He wrote the play in the months that followed his father's death. [. . .] The
> corpse of John Shakespeare does not walk the night. From hour to hour it
> rots and rots.[85]

The father's bequest is that of a state rather than an estate: the state of
fatherhood. And the key to that new state involves the recognition of
filiation, the assumption of a place in the 'apostolic succession'.[86] There is
no suggestion of an anxious struggle *á la* Harold Bloom in Stephen's
description of this process, except in the adjective 'disarmed', which
intimates that death thankfully removes all need for generational warfare.

One of the purports of the passage is that sons choose their fathers
whereas fathers do not choose their sons: 'Who is the father of any son that
any son should love him or he any son?'[87] As in the later musings of VI.
B.8, filiation is a choice, and filiation is a choice that occurs after the
demise of the paternal figure:

> Well: if the father who has not a son be not a father can the son who has not a
> father be a son? When Rutlandbaconsouthamptonshakespeare [. . .] wrote
> *Hamlet* he was not the father of his own son merely but, being no more a
> son, he was and felt himself the father of all his race, the father of his own
> grandfather, the father of his unborn grandson.[88]

The withdrawal to rest of the father who has done his fathering enables the
son to accede to fatherhood. The mode of fatherhood in which Stephen
is interested (and the kind of fatherhood in which VI.B.8 shows Joyce
also to have been invested) is both artistic and religious. It is one that, like
the doctrine of consubstantiality which so exercises Stephen's imagination
throughout 16 June 1904, circumvents human reproduction and its
'strandentwining cables', but does not forfeit intellectual and spiritual
connection. The kind of paternity Stephen more immediately foresees
and desires for himself, however, does not involve another human being,

[85] *U* 9: 829–35.   [86] *U* 9: 838.
[87] *U* 9: 844–5.   [88] *U* 9: 864–9.

but a work of art envisaged as a sacred child of the mind. Mulligan, hearing Stephen declaim, accurately ventriloquizes his fantasy of clean, heady parturition:

> – Himself his own father, Sonmulligan told himself. Wait. I am big with child. I have an unborn child in my brain. Pallas Athena! A play! The play's the thing! Let me parturiate![89]

Thus does Stephen unknot the tortured tangle of his thoughts about creation in 'Proteus' and move towards a theoretical model that would allow him both to choose a father for himself (Bloom, Shakespeare) and in due course to father imagined worlds, and through them other artists. This seems to be the gist of Joyce's own meditations in VI.B.8. A dead father (G.F) and a living father (J.S.J) are dispatched to their graves, secretly enjoined to rest in peace so that their son may, with their mystical assistance, bring an apostolic successor of his own into the world:

> Larbaud result of
> J.J + G.F

The cycle, by Joyce's own evaluation, has been successfully completed.

The centrality of the issue of recognition in these Ulyssean and proto-Wakean musings constitutes another point at which Joyce's published text and private notebooks intersect with Flaubert's 'Légende de saint Julien'. The theme of physical recognition—recognition enabled by the bodily marks of kinship—pervades Flaubert's tale. The first manifestation of this theme indicates Julian's split affinities: he is at once his parents' son and the son of God. Indeed, both parents look upon him as 'marked out by God'.[90] Stains and spots form a prominent motif throughout the story. After his first killing of an animal, guilt causes Julian to hastily wipe away the single tell-tale spot of blood: 'A drop of blood stained the flagstones. He quickly wiped it off with his sleeve.'[91] *Ulysses* features its own imagined re-enactment of Lady Macbeth's efforts to erase compromising spots—in 'Telemachus', Stephen, reacting to Haines's professed wish to collect his witticisms for a book (and with his own awkwardly culpable feelings regarding his behaviour at his mother's deathbed in mind), thinks of post-colonial remorse in Shakespeare's terms: 'They wash and tub and scrub. Agenbite of inwit. Conscience. Yet here's a spot.'[92] When Julian encounters the family of deer that so neatly replicates his own, the child figure of the group—'the dappled

---

[89]   *U* 9: 875–7.

[90]   *TCE*, 44 ['marqué de Dieu' (*TC*, 88)].

[91]   *TCE*, 45 ['Une goutte de sang tachait la dalle. Il l'essuya bien vite avec sa manche' (*TC*, 90)].

[92]   *U* 1: 481–2; 'Yet here's a spot', *Macbeth*, Act V, scene 1, line 31.

fawn'[93]—mirrors his own 'marked' body. Later Julian's wife, asking for proof that Julian's parents are who they claim to be, is reassured by their description of marks on his body (they identify themselves, that is, by identifying their son): 'They proved it was so by describing distinguishing marks on his skin.'[94] Once the double murder has been committed, the evidence of the egregious misdeed—bloody stains multiplied by the light that shines through the castle's stained-glass windows—is everywhere:

> *Splashes* and *stains* of blood showed starkly against the whiteness of their skin, on the sheets, on the floor, down an ivory crucifix hanging in the alcove. The crimson reflection from the stained-glass window, just then catching the sun, lit up these red *patches* and scattered others still more plentifully about the room.[95]

The bodies of the parents whose child was 'marked' from the start become riddled with the horrific traces of his murdering frenzy. In a symbolic development that paradoxically signifies both Julian's lapse and his saintly vocation, the body of Christ on the crucifix above the bed, like his parents' bodies (in a further confusion of the boundaries between the generations), is spattered by the carnage. Julian turns violently against the various fatherhoods—biological and spiritual—that have forged his identity. The brutal slaughter constitutes an extreme expression of his struggle with these influences.

Although Joyce also has marks on his mind in VI.B.8 ('Leopardi changes not his spots'), his phrasing of the problem involves no sense of strife. His response to the question ('Can a leopard change his spots?') deals playfully with the terms of the idiom, which remains recognizable even as it is modified. The jotting, like a number of others in the notebook that have bearing on intertextuality, is suggestive of serenity rather than of conflict. Joyce recognizes that his development as a person and as a writer—as son to both John Stanislaus Joyce and Gustave Flaubert—will not efface or erode the marks of his debts and allegiances to them. What VI.B.8 makes clear is that these 'spots' are consciously displayed, positively viewed, and accepted and embraced as enduring, indeed lifelong, indications of the lives of Joyce's fathers within him.

---

[93] *TCE*, 51 ['le faon tacheté' (*TC*, 99)].

[94] *TCE*, 58 ['Ils en donnèrent la preuve, en décrivant des signes particuliers qu'il avait sur la peau.' (*TC*, 110)].

[95] *TCE*, 63 (my emphasis) ['Des *éclaboussures* et des *flaques* de sang s'étalaient au milieu de leur peau blanche, sur les draps du lit, par terre, le long d'un Christ d'ivoire suspendu dans l'alcôve. Le reflet écarlate du vitrail, alors frappé par le soleil, éclairait ces *taches* rouges, et en jetait de plus nombreuses dans tout l'appartement.' (*TC*, 117)]

Finnegans Wake notebook VI.B.5, which Joyce used over the preceding summer of 1924, features a jotting that reads:

> James Joyce the Joker
> Killed his father with
> A blow of the poker[96]

Within a year, jocoserious parricide had given way to jocoserious peace of mind:

> J[ohn]. S[tanislaus]. J[oyce] can rest having made me
> G[ustave]. F[laubert can rest having made me]

VI.B.8 reveals an author attuned to the inevitable and desirable dynamics of influence and intertextuality—a cheerfully tranquil 'holiday wisdom'.[97]

BOUVARD AND PÉCUCHET IN *FINNEGANS WAKE*

Joyce's notes about Flaubert in VI.B.8 are retrospective: they are cast either in the past tense:

> G.F [can rest having made me]

or in the form of factual, non-verbal statements:

> Flaub. treatment
> of language as a kind
> of despair
> J.J contrary

> Larbaud result of
> J.J + G.F[98]

But these notes are also prospective, appearing as they do in the midst of the *avant-textes* of the *Wake*, and thereby belonging to the vast collection of words and phrases Joyce was assembling for use in composition.

---

[96] VI.B.5, 72; *JJA 30*, 38; *The 'Finnegans Wake' Notebooks at Buffalo*, ed. Vincent Deane, Daniel Ferrer, and Geert Lernout (Turnhout: Brepols, 2001–), *Notebook VI.B.5* (2004), 79.
[97] VI.B.8, 27; *JJA 30*, 207.
[98] VI.B.8, 71, 42, 88; *JJA 30*, 329, 315, 338.

By the summer of 1925, Joyce was well launched on his new project: the 'mechanics of creativity', to coin Luca Crispi's phrase,[99] were in motion. As Danis Rose has shown, VI.B.8, as a fully fledged working notebook for the *Wake*, reflects many preoccupations other than the Flaubertian,[100] as evidenced by, amongst other things, Joyce's use of the system of sigla first inaugurated around March 1924.[101] Neither the unusually personal ring of Joyce's 'Flaubert' jottings, nor the fact that these were not directly integrated into the *Wake* (as indicated by the fact that all three notes remained uncrossed), detract from their significance as notes belonging to the work's *avant-textes* and thereby impinging on the project in which Joyce was then immersed. These jottings cannot be dismissed as merely whimsical exercises in authorial stock-taking (important though that process undoubtedly is): they must be examined in the light of the creative context in which they emerged. On page 443 of *Finnegans Wake*, the text itself seems to beg the question: 'what about our trip to Normandy style conversation'.[102] This inquiry, as the foregoing section of this chapter sought to demonstrate, invites important answers regarding Joyce's understanding of his relationship to Flaubert. The following analysis examines the ways in which Joyce's final work bears traces of his Flaubertian 'holiday wisdom'.[103]

To look for a single author's mark in *Finnegans Wake* may seem a foolhardy enterprise. In a work in which intertextuality seems to have gone haywire—in which thousands of borrowed phrases swarm the text, radically severed from their sources—the reader in search of one particular, legible, intertextual signature may seem to be clutching at straws. Intertextuality is a generalized phenomenon in the *Wake*, yet despite its all-pervasiveness, its function remains uncertain, the meanings it generates ineluctably plural and ambiguous. In the *Wake*'s multilingual, portmanteau world, single words often have many more than one, two, or three possible referents, several of which may derive from intertextual sources. The very possibility of casting Joyce's kaleidoscopic carousel of quotations[104] into an interpretative framework is undermined by the sheer

---

[99] Luca Crispi, 'The Mechanics of Creativity: A Genetic Study of *Finnegans Wake*, II.2' (unpublished doctoral thesis, SUNY-Buffalo, 2001).

[100] Rose, *Textual Diaries*, 82–3.

[101] See *L1*, 213, 216.

[102] *FW* 443: 32–3.

[103] VI.B.8, 27; *JJA 30*, 207.

[104] According to Roland Barthes and Maurice Nadeau, 'every novel is a kind of carousel of imitated languages' ['tout roman est une espèce de carrousel de langages imités' (Roland Barthes and Maurice Nadeau, *Sur la littérature* [Grenoble: Presses universitaires de Grenoble, 1980], 17)]. In *Ulysses* and *Finnegans Wake*, Joyce provides this view with two of its most extreme exemplars.

number of borrowings involved, by these allusions' dissociation from their original textual environments, and by the distortions brought to bear on each grafted snippet.

The full extent of Joyce's intertextuality and the dizzying variety of the materials incorporated into the *Wake* have come to light only gradually. In an article on 'Joyce's Sources' published in 1995, Inge Landuyt and Geert Lernout contrast the assurance that characterized early evaluations of the *Wake*'s allusiveness with the caution of subsequent reassessments. In particular, Landuyt and Lernout question James Atherton's claim that:

> Joyce's usual method was to make use of a book without mentioning it to anyone [...] and then to insert a reference to the book, as a kind of acknowledgement, somewhere in his own text.[105]

'Atherton's law', as Landuyt and Lernout explain, has been largely discredited. Whereas Atherton delineates a system of reference involving a one-to-one mapping of book titles featured in *Finnegans Wake* onto the texts Joyce actually read, the author 'seems to have worked according to different and much more haphazard rules':[106] an allusion to a title does not necessarily imply that Joyce used the book in question, nor does the fact that Joyce read a book constitute any sort of guarantee that its title or contents will make an appearance in the *Wake*. Furthermore, the make-up of the *Wake* is such that even in those cases where textual sources have been precisely identified, their bearing on it remains unclear, tangential at best. Luca Crispi, for instance, warns against an overly interpretative reading of the *Wake*'s references to W. B. Yeats's *A Vision* in Chapter II.2, in which allusions to the Irish poet and his text cluster around the diagram featured on page 293 (a figure Crispi tentatively relates to the illustrations in *A Vision*). Although the connection seems indubitable (as Joyce made notes on the 1938 edition of Yeats's text in notebook VI.B.42),[107] it does not, as Crispi argues, underpin a relationship of commentary between the two texts, which:

> are not mutually explanatory and are dependent upon one another only in the most superficial manner.[108]

The elusiveness of Joyce's sources and the insoluble ambiguity of their function in the *Wake* suggest that a quest for traces of Joyce's engagement with Flaubert in his final work, and for and clues as to its nature, may

---

[105] Atherton, *Books at the Wake*, 19, quoted in Landuyt and Lernout, 'Joyce's Sources: *Les grands fleuves historiques*', in *Joyce Studies Annual*, vol. 6 (Summer 1995), 99.
[106] Landuyt and Lernout, 'Joyce's Sources', 100.
[107] Luca Crispi, 'Storiella as She Was Wryt: *Chapter II.2*', in *HJWFW*, 238.
[108] Crispi, 'Storiella', *HJWFW*, 238–9.

prove a wild goose chase. Hints—in the form of recognizable quotation or misquotation—are necessarily scarce,[109] given the distorting effects of Joyce's 'automatic word machine'.[110] And yet *Finnegans Wake* arguably marks the climax of Joyce's Flaubertian intertextuality.

The form of this response is signposted—in a way that seems to accord with 'Atherton's law'—on page 302, when Bouvard and Pécuchet appear in the midst of Shem and Shaun's scientific experiments: 'From here Buvard to dear Picuchet. Blott.'[111] A little further down the page, the italicized marginalia to the left spells out: '*Sesama to the Rescues. The Key Signature*,'[112] in apparent response to the phrase 'Exquisite Game of inspiration' that appears at centre on the same level. The names of Flaubert's two 'clerricals'[113] (copying clerks, with a suggestion of monk-ishness) feature in a section of Joyce's work devoted to the fumbling learning processes of the *Wake*'s own twin-pair. Bouvard and Pécuchet appear disguised amid references to the writing materials they so highly value: 'buvard' is French for a sheet of blotting paper—a fitting implement with which to deal with the 'blott' that closes the paragraph. Further down the page, the text evokes handwriting, pens, and the act of cribbing, all of which are central concerns to Flaubert's protagonists, who pride them-selves on their penmanship and revel in the act of copying:

> I always adored your hand. So could I too without the scrope of a pen. Ohr for oral, key for crib [...] Can you write us a last line?[114]

'A last line', of course, is precisely what Flaubert could not provide in *Bouvard et Pécuchet*. The work remained unfinished, cut short by Flaubert's death, in 1880, at his writing desk.

Bouvard et Pécuchet and *Finnegans Wake*: Similarities

Joyce's inclusion of the title of Flaubert's last work in *Finnegans Wake* is at once intriguing and logical. Although the book is not known to have

---

[109] Atherton identifies just one other probable *clin d'oeil* to Flaubert in *Finnegans Wake*. The evocation of Hannibal and ancient Carthage at *FW* 538: 9–13, as he points out, seems a likely reference to *Salammbô*: 'Twere a honnibel cruelty [...] in the mightyevil roohms of encient cartage.'—*Books at the Wake*, 249. R. J. Schork notes a possible reference to *La Tentation*'s Saint Antony at *FW* 86: 13–14: 'Anthony out of a tellafun book, ellegedly with a pedigree pig (unlicensed)'—*Joyce and Hagiography*, 76.

[110] The phrase is Jean-Michel Rabaté's in 'The Fourfold Root of Yawn's Unreason: Chapter III.3', in *HJWFW*, 398.

[111] *FW* 302: 9–10.

[112] *FW* 302: 19–21.

[113] *FW* 302: 6.

[114] *FW* 302: 19–23.

featured in any of Joyce's libraries,[115] *Bouvard et Pécuchet* has often been identified as a likely source of inspiration for Joyce in *Ulysses* and *Finnegans Wake*.[116] Constantine Curran recalls Joyce's interest in 'the fatuous doings of Bouvard and Pecuchet'.[117] Cyril Connolly describes *Bouvard et Pécuchet* as Joyce's favourite book (without giving any indication of his source for such a statement):

> Polymath pessimism is irradiated by gleams of poetry: slapstick fused with the sadness of things: understandably Joyce's favourite book.[118]

The combination of comedy and sadness is but one of many bouvard-et-pécuchetian characteristics that make Joyce's putative interest in *Bouvard et Pécuchet* signally plausible.

A number of other reasons may explain Joyce's presumed interest in *Bouvard* during the writing of the *Wake*. There are three substantive parallels worthy of mention. Both texts, to begin with, are broad in content and ambition, driven by totalizing aspirations. While Flaubert wanted *Bouvard* to be an 'encyclopaedia of human Stupidity',[119] Joyce famously intended the *Wake* as a 'history of the world'.[120]

Secondly, the texts present significant formal similarities. The form of the *Wake*, which begins where it ends and ends where it begins by way of a 'commodius vicus of recirculation' 'of course by recourse',[121] is analogous to the cyclical form of *Bouvard et Pécuchet*, in which the protagonists start out and end up as copyists.

Thirdly, both texts are structured by the irony of contradiction.[122] As Maupassant eloquently wrote of *Bouvard*, the book is:

> a prodigious critique of all scientific systems, which, opposed to each other, destroy each other because of the eternal contradictions between their authors, because of the contradictions between facts, because of the contra-

---

[115] For the main catalogues of Joyce's libraries, see Chapter 1, footnote 12.

[116] Most notably by Pound and by Kenner—see Chapter 5.

[117] Curran, *James Joyce Remembered*, 29.

[118] Cyril Connolly, *100 Key Books of the Modern Movement from England, France, and America 1880–1950* (London: Allison & Busby, 1986), 110.

[119] Flaubert to Edgard Raoul-Duval, 13 February 1879 ['encyclopédie de la Bêtise humaine' (*C5*, 535)].

[120] *JJ*, 537.

[121] *FW* 3: 2 and 49: 35.

[122] That this structure is the outcome of a deliberate choice on Flaubert's part is clear from a letter to Edma Roger des Genettes of 22 February 1880: 'I need a lot of contradictory pieces of information.' ['Il me faut des tas de renseignements qui se contredisent.' (*C5*, 845)].

dictions inherent in recognized, undisputed laws. It is the tale of the weakness of human intelligence.[123]

Bouvard and Pécuchet's attempts to become intelligent, to master their chosen domains of inquiry, flounder under the pressure of the oppositions inherent to human knowledge and to human discourse. At the start of their studies, the contradictions Flaubert's *bonshommes* encounter prove convenient aids to debate, enabling each to adopt a clearly partisan, predetermined point of view. In reading about the French Revolution, for example, Bouvard and Pécuchet simply replicate the disagreements that obtain between the historical accounts they peruse:

> the contradictions in these books did not worry them a bit. Each took from them whatever might defend his cause.[124]

Such blind equanimity does not last. The pursuit of truth gradually leads to the discovery of too many glaringly conflicting, mutually debunking positions among the scholarly volumes Bouvard and Pécuchet consult. The narrator sums up these incompatible attitudes in swift impersonal paragraphs, leaving the reader to deduce (without it being clear whether Bouvard and Pécuchet themselves deduce) the irony implicit in such juxtapositions:

> The Revolution is for some a satanic event. Others proclaim that it was a sublime exception. The defeated ones on each side are, of course, martyrs.[125]

Disheartened by this encounter with contradiction and complexity, Bouvard and Pécuchet, overwhelmed by insuperable doubts, give up their efforts to understand the revolutionary period. The *bonshommes'* return to copying at the end of the book is prompted by a succession of such defeats: 'everything has come to pieces in their hands'.[126] The quest for knowledge is abandoned, and Bouvard and Pécuchet decide to focus instead on 'the material pleasure of the material act of copying':[127]

---

[123] ['une prodigieuse critique de tous les systèmes scientifiques opposés les uns aux autres, se détruisant les uns les autres par les éternelles contradictions des auteurs, les contradictions des faits, les contradictions des lois reconnues, indiscutées. C'est l'histoire de la faiblesse de l'intelligence humaine.' (Guy de Maupassant, review of *Bouvard et Pécuchet, Le Gaulois*, 6 April 1881, in *BP*, 445)].

[124] *BPE*, 120 ['les contradictions de ces livres ne les embarrassaient nullement. Chacun y prenait ce qui pouvait défendre sa cause.' (*BP*, 172)].

[125] *BPE*, 120 ['La Révolution est pour les uns, un évènement satanique. D'autres la proclament une exception sublime. Les vaincus de chaque côté, naturellement sont des martyrs.' (*BP*, 173)].

[126] *BPE*, 287 ['tout leur a craqué dans les mains' (*BP*, 388)].

[127] Passage not featured in *BPE* ['le plaisir matériel qu'il y a dans l'acte matériel de copier' (*BP*, 389)].

No thinking! Let us copy! [...] Equality of all things, of the good and the bad, the beautiful and the ugly, the insignificant and the characteristic. There is no truth only phenomena.

End with a view of the two bonshommes bent over their desk, copying.[128]

These sentences, which belong to Flaubert's fragmentary drafts for the end of the book, have been published with the reading text ever since the book's first (posthumous) publication in 1881. Contradiction remains integral to the closing tableau of the two *bonshommes* working on their handwritten 'copie'. For Yvan Leclerc, their intransitive, self-addressed imperative, 'Copions!', implies an endless series of opposing statements, 'the pros and cons neutralized on the ecumenical space of the page'.[129] In other drafts, Flaubert conjures a more detailed vision of Bouvard and Pécuchet juxtaposing contrasting quotations on the very same page, creating elaborate collages of contradiction:

> But as two texts of the same category that they've copied often contradict each other, they copy them out one after the other on the same register.[130]

These extracts from the manuscript archive accord with Flaubert's much-quoted distrust of conclusions ('stupidity consists in wanting to reach conclusions').[131] Even had Flaubert been able to complete his work, Bouvard and Pécuchet's 'copie', projected into an endless future, would theoretically go on forever. Fascinatingly, the manuscripts also show that Flaubert considered maximizing the grotesque effect of the discrepancies between these contradictory quotations by giving their expression an oral and simultaneous dimension: 'as they read simultaneously, they read contradictory texts out loud to each other'.[132] The burlesque cacophony imagined here vividly images the disquieting disharmony that Flaubert's *bonshommes* discover in the course of their reading. In another draft snippet, Flaubert had taken this simultaneous coincidence of

---

[128] Passage not featured in *BPE* ['Pas de réflexion! Copions! [...] Egalité de tout, du bien et du mal, du beau et du laid, de l'insignifiant et du caractéristique. Il n'y a pas de vrai que les phénomènes. –/Finir par la vue des deux bonshommes penchés sur leur pupitre et copiant.' (*BP*, 390)].

[129] Yvan Leclerc, *La Spirale*, 140 ['le pour et le contre neutralisés dans l'espace oecuménique de la page'].

[130] ['Mais comme, souvent, deux textes de la même classe qu'ils ont copié s'opposent, se contrarient, ils les recopient l'un au bout de l'autre sur le même registre.' (Gustave Flaubert, *Oeuvres complètes*, 16 vols [Paris: Club de l'honnête homme, 1971–5], vol. 6 [1972], 752, quoted in Leclerc, *La Spirale*, 139)].

[131] Flaubert to Louis Bouilhet, 4 September 1850 ['la bêtise consiste à vouloir conclure' (*CI*, 680)].

[132] ['comme ils lisent simultanément, ils se lisent tout haut les textes contradictoires' (Flaubert, *Oeuvres complètes* [Club dé l'honnête homme], vol. 6, 772, quoted in leclerc, *La Spirale*, 140)].

contraries to its logical limit, imagining a mode of scriptural as well as oral superimposition:

> Readers' reflections about these passages are written, contradictorily, on top of each other.[133]

In Leclerc's words, the ending of the book is—in an invocation of one of those images that have, since Gérard Genette's *Palimpsestes* (1982), become emblematic of intertextuality—'Not so much synthesis as *palimpsest*.'[134]

In *Finnegans Wake* contradiction unfolds in a manner that at least matches the superimpositions of Flaubert's paroxysmic closing vignette. In the Wakean world contradiction (between, say, single or multiple selves, mind and body, life and death) operates across the text but also within short phrases and even single words. A passage from page 49— chosen from a dizzyingly wide array of possible examples—illustrates the *Wake*'s predilection for opposition, and its constant implied refutation of the idea that anything is so simple as to be merely double (rather than triple, quadruple, or infinite):

> Now let the centuple celves of my egourge as Micholas de Cusack calls them,—of all of whose I in my hereinafter of course by recourse demission me—by the coincidence of their contraries reamalgamerge in that indentity of undiscernibles.[135]

Tensions between units, binaries and multiples abound in these lines. The self ('celves') is neither singular nor dual but 'centuple': a hundred cell-like 'celves' or elves make up, or co-own, an 'I' or 'ego', which has an afterlife ('my hereinafter') as well as a present, and which they may forsake ('demission me'). Contraries coincide, which is to say that they 'occur or exist at the same time', but also that (as on a palimpsest) they 'occupy the same place' (*OED*). They may, in the *Wake*'s words, 'amalgamate' and 'merge', or 'reamalgamerge', in a process of double fusion. Thus, 'indentity' telescopes identity and its contrary, 'in-identity'. If Joyce is Flaubert's self-proclaimed 'contrary', as VI.B.8 suggests, then surely in the Wakean world their meeting, merging, or reamalgamerging may be read as a multilayered riot of contradiction: as a fruitful coincidence of contraries; as a 'coincidence of their contraries'; as a glorious coincidence of contrariness; and even as a 'coincidence' of contrariness.

---

[133] ['Des réflexions de lecteurs sont écrites, les unes sur les autres, contradictoirement, à propos de ces passages.' (Flaubert, *Oeuvres complètes* [Club de l'honnête homme], vol. 6, 752, quoted in Leclerc, *La Spirale*, 140].
[134] ['Non pas synthèse mais *palimpseste*.' (Leclerc, *La Spirale*, 140 [my emphasis])].
[135] *FW* 49: 33–6, 50: 1–2.

Joyce's and Flaubert's predilection for opposition and contradiction is nowhere more obvious than in their twin pairings: Shem and Shaun constitute a unit strikingly similar to that formed by Bouvard and Pécuchet. Like Bouvard and Pécuchet, Shem and Shaun are at once extremely similar and utterly different—a paradox perfectly encapsulated in Anna Livia's description of her sons:

> Them boys is so contrairy. [...] Unless they changes by mistake. I seen the likes in the twinngling of an aye. [...] The sehm asnuh. Two bredder as doffered as nors in soun.[136]

Like Joyce himself ('J.J contrary'), Shem and Shaun are contraries and yet they are 'contrairy' as a unit, in the singular: they 'is' 'contrairy'. And yet, like Joyce and Flaubert, they are also 'contrairy'—poles apart—in relation to each other, as different as north and south ('as doffered as nors in soun'). Here again, such 'contrairiness' (the added 'i' making the French 'contraire' shadowily but visibly present) does not preclude likeness: Shem and Shaun are so alike ('the likes') that, like twins 'twinngling', they may change into one another 'by mistake'. It seems no coincidence, in the light of all this—or only a 'coincidance' of contraries—that Bouvard and Pécuchet, who are also as different as they are identical, should appear as avatars of Shem and Shaun when they make their appearance in the *Wake*.

There is another possible reason, aside from these similarities, for the *Wake*'s allusion to *Bouvard*. Joyce's book, as John Nash and others have noted,[137] makes numerous references to the critical reception of *Ulysses*. Snippets excerpted from reviews of the book are woven into the new work as a mode of ironizing, neutralizing rebuttal. In 1925 Joyce wrote to Harriet Shaw Weaver to articulate an explicit request for assistance in this regard:

> I should be glad to hear Mr Muir's article read to me before I send off the piece which is an indirect reply to criticisms.[138]

Landuyt has identified the location of a number of preparatory notes for these 'indirect replies'.[139] Pages 116 to 169 of notebook VI.B.6 feature words extracted from Aramis's piece on 'The Scandal of *Ulysses*' in *The Sporting Times*, from John Middleton Murry's review in *Nation and*

---

[136] *FW* 620: 12–16.
[137] John Nash, *James Joyce and the Act of Reception: Reading, Ireland, Modernism* (Cambridge and New York: Cambridge University Press, 2006); Ingeborg Landuyt, 'Cain-Ham-(Shem)-Esau-Jim the Penman: *Chapter I.7*', in *HJWFW*.
[138] Joyce to Harriet Shaw Weaver, 26 February 1925, *L1*, 114.
[139] Landuyt, 'Cain-Ham-(Shem)-Esau-Jim the Penman', *HJWFW*, 160.

Athanaeum, and from pieces by Stephen Gwynn and Arnold Bennett. Joyce also made note of Virginia Woolf's reaction to *Ulysses* in her essay, 'Modern Novels', which was published in the *Times Literary Supplement* on 10 April 1919. Woolf's essay famously called for authors to:

> record the atoms as they fall upon the mind in the order in which they fall, let us trace the pattern, however disconnected and incoherent in appearance.

Ulysses was a failure, she went on to state:

> because of the comparative poverty of the writer's mind.[140]

Joyce jotted down 'incoherent atoms' and 'poverty of mind' on a leaf of VI.B.6, and the latter note enters the *Wake* almost verbatim. The addition of two tautological adjectives—'your *horrible awful* poverty of mind'[141]— imitates upper-class phrasing in an act of parody presumably intended as retaliation for Woolf's condescending, class-inflected dismissal of Joyce's intellect.[142] It is with Wyndham Lewis's scathing comments in *Time and Western Man*, which was published several years later, in 1927, that *Finnegans Wake* engages most extensively—indeed, the 'Mookse and the Gripes' was crafted specifically as a riposte to Lewis's criticism, after Joyce actively sought out the materials with which to forge his comeback.[143]

Pound, Descharmes, and Pécuchet

Joyce's acknowledgements of, and responses to, reviews of *Ulysses* by way of quotation and misquotation constitute an important strand of the book's composition. Despite the fact that no manuscript evidence specifically evidences such a process in relation to *Bouvard et Pécuchet*, it seems entirely plausible, in the light of these various other 'acts of reception', that Bouvard and Pécuchet entered the text as just such a gesture: as an acknowledgement of one particularly insistent strain of contemporary

---

[140] 'Aramis' (pseudonym), 'The Scandal of *Ulysses*', *Sporting Times*, 1 April 1922; John Middleton Murry, review of *Ulysses*, *Nation and Athenaeum*, 22 April 1922; Stephen Gwynn, 'Modern Irish Literature', *Manchester Guardian*, 15 March 1923; Arnold Bennett, 'James Joyce's *Ulysses*', *Outlook*, 29 April 1922; Virginia Woolf, 'Modern Novels', *Times Literary Supplement*, 10 April 1919.

[141] *FW* 192: 10 (my emphasis).

[142] An entry from Woolf's diary for 16 August 1922 describes *Ulysses* as: 'An illiterate, underbred book it seems to me: the book of a self taught working man, & we all know how distressing they are, how egotistic, insistent, raw, striking, & ultimately nauseating.' – *The Diary of Virginia Woolf*, ed. Anne Olivier Bell, 5 vols (London: Hogarth Press, 1977–84), vol. 2 (1978), 189.

[143] See Landuyt, 'Cain-Ham-(Shem)-Esau-Jim the Penman', 155, and Dirk Van Hulle, *Textual Awareness: A Genetic Study of Late Manuscripts by Joyce, Proust, and Mann* (Ann Arbor: University of Michigan Press, 2004), 96.

response to Joyce's work: as a trace, that is, of that Flaubertian leitmotif that runs through all of Ezra Pound's reviews of Joyce's works. As early as May 1918, Pound declared that in *Ulysses*:

> Joyce has done what Flaubert had set out to do in *Bouvard et Pécuchet*, done it better, more succinct. An epitome.[144]

Joyce was pleased enough with this assessment to single it out for inclusion in the 'Advance Press Notice' put together in 1921 to advertise the forthcoming publication of *Ulysses* in book form.[145] Immediately after the publication of *Ulysses*, Pound published two essays that continued to emphasize the importance of Flaubert's final work. The first of these was his 'Paris Letter', which appeared in *The Dial* in June 1922, and which reiterated the view that 'in *Ulysses* [Joyce] has carried on a process begun in *Bouvard et Pécuchet*'.[146] The second and most detailed of Pound's articulations of the specific connection between *Ulysses* and *Bouvard et Pécuchet* features in an article entitled 'James Joyce et Pécuchet', which appeared in the Parisian *Mercure de France* that same month. The novelty of 'James Joyce et Pécuchet' resides in Pound's engagement with contemporary Flaubertian criticism. In particular, Pound gave an admiring account of René Descharmes' influential study, *Autour de Bouvard et Pécuchet*, which was published in 1921 at the beginning of Flaubert's centenary year.

Descharmes may well have played a key role in Joyce's response to *Bouvard et Pécuchet*. His call for a meticulous exploration of the Flaubertian archive, involving analysis of the various manuscript stages of his works' development ('one would have to rehearse all the planning and writing that Flaubert put into the very foundations of his work'),[147] reads like a manifesto for genetic criticism:

---

[144] Pound, '*Ulysses*', *P/J*, 139. Pound expressed the same view a few months later in a private letter to Joyce—Pound to Joyce, 22 November 1918, *P/J*, 145.

[145] Quotation from Ezra Pound's essay '*Ulysses*' for the 'Advance Press Notice', in Joyce's hand, with notation in Sylvia Beach's hand; n.d. [1921], University of Buffalo, The State University of New York, The Poetry Collection, PCMS-0020, James Joyce Collection, 1900–59, Box XVIII (Miscellaneous Material Related to Joyce's Works), E.1 (*Ulysses*: The First Edition), Folder 6. Joyce had responded in similar fashion to an earlier evocation of the Flaubertian analogy. In December 1917 Pound sent the first two episodes of *Ulysses* to *The Little Review* for publication. In the January issue, the announcement of the forthcoming serialization consisted of words excerpted from the poet's accompanying letter to the editor: 'Compression, intensity. It looks to me rather better than Flaubert.'—*P/J*, 130. In an unpublished letter of 6 January 1918, Joyce responded to Pound with gratitude: 'let me thank you for your kind words about my book. I am very grateful to you for your encouragement.'—YCAL MSS 43, box 26, ff. 1,112–14.

[146] Pound, 'Paris Letter', *P/J*, 194.

[147] ['il faudrait reprendre, en sous-oeuvre, tout le travail de composition et d'écriture de Flaubert' (Descharmes, *Autour de 'Bouvard et Pécuchet'*, 99)].

is it possible to establish a bibliography of *Bouvard et Pécuchet*? How did he make use of the materials that were offered him? How did this documentary Realism combine with the principles of Art that are also known to have been his?[148]

Such questions are typical of the latest trends in genetic criticism, which 'explore the *avant-texte*'s starting points in the author's personal library'.[149] As Dirk Van Hulle notes:

> The edition of *The 'Finnegans Wake' Notebooks at Buffalo* is an example of these efforts to establish what a writer reads, what he deems interesting enough to excerpt, and how these reading notes are processed and incorporated in the manuscripts.[150]

Descharmes is interested in the 'literary and documentary sources of *Bouvard et Pécuchet*'[151] but also, crucially, in the distortion incurred by the original as it is woven into its new context: 'As he transcribes and interprets, does Flaubert not falsify the character of what he quotes?'[152] Descharmes' book, in other words, is all about the poetics of intertextuality. And Joyce's engagement with Flaubert in the *Wake* relates precisely to such poetics. In this light Joyce's allusion to *Bouvard et Pécuchet*, whether it be an instance of Atherton's law or, via Pound, an act of reception, constitutes a self-conscious signpost to these authors' shared understanding of the part played by intertextuality in all literary endeavours.

Intra- and Intertextual Systems of Writing

Finnegans Wake and *Bouvard et Pécuchet* emerged from extremely systematic networks of intra- and intertextual writing: in these works, intertextuality becomes a principle—an end as well as a means. In *Autour de Bouvard et Pécuchet*, Descharmes made a list of the numerous points of connection between *Bouvard* and the *Dictionnaire des Idées Reçues*. His account of these intratextual linkages is presented in a table covering seven pages.[153] Descharmes' intention, however, is not simply to suggest a

---

[148] ['est-il possible de préciser la bibliographie de *Bouvard et Pécuchet*? Comment a-t-il tiré parti des matériaux qui lui étaient offerts? Comment ce Réalisme documentaire s'est-il combiné avec les principes d'Art que nous connaissons par ailleurs?' (Descharmes, *Autour de 'Bouvard et Pécuchet'*, 56)].

[149] Dirk Van Hulle, Introduction (with Luca Crispi and Sam Slote), *HJWFW*, 39.

[150] Van Hulle, Introduction, *HJWFW*, 39.

[151] ['sources livresques et documentaires de *Bouvard et Pécuchet* (Descharmes, *Autour de 'Bouvard et Pécuchet'*, 89)].

[152] ['En transcrivant et en interprétant, Flaubert ne fausse-t-il pas le caractère de ce qu'il cite?' (Descharmes, *Autour de 'Bouvard et Pécuchet'*, 91)].

[153] Descharmes, *Autour de 'Bouvard et Pécuchet'*, 233–9.

binary intratextual relationship between these two works: this first table is immediately followed by a second, which lists the numerous instances of intratextuality connecting the *Dictionnaire* to Flaubert's earlier works.[154] Pierre-Marc de Biasi has since confirmed and expanded these findings by tracing the workings of intratextuality through all of Flaubert's drafts. Commenting on the 'documentary construction site' of *Bouvard et Pécuchet*, he observes that:

> Flaubert seems to have gradually annexed the near totality of his earlier research: that relating to *Salammbô*, *L'Éducation sentimentale*, *La Tentation*, etc.[155]

Descharmes' and de Biasi's work shows that the *Dictionnaire* was far more than a mere source for *Bouvard*, and that the project functioned both as a prospective and as a retrospective repository for those clichés that Flaubert saw as constitutive of the bourgeois world-view he abhorred. Leclerc agrees with these analyses, declaring that the *Dictionnaire* is both 'source and estuary' of everything Flaubert wrote, and that 'Everything is in *Bouvard* and conversely'—so much so that the novel can be seen as an 'anthology of Flaubert compiled by the author himself'.[156] Thus, *Bouvard* can be read partly as a pastiche of Flaubert by himself, written not only (as Flaubert hoped in relation to the *Dictionnaire*) 'with the materials arranged so that the reader has no idea whether or not we're taking the piss',[157] but also in such a way that 'the reader is unable to determine whether Flaubert is mocking himself or not'.[158]

The same intratextual principle prevails through Joyce's writing. The VI.A 'Scribbledehobble' notebook, long thought to have been the first used in preparation for the *Wake* (specialists now tend to think VI.A was preceded by VI.B.10),[159] exemplifies this mode of composition. The notebook consists of 'indexes' of linguistic materials—some of them accumulated years before—distributed under headings that refer to the titles of Joyce's previously published works. This way of working from lists of reusable elements was not new to Joyce. One need only remember how

[154] Descharmes, *Autour de 'Bouvard et Pécuchet'*, 240–50.
[155] ['chantier documentaire'; 'Flaubert semble y avoir petit à petit annexé la quasi-totalité de ses anciennes recherches: celles de *Salammbô*, de *L'Éducation sentimentale*, de *La Tentation*, etc.' (*Carnets de Travail*, ed. Pierre-Marc de Biasi, 766)].
[156] ['source et estuaire'; 'Tout est dans *Bouvard* et réciproquement'; 'anthologie de Flaubert par lui-même' (Leclerc, *La Spirale*, 23, 19, 23)].
[157] Flaubert to Louis Bouilhet, 4 September 1850, *GW*, 155 ['de telle manière que le lecteur ne sache pas si on se fout de lui, oui ou non' (*CI*, 678–9)].
[158] ['le lecteur n'est [pas] en mesure de décider si Flaubert se fout de lui-même, oui ou non' (Leclerc, *La Spirale*, 26)].
[159] See Sam Slote, Introduction, *HJWFW*, 5, and Van Hulle, *Textual Awareness*, 77.

Stephen Hero was condensed into 'A Portrait of the Artist', which was in turn remoulded and expanded into *A Portrait of the Artist as a Young Man*; or how the tower scene at first intended for the end of *A Portrait* became the opening of *Ulysses*, itself a book initially envisaged as a short story for *Dubliners*.[160] Joyce's tendency to look for recyclable[161] material in earlier writing is manifest throughout the *avant-textes* of the *Wake*. The titles of several of the *Dubliners* short stories, to choose but one example, appear in VI.B.8.[162]

In the introduction to *How Joyce Wrote Finnegans Wake*, Sam Slote distinguishes *Finnegans Wake* from *Ulysses* by arguing that whereas *Ulysses* gathered momentum from an intertextual scaffolding (essentially derived from Homer), the impetus for the *Wake* was primarily intratextual. Using the sketches written in 1923 as starting points or 'nodes' (to use David Hayman's term),[163] Joyce produced a self-generating textual yarn or 'concatenated series of *intratextual* echoes'.[164]

Thus both *Finnegans Wake* and *Bouvard et Pécuchet* were erected upon trellises and around 'nodes' derived from Joyce's and Flaubert's earlier works. In both authors' works the tendency to recycle lexical and thematic units is pronounced and in both cases the propensity seems to have grown exponentially, reaching its most radical form in the final works. Yet this predilection for intratextual writing pales in comparison with both authors' drive to appropriate other writers' words.

Massive archives testify to these highly idiosyncratic and labour-intensive working methods. In Joyce's case, twenty-five thousand pages of manuscript material, in the form of notebooks and drafts, are extant for *Finnegans Wake* alone. Of the *James Joyce Archive*'s sixty-three volumes, sixteen are devoted to the *Wake* notebooks, and twenty more to the

---

[160] See Hans Walter Gabler, 'The Seven Lost Years of *A Portrait of the Artist as a Young Man*', in *Approaches to Joyce's 'Portrait': Ten Essays*, ed. Thomas F. Staley and Bernard Benstock (Pittsburg: University of Pittsburg Press, 1976); 'Toward a Critical Text of James Joyce's *A Portrait of the Artist as a Young Man*', in *Studies in Bibliography* 27 (1974); Introduction, James Joyce, *A Portrait of the Artist as a Young Man*, ed. Hans Walter Gabler with Walter Hettche (Garland: New York and London, 1993); and *The Rocky Road to 'Ulysses'* (Dublin: National Library of Ireland, 2004), especially 3–5, 18–23. Also see *JJ*, 230.

[161] The term is borrowed from Dirk Van Hulle—see the section on 'The Encyclopaedic Recycling of Wyndham Lewis's Early Joyce Criticism', in *Textual Awareness*, 96–102.

[162] 'Two gallants', 'encounter', 'his boardelhouse', and 'mother' appear on VI.B.8, 17; *JJA 30*, 302.

[163] David Hayman, 'Nodality and the Infrastructure of *Finnegans Wake*', *JJQ*, vol. 16, no. 2 (Fall 1978–Winter 1979).

[164] Slote, Introduction, *HJWFW*, 14–15.

various stages of its drafting and proofing. These materials provide the information from which a 'profile of the creative moment'—to use Hayman's phrase[165]—may be drawn. The genetic situation is similar as regards Flaubert. In 1910 *La Revue des Deux Mondes* published an article by Louis Bertrand entitled 'Les Carnets de Flaubert', which bore intimations of the volumes of unpublished material that would soon come to light.[166] Over time, Bertrand's forecast was realized, with the Flaubertian dossier gradually amounting to around twenty thousand pages, 3,848 of which relate specifically to the genesis of *Bouvard et Pécuchet*. Between 1971 and 1975, the *Société des études littéraires françaises* published extensive transcriptions of the Flaubertian *Carnets* as part of its sixteen-volume edition of the author's *Oeuvres complètes*,[167] but by dint of numerous misreadings and other acts of editorial licence, Flaubert's fragmented and sometimes erratic and illegible working notes were turned into a continuous reading text. In 1988 Pierre-Marc de Biasi rectified this flawed representation of the Flaubertian *avant-textes* in his edition of Flaubert's *Carnets de Travail*, a heavy tome that has become as essential to Flaubertian scholarship as the *James Joyce Archive* is to Joycean critics.

These working documents bear witness to the scales and mechanisms of Joyce's and Flaubert's intertextual practices. In Flaubert's case, reading notes confirm what the author himself so often stated in his letters: that he read extensively and painstakingly, driven by a thirst for erudition and exactitude that underpins his 'documentary Realism'.[168] Even by Flaubert's own standards, the research involved in the preparation of *Bouvard* was unprecedented. No sooner had he envisioned the project than he realized how much preliminary reading it would entail: 'I am about to start

---

[165] Hayman, 'Genetic Criticism and Joyce', 6.

[166] Louis Bertrand, 'Les Carnets de Gustave Flaubert', *La Revue des Deux Mondes*, vol. 58 (15 July 1910).

[167] Flaubert, *Oeuvres complètes* (Club de l'honnête homme). A prefatory note introduces the sixteen volumes as a 'new edition established from Flaubert's unpublished manuscripts, by the *Société des études littéraires françaises*, comprising the scénarios and plans of the various novels, Flaubert's notes and documents, with historical and critical annotations, and illustrated with contemporary images' ['édition nouvelle établie d'après les manuscrits inédits de Flaubert, par la *Société des études littéraires françaises*, contenant les *scénarios* et plans des divers romans, les notes et documents de Flaubert, avec des notices historiques et critiques, et illustrée d'images contemporaines']. New transcriptions from Flaubert's manuscripts appear in a number of the edition's volumes: vol. 6 (1972), for instance, consists in 'La Copie de "Bouvard et Pécuchet" d'après le dossier de Rouen'; vol. 8 (1973) includes Flaubert's 'reading notebooks' ['carnets de lecture'] for the first version of *L'Éducation sentimentale*; vol. 10 (1973) comprises Flaubert's 'travel notebooks' ['carnet de voyages']; vol. 12 (1974) prints various of Flaubert's 'fragments and drafts' ['fragments et ébauches'].

[168] ['Réalisme documentaire' (Descharmes, *Autour de 'Bouvard et Pécuchet'*, 56)].

a book which will require much reading.'[169] Throughout his work on the book Flaubert uses adjectives such as 'colossal' and 'immense' to describe his reading. In March 1873 he read twenty books. Between September 1872 and August 1873 he claimed to have 'swallowed' ['avalé'] 194, making incessant notes as he tore through every volume. A year later, his tally stood at 294. In 1880 he sent his final reckoning to Edma Roger des Genettes:

> Do you know how many books I have had to absorb for the sake of my two heroes? More than one thousand five hundred. I have a pile of notes which is eight inches high.[170]

Joyce's reading, as James Atherton comments, was also 'extraordinarily wide'.[171] Many of the key works of annotation relating to the *Wake*—Atherton's *Books at the Wake*, Adaline Glasheen's *Census*, and Roland McHugh's *Annotations* (both in their third editions), as well as the more recent and ongoing edition of *The Finnegans Wake Notebooks at Buffalo*—are massive source-hunting enterprises, with no end to their endeavours as yet in sight.

Breadth is another striking characteristic of both authors' reading. In a review of de Biasi's edition of the *Carnets de Travail*, Julian Barnes gives a representative example of the heteroclite assemblage of books Flaubert consulted:

> The background reading-list is immense and immensely various—Comte's *Principes de la philosophie positive* on the same three-monthly roster as Visca's *Du Vaginisme* and *Histoire d'un atome de carbone*.[172]

Almost any snapshot of Joyce's reading through the years of the *Wake*'s composition could match this for variety.

Although Joyce and Flaubert appear to have had analogous reading habits, the ways in which each author turned these swathes of textual material into the fabric of literature diverge significantly. Flaubert's reading may seem outlandish, but his research was in fact highly organized

---

[169] Flaubert to George Sand, 12 July 1872 ['je vais commencer un bouquin qui exigera de moi de grandes lectures' (*C5*, 548)].

[170] Flaubert to Edma Roger des Genettes, 24–25 January 1880, *GW*, 421 ['Savez-vous à combien se montent les volumes qu'il m'a fallu absorber pour mes deux bonshommes?—A plus de 1500. Mon dossier de notes a huit pouces de hauteur.' (*C5*, 796)].

[171] Atherton, *Books at the Wake*, 19.

[172] Julian Barnes, 'The Cost of Conscientious Literature', in *Something to Declare* (London: Picador, 2002), 266. Barnes's comment is clearly inspired by page 510 of de Biasi's edition of Flaubert's *Carnets de Travail*, which transcribes a page from one of Flaubert's notebooks consisting entirely of a list of his reading between August and 23 October 1872.

and systematic, in keeping with a pattern established in earlier years. For *Salammbô*, Flaubert read with Carthage in mind. For 'Hérodias', he read to augment his knowledge of the biblical story and of history. For 'La Légende de saint Julien l'Hospitalier', he read about myths and legends and his chosen saint. For *Bouvard*, Flaubert researched his materials chapter by chapter. His reading focused around those branches of know-ledge singled out for their pertinence to his *bonshommes'* curiosity. As such it focused on horticulture, agriculture, arboriculture, chemistry, medicine, geology, archaeology, and history.[173] Within these predetermined areas of inquiry, Flaubert was particularly attracted to those works that promised prime examples of the intellectual grotesque. His notes feature the titles of the works he was reading, page numbers, quotations, and other detailed references. After making a first round of notes, the harvest would be condensed into a more compact selection: his 'notes de notes'.[174] These were then turned into prose summaries ('resumés'), before becoming part of an expanding series of manuscript drafts: first the Flaubertian *scénarios*, and then endlessly revised continuous drafts.

Joyce's reading routine, by contrast, appears to have been less regular, and very much less scholarly. He often seems to have been content to read anything that came his way: the notebooks bear traces of his encounters with thousands of oddly entitled publications. One of the books from which Joyce took notes is entitled *Queer Fish: And Other Inhabitants of the Rivers and Oceans.*[175] Joyce extracted phrases such as 'no eyelids', 'plaice', 'sole', 'pectoral fins', 'bullhead', and 'He's queer, that fish'.[176] These cohabit and criss-cross in the notebook with entries from the *Encyclopaedia Britannica*'s account of Ancient Rome, unsourced entries concerning 'English Restoration Comedy',[177] entries extracted from newspaper articles, and other entries relating to Joyce's travels. He rarely made note of the titles of the texts he was reading. The notebooks betray no attempt to summarize a storyline or encapsulate an argument. Words and phrases are extracted from bizarre-sounding books according to a logic that almost

---

[173] See the table established by Descharmes in *Autour de 'Bouvard et Pécuchet'*, 63, and de Biasi's more detailed 'Schematic index of elements and research themes featured in the novel' ['Index schématique des éléments et des thèmes d'enquête contenus dans le roman' (*Carnets de Travail*, 767–9)].

[174] 'These are the notes I make from my own notes, which I am coordinating in order to draw up a plan for my chapter!' ['Ce sont les notes de mes notes, que je coordonne, pour dresser le plan de mon chapitre!' (Flaubert to Caroline de Commanville, 21 March 1879, C5, 587)].

[175] E. G. Boulanger, *Queer Fish: And Other Inhabitants of the Rivers and Oceans* (London: Partridge, 1925).

[176] VI.B.8, 62, 63, 64; *JJA 30*, 320–2.

[177] VI.B.8, 38–9; *JJA 30*, 313.

always remains elusive. Ideas that seem relevant to Joyce's project are sometimes not excerpted: Landuyt and Lernout remark that 'now and then there are ideas in Metchnikoff one feels Joyce *should have* made note of'.[178] Conversely, many of the words Joyce chooses to extract from his sources are unaccountably banal. Why take the trouble to make note of such commonplace fish names as 'plaice' and 'sole' rather than record some of the reasons for these species' inclusion in a book entitled *Queer Fish*? The aim seems to have consisted entirely in the accumulation of a stockpile of words and phrases for redistribution across *Work in Progress*. These were mobilized at all stages of the writing process: during the initial drafting, and then again during additions, revisions, reworkings, and proofing.[179]

One of the more curious aspects of Joyce's reading practice resides in his willingness to work from second-hand sources. In this Joyce replicates the ways of Stephen Dedalus in *A Portrait of the Artist as a Young Man*. According to Jacques Aubert, Stephen owes his knowledge of Aquinas not to the *Summa Theologica* but to Bernard Bosanquet's *A History of Aesthetic* (1892).[180] Similarly, as was noted in Chapter 2, Stephen derives his notion of Plato's (putative) connection between truth and beauty as well as his image of the author as the God of creation from Flaubert. Likewise, the Homeric intertext of *Ulysses* was shaped in part by Joyce's childhood experience of Charles Lamb's *Adventures with Ulysses*[181] and in part by Victor Bérard's *Les Phéniciens de l'Odyssée*.[182] As Landuyt and Lernout point out, this aspect of Stephen's personality gave Joyce pause in the months following the publication of *Ulysses*. In VI.B.10, Joyce wrote:

discussing Alden War
SD said that he
had read Motley's Rise
of the Dutch Republic (had read title)[183]

(This aptly pinpoints another problem with Atherton's law: Joyce's engagement with a particular work quite often does not extend beyond its title.) This self-awareness accords with Landuyt and Lernout's discovery of Joyce's source for the Edgard Quinet sentence that features in the *Wake* in six variously distorted versions. By identifying Léon Metchnikoff's

[178] Landuyt and Lernout, 'Joyce's Sources', 101.
[179] Crispi, 'Storiella', *HJWFW*, 228.
[180] Jacques Aubert, *The Aesthetics of James Joyce* (Baltimore: Johns Hopkins University Press, 1992), 107. Fran O'Rourke has recently contested this view in 'Joyce's Early Aesthetic', *Journal of Modern Literature*, vol. 34, no. 2 (Winter 2011).
[181] *JJ*, 46.
[182] Gilbert, *James Joyce's 'Ulysses'*, vii. See also Michael Seidel, *Epic Geography in James Joyce's 'Ulysses'* (Princeton: Princeton University Press, 1976).
[183] VI.B.10, 86. Bloom refers to this title in 'Circe', as Landuyt and Lernout point out—'Joyce's Sources', 101; *U* 15: 1,390–1.

La Civilisation et les grands fleuves historiques (1889) (rather than Quinet's own 1825 text, *Introduction à la philosophie de l'histoire de l'humanité*) as Joyce's source for the quotation, thereby highlighting the second-handedness of even such a prominent borrowing, Landuyt and Lernout knock another hole in the conception of Joyce as an 'all-round renaissance man who knows huge chunks of learning by heart'.[184]

These differences in the initial stages of the intertextual process go some way towards explaining the variations in the extents and modes of the intertextualities deployed by Joyce and Flaubert in their final works. Flaubert begins by keeping track of his sources and by excerpting exact quotations, even if these details are later elided or deliberately altered.[185] Joyce's treatment of his sources, by contrast, suggests a nonchalant, carefree—even wilfully careless—attitude. This genetic fact suggests that the all-pervasive intertextuality of the *Wake* was intentional from the first: Joyce's method, as reflected in his note-taking habits, seems to have been geared entirely towards the production of a radical intertextuality[186]—a state in which borrowed words are ineluctably severed from their sources.

Joyce need not necessarily have read Descharmes to have been aware of *Bouvard*'s intertextual make-up. Indeed, *Bouvard* wears its intertextuality on its sleeve: the text swarms with scholarly references that map the protagonists' progress through a library prepared for them by Flaubert's reading. The novel is full of bibliographical information (titles, author names, page numbers) and quotations clearly demarcated by inverted commas. Although this veneer of scholarly accuracy suggests reliability, the information provided is in fact of little use. The author names volunteered by the text are often obscure. Page numbers are offered where no specific edition is indicated ('Monsieur Villemain scandalized them by showing, on page eighty-five of his *Lascaris*, a Spanish woman [*a*

---

[184] Landuyt and Lernout, 'Joyce's Sources', 101.

[185] The appearance of meticulousness in Flaubert's note-taking disguises a disorderliness which, much like the negligence that characterizes Joyce's notebook jottings, facilitated the elision of textual sources. As Anne Herschberg-Pierrot explains, Flaubert's manner of condensing his reading notes into 'notes de notes' was conducive to the gradual occlusion and transformation of the original text on which a given passage was based. The page numbers used in Flaubert's 'notes de notes' tend, for instance, to refer to his previous batch of notes rather than to the text from which the transferred quotations are excerpted. See 'Les Dossiers de *Bouvard et Pécuchet*', *The Romanic Review*, vol. 86, no. 3 (1 May 1995).

[186] Paul Saint-Amour uses this phrase (and its adjectival and adverbial cognate, 'radically intertextual') three times in *The Copyrights: Intellectual Property and the Literary Imagination* (London and Ithaca: Cornell University Press, 2003), 26, 47, 97. It is not defined, but is used to describe the extreme kinds of literary and linguistic collage that went into the making of the nineteenth-century poetic form called the 'cento', Joyce's *Ulysses*, and Wilde's *De Profundis*.

Spaniard] smoking a pipe').[187] Inverted commas are used confusingly, as when Flaubert quotes from a letter sent to Bouvard and Pécuchet by a friend of a friend, on the subject of the divine right of kings. Within the quotation marks that frame the extended excerpt from this letter, other sets of inverted commas are inconsistently deployed. The quoted passages are variously attributed to one or to several authors (without the titles of the relevant works being named), while summaries of other reported views feature without the substantiation of an accompanying quotation:

> 'Thus power comes from the people. They have the right "to do anything they wish", says Helvétius, "to change their constitution", says Vattel, to revolt against injustice, claim Glafey, Hotman, Mabley, etc.! St Thomas Aquinas authorizes them to deliver themselves from a tyrant. They are even, says Jurieu, dispensed from being right.'[188]

In its layering of quotations and in its inconsistent treatment of individual quoted snippets, this passage is typical of Flaubert's baffling use of quotation marks throughout *Bouvard et Pécuchet*—as indeed throughout his entire oeuvre.

Flaubert and Quotation Marks

Flaubert's idiosyncratic use of quotation marks was unsettlingly novel and pioneering at a time when standard, classical economies of quotation prevailed (indeed it remains defamiliarizing to this day). His departures from the current regime of quotation are related to the various aesthetic principles expounded in his *Correspondance*. In particular, Flaubert's deviation from established practice is connected to his passionate advocacy of authorial impersonality. As is well known, Flaubert's determination to banish the traditional omniscient narrator from his fiction led to the development and extensive deployment of *style indirect libre* as a means of using point of view (that is, many different points of view, none of them assimilable to the author's own) to order narrative. '[F]ree indirect discourse', as Stephen Heath simply states, 'followed from the Flaubertian imperative of impersonality'.[189] The role of Flaubert's technical discovery as a precursor to later modes of writing has aroused much critical com-

---

[187] *BPE*, 131 ['M. Villemain les scandalisa en montrant page 85 de son *Lascaris*, un Espagnol qui fume une pipe' (*BP*, 187–8)].

[188] *BPE*, 167 ['Donc le pouvoir vient du peuple. Il a le droit "de faire tout ce qu'il veut", dit Helvétius, "de changer sa constitution", dit Vattel, "de se révolter contre l'injustice", prétendent Glafey, Hotman, Mably, etc.! Et saint Thomas d'Aquin l'autorise à se délivrer d'un tyran. Il est même, dit Jurieu, dispensé d'avoir raison.' (*BP*, 236–7)].

[189] Heath, *Madame Bovary*, 117.

ment, with *Madame Bovary* in particular being praised for the impression of psychological depth conveyed by Flaubert's use of the technique to portray Emma's inner consciousness.

But focalization, and the sense of intimacy between reader and character that it fosters, are not the only effects of free indirect discourse. As Tzvetan Todorov explains:

> All cases of *style indirect libre* range between two limits: on the one side, a reported discourse that has the syntactic forms of indirect discourse [...] on the other side, a vision of reality that is not the narrator's own, but that of a fictional character.[190]

Victor Brombert concurs, describing the technique as used by Flaubert both 'as an elliptic abstract of conversation' and 'as an equivalent for interior monologue'.[191] The implications for quotation marks are several. With free indirect discourse providing an elegant way of reporting speech indirectly, such markers are no longer needed to relay the content of conversations. Neither are they needed to 'quote' from a character's mental processes—a function free indirect discourse can also fulfil without them. They are also frequently omitted within passages of *style indirect libre* when they might otherwise have been used to distinguish between obvious acts of mental quotation and the personal thoughts within which these are embedded. Thus *style indirect libre* has the potential to generate a spiral of telescoped quotations, with reported speech, inner thought, and snippets of common parlance seamlessly woven together within the surrounding context of third-person narration. Moreover, Flaubert's use of the technique often makes it difficult or impossible to ascertain where psychological *style indirect libre* begins and ends, an indeterminacy that fosters a generalized sense of uncertainty as to which of his characters (if any) is exerting its gravitational pull over the narrative at any given moment. As Heath explains, this ambivalence is essential to Flaubert's aesthetics and poetics. Flaubertian *style indirect libre*:

> becomes the very mode of impersonality as undecidable, beyond conclusions; orders of language, versions of sense, can be set down with no commitment, so many quotations which the writer neither accepts nor evidently condemns [...] remaining in suspense in the work.[192]

---

[190] Tzvetan Todorov, 'Les registres de la parole', *Journal de la Psychologie* (1967) 271–2, quoted in Dorrit Cohn, *Transparent Minds: Narrative Modes for Presenting Consciousness in Fiction* (Princeton: Princeton University Press, 1978), 110.

[191] Victor Brombert, *Novels of Flaubert*, 76.

[192] Heath, *Madame Bovary*, 118–19.

Crucial though it is (not least to Joyce's later refinements of focalizing techniques), *style indirect libre* does not account for the full range of Flaubert's anomalous usage of quotation marks. To begin with, the status of those quotations that do remain is sometimes signalled by italics rather than by quotation marks. Words and phrases marked off in this way frequently transcribe received ideas. In Heath's words, Flaubert's italics 'nail the commonplace', 'identify the *on-dit* of language', whether it be encased in a character's thoughts or in stretches of third-person narration not governed by *style indirect libre*. This extension of Flaubert's 'citational method'[193] of writing raises the same kinds of issue as pertain to the blurring of boundaries effected by *style indirect libre*. Italics are at once markers of a borrowing—an owning up to the act of quotation—and a disowning of the borrowed words they inflect. Flaubert's use of italics, as Heath intimates, is inconsistent, and begs the question:

> where should the italics begin and end? [...] The whole book should be in italics, which is the very project of the *Dictionnaire des Idées Reçues*, but also of *Madame Bovary* in its impersonality of free indirect style, with Flaubert not owning to any of the words he thereby quotes, puts into silent italics, avoiding any loud positions.[194]

The confusion that pertains to such a situation is compounded by the fact that italics are often omitted precisely where the reader might expect them most—in cases where phrases are instantly recognizable as clichés. When even italics—already an attenuated, ambiguous substitute for quotation marks—disappear, the reader is left confounded by a sense of recognition that the text would seem to deny. As Christopher Prendergast notes, quotations:

> although for the most part formally unmarked [...] are none the less instantly recognisable as such, and it is largely in and through such recognitions that the realisation of Flaubert's ironic project is guaranteed.[195]

Roland Barthes famously referred to the kind of ambiguously marked and unmarked quotation deployed in Flaubert's texts as 'quotations without inverted commas'.[196] Although it is accurate to the impression of phantasmal presence paradoxically conveyed by Flaubert's elision of quotation

---

[193] Prendergast, *Order of Mimesis*, 202.
[194] Heath, *Madame Bovary*, 121.
[195] Prendergast, *Order of Mimesis*, 185.
[196] Barthes, 'From Work to Text', 160 ['citations sans guillemets' ('De l'oeuvre au texte', 76)].

marks, Barthes' neat phrase occludes the oscillation that characterizes Flaubert's use of citational markers. It is by virtue of this very inconsistency that Flaubert's texts are so challenging to the reader, their ironies so difficult to decipher. In each work Flaubert forces the reader to make sense of:

> a huge, mobile network of citations drawn from a diffuse corpus of other texts, but which, as they enter the space of the Flaubert text, are ironically displayed as, precisely, citations, or, at a further self-reflexive move, as instances of Quotation itself.[197]

Such an interpretation reads as an adumbration of the purpose of Joyce's later deployment of even more radical and unbounded forms of intertextuality and of the intertextual theory Joycean and Flaubertian practices brought in their wake. To quote Prendergast again, Flaubert's cultivation of self-conscious Quotation throws into sharp relief the fact that:

> all utterance (and therefore all intelligibility) is in some way derivative or 'citational', articulated from a system that is socially established and maintained by means of convention, habit and repetition.[198]

Quotation, as Prendergast goes on to explain, has two principal functions. On the one hand, 'quotation signifies a borrowing' so that 'to quote is to accept and to endorse'. Conversely, 'quotation can have the opposite function: it represents the insertion of a certain distance between the speaker and what is being said, and thus opens up the possibility of ironic negation'.[199] The elision of quotation marks removes a crucial interpretative foothold, considerably complicating the reader's efforts to reach any conclusions about the text's meaning.

In *Bouvard et Pécuchet*, Flaubert's blurring of the conventional boundaries between discourses is rendered even more complex by two of the book's distinguishing features: the fact that the act of copying ('citation sans guillemets' par excellence) rests at the heart of the book, and the paradoxical (if related) fact that Bouvard and Pécuchet harbour scholarly ambitions which involve the desire to do more than merely copy—to write academically in their own right—and the concomitant need to quote rigorously, conventionally, and trustworthily, in such a way as to separate what is borrowed from what is original. Yet scholarly trustworthiness is a far cry from what confronts the reader of the book: as the novel unfolds,

---

[197] Prendergast, *Order of Mimesis*, 185–6.
[198] Prendergast, *Order of Mimesis*, 193.
[199] Prendergast, *Order of Mimesis*, 202.

any expectations he or she might have had regarding the exactness of Bouvard and Pécuchet's citations crumble. Their error-ridden ways soon infiltrate every aspect of the text, so that the reader insensibly begins to assume that quotations are not necessarily quotations and that the books cited as sources are not necessarily actual sources. The reader comes to assume confusion to be a trademark of Bouvard and Pécuchet's citational and bibliographic efforts, just as it is a trademark of everything else that they do. In this light, the book's quotational practices seem inflected by a form of mimicry related to *style indirect libre*: the text, in other words, is irregular in its handling of quotation because Bouvard and Pécuchet are unreliable in theirs. This *mise en abyme* turns the Flaubertian spiral of quotation into a vortex. Not for nothing is Barthes' description of 'the text' as 'a tissue of quotations drawn from the innumerable centres of culture' immediately followed by mention of *Bouvard et Pécuchet*:

> Similar to Bouvard and Pécuchet, those eternal copyists, at once sublime and comic and whose profound ridiculousness indicates precisely the truth of writing, the writer can only imitate a gesture that is always anterior, never original.[200]

Joyce and 'Perverted Commas'

It is possible, in a tantalizing literary-critical twist, that Barthes may have forged his insight regarding the technique of 'citations sans guillemets' from one of Pound's comments about Joyce in 'James Joyce et Pécuchet'. Indeed, Pound's essay evokes Joyce's own 'determined elimination of quotation marks'.[201] The observation accords with Joyce's distaste for what he termed 'perverted commas'.[202] The punning, epigrammatical turn of phrase was no mere whimsy. A prime example of Joyce's own destabilization of the conventional categories of discourse may be found in his development of the Uncle Charles Principle in *Dubliners* and then, much more extensively, in *A Portrait of the Artist as a Young Man*.[203] The Uncle Charles Principle is a direct successor to Flaubert's *style indirect libre*. It performs the same elision of introductory grammatical forms, but

---

[200] Barthes, 'The Death of the Author', 146 ['le texte est un tissu de citations, issues de mille foyers de la culture. Pareil à Bouvard et Pécuchet, ces éternels copistes, à la fois sublimes et comiques et dont le profond ridicule désigne précisément la vérité de l'écriture, l'écrivain ne peut qu'imiter un geste toujours antérieur, jamais original.' ('La Mort de l'auteur', 67)].

[201] ['élimination acharnée des guillemets' (Pound, 'James Joyce et Pécuchet', *P/J*, 207)].

[202] Joyce to Harriet Shaw Weaver, 11 July 1924, *L3*, 99.

[203] See Chapter 2, footnote 101.

the reported thoughts that follow are conveyed in words the character in question might actually use were he or she in a position to do so. Emma Bovary's thoughts come to us through a *style indirect libre* which mobilizes syntactical and lexical structures that she herself could not have summoned. Joyce, by contrast, uses words and structures that are carefully calibrated to what the reader can infer of his characters' intellectual and lexical abilities. Thus, in Hugh Kenner's example, Uncle Charles in *A Portrait* 'repairs to his outhouse' by way of a Victorian phrase that captures the antiquated quaintness of his language and habits. In the same way, Lily, at the beginning of 'The Dead', is 'literally run off her feet'—a phrase she might have uttered aloud had reported speech been Joyce's chosen mode of narration.[204] Likewise, the language of *A Portrait of the Artist as a Young Man* adapts seamlessly to the development of Stephen's mind, from the babbling inarticulacy of early infancy to the complicated clausal convolutions of his thoughts about aesthetics at the end of the book.

This mode of narration is mobilized extensively in *Ulysses*. Gerty MacDowell's musings, for instance, are rendered largely in her own idiom. Joyce's innovation in *Ulysses* is to have made quotation an endlessly regressive phenomenon. Gerty's idiom is her own, yet it is also an idiom extensively made up of quotations from the women's magazines she reads. Similarly, 'Eumaeus' applies the Uncle Charles Principle to Bloom, whose mind appears to be entirely constituted by grammatical and idiomatic clichés. What Sartre identifies in *L'Idiot de la famille* as one of Flaubert's insights ('Flaubert does not believe that one speaks: one is spoken')[205] is borne out by Joyce's use of focalizing techniques as ways of rendering minds utterly shaped by their linguistic environments. This phenomenon of quotation within quotation—quotations from the minds of characters, which are themselves quotations from the discourses of culture—is taken even further in Joyce's works through the use of interior monologue, which articulates the thoughts of characters directly, maximizing the author's effacement, and leaving quotations to stand *tel quel* in the text.

Finnegans Wake marks the next stage in Joyce's development of ever more radical modes of intertextual writing. In a work in which virtually every word originates from a written source,[206] it is noteworthy that the use of inverted commas or italics as markers of quotation is extremely

---

[204] Both examples are Kenner's in *Joyce's Voices*, 15–18.

[205] ['Flaubert ne croit pas qu'on parle: on est parlé' (Jean-Paul Sartre, *L'Idiot de la famille*, vol. 1 [1971], 353)].

[206] This is Rose's hypothesis in *James Joyce's The Index Manuscript: 'Finnegans Wake' Holograph Workbook VI.B.46*, ed. Danis Rose (Colchester: A Wake Newslitter Press, 1978), xiii, and in Danis Rose and John O'Hanlon, *Understanding 'Finnegans Wake': A Guide to the Narrative of Joyce's Masterpiece* (New York: Garland, 1982), ix.

scarce. The *Wake*'s 628 pages contain very few acts of conventional quotation. For that very reason exceptions are revealing. On page 281, Joyce's quotation from Quinet occurs in a version that remains very close to its French original:

> *Aujourd'hui comme aux temps de Pline et de Columelle la jacinthe se plaît dans les Gaules, la pervenche en Illyrie, la marguerite sur les ruines de Numance.*[207]

As was mentioned above, Joyce did not find this sentence in Quinet's *Introduction à la philosophie de l'histoire de l'humanité* but derived it instead from a quotation in Léon Metchnikoff's *La Civilisation et les grands fleuves historiques*. Like Joyce's debt to Flaubert in *A Portrait*, the provenance of this passage can be ascertained with some certainty owing to an error: in writing 'aux temps de Pline', Joyce replicates Metchnikoff's mistake in substituting the phrase for Quinet's original 'aux jours de Pline'.[208] In fact, Joyce made many more transcription mistakes in copying from Metchnikoff than Metchnikoff had made in quoting from Quinet. Joyce's accidental changes were compounded by further spelling emendations introduced by his amanuensis, Mme France Raphaël, as she transcribed the sentence from one notebook to another.[209] But as Landuyt and Lernout explain, Joyce went to great lengths to try to make this particular quotation impeccably accurate. His correspondence with Paul Léon on the subject makes clear Joyce's eagerness for at least one of the quotations in the *Wake* to be exact.[210] There is considerable irony, then, in finding that Joyce should have failed in the one obvious instance in which he intended to quote scrupulously. His apparent determination to insert the sentence into the text as he had read it in Metchnikoff acts as confirmation of the importance of citational issues in the *Wake*. Amid thousands of unidentifiable quotations, Joyce wished to include one sentence that would highlight the difference between the *Wake*'s principal system of quotation (a system marked by wilful negligence) and more classical economies of quotation. The Quinet sentence was presumably intended to function as a reminder that the author of the *Wake* knew what an ordinary quotation might look like—as a yardstick by which to gauge the extent of his general disregard for the conventions adhered to on this single occasion.

The *Wake* combines total intertextuality with utter originality. The process of alchemy whereby old words are freshly minted is effected by

---

[207] *FW* 281: 4–13 ['Today as in the days of Pliny and Columella the hyacinth thrives in Gaul, the periwinkle in Illyria, the daisy on the ruins of Numantia.'].

[208] Landuyt and Lernout, 'Joyce's Sources', 112.

[209] See Landuyt and Lernout, 'Joyce's Sources', 113, for an account of Joyce's and Mme Raphaël's successive distortions of Metchnikoff's quotation from Quinet.

[210] See Landuyt and Lernout, 'Joyce's Sources', 113–14.

three essential means: the elision of quotation marks discussed above, distortion, and decontextualization. Stuart Gilbert describes the distortion process in his *Paris Journal*:

> He has made a list of 30 towns, New York, Vienna, Budapest, and Mrs. [Helen] Fleischmann has read out the articles on some of these. I 'finish' Vienna and read Christiania and Bucharest. Whenever I come to a name (of a street, suburb, park, etc.) I pause. Joyce thinks. If he can Anglicize the word, i.e. make a pun on it, Mrs. F. records the name or its deformation in the notebook. Thus 'Slotspark' (I think) at Christiania becomes Sluts' park. He collects all queer names in this way and will soon have a notebook full of them.[211]

By the late 1920s Joyce considered this mode of writing to be so mechanical as to make the project suitable for transfer to someone else—specifically, the Irish novelist and poet James Stephens.[212] This did not happen: if the *Wake* was in part a self-propelling machine, it was a machine of which Joyce was clearly an essential constituent part.

The distortions imposed upon ordinary words are crucial to Joyce's handling of quotation in the *Wake*. 'Buvard to dear Picuchet' is a quotation, yet the distortion Joyce effects by the mere substraction or substitution of a vowel or two makes it something newly made as well. Thus is the *Wake* all at once old and new, full of *déjà-lus*, and yet brimming with meanings that go beyond—and often do not depend on—recognition.[213]

The decontextualization of the textual fragments Joyce jotted down in his notebooks forms the third crucial intertextual process involved in the genesis of the *Wake*. Joyce's erratic methods in the note-taking stages of his work made some degree of decontextualization inevitable, even had it not become an actual working principle. Dirk Van Hulle gives a salient example of Joyce's apparent indifference to the order in which his notes were arranged within the notebooks. Joyce's notes in VI.B.46 are a mixture of material neatly organized under headings, and other material anarchically inserted wherever space allowed:

---

[211] Stuart Gilbert, *Reflections on James Joyce: Stuart Gilbert's Paris Journal*, ed. Thomas F. Staley and Randolph Lewis (Austin: University of Texas Press, 1993), entry for 31 January 1930, 20–1, quoted in Rabaté, 'The Fourfold Root of Yawn's Unreason', *HJWFW*, 392.

[212] *JJ*, 591–2.

[213] Joyce's distorting procedures are discussed in, amongst others, Margot Norris, *The Decentered Universe of 'Finnegans Wake': A Structuralist Analysis* (Baltimore and London: Johns Hopkins University Press, 1976); John Bishop, *Joyce's Book of the Dark: 'Finnegans Wake'* (Madison: University of Wisconsin Press, 1986); and Finn Fordham, *Lots of Fun at 'Finnegans Wake' Unravelling Universals* (Oxford: Oxford University Press, 2007).

Joyce's notes in VI.B.46 are divided quite systematically into different sections or 'indexes' [...] The Mauthner notes are probably of a later date than the indexes, since they were jotted down wherever Joyce found some blank space, starting on pages 60 and continuing in retrograde direction on pp. 54–55, 50, 49, 48, and 46.[214]

There are also occasions on which Joyce seems to have deliberately sought to make the original contexts of his notes irretrievable. His call upon Mme Raphaël as an amanuensis from 1933 onwards is a case in point.[215] According to a widespread view, Joyce hired Mme Raphaël to copy unused jottings from his early notebooks, suspecting full well that she might make mistakes in the process. While Ian MacArthur argues that Joyce 'uses the accidental mistranscriptions'[216] (implying that Joyce intentionally provoked them by hiring a third-party collaborator), Danis Rose has shown that in several instances Joyce restored units distorted by Raphaël to their original form.[217] Van Hulle concludes that although 'it would be an over-interpretation to conclude that Raphaël's transcriptions were planned as a systematical technique of distortion', Joyce's use of some of her distortions 'seems to indicate that he allowed some sort of (anti) collaboration to become part of his work'.[218]

Even if accidental changes are left out of the equation, the nature of Mme Raphaël's task was bound to produce decontextualization. It is difficult to see how the arrangement could have been made without this effect in mind. Her job—to copy and transfer the unused materials of earlier notebooks into new notebooks—is evidently an exercise in simple cut-and-paste (simple in principle, but anything but straightforward in practice, given Joyce's handwriting and his habit of mixing languages and sources indiscriminately). Chapter II.2 of the *Wake*, which was made entirely from the stuff of such collaborative coincidences, constitutes an extreme example of the use Joyce sometimes made of the incongruous juxtapositions yielded by Mme Raphaël's transcriptions:

Raphaël filled notebook C.10 with notes from notebooks B.28, B.26, B.23, and D.5. On the basis of this accidental collection, Joyce wove a new text, thereby effacing the original context and meaning of the entries entirely.[219]

---

[214] Van Hulle, 'The Lost Word: *Book IV*', in *HJWFW*, 439.

[215] *JJ*, 671, and Slote, Introduction, *HJWFW*, 26.

[216] Ian MacArthur, 'Mutant Units in the C Notebooks', *A 'Finnegans Wake' Circular* 2.4 (1987), 76–7.

[217] Rose, *Textual Diaries*, 176–7.

[218] Van Hulle, *Textual Awareness*, 107.

[219] Van Hulle, *Textual Awareness*, 107.

Writing about another section of the book, II.4, Jed Deppman traces the stages of the process whereby Joyce 'unhooks' textual fragments from their initial context in the *Wake*—in which they cohabit with elements derived from the same original source—in order to graft them into a different section of the book. In Deppman's view, this cavalier treatment of the text's sources suggests a willingness, or even a desire, to forget—or at least a complete lack of interest in remembering—where its origins lay. On this reading, Joyce valued his sources precisely as providers of echoes from texts that were no longer known to him:

> counting on some turns of phrase [...] to reproduce or represent circumstances, texts, contexts that he himself had forgotten or failed to fully imagine or notice in the first place. He may have been hoping or expecting, even in the early years of the writing of the *Wake*, that his language was pregnant with meanings to which he himself was or would become blind.[220]

Intertextuality and Plagiarism

In his letters Flaubert expressed disapproval of the kind of procedure Joyce uses to compile his notebooks. Commenting on his friend Edmond de Goncourt's habit of finding a word on the street and introducing it *tel quel* into his work, Flaubert wrote condescendingly that:

> Goncourt, for instance, is so pleased when he has picked up a word in the street that he can shove into a book.[221]

Reality, in Flaubert's view, was only a starting point, which needed to be synthesized and remoulded to create a new artistic vision representative of, but not solely confined to, a mirroring of the real world:

> It's not just a question of seeing. One must order and combine one's perceptions. Reality, according to me, should be only a *springboard*. Our friends are convinced that it in itself constitutes all of Art![222]

As is hinted by Shem's description as an 'odious and still today insufficiently malestimated notesnatcher',[223] the modus operandi criticized by Flaubert corresponds to Joyce's own working practice during some of the

---

[220] Jed Deppman, 'A Chapter in Composition: *Chapter II.4*', in *HJWFW*, 335.

[221] Flaubert to George Sand, late December 1875, *GW*, 401 ['Goncourt, par exemple, est très heureux quand il a saisi dans la rue un mot qu'il peut coller dans un livre.' (*C4*, 1,000)].

[222] Flaubert to Ivan Turgenev, 8 December 1877, *FS2*, 242 ['Il ne s'agit pas seulement de voir, il faut arranger et fondre ce que l'on a vu. La Réalité, selon moi, ne doit être qu'un *tremplin*. Nos amis sont persuadés qu'à elle seule elle constitue tout l'Art!' (*C5*, 337)].

[223] *FW* 125: 21–2.

stages of the *Wake's* composition.[224] He was content, for instance, to depend on notes Samuel Beckett took while reading Fritz Mauthner's *Beiträge zu einer Kritik der Sprache* in order to avoid having to study the book himself.[225] Similarly, he embraced words that inadvertently made their way into the text of Beckett's script while the younger writer was serving as his amanuensis:

> there was a knock at the door which Beckett didn't hear. Joyce said, 'Come in', and Beckett wrote it down. Afterwards he read back what he had written and Joyce said, 'What's that "Come in"?' 'Yes, you said that,' said Beckett. Joyce thought for a moment, then said, 'Let it stand.'[226]

Joyce may have embarked upon the writing process by snatching notes off the streets, off people's lips, or, more often, from written sources, but the subsequently applied procedures of elision, distortion, and decontextualization eclipse the threat of any allegation of plagiarism being brought against the *Wake* (the theme, however, remains in play throughout the book). Ironically, it was Flaubert, who so objected to 'Shemish notes-natching', who was confronted with such a charge. In 1912 Descharmes rediscovered an affair that had caused Flaubert to come under posthumous attack for plagiarism in 1887, seven years after his death. The plot of *Bouvard et Pécuchet*, as (none other than) Edmond de Goncourt discovered, was the same as that of a short story published on three occasions in the 1840s and 1850s, in journals of which Flaubert is known to have been a reader.[227] Descharmes comments on:

> the curious analogy that exists between the subject of *Bouvard* reduced to its essential structure, and the subject of the short story entitled *Les Deux Greffiers*, published by the lawyer Maurice on 14 April 1841 in the *Gazette des Tribunaux*, reproduced the following month in the *Journal des Journaux*, and finally reprinted on 7 February 1858 in the *Audience*.[228]

---

[224] While *Ulysses* is manifestly full of words 'snatched' from many different sources, *Stephen Hero* and *A Portrait* both depict an aspiring artist struck with wonderment at the mere sight and sound of words encountered in everyday contexts. In the former, Stephen's mind is 'often hypnotised by the most commonplace conversation'—*SH*, 26. In the latter, a peripatetic Stephen finds himself 'glancing from one casual word to another on his right or left in stolid wonder that they had been so silently emptied of instantaneous sense until every mean shop legend bound his mind like the words'—*P*, 150.

[225] *JJ*, 649.

[226] *JJ*, 649.

[227] The story, entitled 'Les Deux Greffiers', was by Barthélemy Maurice. It is reproduced in Flaubert, *Oeuvres complètes* (1971–5), vol. 6, 843–50.

[228] ['l'analogie curieuse qui existe entre le sujet de *Bouvard* réduit à sa charpente essentielle, et le sujet d'une nouvelle intitulée *Les Deux Greffiers*, publiée par le publiciste Maurice, le 14 avril 1841, dans la *Gazette des Tribunaux*, reproduite le mois suivant dans le

Goncourt's journal entry for 14 April 1887 records the shock caused by the discovery of Maurice's story among Flaubert's entourage, and its outrage at what appeared to be a shameful act of plagiarism:

> There can be no doubt about it... the two bonshommes copying [...] It is odd that Flaubert should not have been stopped in his tracks by the thought that this kind of plagiarism would some day be discovered.[229]

In his friends' eyes, Flaubert had become 'a text thief'.[230] The problem was not a legal one, but, to quote the *Wake*, one of 'malestimation': Flaubert, like Shem, now cut the figure of a 'malestimated notes-natcher'.[231] René Dumesnil offers the commonsensical explanation that Flaubert read Maurice's story and forgot all about it until the idea returned to him as his own many years later.[232] Leclerc argues that Flaubert's use of *Les Deux Greffiers* deserves no scandalized response: that in a book in which virtually every sentence derives from textual sources, the story that provided Flaubert with its plot ought not be considered a special case.[233] The story should be listed in the catalogue of Flaubert's working library, having been 'submitted, whether consciously or unconsciously, to the same labour of forgetting—the labour involved in the erasure of its origin and of the author of that origin',[234] as all the other books on the basis of which *Bouvard* was built.

As Leclerc explains, it was the realization that Flaubert's borrowings extended beyond the immense body of erudite fact to include the book's plot and protagonists which so unnerved the Goncourts and their circle: such an appropriation turned quotation into a veritably boundless process. Intertextuality, as they discovered, was more than a necessary means to Flaubert's composition of a book about knowledge: it was a principle subtending the entire book. In making every part of his work a repetition,

---

Journal des Journaux, reprise enfin le 7 février 1858 par l'*Audience*' (Descharmes, *Autour de 'Bouvard et Pécuchet'*, 90–1)].

[229] ['Il ne peut y avoir de doute... les deux bonshommes qui recopient [...] C'est bien curieux que Flaubert n'ait pas été arrêté par la prévision qu'un jour ou l'autre, cette espèce de plagiat serait découvert.' (Edmond de Goncourt, *Journal: mémoires de la vie littéraire*, 22 vols [Monaco: Imprimerie nationale de Monaco, 1956–8], vol. 14 [1885–7], 219, quoted in Leclerc, *La Spirale*, 142)].

[230] Leclerc, *La Spirale*, 142 ['un voleur de texte'].

[231] *FW* 125: 22.

[232] René Dumesnil, Introduction, *Bouvard et Pécuchet*, in Gustave Flaubert, *Oeuvres* (Paris: Gallimard, 1951–2), vol. 2, 701, quoted in Leclerc, *La Spirale*, 143.

[233] Leclerc, *La Spirale*, 143.

[234] ['soumise au même travail, conscient ou inconscient, d'oubli, d'effacement de l'origine, du nom d'auteur' (Leclerc, *La Spirale*, 143)].

an appropriation, a quotation, a borrowing, Flaubert took the effacement of the author further than his followers could comprehend:

> *l'auteur n'est à l'origine de rien.* [...] C'est bien ce qui fait problème, et scandale, autant que le non-respect de la propriété des autres: comment reconnaître le bien de Flaubert, sa voix originelle, sans interférences (on dirait aujourd'hui: sans intertextualité)?[235]

The allegation of plagiarism emitted in private circles in 1887 marked the beginnings of a gradual recognition of the extent of Flaubert's intertextual practices—of his willingness to create a work constituted entirely by processes of absorption and remoulding. Intertextuality gone haywire: Flaubert, before Joyce, had done this—as Joyce, if he read Descharmes or even just *Bouvard et Pécuchet*, would have known.

There is evidence in Flaubert's and Joyce's last works that each knew what the modes of their writing implied, and what reactions their works might arouse if and when the full extent of their intertextuality was understood.

Indeed, *Bouvard* and *Finnegans Wake* manifest a heightened degree of self-consciousness regarding their appropriating procedures. In *Bouvard*, a book made up of copied textual fragments, the two protagonists in the copied plot are retired copying clerks by profession who eventually return to their 'copie' for pleasure. Bouvard and Pécuchet imitate their author in all their reading and writing methods: the manners in which they read, annotate, and summarize are recognizably Flaubertian. In the same way, Shem, Joyce's most obvious avatar in *Finnegans Wake*, is depicted in terms that anticipate, and arguably thereby neutralize, those allegations of plagiarism, imposture, and forgery that might be brought against a book compiled in the fashion of the *Wake*. Shem is a 'notesnatcher', a thief, a copyist, a forger. He uses 'borrowed plumes' and 'pelagiarist pen[s]' to 'cutely copy' 'counterfeit franks', 'quashed quotatoes, messes of mottage', 'styles of signature', 'cantraps of fermented words', and thereby produce 'stolen fruit', 'epical forged cheque[s]', 'public impostures', and 'piously forged palimpsests'.[236] Joyce's portrait of Shem echoes his descriptions of the *Wake* and of the kind of writer it was making him. In 1931 Joyce famously told George Antheil that he expected to go down in history as 'a scissors and paste man',[237]

---

[235] ['*nothing originates with the author.* [...] That is where the true problem lies, and the scandal, as much as in the breach of other people's property: how can one recognize what belongs to Flaubert, his original voice, without interference (without intertextuality, as one might say today)?' (Leclerc, *La Spirale*, 143 [my emphasis])].

[236] *FW* 125: 21–2; *FW* 183: 32; *FW* 182: 3; *FW* 181: 15; *FW* 183: 19; *FW* 183: 22–3; *FW* 181: 15; *FW* 184: 26; *FW* 181: 14–15; *FW* 181: 16; *FW* 182: 1–2; *FW* 182: 2.

[237] Joyce to George Antheil, 3 January 1931, *L1*, 297.

an assessment with which his literary critics have increasingly concurred. Rabaté, for instance, calls Joyce a 'bricoleur' who 'simply salvage[s] trivia',[238] and for Crispi, Joyce extends 'the technique of composing by collage'.[239]

There are differences as well analogies between Joyce's and Flaubert's conceptions of the intertextual project. One of the most notable differences is tonal. The metaphors Flaubert used to describe *Bouvard*'s intertextuality are charged with searing contempt for the texts he made himself read and recycle. Flaubert's intertextuality was gargantuan in intent as well as in scale. *Bouvard*, as the letters Flaubert wrote during the book's composition clearly show, depended on a readerly equivalent of the digestive process. Books and pages are ingested, digested, and regurgitated: 'I swallow printed pages [...] I will make sure to *regurgitate my bile* over my contemporaries [...] this spewing up will take several years'.[240] Revulsion and venomous hatred are intermixed in Flaubert's scatological vision of literary creation as a mode of punishment:

> I feel suffocating waves of hatred against the stupidity of my times. Shit rises to my mouth [...] I want to keep it, to let it settle, to let it harden. I want to make a paste out of it with which to coat the nineteenth century.[241]

By contrast, Joyce's neutrally stated aspiration to 'write a history of the world'[242] in the *Wake* may, if Joyce knew of Flaubert's disgust at the life led by people around him, offer another explanation for the notebook jotting that opposes Flaubert's 'treatment of language [a]s a kind of despair' to his own 'contrary' position'. Joyce's intertextuality was carefully planned and yet also, in an important sense, carefree. Plagiarism, like everything else in the *Wake*, is at least partly a joking matter.

In spite of these differences, Flaubert's inauguration of a radical mode of intertextual writing sowed the seeds for Joyce's own compositional

---

[238] Rabaté, 'The Fourfold Root of Yawn's Unreason', *HJWFW*, 403–4.

[239] Crispi, 'Storiella', *HJWFW*, 233.

[240] Flaubert to Ernest Feydeau, 29 December 1872 ['J'avale des pages imprimées [...] je tâcherai de *vomir ma bile* sur mes contemporains [...] ce dégueulage me demandera plusieurs années' (*C4*, 627)].

[241] Flaubert to Louis Bouilhet, 30 September 1855 ['Je sens contre la bêtise de mon époque des flots de haine qui m'étouffent. Il me monte de la merde à la bouche [...] je veux la garder, la figer, la durcir. J'en veux faire une pâte dont je barbouillerais le XIXe siècle.' (*C2*, 600)]. Flaubert's vision of himself coating the nineteenth century in regurgitated excremental matter has a parallel in Joyce's description of Shem writing with the waste of his own body. Shem uses 'synthetic ink and sensitive paper for his own end out of his wit's waste' and in future 'shall produce nichthemerically from his unheavenly body a no uncertain quantity of obscene matter not protected by copriright in the United Stars of Ourania or bedeed or bedood and bedang and bedung to him [...] through the bowels of his misery' – *FW* 185: 7–8 and 185: 29–33.

[242] *JJ*, 537.

processes. Flaubert became increasingly aware that if to write is necessarily to copy, then the true artist should at least copy knowingly:

> From *Novembre* and the first *Education* to *Bouvard*, one can see a sort of reversal of the hierarchy between writer and copyist: given that the author, thinking to draw his brilliant ideas from his own mind, discovers himself to be the involuntary copyist of other people's writing (of Balzac's writing, at the time, for Gustave), it is by making himself their voluntary copyist that he will have a chance to achieve the status of writer. If all writers are unwittingly copyists, then he who aspires to become and indeed becomes a copyist is truly a writer. Having realized this, in order not to copy unknowingly, in order to copy in full textual knowledge, Flaubert devours books.[243]

This interpretation of Flaubert's path to the massive intertextuality of *Bouvard* corresponds to the understanding of Joyce's writing that has been rehearsed throughout this study. Joyce, like Flaubert before him, became ever more aware of language as a web of inevitable quotation, and decided, with exponential consequences, to turn the unavoidable into a deliberate, playful, daring, self-conscious process. Joyce saw, as Flaubert had seen before him, how by such paradoxical means originality could be gleaned.

---

[243] Leclerc, *La Spirale*, 146 ['De *Novembre* et de la première *Éducation* à *Bouvard*, on assiste à une sorte de renversement de hiérarchie entre écrivain et copiste: puisque l'auteur, croyant tirer les pensées géniales de son propre fonds, se retrouve le copiste involontaire des autres (pour Gustave, à l'époque, de Balzac), c'est en se faisant leur copiste volontaire qu'il aura une chance d'accéder au statut d'écrivain. Si tous les écrivains sont des copieurs qui s'ignorent, seul celui qui se veut et se fait copiste est véritablement écrivain. Dès lors, pour ne pas copier sans le savoir, pour copier en connaissance de texte, Flaubert se bourre de livres.'].

Conclusion: Linking Forward

This study has argued that James Joyce's radically intertextual poetics found fruitful points of departure in the works of Gustave Flaubert. The emphasis at all points has been on elaboration, transformation, deviation. Neither author comes out of this study the weaker for the connections that are discerned between them: it is hoped, rather, that this account of their artistic intersections will enhance appreciation of the dazzling complexity of their respective enterprises.

Flaubert self-evidently does not have the kind of relationship to Joyce that Joyce has to Flaubert. Nonetheless he did have an assured sense of the seminal place he would come to assume in the literary tradition. He had confidence that what he was doing was new and wholly worthwhile, and dared to hope that a successor might come to relay his efforts and see his endeavours through. In a letter written to Louise Colet in 1853, he struck a prophetic tone to presage the summation of his own artistic vision in someone else's art:

> the task which I am undertaking will be carried through by someone else. I will have shown somebody the way, someone more gifted and more *born to it* than I am. Perhaps it is an absurdity, to want to impart to prose the rhythm of verse (leaving it still prose and very prosey), to want to write about ordinary life as we write history or epic (without distorting the subject). [...] But perhaps it is also a great and a very original undertaking![1]

Long before Joyce came to think about the 'strandentwining cables' that connect authors to each other, Flaubert envisioned his own work as a cord hurled forward, showing somebody the way. Among the great chorus of voices that has, over the decades, claimed Flaubert as the founding father of a wide range of literary styles and movements, Joyce's response stands out. It does so partly by virtue of its breadth, partly by virtue of

---

[1] Flaubert to Louise Colet, 27 March 1853, *GW*, 203 ['la tâche que j'entreprends sera exécutée par un autre. J'aurai mis sur la voie quelqu'un de mieux doué et de plus *né*. Vouloir donner à la prose le rythme du vers (en la laissant prose et très prose) et écrire la vie ordinaire comme on écrit l'histoire ou l'épopée (sans dénaturer le sujet) est peut-être une absurdité. [...] Mais c'est peut-être aussi une grande tentative et très originale!' (*C2*, 287)].

the magnitude of Joyce's achievement, and partly because his intertextual engagement arrestingly accords with Flaubert's prescient-sounding
missive.

The most significant effect of the crucial, many-faceted, ever more self-
conscious literary relationship between Joyce and Flaubert arguably resides
in those thoughts about intertextuality that it helped crystallize in Joyce's
mind. Throughout his works, Joyce uses Flaubert to think through the
dynamics and implications of any text's inevitable relations to other texts.
These musings about language and literature as meshing webs of echo and
quotation are reflected at many points in his works, as for instance in
Leopold Bloom's realization, in the 'Ithaca' episode of *Ulysses*, that he is:

> neither first nor last nor only nor alone in a series originating in and repeated
> to infinity.[2]

Joyce, like Bloom, renounces possession. Bloom reflects that he can no
more own his wife than he can her sexual past and future—nor can his
imagination even begin to compass the long series of cuckolded husbands
into which her act of adultery inscribes him. Analogously, Joyce recognizes
that in the infinite constellation of literature he can no more lay claim to
the possession of his own ingenious arrangements of words than he can lay
claim to the possession of words themselves—some will have been appropriated from other authors, some will be adopted by future writers. Joyce,
like Bloom, is but a point in a series—a single stitch in the expanding,
woven fabric of textuality. Like Stephen in 'Proteus', he accepts and
embraces the fact that 'The cords of all link back', that literature, like
life itself, is a matter of 'strandentwining cables' that twist and turn,
tweaking the original to produce difference amid the continuity of
human and textual descent.

The creation of such difference through the artistic processes of appropriation, grafting, and adaptation is essential to the effect of Joyce's
intertextuality. As has been argued throughout this study, the archness
and command that Joyce brings to his connections to Flaubert renders
inadequate a discussion of their relations in terms of influence alone. Over
and above the impact he exerted on each successive work, Flaubert
prompted Joyce to think about what literary influence might mean—
what the fact of coming after or 'behind' other writers might entail. Like
Flaubert before him, Joyce turns the inevitability of literary belatedness to
benefit, transforming what might have remained a purely passive phenomenon into a working principle. The range of images Joyce uses to

---

[2] *U* 17: 2,130–1.

describe literary relations (linking cords, strandentwining cables, serial mathematical sequences, forged cheques, neutral palimpsests) self-reflexively suggests as much, portraying his dealings with earlier texts as a combination of deliberate, consciously conducted engagements and of inevitable, unconscious, unattributed quotation. Although this study has focused on Joyce's relationship with Flaubert, this is not intended to occlude the fact that both open their writings up to precursor texts from 'the innumerable centres of culture',[3] thereby upsetting the binary which lies at the core of the influence model of literary relations. Both authors respond to the realization that writing can never escape its own ineluctable second-hand status. In Joyce's case, if not in Flaubert's, this awareness is entertained and cultivated with 'equanimity'[4] and without despair.

By writing as intertextually as they do, Joyce and Flaubert inaugurate and develop a trend in literature that rendered possible the emergence of intertextual theory in the 1960s. Intertextual theory, denying the possibility of originality in writing, considered itself to be a fundamentally innovative literary-critical hypothesis. But the excavation of the literary history of these theoretical statements reveals how many of their intellectual insights and defining images derive from the literary texts that preceded them. Joyce and Flaubert are the most extreme exponents and exemplars of intertextual theory—all at once its midwives and its *raisons d'être*. Their works constitute two of the triggers that set the wheels of the theory in motion, provoking the need for a new term to replace—or rather expand—traditional conceptions of literary influence.

Joyce and Flaubert forged similes that assume pride of place in the writings of Roland Barthes, Julia Kristeva, and their followers. The Barthesian idea of a dead or invisible 'Author-God',[5] for instance, has clear and memorable antecedents in both Joyce ('The artist, like the God of creation')[6] and Flaubert ('The author in his work must be like God in creation').[7] His proclamation of 'the death of the author' makes impersonality one of intertextuality's key correlative concepts; but the combination of authorial effacement and intertextuality that already prevails in the works of Joyce and Flaubert makes Barthes' provocative statement seem less revolutionary than descriptive. Similarly, Barthes' attack on the 'myth of filiation' echoes Joyce's ambivalence about paternity, as encapsulated in

---

[3]   Barthes, 'The Death of the Author', 146 ['mille foyers de la culture' ('La Mort de l'auteur', 67)].

[4]   *U* 17: 2,155.

[5]   Barthes, 'The Death of the Author', 146 ['Auteur-Dieu' (La Mort de l'auteur', 67)].

[6]   *P*, 181.

[7]   Flaubert to Leroyer de Chantepie, 18 March 1857, *GW*, 258 [L'artiste doit être dans son oeuvre comme Dieu dans la création (*C2*, 691)].

Stephen Dedalus's statement in *Ulysses* that 'Paternity may be a legal fiction.'[8] Throughout his works and notebooks Joyce problematizes and complicates (without wholly forsaking) the traditional, filial model of literary relations, writing in ways that ever more clearly reflect his conception of language and literature as matrices of intricately interlinking verbal materials.

Mikhail Bakhtin's contention that 'The word in language is half someone else's' accords with Stephen's suspicion, expressed in conversation with an English priest in *A Portrait of the Artist as a Young Man*, that 'The language in which we are speaking is his before it is mine.'[9] Irrespective of the colonial situation of Ireland that compounds the significance of Stephen's words, the statement resonates as a diagnosis of the human experience of language, into which all are born as into one of those all at once constraining and enabling nets by which Stephen resolves to fly ('You talk to me of nationality, language, religion. I shall try to fly by those nets.').[10] Such a view is congruent with the tenor of Joyce's statements on related matters. Thus his 1907 essay, 'Ireland: Island of Saints and Sages', betrays a calm apolitical lucidity concerning the inextricable hybridity of all civilizations, races, and languages:

> Our civilization is an immense woven fabric in which very different elements are mixed [. . .] In such a fabric, it is pointless searching for a thread that has remained pure, virgin and uninfluenced by other threads nearby. What race or language [. . .] can nowadays claim to be pure?[11]

Joyce puts paid to the illusion of purity, asserting the inevitable adulteration involved in the making of literature—its ineluctable intertextuality.

As for Barthes and Bakhtin, so for other theorists. The symbolism of Stephen's inheritance of second-hand clothes at the end of *A Portrait* gestures towards the second-handedness of all literature evoked by Antoine Compagnon in *La Seconde Main*. Likewise, Stephen's determination to go forth to Paris to '*forge* [. . .] the uncreated conscience of [his] race',[12] and *Finnegans Wake*'s mention of 'piously forged palimpsests'[13] foreshadow the purport of Gérard Genette's

---

[8] Barthes, 'From Work to Text', 160 ['mythe de la filiation' ('De l'oeuvre au texte', 76)]; *U* 9: 844.

[9] Mikhail Bakhtin, 'Discourse in the Novel', in *The Dialogic Imagination: Four Essays*, trans. C. Emerson and M. Holquist, ed. M. Holquist (Austin: University of Texas Press, 1981), 293; *P*, 159.

[10] *P*, 171.

[11] James Joyce, 'Ireland: Island of Saints and Sages', in *OCPW*, 118.

[12] *P*, 213 (my emphasis).

[13] *FW* 182: 2.

study, *Palimpsestes*. Similarly, the same theorist's analysis of intertextuality in terms of *bricolage*[14] agrees with Joyce's description of himself as a 'scissors and paste man'.[15]

For few authors do Barthes' and Kristeva's descriptions of texts as 'mosaics' or 'tissues' of quotation[16] ring true as they do for Flaubert and for Joyce. This is not to deny other writers a role in providing the conditions that made possible—and indeed necessary—the emergence of the concept: Lautréamont, Mallarmé, Wilde, Pound, Eliot, the Surrealists, Woolf, and many more, thought and wrote about textual relations in ways that contributed to the need for the new notion. But Joyce and Flaubert are surely the prime movers behind intertextual theory, as well as its paradigm cases.

The combined legacy of these two masters extends further still: their writing has instigated a trend in literature—for densely intertextual writing that makes intertextuality a central theme—which, reinforcing and reinforced by the theory whose seeds they sowed, shows no sign of abating. One need only think of Jorge Luis Borges's *Fictions* with their elaborate, thoughtful, ludic meditations on the themes of literary interconnectedness and repetition: of Pierre Menard's ambition 'to produce a number of pages which coincided—word for word and line for line with those of Miguel de Cervantes';[17] of the certainty, expressed in 'The Library of Babel', that 'everything has already been written'.[18] One might also think of Umberto Eco's *The Name of the Rose*, in which the narrator realizes that 'not infrequently books speak of books: it is as if they spoke among themselves'.[19] Or of Georges Perec's *La Vie Mode d'Emploi*, in which a list of quoted authors is provided in an appendix to the novel.

It is touching, given the innumerable Flaubertian resonances that traverse Joyce's works, and given the many echoes both authors have sent rippling through the literary and critical worlds in their wake, to find that the unmarried, childless hermit of Croisset conceived of future readers and writers as members of an immortal family:

And, who knows? Every voice finds its echo!—I often think with tenderness of those unknown beings, as yet unborn, or foreign, etc., who are moved or

---

[14] Gérard Genette, 'Structuralisme et critique littéraire', *Figures I* (Paris: Seuil, 1966).

[15] Joyce to George Antheil, *L1*, 297.

[16] Kristeva, 'Word, Dialogue, Novel', 66 ['Le Mot, le dialogue, et le roman', 85]; Barthes, 'The Death of the Author', 146 ['La Mort de l'auteur', 67].

[17] Jorge Luis Borges, 'Pierre Menard, Author of the *Quixote*', in *Fictions* (London: Penguin Books, 2000), 37.

[18] Borges, 'The Library of Babel', in *Fictions*, 73.

[19] Umberto Eco, *The Name of the Rose* (1980), trans. William Weaver (London: Vintage, 2004), 286.

will be moved by the same things as I. A book creates an eternal family for one among humanity. All those who will live through your thinking, they are like children seated around your own fireplace.—And what gratitude do I myself feel towards those poor old souls whose books one tears through so voraciously, those people one feels one has known, of whom one dreams as one dreams of dead friends![20]

Although it is articulated here in the familial terms prized by proponents of the influence model of literary relations, the breadth and open-endedness of Flaubert's vision of an everlasting community of past, present, and future readers and writers more aptly prefigures the inter-textual view of art as an infinite, simultaneous system. While Stephen wonders whether he is 'walking into eternity along Sandymount strand' and whether anyone 'ever anywhere will read [his] written words',[21] his author's hopes about his own posterity are not known.[22] But Joyce did, in the privacy of one of his working notebooks, recognize 'G. F' as a literary father, or, to quote the *Wake*, as a 'family furbear'[23]—an artistic progenitor deserving of aeons of peaceful rest for having shown Joyce the intertextual way. In 'Proteus', Stephen ambivalently reflects that 'The cords of all link back'. In Flaubert, Joyce found a cord flung toward the future. Seizing and absorbing it, stranding and twining it with countless other threads, he formed a strandentwining cable, a trailing navelcord proffered forward to new generations of readers and writers.

---

[20] Flaubert to Louise Colet, 25 March, 1854 ['Et puis, qui sait? Chaque voix trouve son écho!—Je pense souvent avec attendrissement aux êtres inconnus, à naître, étrangers, etc., qui s'émeuvent ou s'émouvront des mêmes choses que moi. Un livre, cela vous crée une famille éternelle dans l'humanité. Tous ceux qui vivront de votre pensée, ce sont comme des enfants attablés à votre foyer.—Aussi quelle reconnaissance j'ai, moi, pour ces pauvres vieux braves, dont on se bourre à si large gueule, qu'il semble que l'on a connus, et auxquels on rêve, comme à des amis morts!' (*C2*, 541)].

[21] *U* 3: 8–9, 414–15.

[22] Joyce did, however, allow himself a chuckle about the academic readers who would ensure his immortality by puzzling their baffled heads over his inscrutable meanings—*JJ*, 521.

[23] *FW* 132: 32.

Appendix

A sample of some of the many likely connections between Joyce's 'Circe' notesheet jottings and Flaubert's *Tentation de saint Antoine*.

'Circe' notesheet number, line number, and page reference (in Herring)	Joyce's notesheet jotting	Likely source of the jotting in *TA*	Page number in *TA*	Page number in *TAE*
'Circe' 1, l. 73, 267	nabuchodonosor rex	Nabuchodonosor se prosterna le visage	50	82
'Circe' 4, l. 49, 287	on all fours	Antoine se met à quatre pattes sur la table, et beugle comme un taureau	50	82
		une Femme toute nue, – à quatre pattes comme une bête	167	198
'Circe' 6, l. 20, 297	Jesus, S of Pantherus & parfumeuse	sa mère, la parfumeuse, s'est livrée à Pantherus, un soldat romain, sur des gerbes de maïs, un soir de moisson.	88	119
'Circe' 6, l. 21, 297	fille d'Israel qui se donna aux porcs	cette fille d'Israël qui s'abandonnait aux boucs	107	137
'Circe' 6, l. 26, 297	quel homme? juste, hein?	quel homme juste ! hein?	112	143
'Circe' 6, l. 55, 298	eleph. bull to knees	l'éléphant plie les genoux	52	83
'Circe' 6, l. 57, 298	Roman wives prefer eunuchs	Un eunuque!	83	113

'Circe' 6, l. 82, 299	Agamemnon du ciel	Agamemnon du ciel!	158	189
'Circe' 6, l. 83, 299	Anthony says creed	il répète le symbole de Jérusalem	157	188–9
'Circe' 7, l. 9, 302	Waxworks horrors	un groupe en cire	47	79
		un cadavre de cire	149	182
'Circe' 10, l. 86, 322	waxworks	les aïeux de cire peinte	169	200
'Circe' 8, l. 105, 310	S. Anthony	passim	passim	passim
'Circe' 8, l. 109, 310	heretic catechism	*épisode des hérésiarques*	71–104 (and passim)	101–133 (and passim)
'Circe' 9, l. 154, 317	Venus, Juno, Ceres	Vénus-Anadyomène	155	187
		Vénus	163, 165	195, 197
		Junon	158	190
		Cérès	162	193
'Circe' 10, l. 69, 322	Arius	Arius	86–7	116–7
'Circe' 10, l. 80, 322	caparisoned horse	Un éléphant blanc, caparaçonné d'un filet d'or	52	83
'Circe' 11, l. 56, 326	hallucination	si bien que l'hallucination le reprenant	95	125
'Circe' 13, l. 23, 333	heresiarchus	hérésiarques	86, 88, 104	116, 119, 134
'Circe' 14, l. 90, 338	wash in blood	Le sang lave tout	146	179
'Circe' 15, l. 28, 342	hyena!	une hyène en reniflant, avance la gueule!	182	214

Bibliography

1. PRIMARY SOURCES

(a) Manuscripts

Joyce, James, 'Notebook with Accounts, Quotations, Book Lists, etc. 1903–1904' ('Paris and Pola Commonplace Book: 1903–1904'), 'Joyce Papers 2002', Dublin, National Library of Ireland, NLI MS 36,639/2/A.

—— '"Cyclops": Partial Draft', 'Joyce Papers 2002', Dublin, National Library of Ireland, NLI MS 36,639/10.

—— Letters to Ezra Pound, 'Ezra Pound Papers', Yale University, Beinecke Rare Book and Manuscript Library, YCAL MSS 43, Box 26, Folders 1,112–14.

—— Quotation from Ezra Pound's essay '*Ulysses*' for the 'Advance Press Notice' in Joyce's hand, with notation by Sylvia Beach, n.d. [1921], University of Buffalo, The State University of New York, The Poetry Collection, PCMS-0020, James Joyce Collection, 1900–1959, Box XVIII (Miscellaneous Material Related to Joyce's Works), E.1 (*Ulysses*: The First Edition), Folder 6.

(b) Printed texts

• *Flaubert*

Flaubert, Gustave, *Premières Oeuvres*, 4 vols (Paris: Fasquelle, 1913–19).

—— *Madame Bovary* (1857) (Paris: Bibliothèque-Charpentier, 1874).

—— *Madame Bovary* (1857) (Paris: Bibliothèque-Charpentier, 1900).

—— *Madame Bovary* (1857) (Paris: Bibliothèque-Charpentier, 1903).

—— *Madame Bovary* (1857) (Paris: Louis Conard, 1910).

—— *Madame Bovary* (1857) (Paris: Gallimard, 1972).

—— *Salammbô* (1862) (Paris: Bibliothèque Charpentier, 1897).

—— *Salammbô* (1862) (Paris: Bibliothèque Charpentier, 1914).

—— *Salammbô* (1862) (Paris: Garnier-Flammarion, 1964).

—— *L'Éducation sentimentale* (1869) (Paris: Bibliothèque-Charpentier, 1901).

—— *L'Éducation sentimentale* (1869) (Paris: Gallimard, 1965).

—— *La première Tentation de saint Antoine*, ed. Louis Bertrand (Paris: Charpentier, 1908).

—— *La Tentation de saint Antoine* (1874) (Paris: Louis Conard, 1910).

—— *La Tentation de saint Antoine* (1874) (Paris: Fasquelle, 1913).

—— *La Tentation de saint Antoine* (1874) (London: J. M. Dent, and Paris: G. Crès, 1913).

—— *La Tentation de saint Antoine* (1874) (Paris: Pocket, 1999).

—— *Trois Contes* (Paris: G. Charpentier, 1877).

—— *Trois Contes* (1877) (Paris: Bibliothèque-Charpentier, 1899).

—— *Trois Contes* (1877) (Paris: Gallimard, 1973).

—— *Bouvard et Pécuchet,* with the *Dictionnaire des Idées Reçues* (1881) (Paris: Flammarion, 1999).

—— *Oeuvres complètes,* 18 vols (Paris: Louis Conard, 1910).

—— *Oeuvres,* ed. Albert Thibaudet and René Dumesnil, 2 vols (Paris: Gallimard, 1951–2).

—— *Oeuvres complètes,* 16 vols (Paris: Club de l'honnête homme, 1971–5).

—— *Correspondance,* 4 vols (Paris: Bibliothèque-Charpentier, 1891–3).

—— *Correspondance,* ed. Jean Bruneau, vol. 1 (Paris: Gallimard, 1973).

—— *Correspondance,* ed. Jean Bruneau, vol. 2 (Paris: Gallimard, 1980).

—— *Correspondance,* ed. Jean Bruneau, vol. 3 (Paris: Gallimard, 1991).

—— *Correspondance,* ed. Jean Bruneau, vol. 4 (Paris: Gallimard, 1998).

—— *Correspondance,* ed. Jean Bruneau and Yvan Leclerc, vol. 5 (Paris: Gallimard, 2007).

—— and George Sand, *Gustave Flaubert-George Sand: Correspondance,* ed. Alphonse Jacobs (Paris: Flammarion, 1981).

—— *Carnets de Travail,* ed. Pierre-Marc de Biasi (Paris: Balland, 1988).

English translations of Flaubert's works

—— *Madame Bovary,* trans. Eleanor Marx-Aveling (London: Vizetelly, 1886).

—— *Madame Bovary,* trans. Henry Blanchamp (London: Greening, [n.d]).

—— *Madame Bovary,* trans. Margaret Mauldon (Oxford: Oxford University Press, 2004).

—— *A Sentimental Education,* trans. Douglas Parmée (Oxford: Oxford University Press, 2008).

—— *Salammbo,* trans. A. J. Krailsheimer (London: Penguin, 1977).

—— *The Temptation of St Antony,* trans. Kitty Mrosovsky (Harmondsworth: Penguin, 1980).

—— *Three Tales,* trans. A. J. Krailsheimer (Oxford: Oxford University Press, 1991).

—— *Bouvard and Pécuchet,* trans. D. F. Hannigan (London: Nichols, 1896).

—— *Bouvard and Pécuchet,* with the *Dictionary of Received Ideas,* trans. A. J. Krailsheimer (Harmondsworth: Penguin, 1977).

English translations of Flaubert's letters

—— *The Letters of Gustave Flaubert 1830–1857,* trans. Francis Steegmuller (London: Faber and Faber, 1981).

—— *The Letters of Gustave Flaubert 1857–1880,* trans. Francis Steegmuller (London: Faber and Faber, 1984).

—— *Selected Letters,* trans. Geoffrey Wall (Harmondsworth: Penguin, 1997).

• *Joyce*

Joyce, James, *Occasional, Critical, and Political Writing,* ed. Kevin Barry (Oxford: Oxford University Press, 2000):

'Royal Hibernian Academy "Ecce Homo"' (written 1899), 17–22.

'Drama and Life' (written January 1900), 23–9.

'The Day of the Rabblement' (privately printed 1901), 50–2.

'James Clarence Mangan (1902)', 53–60 (first pub. in *St Stephens* 1/6, May 1902, 116–18).

'An Irish Poet', 61–3 (first pub. in *Daily Express*, 11 December 1902).

'The Bruno Philosophy', 93–4 (first pub. in *Daily Express*, 30 October 1903).

'Ireland: Island of Saints and Sages' (written 1907), 108–26.

'A Curious History', 160–2 (first pub. in *Sinn Féin*, 2 September 1911).

'The Universal Literary Influence of the Renaissance' (written 1912), 187–90.

—— *The Critical Writings of James Joyce*, ed. Ellsworth Mason and Richard Ellmann (London: Faber and Faber, 1959).

—— *Poems and Shorter Writings*, ed. Richard Ellmann, A. Walton Litz, and John Whittier-Ferguson (London: Faber and Faber, 2001).

—— *Dubliners* (1914) (Harmondsworth: Penguin Classics, 2000).

—— *Dubliners* (1914), ed. Jeri Johnson (Oxford: Oxford University Press, 2000).

—— *Stephen Hero*, ed. Theodore Spencer (1944), revd edn incorporating additional manuscript pages from Yale and Cornell University libraries, ed. John J. Slocum and Herbert Cahoon (New York: New Directions Publishing Corporation, 1969).

—— *A Portrait of the Artist as a Young Man* (1916), ed. Jeri Johnson (Oxford: Oxford University Press, 2000).

—— *Exiles* (1918) (London: Jonathan Cape, 1952).

—— *Ulysses* (1922), ed. Hans Walter Gabler with Wolfhard Steppe and Claus Melchior (New York: Random House, 1986).

—— *Ulysses* (1922), ed. Jeri Johnson (Oxford: Oxford University Press, 1993).

—— *Ulysses* (1922) (New York: Random House, 1934).

—— *Ulysses* (1922) (New York: The Modern Library, 1961).

—— *Finnegans Wake* (1939) (London: Faber and Faber, 1975).

—— *Oeuvres*, ed. Jacques Aubert, 2 vols (Paris: Gallimard, 1982–95).

—— *Letters of James Joyce*, ed. Stuart Gilbert (London: Faber and Faber, 1957).

—— *Letters of James Joyce*, vol. 2, ed. Richard Ellmann (London: Faber and Faber, 1966).

—— *Letters of James Joyce*, vol. 3, ed. Richard Ellmann (London: Faber and Faber, 1966).

—— *Selected Letters of James Joyce*, ed. Richard Ellmann (London: Faber and Faber, 1975).

—— *The Workshop of Daedalus: James Joyce and the Raw Materials for 'A Portrait of the Artist as a Young Man'*, ed. Robert Scholes and Richard M. Kain (Evanston: Northwestern University Press, 1965).

—— *The James Joyce Archive*, ed. Michael Groden et al., 63 vols (New York and London: Garland, 1977–9):

JJA 2: Notes, Criticism, Translations, and Miscellaneous Writings.

JJA 7: A Portrait of the Artist as a Young Man: Epiphanies, Notes, Manuscripts, and Typescripts.

JJA 8: A Portrait of the Artist as a Young Man: A Facsimile of the Manuscript Fragments of *Stephen Hero*.

JJA 11: Exiles: Notes, Manuscripts, and Proofs.

JJA 13: Ulysses: 'Wandering Rocks' through 'Nausicaa', Manuscripts and Typescripts.

JJA 30: Finnegans Wake: Buffalo Notebooks VI.B.5–VI.B.8.

——*The 'Finnegans Wake' Notebooks at Buffalo*, ed. Vincent Deane, Daniel Ferrer, and Geert Lernout (Turnhout: Brepols, 2001–):
Notebook VI.B.5 (2004).

2. SECONDARY SOURCES

Adams, Robert M., 'Light on Joyce's *Exiles*? A New MS, a Curious Analogue, and Some Speculations', *Studies in Bibliography*, vol. XVII (1964), 83–105.

Améry, Jean, *Charles Bovary, médecin de campagne: portrait d'un homme simple*, trans. Françoise Wuilmart (Paris: Actes Sud, 1991).

'Aramis' (pseudonym), 'The Scandal of *Ulysses*', *Sporting Times*, 1 April 1922, 4 (repr. in *James Joyce: The Critical Heritage*, 2 vols, ed. Robert H. Deming [London: Routledge and Kegan Paul, 1970], vol. 1, 192–4).

Atherton, James, *The Books at the Wake: A Study of Literary Allusions in James Joyce's 'Finnegans Wake'*, 3rd edn (London: Faber and Faber, 1959).

Attridge, Derek (ed.), *The Cambridge Companion to James Joyce*, 2nd edn (Cambridge: Cambridge University Press, 2004).

Aubert, Jacques, *The Aesthetics of James Joyce* (Baltimore: Johns Hopkins University Press, 1992).

Auden, W. H., *The Enchafèd Flood* (London: Faber and Faber, 1951).

Bakhtin, Mikhail, 'Discourse in the Novel', in Mikhail Bakhtin, *The Dialogic Imagination: Four Essays*, trans. C. Emerson and M. Holquist, ed. M. Holquist (Austin: University of Texas Press, 1981) 259–422.

Baldick, Chris, *The Oxford Dictionary of Literary Terms*, 3rd edn (Oxford: Oxford University Press, 2008).

Barnes, Julian, 'The Cost of Conscientious Literature', in Julian Barnes, *Something to Declare* (London: Picador, 2002), 251–67 (first pub. as 'The Thunderous Presence of *l'homme-plume*', *Times Literary Supplement*, 7–13 October 1988, 1,090–2).

Baron, Scarlett, 'Gnomonic Structures: Flaubert's *Trois Contes* and Joyce's *Dubliners*', *Papers on Joyce*, no. 13, 2007, 43–60.

—— 'Joyce's "holiday wisdom": "Gustave Flaubert can rest having made me"', *Genetic Joyce Studies*, issue 7, Spring 2007, http://www.geneticjoycestudies.org/ GJS7/GJS7baron.html (July 2011).

—— 'Flaubert, Joyce – Vision, Photography, Cinema', *Modern Fiction Studies*, vol. 54, no. 4 (Winter 2008) 689–714.

Baron, Scarlett, "'Will you be as gods": Joyce Translating Flaubert', *James Joyce Quarterly*, vol. 47, no. 4 (Summer 2010).

—— 'Invisible Author-Gods: Flaubert, Joyce, and Intertextual Theory', special issue of *Dix Neuf, Journal of the Society of Dix-Neuviémistes*, ed. Mary Orr, Anne Green, and Timothy Unwin, vol. 15, no. 1, April 2011, 92–103.

——'Radical Intertextuality: From *Bouvard et Pécuchet* to *Finnegans Wake*', in *James Joyce and the Nineteenth-Century French Novel*, ed. Finn Fordham and Rita Sakr, *European Joyce Studies* 19 (Amsterdam and New York: Rodopi, 2011), 128–45.

Barthes, Roland, *Mythologies* (Paris: Éditions du Seuil, 1957).

—— *Mythologies*, trans. Annette Lavers (London: Jonathan Cape, 1972).

—— *S/Z* (Paris: Editions du Seuil, 1970).

—— *S/Z*, trans. Richard Miller (London: Jonathan Cape, 1975).

—— *Image Music Text*, ed. and trans. Stephen Heath (London: Fontana, 1977): 'The Death of the Author', 142–8.

'From Work to Text', 155–64.

—— *Le Bruissement de la langue* (Paris: Éditions du Seuil, 1984): 'La Mort de l'auteur', 63–9 (first pub. in *Mantéia*, vol. 5, no. 4 [1968], 12–17). 'De l'oeuvre au texte', 71–80 (first pub. in *Revue d'esthétique* 3 [1971], 225–32).

—— and Maurice Nadeau, *Sur la littérature* (Grenoble: Presses universitaires de Grenoble, 1980).

Baxandall, Michael, *Patterns of Intention: On the Historical Explanation of Pictures* (New Haven and London: Yale University Press, 1985).

Bennett, Arnold, 'James Joyce's *Ulysses*', in *Outlook*, 29 April 1922, 337–9 (repr. in *James Joyce: The Critical Heritage*, 2 vols, ed. Robert H. Deming [London: Routledge and Kegan Paul, 1970], vol. 1, 219–22).

Berg, William J., Michel Grimaud, and George Moskos (eds.), 'The Family Idiot: Julian and Gustave', in *Saint/Oedipus: Psychocritical Approaches to Flaubert's Art* (Ithaca and London: Cornell University Press, 1982), 176–202.

Bertrand, Louis, 'Les Carnets de Gustave Flaubert', *Revue des Deux Mondes*, vol. 58 (15 juillet 1910), 371–92.

Billot, Antoine, *Monsieur Bovary* (Paris: Gallimard, 2006).

Bishop, John, *Joyce's Book of the Dark: 'Finnegans Wake'* (Madison: University of Wisconsin Press, 1986).

Block, Haskell M., 'Théorie et technique du roman chez Flaubert et James Joyce', unpublished doctoral thesis, University of Paris, Sorbonne, 1948.

—— 'Flaubert, Yeats, and the National Library', *Modern Language Notes*, vol. 67, no. 1 (January 1952), 55–6.

—— 'Theory of Language in Gustave Flaubert and James Joyce', *Revue de Littérature Comparée*, xxxv (1961), 197–206.

Bloom, Harold, *The Anxiety of Influence: A Theory of Poetry* (New York: Oxford University Press, 1973).

Borges, Jorge Luis, *Fictions* (1944) (London: Penguin Books, 2000).

Bourget, Paul, 'Gustave Flaubert', in *Studies in European Literature, being the Taylorian Lectures, 1889–1899* (Oxford: Clarendon Press, 1900), 253–74.

Boyd, Ernest, 'Adult or Infantile Censorship?', *The Dial*, 70: 4 (April 1921), 381–5.

Brandes, Georg, *Main Currents in Nineteenth-Century Literature*, English trans., 4 vols (London: William Heinemann, 1901–5).

—— *Creative Spirits of the Nineteenth Century*, trans. Rasmus B. Anderson (London: T. Fisher Unwin, 1924).

Brombert, Victor, *The Novels of Flaubert: A Study of Themes and Techniques* (Princeton: Princeton University Press, 1966).

Brown, Richard, *James Joyce and Sexuality* (Cambridge: Cambridge University Press, 1985).

—— 'Shifting Sexual Centres: Joyce and Flaubert', in *'Scribble' 2: Joyce et Flaubert*, ed. Claude Jacquet and André Topia (Paris: Minard, 1990), 65–84.

—— ' "Everything" in "Circe" ', in *Reading Joyce's 'Circe'*, ed. Andrew Gibson, *European Joyce Studies* 3 (Amsterdam: Rodopi, 1994), 222–40.

Brunazzi, Elizabeth, 'The Autogenetic Text in Flaubert's *La Tentation de saint Antoine* and Joyce's *Ulysses*', doctoral thesis, Princeton University (Ann Arbor: U.M.I. Research Press, 1988).

Budgen, Frank, *James Joyce and the Making of 'Ulysses'* (London: Grayson and Grayson, 1934).

Bush, Ronald, 'James Joyce, Eleanor Marx, and the Future of Modernism', in *The Future of Modernism*, ed. Hugh Witemeyer (Ann Arbor: University of Michigan Press, 1997), 49–77.

—— 'Joyce's Modernisms', in *Palgrave Advances in James Joyce Studies*, ed. Jean-Michel Rabaté (Basingstoke and New York: Palgrave Macmillan, 2004), 10–38.

Camerani, Marco, *Joyce e il cinema delle origini: 'Circe'* (Firenze: Cadmo, 2008).

Cixous, Hélène, 'At Circe's, or the Self-Opener', *boundary 2*, vol. 3, no. 2 (Winter 1975), 387–97.

—— *The Exile of James Joyce*, trans. Sally A. Purcell (London: John Calden, 1976).

—— 'Joyce: The (R)use of Writing', in *Post-Structuralist Joyce*, ed. Derek Attridge and Daniel Ferrer (Cambridge: Cambridge University Press, 1984), 15–30.

Clayton, Jay, and Eric Rothstein, 'Figures in the Corpus: Theories of Influence and Intertextuality', in *Influence and Intertextuality in Literary History*, ed. Jay Clayton and Eric Rothstein (Madison: The University of Wisconsin Press, 1991), 3–36.

Cohn, Dorrit, *Transparent Minds: Narrative Modes for Presenting Consciousness in Fiction* (Princeton: Princeton University Press, 1978).

Colet, Louise, 'Souvenirs', http://flaubert.univ-rouen.fr/correspondance/conard/autour/mantes.html (July 2011).

Compagnon, Antoine, *La Seconde Main: ou Le Travail de la citation* (Paris: Éditions du Seuil, 1979).

Connolly, Cyril, *100 Key Books of the Modern Movement from England, France, and America 1880–1950* (London: Allison & Busby, 1986).

Connolly, Thomas E., *The Personal Library of James Joyce: A Descriptive Bibliography* (Buffalo: University of Buffalo, 1957).

Crispi, Luca, 'The Mechanics of Creativity: A Genetic Study of *Finnegans Wake*, II.2', unpublished doctoral thesis, SUNY-Buffalo, 2001.

—— 'Storiella as She Was Wryt: *Chapter II.2*', in *How Joyce Wrote Finnegans Wake*, 214–49.

—— and Slote, Sam (eds), *How Joyce Wrote 'Finnegans Wake': A Chapter-by-Chapter Genetic Guide* (Madison: University of Wisconsin Press, 2007).

Cross, Richard K., *Flaubert and Joyce: The Rite of Fiction* (Princeton: Princeton University Press, 1971).

Culler, Jonathan, *Flaubert: The Uses of Uncertainty* (London: Paul Elek, 1974).

—— 'Presupposition and Intertextuality', in *The Pursuit of Signs: Semiotics, Literature, Deconstruction* (1981), augmented edn (New York and Ithaca: Cornell University Press, 2002), 100–18.

Curran, Constantine, *James Joyce Remembered* (London: Oxford University Press, 1968).

Danger, Pierre, *Sensations et objets dans le roman de Flaubert* (Paris: A. Colin, 1973).

Darwin, Charles, *On the Origin of Species*, ed. Gillian Beer (Oxford: Oxford University Press, 2008).

Daunais, Isabelle, *Flaubert et la scénographie romanesque* (Paris: Nizet, 1993).

D'Aurevilly, Jules Barbey, review of *Bouvard et Pécuchet*, *Le Constitutionnel*, 10 Mai 1881 (partially repr. in Gustave Flaubert, *Bouvard et Pécuchet*, with the *Dictionnaire des Idées Reçues* [Paris: Flammarion, 1999], 452–4).

Dean, Tim, 'Paring His Fingernails: Homosexuality and Joyce's Impersonalist Aesthetic', in *Quare Joyce*, ed. Joseph Valente (Ann Arbor: University of Michigan Press, 1998), 241–72.

Deane, Seamus, Introduction, *Finnegans Wake* (London: Penguin Classics, 2000), vii-l.

Deane, Vincent, 'Editorial', *A 'Finnegans Wake' Circular*, vol. 1, no. 1 (1985), 1.

De Banville, Théodore, '*Trois Contes* par Gustave Flaubert', *Le National*, 14 May 1877.

De Biasi, Pierre-Marc 'L'élaboration du problématique dans "La Légende de saint Julien l'Hospitalier"', in *Flaubert à l'oeuvre* (Paris: Flammarion, 1980), 69–102.

—— (ed.), Gustave Flaubert, *Carnets de Travail* (Paris: Balland, 1988).

Debray-Genette, Raymonde, 'Du mode narratif dans les *Trois Contes*', in *Travail de Flaubert*, ed. Gérard Genette and Tzvetan Todorov (Paris: Seuil, 1983), 135–65 (first pub. in *Littérature*, no. 2 [May 1971], 39–62).

De Bujanda, J. M., with Marcella Richter (eds), *Index Librorum Prohibitorum, 1600–1966* (Montréal: Médiaspaul, 2002).

De Goncourt, Edmond, *Journal: Mémoires de la vie littéraire*, 22 vols (Monaco: Imprimerie nationale de Monaco, 1956–8), vol. 14 (1885–7).

De Kock, Paul, *Le Cocu* (1813) (Paris: Gustave Barba, 1931).

De Maupassant, Guy, *Oeuvres poétiques complètes: Des Vers et autres poèmes* (1880), ed. Emmanuel Vincent (Rouen: Publications de l'Université de Rouen, 2001).

—— review of *Bouvard et Pécuchet*, *Le Gaulois*, 6 April 1881 (repr. in *Bouvard et Pécuchet, Dictionnaire des Idées Reçues* [Paris: Flammarion, 1999], 444–8).

—— *Pierre et Jean* (1888) (Paris: Flammarion, 1992).

—— *Pierre et Jean* (1888), trans. Julie Mead (Oxford: Oxford University Press, 2001).

Deming, Robert H. (ed.), *James Joyce: The Critical Heritage*, 2 vols (London: Routledge and Kegan Paul, 1970).

Deppman, Jed, 'A Chapter in Composition: *Chapter II.4*', in *How Joyce Wrote 'Finnegans Wake': A Chapter-by-Chapter Genetic Guide*, ed. Luca Crispi and Sam Slote (Madison: University of Wisconsin Press, 2007), 304–46.

Derrida, Jacques, *De la grammatologie* (Paris: Éditions de Minuit, 1967).

—— *L'écriture et la différence* (Paris: Éditions du Seuil, 1967).

Descharmes, René, *Flaubert, sa vie, son caractère et ses idées, avant 1857* (Paris: Librairie des Amateurs, 1909).

—— *Autour de 'Bouvard et Pécuchet'* (Paris: Librairie de France, 1921).

De Staël, Madame, 'De l'esprit des traductions', in *Oeuvres complètes de Madame la baronne de Staël-Holstein*, 2 vols (Paris: F. Didot, and Strasbourg: Treuttel et Würtz, 1836), vol. 2, 294–7 (first pub. in *Biblioteca Italiana*, Issue 1 [January 1816]).

Downes, Gareth, 'James Joyce, Catholicism, and Heresy: With Specific Reference to Giordano Bruno', unpublished doctoral thesis, University of St Andrews, 2001.

—— 'The Heretical *Auctoritas* of Giordano Bruno', *Joyce Studies Annual* (2003), 37–73.

Du Camp, Maxime, *Souvenirs littéraires*, 2 vols (Paris: Hachette et Cie, 1882–3).

Dujardin, Édouard, *Les Lauriers sont coupés* (1888) (Paris: Albert Messein, 1925).

Dumas, Alexandre, *The Count of Monte Cristo* (1844–5), trans. Robin Buss (London: Penguin Classics, 2003).

Dumesnil, René, Introduction, *Bouvard et Pécuchet*, in Gustave Flaubert, *Oeuvres*, 2 vols (Paris: Gallimard, 1951–2), ed. Albert Thibaudet and René Dumesnil, vol. 2, 695–710.

Eco, Umberto, *The Name of the Rose* (1980), trans. William Weaver (London: Vintage, 2004).

Eisenstein, Sergei, 'Through Theatre to Cinema', in *Film Form: Essays in Film Theory*, ed. and trans. Jay Leyda (London: Dennis Dobson, 1949), 3–17 (first pub. in Russian in *Sovyet skoye kino* [November–December 1934], and subsequently in *Theatre Arts Monthly*, vol. 20, no. 9 [September 1936], 735–47).

Ellmann, Maud, 'Polytropic Man: Paternity, Identity, and Naming in *The Odyssey* and *A Portrait of the Artist as a Young Man*', in *James Joyce: New Perspectives*, ed. Colin MacCabe (Brighton: Harvester Press, 1982), 73–104.

Ellmann, Richard, *James Joyce* (New York: Oxford University Press, 1959).

—— *Ulysses on the Liffey* (London: Faber and Faber, 1972).

—— *The Consciousness of Joyce* (London: Faber and Faber, 1977).

—— *James Joyce*, revd. edn (Oxford: Oxford University Press, 1982).

—— *Oscar Wilde* (New York: Alfred A. Knopf, 1988).

Felman, Shoshana, 'Flaubert's Signature: *The Legend of Saint Julian the Hospitable*', trans. Brian Massumi et al., in *Flaubert and Postmodernism*, ed. Naomi Schor and Henry F. Majewski (Lincoln and London: University of Nebraska Press, 1984), 46–75.

Ferrer, Daniel, 'Peut-on parler de métalepse génétique?' in *Métalepses: Entorses au pacte de la représentation*, ed. John Pier and Jean-Marie Schaffer (Paris: Éditions de l'EHESS, 2005), 109–19.

Ford, Jane, 'James Joyce's Trieste Library: Some Notes on its Use', in *Joyce at Texas: Essays on the James Joyce Materials at the Humanities Research Centre*, ed. Dave Oliphant and Thomas Zigal (Austin: The University of Texas at Austin, 1983), 141–57.

Fordham, Finn, *Lots of Fun at 'Finnegans Wake': Unravelling Universals* (Oxford: Oxford University Press, 2007).

Foster, R. F., *Modern Ireland, 1600–1972* (Harmondsworth: Penguin Press, 1988).

Foucault, Michel, *La Bibliothèque fantastique: A propos de 'La Tentation de saint Antoine' de Gustave Flaubert* (Bruxelles: La Lettre volée, 1995) (first pub. in *Les Cahiers Renault-Barrault*, no. 59, March 1967).

—— 'Qu'est-ce qu'un auteur?', in *Dits et Écrits 1954–1988*, 4 vols (Paris: Gallimard, 1994), ed. Daniel Defert, François Ewald with Jacques Lagrange, vol. 1, 789–820 (first given as a talk at the *Société française de philosophie* and published in its *Bulletin de la Société française de philosophie*, no. 3 [July–September 1969], 73–104, before being revised for translation into English).

—— 'What is an Author?', in *Textual Strategies, Perspectives in Post-Structuralist Criticism*, ed. Josué V. Harari (London: Cornell University Press, 1979), 141–60.

Gabler, Hans Walter, 'Toward a Critical Text of James Joyce's *A Portrait of the Artist as a Young Man*', in *Studies in Bibliography* 27 (1974), 1–53.

—— 'The Seven Lost Years of *A Portrait of the Artist as a Young Man*', in *Approaches to Joyce's 'Portrait': Ten Essays*, ed. Thomas F. Staley and Bernard Benstock (Pittsburg: University of Pittsburg Press, 1976), 25–60.

—— Preface, *The James Joyce Archive*, ed. Michael Groden et al., 63 vols. (New York and London: Garland, 1977–9), vol. 7, xxiii–xxv.

Gabler, Hans Walter, (ed.), with Wolfhard Steppe and Claus Melchior, *Ulysses* (New York: Random House, 1986).

—— Introduction, James Joyce, *A Portrait of the Artist as a Young Man*, ed. Hans Walter Gabler with Walter Hettche (Garland: New York and London, 1993), 1–18.

—— *The Rocky Road to 'Ulysses'* (Dublin: National Library of Ireland, 2004).

Garrett, Peter, *Scene and Symbol from George Eliot to James Joyce* (Yale: Yale University Press, 1969).

Genette, Gérard, 'Structuralisme et critique littéraire', in *Figures I* (Paris: Seuil, 1966), 45–70 (first pub. in *L'Arc*, no. 26 [1965], 30–44).

—— *Palimpsestes: La Littérature du second degré* (Paris: Éditions du Seuil, 1982).

Gide, André, *Journal, 1889–1939* (Paris: Gallimard, 1948).

Gifford, Don, with Robert J. Seidman, *'Ulysses' Annotated: Notes for James Joyce's 'Ulysses'*, 2nd edn (Berkeley/Los Angeles, and London: University of California Press, 1988).

Gilbert, Stuart, *James Joyce's 'Ulysses': A Study* (1930) (New York: Vintage Books, 1955).

—— *Reflections on James Joyce: Stuart Gilbert's Paris Journal*, ed. Thomas F. Staley and Randolph Lewis (Austin: University of Texas Press, 1993).

Gillespie, Michael Patrick, *Inverted Volumes Improperly Arranged: James Joyce and his Trieste Library* (Ann Arbor: UMI Research Press, 1983).

—— with Erik Bradford Stocker, *James Joyce's Trieste Library: A Catalogue of Materials at the Harry Ransom Humanities Research Centre*, ed. Dave Oliphant (Austin: Harry Ransom Humanities Research Centre, 1986).

Glasheen, Adaline, *Third Census of 'Finnegans Wake': An Index of the Characters and their Roles* (Berkeley: University of California Press, 1977).

Grimaldi, Laura, *Monsieur Bovary*, trans. (into French from Italian) Geneviève Leibrich (Paris: Métailié, 1995).

Groden, Michael, '"Cyclops" in Progress, 1919', *James Joyce Quarterly*, vol. 12, nos 1 and 2 (Fall 1974 and Winter 1975), 123–68.

—— 'Joyce at Work on "Cyclops": Toward a Biography of "*Ulysses*"', *James Joyce Quarterly*, vol. 44, no. 2 (Winter 2007), 217–45.

Gwynn, Stephen, 'Modern Irish Literature', *Manchester Guardian*, 15 March 1923, 38–9 (repr. in *James Joyce: The Critical Heritage*, 2 vols, ed. Robert H. Deming [London: Routledge and Kegan Paul, 1970], vol. 1, 299–301).

Hall, H. S., and Stevens, F. H., *A Textbook of Euclid's Elements for the Use of Schools* (1887) (London: Macmillan, 1903).

Hayman, David, *Joyce et Mallarmé*, 2 vols (Paris: Lettres Modernes, 1956).

—— '*A Portrait of the Artist as a Young Man* and *L'Éducation sentimentale*: The Structural Affinities', *Orbis Litterarum* XIX, no. 4 (1964), 161–75.

—— Preface, *The James Joyce Archive*, ed. Michael Groden et al., 63 vols. (New York and London Garland, 1977–9), vol. 30, vii–xxviii.

Hayman, David, 'Nodality and the Infrastructure of *Finnegans Wake*', *James Joyce Quarterly*, vol. 16, no. 2 (Fall 1978–Winter 1979), 135–49.

—— 'Toward a Postflaubertian Joyce', in *'Scribble' 2: Joyce et Flaubert*, ed. Claude Jacquet and André Topia (Paris: Minard, 1990), 13–32.

—— 'Genetic Criticism and Joyce: An Introduction', in *Probes: Genetic Studies in Joyce*, ed. David Hayman and Sam Slote, *European Joyce Studies* 5 (Amsterdam: Rodopi, 1995), 3–18.

—— and Slote, Sam (eds), *Probes: Genetic Studies in Joyce*, in *European Joyce Studies* 5 (Amsterdam: Rodopi, 1995).

Heath, Stephen, (under the pseudonym 'Cleanth Peters'), 'Structuration of the Novel-Text', in *Signs of the Times: Introductory Readings in Textual Semiotics*, ed. Stephen Heath, Colin MacCabe, and Christopher Prendergast (Cambridge: Granta, 1971), 52–78.

—— *Madame Bovary* (Cambridge: Cambridge University Press, 1992).

Herring, Philip, *Joyce's 'Ulysses' Notesheets in the British Museum* (Charlottesville: University Press of Virginia, 1972).

Herschberg-Pierrot, Anne, 'Les Dossiers de *Bouvard et Pécuchet*', *The Romanic Review*, vol. 86, no. 3 (1 May 1995), 537–49.

Heywood, C., 'Flaubert, Miss Braddon, and George Moore', *Comparative Literature*, vol. 12, no. 2 (Spring 1960), 151–8.

Hill, W. H., *Elements of Philosophy Comprising Logic and Ontology or General Metaphysics* (Baltimore: John Murphy, and London: R. Washburne, 1873).

Huss, Roger, 'Some Anomalous Uses of the Imperfect and the Status of Action in Flaubert', *French Studies* 31 (1977), 139–48.

Irwin, William, 'Against Intertextuality', *Philosophy and Literature*, 28 (2004), 227–42.

Jacquet, Claude, and André Topia (eds), *'Scribble' 2: Joyce et Flaubert* (Paris: Minard, 1990).

—— 'Joyce et Flaubert', in *'Scribble' 2* (1990), 5–12.

James, Henry, 'Gustave Flaubert', *Macmillan's Magazine*, vol. 67, no. 401 (March 1893), 332–43.

Jameson, Fredric, *'Ulysses* in History', in *James Joyce and Modern Literature*, ed. W. J. McCormack and Alistair Stead (London: Routledge and Kegan Paul, 1982), 126–41.

Johnson, Jeri, Introduction, *Dubliners* (1914), ed. Jeri Johnson (Oxford: Oxford University Press, 2000), vii–xl.

—— 'Joyce and Feminism', in *The Cambridge Companion to James Joyce*, ed. Derek Attridge, 2nd edn (Cambridge: Cambridge University Press, 2004), 196–212.

Joyce, Stanislaus, *My Brother's Keeper* (London: Faber and Faber, 1958).

Kenner, Hugh, *Dublin's Joyce* (London: Chatto and Windus, 1955).

—— *Flaubert, Joyce, and Beckett: The Stoic Comedians* (London: W. H. Allen, 1964).

Kenner, Hugh, *Joyce's Voices* (London: Faber and Faber, 1978).

—— *Ulysses* (London: George Allen & Unwin, 1980).

Kershner, R. Brandon, 'Dialogical and Intertextual Joyce', in *Palgrave Advances in James Joyce Studies*, ed. Jean-Michel Rabaté (Basingstoke and New York: Palgrave Macmillan, 2004), 183–202.

Kockelmans, Joseph J., *Heidegger on Art and Art Works* (Dordrecht and Boston: M. Nijhoff, 1995).

Kristeva, Julia, *Sémeiótiké: Recherches pour une sémanalyse* (Paris: Éditions du Seuil, 1969):

'Le Mot, le dialogue et le roman', 82–112 (dated 1966, first pub. as 'Bakhtine, le mot, le dialogue, le roman', in *Critique* XXIII, 239 [April 1967], 438–65).

'Poésie et Négativité', 185–216 (first pub. in *L'Homme* VIII, 2 [April–June 1968], 36–63).

—— *La Révolution du langage poétique: l'avant-garde à la fin du XIXe siècle: Lautréamont et Mallarmé* (Paris: Éditions du Seuil, 1974).

—— 'Word, Dialogue, and Novel', *Desire in Language: A Semiotic Approach to Literature and Art*, ed. Leon S. Roudiez, trans. Thomas Gora, Alice Jardine, and Leon S. Roudiez (New York: Columbia University Press, 1980), 64–91.

—— *Revolution in Poetic Language*, trans. Margaret Walker (New York: Columbia University Press, 1984).

Landuyt, Ingeborg, 'Cain-Ham-(Shem)-Esau-Jim the Penman: *Chapter I.7*', in *How Joyce Wrote 'Finnegans Wake': A Chapter-by-Chapter Genetic Guide*, ed. Luca Crispi and Sam Slote (Madison: University of Wisconsin Press, 2007), 142–62.

—— and Geert Lernout, 'Joyce's Sources: *Les grands fleuves historiques*', in *Joyce Studies Annual*, vol. 6 (Summer 1995), 99–138.

Larbaud, Valery, Preface to Édouard Dujardin, *Les Lauriers sont coupés* (Paris: Albert Messein, 1925), 5–16.

—— *Oeuvres*, ed. Jean-Aubry and Robert Mallet (Paris: Gallimard, 1957).

Lawrence, Karen, 'Style and Narrative in the "Ithaca" Chapter of Joyce's *Ulysses*', *ELH*, vol. 47, no. 3 (Autumn 1980), 559–74.

Leclerc, Yvan, *La Spirale et le Monument: Essai sur 'Bouvard et Pécuchet'* (Paris: SEDES, 1988).

—— et al. (eds), *Flaubert, Le Poittevin, Maupassant: Une affaire de famille littéraire: Actes du Colloque de Fécamp, 27–28 octobre 2000* (Rouen: Publications de l'Université de Rouen, 2002).

Leopardi, Giacomo, *Pensieri*, trans. W. S. di Piero (New York: Oxford University Press, 1984).

Leopardi, Giacomo, 'Lettera ai Sigg. Compilatori della Biblioteca Italiana in Riposta a quella di Mad. La Baronessa di Staël Holstein ai Medesimi', in *Poesie e Prose*, ed. Rolando Damiani and Mario Andrea Rigoni, 2 vols (Milan: Arnoldo Mondadori, 1987–8), vol. 2 (1988), 434–40.

Lernout, Geert, *The French Joyce* (Ann Arbor: University of Michigan Press, 1990).

—— 'The *Finnegans Wake* Notebooks and Radical Philology', in *Probes: Genetic Studies in Joyce*, ed. David Hayman and Sam Slote, *European Joyce Studies* 5 (Amsterdam: Rodopi, 1995), 19–48.

—— 'The Beginning: *Chapter I.1*', in *How Joyce Wrote Finnegans Wake: A Chapter-by-Chapter Genetic Guide*, ed. Luca Crispi and Sam Slote (Madison: University of Wisconsin Press, 2007), 49–65.

—— and Wim Van Mierlo (eds), *The Reception of James Joyce in Europe*, 2 vols (London: Thoemmes Continuum, 2004).

Levin, Harry, *The Gates of Horn: A Study of Five French Realists* (New York: Oxford University Press, 1966).

Lewis, Wyndham, *Time and Western Man* (London: Chatto & Windus, 1927).

Llosa, Mario Vargas, 'Flaubert, Our Contemporary', in *The Cambridge Companion to Flaubert*, ed. Timothy Unwin (Cambridge: Cambridge University Press, 2006), 220–4.

Lobner, Corinna del Greco, *James Joyce's Italian Connection: The Poetics of the Word* (Iowa City: University of Iowa Press, 1989).

Lynch, Michael, '"Here is Adhesiveness": From Friendship to Homosexuality', *Victorian Studies*, vol. 29, no. 1 (Autumn, 1985), 67–96.

MacArthur, Ian, 'Mutant Units in the C Notebooks', *A 'Finnegans Wake' Circular* 2.4 (1987), 76–7.

MacCabe, Colin (ed.), *James Joyce: New Perspectives* (Brighton: Harvester Press, 1982).

MacCourt, John, *The Years of Bloom: James Joyce in Trieste 1904–1920* (Dublin: Lilliput Press, 2000).

—— 'Giacomo of Trieste: James Joyce on the Adriatic', *Istria on the Internet, Relevant Non-Istrians, James Joyce*, http://www.istrianet.org/istria/illustri/nonistrian/joyce/mccourt_giacomo.htm (July 2011).

MacFarlane, Robert, *Original Copy: Plagiarism and Originality in Nineteenth-Century Literature* (Oxford: Oxford University Press, 2007).

McHugh, Roland, *Annotations to 'Finnegans Wake'*, 3rd edn (Baltimore and London: Johns Hopkins University Press, 2006).

McIntyre, J. Lewis, *Giordano Bruno* (London: Macmillan, 1903).

Mandle, W. F., *The Gaelic Athletic Association and Irish Nationalist Politics 1884–1924* (London: Christopher Helm, 1987).

Manganiello, Dominic, *Joyce's Politics* (London: Routledge and Kegan Paul, 1980).

Mason, Michael, 'Why is Leopold Bloom a Cuckold?', *ELH*, no. 1 (1977), 171–8.

Maume, Patrick, *The Long Gestation: Irish Nationalist Life 1891–1918* (Dublin: Gill and Macmillan, 1999).

Morrison, Stephen, 'Heresy, Heretics, and Heresiarchs in the Work of James Joyce', unpublished doctoral thesis, University of London, 2000.

Murry, John Middleton, review of *Ulysses*, *Nation and Athenaeum*, 22 April 1922, 124–5 (repr. in *James Joyce: The Critical Heritage*, 2 vols, ed. Robert H. Deming [London: Routledge and Kegan Paul, 1970], vol. 1, 195–8).

Nash, John, *James Joyce and the Act of Reception: Reading, Ireland, Modernism* (Cambridge and New York: Cambridge University Press, 2006).

Norris, Margot, *The Decentered Universe of 'Finnegans Wake': A Structuralist Analysis* (Baltimore and London: Johns Hopkins University Press, 1976).

—— *Joyce's Web: The Social Unraveling of Modernism* (Austin: University of Texas Press, 1992).

O'Neill, Christine, *Too Fine a Point: A Stylistic Analysis of the 'Eumaeus' Episode in James Joyce's 'Ulysses'* (Trier: Wissenschaftlicher Verlag, 1996).

Osteen, Mark, *The Economy of 'Ulysses'* (New York: Syracuse University Press, 1995).

O'Rourke, Fran, 'Joyce's Early Aesthetic', *Journal of Modern Literature*, vol. 34, no. 2 (Winter 2011), 97–120.

Parandowski, Jan, 'Meeting with Joyce', in Willard Potts (ed.), *James Joyce: Portraits of the Artist in Exile* (Dublin: Wolfhound Press, 1979), 154–62.

Patey, Caroline, Giovanni Cianci, and Francesca Cuojati (eds), *Anglo-American Modernity and the Mediterranean: Milan, 29–30 September 2005* (Milan: Cisalpino, 2006).

Peake, Charles, *James Joyce: The Citizen and the Artist* (London: Edward and Arnold, 1977).

Perec, Georges, *La Vie mode d'emploi: romans* (Paris: Hachette, 1978).

Pilkington, A. E., 'Point of View in Flaubert's "La Légende de saint Julien"', *French Studies* 29 (1975), 266–79.

Pippin, Robert, *Modernism as a Philosophical Problem: On the Dissatisfactions of European High Culture* (Oxford: Blackwell, 1991).

Potts, Willard (ed.), *James Joyce: Portraits of the Artist in Exile* (Dublin: Wolfhound Press, 1979).

Pound, Ezra, *Instigations of Ezra Pound* (New York: Boni and Liveright, 1920).

—— *Pound/Joyce: The Letters of Ezra Pound to James Joyce: with Pound's Essays on James Joyce*, ed. Forrest Read (London: Faber and Faber, 1968):
'*Dubliners* and Mr James Joyce', 27–30 (first pub. in *The Egoist*, I, 14 [15 July 1914], 267).
'The Non-Existence of Ireland', 32–3 (first pub. in *The New Age*, XVI, 17 [25 February 1915], 452).
'Mr James Joyce and the Modern Stage', 49–56 (first pub. in *The Drama*, VI, 2 [February 1916], 122–32).
'James Joyce: At Last the Novel Appears', 88–91 (first pub. in *The Egoist*, IV, 2 [February 1917], 21–2).
'Joyce', 133–9 (first pub. in *The Future*, II, 6 [May 1918], 161–3).
'*Ulysses*', 139–41 (first pub. in 'Joyce' in Ezra Pound, *Instigations of Ezra Pound* [New York: Boni and Liveright, 1920], 203–13).

'James Joyce et Pécuchet', 200–11 (first pub. in *Mercure de France*, CLVI, 575 [1 June , 1922], 307–20).

'Paris Letter', 194–200 (first pub. in *The Dial*, LXXII, 6 [June 1922], 623–9).

'Past History', 245–54 (first pub. in *The English Journal*, XXII, 5 [May 1933], 349–58).

Power, Arthur, *Conversations with James Joyce*, ed. Clive Hart (1974) (Chicago: Chicago University Press, 1982).

Prendergast, Christopher, *The Order of Mimesis* (Cambridge: Cambridge University Press, 1986).

Proust, Marcel, 'A Propos du Style de Flaubert', in *Chroniques* (Paris: Gallimard, 1927), 193–211 (first pub. in *Nouvelle Revue Française* [1 January 1920], 72–90).

Rabaté, Jean-Michel, *Joyce upon the Void: The Genesis of Doubt* (Basingstoke: Macmillan, 1991).

—— 'The Fourfold Root of Yawn's Unreason: *Chapter III.3*', in *How Joyce Wrote 'Finnegans Wake': A Chapter-by-Chapter Genetic Guide*, ed. Luca Crispi and Sam Slote (Madison: University of Wisconsin Press, 2007), 384–409.

—— and Pierre-Marc de Biasi, 'Joyce, Flaubert et *Exiles*', in *'Scribble' 2: Joyce et Flaubert*, ed. Claude Jacquet and André Topia (Paris: Minard, 1990), 165–72.

Restivo, Giuseppina, 'From *Exiles* to *Ulysses*: The Influence of Three Italian Authors on Joyce – Giacosa, Praga, Oriani', in *Anglo-American Modernity and the Mediterranean: Milan, 29–30 September 2005*, ed. Caroline Patey, Giovanni Cianci, and Francesca Cuojati (Milan: Cisalpino, 2006), 133–51.

Riffaterre, Michael, 'Interpretation and Undecidability', *New Literary History* 12 (2) (1980), 227–42.

—— 'Intertextual Representation: On Mimesis as Interpretive Discourse', *Critical Inquiry*, 11 (1) (1984), 141–62.

—— 'Compulsory Reader Response: The Intertextual Drive', in *Intertextuality: Theories and Practices*, ed. Michael Worton and Judith Still (Manchester and New York: Manchester University Press, 1990), 56–78.

Rose, Danis (ed.), *James Joyce's The Index Manuscript: 'Finnegans Wake' Holograph Workbook VI.B.46* (Colchester: A Wake Newslitter Press, 1978).

—— *The Textual Diaries of James Joyce* (Dublin: Lilliput Press, 1995).

—— and John O'Hanlon, *Understanding 'Finnegans Wake': A Guide to the Narrative of Joyce's Masterpiece* (New York: Garland, 1982).

Saint-Amour, Paul, *The Copywrights: Intellectual Property and the Literary Imagination* (London and Ithaca: Cornell University Press, 2003).

Sartre, Jean-Paul, *L'Idiot de la famille: Gustave Flaubert de 1821 à 1857*, 3 vols (Paris: Gallimard, 1971–2).

Scholes, Robert E. (ed.), *The Cornell Joyce Collection: A Catalogue* (Ithaca: Cornell University Press, 1961).

—— and Richard M. Kain (eds), *The Workshop of Daedalus: James Joyce and the Raw Materials for 'A Portrait of the Artist as a Young Man'* (Evanston: Northwestern University Press, 1965).

Schork, R. J., *Greek and Hellenic Culture in Joyce* (Gainesville: University Press of Florida, 1998).

—— *Joyce and Hagiography: Saints Above* (Gainesville: University Press of Florida, 2000).

Scrogham, Ron E., 'The Echo of the Name "Iaokanann"', *The French Review*, vol. 71, no. 5 (April 1998), 775–84.

Sedgwick, Eve Kosofsky, *Epistemology of the Closet* (Berkeley: University of California Press, 1990).

Seidel, Michael, *Epic Geography in James Joyce's 'Ulysses'* (Princeton: Princeton University Press, 1976).

Senn, Fritz, 'Trivia Ulysseana IV, Brood of Tempters', *James Joyce Quarterly*, vol. 19, no. 2 (Winter 1982), 151–3.

—— '"Circe" as Harking Back in Provective Arrangement', in *Reading Joyce's 'Circe'*, ed. Andrew Gibson, *European Joyce Studies* 3 (Amsterdam: Rodopi, 1994), 63–92.

—— *Inductive Scrutinies: Focus on Joyce*, ed. Christine O'Neill (Dublin: The Lilliput Press, 1995).

—— 'Dynamic Adjustments in *Dubliners* "(as Joyce clearly states)"', in *New Perspectives on 'Dubliners'*, ed. Mary Power and Ulrich Schneider, *European Joyce Studies* 7 (Amsterdam: Rodopi, 1997), 1–18.

—— *Ulyssean Close-ups* (Roma: Bulzoni Editore, 2007).

Spiegel, Alan, 'Flaubert to Joyce: Evolution of a Cinematographic Form', *NOVEL*, vol. 6, no. 3 (Spring 1973), 229–43.

—— *Fiction and the Camera Eye: Visual Consciousness in the Film and the Modern Novel* (Charlottesville: University Press of Virginia, 1976).

Stanford Friedman, Susan, 'Weavings: Intertextuality and the (Re)Birth of the Author', in *Influence and Intertextuality in Literary History*, ed. Jay Clayton and Eric Rothstein (Madison: The University of Wisconsin Press, 1991), 147–80.

Tadié, Benoît, 'The Room of Infinite Possibilities: Joyce, Flaubert, and the Historical Imagination', *Études anglaises*, vol. 58, no. 2 (April–June 2005), 131–40.

Taine, Hippolyte, *De l'intelligence*, 2 vols (Paris: Hachette, 1870).

Tanner, Tony, *Adultery in the Novel: Contract and Transgression* (Baltimore and London: Johns Hopkins University Press, 1979).

Tarver, John Charles, *Gustave Flaubert as Seen in his Works and Correspondence* (London: Archibald Constable & Company, 1895).

Texier, Edmond, review of *Madame Bovary*, *L'Illustration*, 9 May 1857 (repr. in *Madame Bovary* [Paris: Louis Conard, 1910], 535–7).

Thornton, Weldon, *Allusions in 'Ulysses' An Annotated List* (Chapel Hill: University of North Carolina Press, 1961).

Todorov, Tzvetan, 'Les registres de la parole', *Journal de la Psychologie* (1967), 265–78.

Topia, André, 'The Matrix and the Echo: Intertextuality in *Ulysses*', in *Post-Structuralist Joyce*, ed. Derek Attridge and Daniel Ferrer (Cambridge: Cambridge University Press, 1984), 103–25.

—— 'Flaubert et Joyce: les affinités sélectives', in *'Scribble' 2: Joyce et Flaubert*, ed. Claude Jacquet and André Topia (Paris: Minard, 1990), 33–64.

—— 'Modèles et écarts: scénarios d'écriture de *Dubliners* à *Ulysses*', unpublished thesis (*doctorat d'état*), University of Paris (Paris VIII, Saint-Denis), 1995.

Unwin, Timothy (ed.), *The Cambridge Companion to Flaubert* (Cambridge: Cambridge University Press, 2006).

Valente, Joseph (ed.), 'Thrilled by His Touch', in *Quare Joyce*, ed. Joseph Valente (Ann Arbor: University of Michigan Press, 1998), 47–76.

Vanderham, Paul, *James Joyce and Censorship: The Trials of 'Ulysses'* (London: Macmillan Press, 1998).

Van Hulle, Dirk, *Textual Awareness: A Genetic Study of Late Manuscripts by Joyce, Proust, and Mann* (Ann Arbor: University of Michigan Press, 2004).

—— 'The Lost Word: *Book IV*', in *How Joyce Wrote 'Finnegans Wake': A Chapter-by-Chapter Genetic Guide*, ed. Luca Crispi and Sam Slote (Madison: University of Wisconsin Press, 2007), 436–61.

Vingtain, Léon, *De la liberté de la presse* (Paris: Michel Lévy, 1860).

Weir, David, 'Gnomon is an Island: Euclid and Bruno in Joyce's Narrative Practice', *James Joyce Quarterly*, vol. 28, no. 2 (Winter 1991), 343–60.

—— *James Joyce and the Art of Mediation* (Ann Arbor: University of Michigan Press, 1996).

Williams, Rowan, *Arius: Heresy and Tradition*, 2nd edn (London: scm press, 2001).

Woolf, Virginia, 'Modern Novels', *Times Literary Supplement*, 10 April 1919, 189–90 (repr. in *James Joyce: The Critical Heritage*, 2 vols, ed. Robert H. Deming [London: Routledge and Kegan Paul, 1970], vol. 1, 125–6).

—— *The Diary of Virginia Woolf*, ed. Anne Olivier Bell, 5 vols (London: Hogarth Press, 1977–84).

Yeats, W. B., 'The Reform of the Theatre', in *Samhain: An Occasional Review* (September 1903), 9–12.

Zola, Émile, *Le Roman expérimental* (1880) (Paris: Flammarion, 2006).

[Collectively authored article], 'Charles Bovary, héros malgré lui', *Magazine littéraire*, no. 458 (November 2006), 62–3.

Film

Huston, John, dir., *The Dead* (Liffey Films: Vestron UK, 1987).

Websites

Le Trésor de la langue française informatisé: http://atilf.atilf.fr/ (July 2011).

The Catholic Encyclopedia: http://www.newadvent.org/cathen/ (July 2011).

Index

Bold numbers denote reference to illustrations.